STATE OF NEW YORK

SECOND REPORT

OF THE

FACTORY INVESTIGATING COMMISSION

1913

VOLUME I

I0754443

TRANSMITTED TO THE LEGISLATURE JANUARY 15, 1913

ALBANY
J. B. LYON COMPANY, PRINTERS
1913

STATE OF NEW YORK

No. 36

IN SENATE

JANUARY 15, 1913

SECOND REPORT

OF THE

New York State Factory Investigating Commission

January 15, 1913

ROBERT F. WAGNER
Chairman

ALFRED E. SMITH
Vice-Chairman

CHARLES M. HAMILTON
EDWARD D. JACKSON
CYRUS W. PHILLIPS
SIMON BRENTANO
ROBERT E. DOWLING
MARY E. DREIER
SAMUEL GOMPERS

FRANK A. TIERNEY
Secretary

ABRAM I. ELKUS
Chief Counsel

BERNARD L. SHIENTAG
Assistant Counsel

CONTENTS OF THE REPORT *

VOLUME I

*The minutes of the testimony taken by the Commission and the following appendices to the Commission's report will be contained in subsequent volumes.

APPENDIX II — Report of the Director of Investigation, by Dr. George M. Price.

APPENDIX III — The Fire Problem, by James P. Whiskeman, C. E.

APPENDIX IV — Manufacturing in Tenement Houses, by Elizabeth C. Watson.

APPENDIX V — Conditions in Canneries, by Zenas L. Potter.

APPENDIX VI — Wood Alcohol, by Prof. Charles Baskerville.

APPENDIX VII — Commercial Acids, by Dr. Chas. F. McKenna.

APPENDIX VIII — Lead Poisoning, by Dr. C. T. Graham Rogers and John H. Vogt.

APPENDIX IX — Report on the Employment of Women and Children in Mercantile Establishments, by Pauline Goldmark and Geo. A. Hall.

APPENDIX X — Briefs and Memoranda submitted to the Commission.

APPENDIX I

REPORT

OF THE

NEW YORK STATE FACTORY INVESTIGATING COMMISSION

To the Legislature of the State of New York:

The Commission appointed pursuant to chapter 561 of the laws of 1911 and to chapter 21 of the laws of 1912, to inquire into the conditions under which manufacturing is carried on throughout the state and to investigate the conditions of labor in mercantile establishments generally, hereby submits the following report.

The Creation of the Commmission

This Commission owes its creation to the demand of the people for an investigation of the conditions of labor in the factories of the state. The public had been profoundly shocked by the fire occurring in New York City on March 25, 1911, in the factory of the Triangle Waist Company, in which 145 employees, chiefly women and children, lost their lives. The conviction was widespread that so appalling a disaster must have been due to conditions resulting from neglect. In full conformity, therefore, with public sentiment, the legislature of the state of New York resolving to leave nothing undone to protect the lives of the men, women, and children working within its bounds, enacted chapter 561 of the laws of 1911 creating the New York State Factory Investigating Commission.

Pursuant to this chapter the following commission was appointed:

From the Senate:

Robert F. Wagner
Charles M. Hamilton.

From the Assembly:
Alfred E. Smith
Edward D. Jackson
Cyrus W. Phillips.

By the Governor:
Simon Brentano
Robert E. Dowling
Mary E. Dreier
Samuel Gompers.

THE AUTHORITY AND SCOPE OF THE COMMISSION

The Commission was authorized by the legislature to inquire into the conditions under which manufacturing was conducted. Its authority was to include the investigation of matters affecting the health and safety of the operatives and the security of the public, to the end that remedial legislation might be enacted to protect from danger to life and health, all workers in existing or future structures used or to be used for manufacturing purposes. It was further empowered to compel the attendance of witnesses, the production of books and papers, and to appoint counsel, secretary, stenographers and necessary assistants. In general it was to have the regular powers of a legislative committee. The members of the Commission were to receive no compensation for their services, but were to be reimbursed for necessary expenses.

The scope of the investigation, as outlined in the act creating the Commission, was properly very broad; for a fire, such as led immediately to the creation of the Commission, is fortunately of rare occurrence. On the other hand, industrial accidents, poisonings, and diseases maim or disable in the state and nation tens of thousands every year. Insufficient ventilation, bad sanitation, and long hours of labor also work their deadly effects. Consideration of these and other constant menaces to the safety and health of industrial workers determined the Commission not to limit itself merely to the study of the fire hazard in factory buildings, but to extend its activities to various other phases of factory life, such as the employment of women and children, sanitation, accident prevention and industrial poisoning and diseases. The labor of the Commission, in brief, was to be devoted to a consideration of measures for the conservation of human life.

ORGANIZATION OF THE COMMISSION

The Commission was organized on the 17th day of August, 1911, by the election of Senator Robert F. Wagner, as Chairman, and Hon. Alfred E. Smith, Vice-Chairman. Frank A. Tierney was selected as Secretary. The Commission appointed Abram I. Elkus, Chief Counsel, and Bernard L. Shientag, Assistant Counsel.

WORK OF COMMISSION IN 1911

The Commission retained Dr. George M. Price as its expert in general charge of the work of inspection and sanitation. Dr. Price immediately organized a corps of inspectors for this purpose. The Commission also retained Mr. H. F. J. Porter as advisory expert on the fire problem.

The Commission held public hearings and executive sessions in New York City and in all other cities of the first and second class in the state, and conducted the following investigations:

1. General sanitary investigation of factories in cities of the first and second class.
2. Fire-hazard in factories.
3. Conditions in bakeries and physical examination of bakers employed therein.
4. Lead poisoning and arsenical poisoning.
5. Women's trades.
6. An industrial survey of a selected area in New York City.
7. Preliminary investigation of child labor in tenement houses.

The results of all these investigations are fully set forth in the Commission's preliminary report. This report together with the minutes of the public hearings and the bills recommended by the Commission were submitted to the legislature on March 1st, 1912. The following bills recommended by the Commission were passed by the legislature and have become laws:

		Labor Law.
1.	Registration of factories......................	Sec. 69
2.	Physical examination of children before employment certificate is issued....................	Sec. 71

3. Fire drills .... Sec. 83a
4. Automatic sprinklers .... Sec. 83b
5. Fire prevention; removal of rubbish; fireproof receptacles for waste material; protection of gas jets; prohibition of smoking in factories........... Sec. 83c
6. Prohibition of the eating of lunch in rooms where poisonous substances are prepared or generated in the process of manufacture; adequate hot and cold washing facilities for such establishments.. Sec. 89a
7. Employment prohibited of women within four weeks after child-birth..................... Sec. 93a
8. Summary power of Commissioner of Labor over unclean and unsanitary factories............ Sec. 95

On March 6th, 1912, chapter 21 of the laws of 1912 was passed extending the time of the Commission within which it might continue its investigations and submit its complete report, to January 15, 1913. This act extended the jurisdiction of the Commission to cities throughout the state and also empowered the Commission to investigate general conditions in mercantile establishments.

WORK OF THE COMMISSION SINCE MARCH 6TH, 1912

After March, 1912, the Commission continued its investigations with the organization previously mentioned; except that James P. Whiskeman, C. E., was retained as advisory expert on the fire problem, and in December, 1912, Mr. Laurence Arnold Tanzer, and Mr. Clarence King of the Legislative Bill-Drafting Bureau of Columbia University, were retained to assist in the drafting of bills to be submitted to the Legislature.

In 1912 the Commission conducted the following investigations:

INVESTIGATIONS

1. GENERAL SANITARY INVESTIGATION

This investigation which was commenced in 1911 was continued in 1912 under the direction of Dr. Price with a staff of six field inspectors, who were assisted from time to time by special investigators and experts.

The investigation of 1911 covered 1,836 industrial establishments in which 63,374 wage earners were employed, and included 9 cities of the state.

The investigation of 1912 covered 1,338 industrial establishments in which 125,961 wage earners were employed, and included 45 cities of the state. The entire number of establishments covered by the general sanitary investigations for 1911 and 1912 was 3,176 in which 189,335 wage earners were employed. These do not include some 400 establishments that were inspected in Rochester in December, 1912, and numerous establishments inspected by experts whom the Commission had retained to examine different phases of the chemical industry in this state.

The general sanitary investigation covered such matters as the location and construction of factories, their light and illumination, heating and ventilation, water supply and washing service, toilet accommodations, dressing and lunch rooms, and general cleanliness.

The results of this investigation will be found in the report of the director of investigation in Appendix II, chapters 1 and 2.

2. The Fire Problem

This investigation was conducted under the direction of James P. Whiskeman, C. E., under whose supervision several hundred factories in New York City and other cities of the state were inspected. Mr. Whiskeman's report will be found in Appendix III.

3. Manufacturing In Tenement Houses

This investigation was conducted under the direction of Miss Elizabeth C. Watson, who was assisted by a force of eleven field inspectors. It covered conditions under which manufacturing was carried on in tenement houses in New York City, and in fifteen other cities of the state. The investigation embraced the employment of women and children in their homes, sanitary conditions under which they worked, and wages.

Miss Watson's report is set forth in Appendix IV.

4. Conditions In the Canneries

This investigation was conducted under the supervision of Zenas L. Potter, with the assistance of nine investigators, several of whom found employment in the canneries in order to observe working conditions at first hand. The investigation was a comprehensive one and included practically every cannery in the state. It covered the employment of women and children in the canneries and cannery sheds, their hours of labor, the sanitary conditions in the canneries, and the housing conditions of the employees. Mr. Potter's report will be found in Appendix V.

5. NIGHT WORK OF WOMEN

This investigation was made by Miss G. Potter and Miss G. E. Smith, who obtained the personal histories of 100 night workers in a large industrial establishment in the central part of the state where there was a regular night shift of women. The results of this investigation are set forth in detail in Appendix II, chapter 3.

6. THE TOBACCO INDUSTRY

This investigation covered 251 establishments consisting of 472 separate shops in which 15,594 persons were employed. In connection with this investigation a physical examination was made by Dr. Fanny Dembo of 600 women workers in the various tobacco factories. This is the first medical examination that has ever been made of so large a number of women workers in factories. The results of the sanitary investigation and physical examination of the workers are set forth in Appendix II, chapter 5.

7. THE PRINTING INDUSTRY

This investigation covered 348 separate printing places in which 9,047 persons, of whom 14.7% were women, were found employed. The printing establishments inspected were distributed in a number of cities, although the majority were in New York City. The results of this investigation are set forth in Appendix II, chapter 6.

8. INVESTIGATION OF DANGEROUS TRADES

The Chemical Industry

Under the supervision of Dr. Price, 142 chemical establishments were inspected. The results of this investigation are set forth in Appendix II, chapter 4.

Wood Alcohol

An important study was made by the Commission of wood alcohol or methyl and its effect on workers. This investigation was made under the supervision of Charles Baskerville, Ph. D., F. C. S., Professor of Chemistry and director of the laboratory of The College of the City of New York, with several assistants. Prof. Baskerville's services were gratuitous and the Commission takes this opportunity to express its appreciation of the valuable contribution he has made to the report. Prof. Baskerville's report will be found in Appendix VI.

Commercial Acids

Dr. Charles F. McKenna was retained as chemical expert by the Commission to make an intensive study of the manufacture and use of various commercial acids and their effects upon those employed to manufacture them or to use them in manufacturing processes. Dr. McKenna's report on "The Dangers to Workers in the Manufacture and Use of Commercial Acids," will be found in Appendix VII.

Lead Poisoning

In 1911 a study of lead poisoning in New York City was made for the Commission by Dr. E. E. Pratt, whose findings appear in the Commission's preliminary report. In 1912 an additional investigation of a large number of lead works and establishments in other cities of the state where lead is used in the process of manufacture was made by C. T. Graham-Rogers, M. D., medical inspector of the state department of labor with the assistance of John H. Vogt, B. S., a factory inspector, who were assigned to the Commission through the courtesy of the Commissioner of Labor. Dr. Rogers' report will be found in Appendix VIII.

Miscellaneous Reports

A number of miscellaneous investigations and studies relating to dangerous trades were made for the Commission as follows:

A.— Report of the inspection of establishments producing, refining, or using wood alcohol, by Frederick E. Breithut, Sc. D., of The College of the City of New York.

B.— Tables compiled by Jacob Feldbaum, B. S., showing the accidents and dangers in the chemical industries in New York State as compared with those of various European countries.

C.— Detailed description of forty accidents occurring in chemical establishments at Niagara Falls, by Miss G. Potter.

D.— Histories of 31 cases of lead poisoning traced to chemical establishments in Niagara Falls, by Miss G. E. Smith.

E.— Personal histories of 132 chemical workers in plants at Niagara Falls, by Marie S. Orenstein, M. A., of the state department of labor.

F.— Diseases of the ear and upper respiratory tract among workers in factories, by Otto Glogau, M. D. This report embraced the physical examination of 155 employees in six factories in the ostrich feather, fur, and cordage industries. The services of Dr. Glogau were rendered without compensation and the Commission desires to express its thanks to him for his valuable assistance and co-operation.

The foregoing reports will be found in Appendix II, chapter 7.

9. MERCANTILE INVESTIGATION

A preliminary investigation of department stores extending over a period of two months, was made by the Commission. The conditions of employment particularly of women and children were studied in 216 establishments in New York, Buffalo, and Rochester, and in six cities of the second class. Attention was directed especially to hours of labor, physical conditions, and wages. The investigation was conducted under the supervision of Pauline Goldmark and George A. Hall. Five investigators were engaged for the field work. The report will be found in Appendix IX.

The Commission desires to express its appreciation of the faithful, conscientious, and able services rendered by all those in charge of the various investigations, and by their assistants.

PUBLIC HEARINGS

In 1912 the Commission held 30 public hearings in the cities of New York, Buffalo, Rochester, Syracuse, Utica, Troy, Albany,

Yonkers, and Niagara Falls. At these hearings 259 witnesses were examined and 3,557 pages of testimony were taken.

HEARINGS IN CONNECTION WITH INSPECTIONS OF FACTORIES

On General Factory Conditions

The Commission decided that it was advisable to make personal inspections of a number of factories throughout the state for the purpose of observing the working conditions at first hand. Accordingly, about fifty factories in all were inspected by the Commission in the cities previously mentioned and also in Little Falls and Auburn. In many cases the testimony of the manufacturers and of the employees was taken in the course of these inspections.

On Conditions in Canneries

The members of the Commission devoted a week in August to a personal inspection of the canneries of the State. In all, six canneries, in the cities of Rome, Canastota, Auburn, Geneva, Albion and Batavia were inspected officially by the members of the Commission. They went from cannery to cannery and took the testimony of the canners, the superintendents, and foremen, and of the women and children found there at work.

EXECUTIVE SESSIONS

In addition to the many executive sessions of the Commission, which had been called to determine its organization, the investigations to be conducted, and the recommendations for remedial legislation, the Commission also held the following executive sessions for employees who wished to appear and to testify to the conditions under which they worked:

1. Executive session for foundry workers, held in Albany.
2. Executive session for employees in department stores, held in New York City.
3. Executive session for those affected by lead poisoning in factories in Niagara Falls, held at Niagara Falls.

ISSUANCE OF TENTATIVE BILLS

The Commission followed the procedure of issuing early in the fall, in the form of proposed bills, the most important recommendations that had been received for remedial legislation. These tentative bills embodied recommendations, none of which had been formally passed upon by the Commission. In fact certain members of the Commission had expressed individually their disapproval of the enactment of some of them. The Commission, however, believed that all those who were interested in its work or who would be affected by the legislation suggested, were entitled to know precisely the recommendations which had been received from various sources and were then under consideration. This method has proved very successful. About thirty tentative bills, dealing with different phases of the Commission's work, were sent to several thousand persons throughout the state. As a result, suggestions and criticisms were received from all of the various interests. Associations of employers and of employees, scientific societies and social organizations formed committees to consider the proposed bills. From many of these were received briefs and memoranda. Beyond doubt the issuance of these tentative bills created great interest in the work of the Commission and gave to it the benefit of the wisdom and experience of very many employers, employees, social workers, and experts throughout the state. The bills proposed were discussed in general at the public hearings referred to above. The following public hearings were also held to discuss in particular the proposed bills dealing with special subjects.

SPECIAL HEARINGS ON TENTATIVE BILLS

1912

November 25, in Albany, the foundry bill and the employment of women in core rooms.

November 26, in Albany, cannery legislation.

December 2nd, in New York City, the reorganization of the labor department.

December 3rd, in New York City, bakeries.

December 4th, in New York City, the fire problem.

December 5th, in New York City, home work in tenement houses.

December 6th, in New York City, the employment of women and children.

APPRECIATION OF ASSISTANCE RENDERED TO THE COMMISSION

The Commission owes much of what it has been able to accomplish to the active assistance and co-operation received throughout its work from numerous civic and social organizations and from many public-spirited men and women who have given it their encouragement and support and placed at its disposal their time, knowledge, and experience.

In particular we desire to express to the Hon. John Williams, Commissioner of Labor of the State of New York, our appreciation of his assistance and counsel, and of his courtesy in assigning to the Commission inspectors from his department who aided us very materially in our investigations.

We also gratefully acknowledge our indebtedness to the National Child Labor Committee, the New York Child Labor Committee and the Consumers' League for their assistance and co-operation in connection with the cannery and homework investigations conducted by the Commission and to the Legislative Bill Drafting Bureau of Columbia University for its assistance in the drafting of bills.

We thank especially Miss Pauline Goldmark not only for her able assistance in the mercantile investigation but also for her advice and counsel on all matters connected with the work of the Commission.

We take this opportunity to express our thanks and appreciation also to the following men and women who have very generously assisted the Commission in its work:

Mr. George W. Alger, Dr. E. M. Alger, Mr. Eugene S. Benjamin, Mr. Reginald Pelham Bolton, Mr. Peter J. Brady, Mr. Frank T. Chapman, Mr. Frank K. Chew, Mr. Julius Henry Cohen, Dr. Thomas Darlington, Mr. John A. Fitch, Mr. Thomas D. Fitzgerald, Miss Josephine Goldmark, Mr. George A. Hall, Mr. Leonard W. Hatch, Mr. Frank P. Hill, Dr. H. E. Ives, Mrs. Florence Kelley, Mr. Paul U. Kellogg, Mr. Paul Kennaday, Mr. D. D. Kimball, Dr. S. Adolphus Knopf, Mr. C. L. Law, Mr. Walter Lindner, Prof. Samuel McCune Lindsay, Mr. Owen R. Lovejoy, Hon. Alexander C. MacNulty, Mr. W. W. Macon, Mr. Louis B. Marks, Mr. F. J. Millar, Mr. V. Everit Macy, Mr. John Martin, Mr. Henry Morgenthau, Mr. D. W. O'Connor, Mr.

Thomas I. Parkinson, Miss Frances Perkins, Mr. Allan Robinson, Mr. I. M. Rubinow, Prof. Henry R. Seager, Prof. Vladimir Simkhovitch, Mr. C. H. Stickney, Dr. W. H. Tolman, Mr. F. S. Tomlin, Miss Mary Van Kleeck, Mr. Lawrence Veiller, Mr. Oswald G. Villard, Miss Lillian D. Wald, Mr. A. F. Weber, Mr. Mornay Williams, Prof. Charles E. A. Winslow.

We also warmly thank the scores of others who assisted us with their views and suggestions at public hearings and at private conferences.

POLICY OF THE COMMISSION

The Commission has endeavored to be fair and just in its investigations and in its findings. In no case has the inquiry been partial. We have given to everyone interested an opportunity to appear at public hearings and at private conferences. Notice of our public hearings was given weeks in advance and they were all largely attended.

At the hearing, for instance, on cannery legislation there were more than twenty canners present accompanied by counsel. At the hearing on the foundry bill twenty-five foundry owners of this state and the representatives of the Molders' Unions appeared. At the hearing on bakery legislation the master bakers of the state and of New York City, representatives of bakers' unions, and health officials were present. At every public hearing, in short, we endeavored to have all sides represented, and to receive the views and suggestions of all divergent interests.

We permitted the cross-examination of our own inspectors and investigators by parties in interest and by their counsel,— a most novel procedure for an investigating commission. We allowed parties in interest to call witnesses and to have their own counsel examine them.

At no time have we lost sight of the fact that we were an investigating commission, not a prosecuting or persecuting commission. As in our investigations, so in the recommendations that we are submitting, we have endeavored to do what was fair and reasonable to all concerned — the manufacturer, the employee, and the public whose representatives we are.

A series of bills that embody our recommendations are set forth in Appendix I. In the drafting of these bills we have had the advice and assistance of a number of experts.

The question has been raised repeatedly: What effect will new laws for the improvement of conditions of working people have on the industries of the state? The Commission believes that nothing should be done to injure any industry. We believe that our industries should be not only unhampered, but even aided and assisted in their growth and development so that they may be able to afford better and more remunerative employment to the people; but we believe just as firmly that no reasonable requirement for the health and safety of the workers will injure any industry. Enlightened manufacturers have appeared before the Commission in different cities of the state and asserted that an improvement in working conditions means an increase in efficiency and pays from the standpoint of dollars and cents. Whether this be true or not, we believe that human life is sacred and must be placed above monetary considerations. The broad aim of government is the happiness and well being of the governed. No government is properly performing its functions when it permits the working people within its bounds to be employed under unsanitary conditions, when it fails to protect them from preventable disease and accident, when it permits the premature employment of young children, and the excessive toil of women. Short sighted indeed is the policy of any state that permits the waste of its human assets.

The Hon. William Sulzer, Governor of the state, in his message to the legislature on January 1st, 1913, said:

"If Americans would excel other nations in commerce, in manufacture, in science, in intellectual growth, and in all other humane attainments, we must first possess a people physically, mentally, and morally fit and sound. Any achievement that is purchased by the continual sacrifice of human life does not advance our material resources but detracts from the wealth of the state. We must now convince employers that any industry that saps the vitality and destroys the initiative of the workers is detrimental to the best interests of the state and menaces the general welfare of the government."

It is in the light of these principles that this report is submitted.

CONTENTS OF THE REPORT

I.

THE LABOR LAW AND ITS ADMINISTRATION

Laws enacted to protect industrial workers and to improve their condition, are of little value unless adequate machinery of government be provided to administer them intelligently and to enforce them effectively. The labor department is charged with administering the statutes dealing with the health and safety of the men, women, and children employed in the industries of the state. There are in this state over 40,000 factories in which 1,250,000 workers are employed. If to these is added the many thousands of employees in mercantile establishments, the workers in tenement houses, those employed in tunnels, mines and caissons and those engaged in the construction of public works, it is safe to say that the Department of Labor is directly responsible for the well-being of upwards of 2,000,000 workers. The Department of Labor should therefore be one of the great departments of the state. Up to the present however, this department has occupied a minor position, and until recent years practically no attempt has been made to raise it to a position of prominence commensurate with its important duties and functions.

In this, the greatest industrial state of the union, but little attention has been paid to the preservation of the state's most precious asset, the workers within its bounds. Consequently, very little attention has been given to the department which is charged with the responsibility for safe and sanitary working conditions.

The annual appropriation for the Department of Labor for the year 1912, covering all its varied activities, was about $320,000. This was a large increase over appropriations in former years but nevertheless, was so utterly inadequate as to make impossible even an attempt to enforce all the laws dealing with the health and safety of workers.

The Commissioner of Labor in his annual report for the year ending October 1st, 1911, says, in referring to the work of the bureau of factory inspection, with which this Commission is most directly concerned:

> "No claim is herein set up that the Bureau has been able to compel the maintenance of proper standards at all times in every place falling within its jurisdiction. I can only repeat what was said before, that one or two visits a year are not enough. We cannot by such insufficient observations find out infractions of the law and apply the remedies. The Legislature of 1911 provided for a substantial increase in the field and office staff of the Bureau, but even when fully equipped according to the improved plan of organization, its field force will remain inadequate to enforce the law."

City departments do practically nothing to remedy defective conditions in factories, and very little with regard to mercantile establishments. The Department of Labor alone must do this important work. The state has properly assumed the duty of looking after the health and safety of its industrial workers and local authorities rely upon the state to see that this duty is performed.

We regret to be compelled to say that the state has not in the past fully discharged this duty. Imperfect laws and inadequate machinery for their enforcement have materially contributed to the annual waste of human life in our industrial establishments, a waste due to unsanitary conditions and preventable accidents and disease.

INADEQUACY OF THE PRESENT SYSTEM OF FACTORY INSPECTION

The principal work of the department consists in the inspection of factories and the enforcement of the statutes relating to the health and safety of employees. To this branch of the department's work the Commission has devoted much attention.

That the present system of factory inspection in this state is inadequate, is the opinion of every witness who appeared before the Commission at public hearings and at executive sessions. This opinion finds expression in the many briefs and memoranda received from various sources. It is shared by representative employees and employers, by civic organizations interested in labor conditions, and by those at the head of the department itself.

This inadequacy of factory inspection is due to the lack of proper statutes and to the lack of a sufficient number of inspectors, especially, inspectors of scientific and technical training. Inspections of factories are infrequent. Some factories are not inspected as often as once a year. No attention has been paid to the prevention of industrial poisoning and diseases, or to the supervision of workers employed in dangerous trades.

The Department of Labor has confined it efforts to acting as a police department, for the detection and punishment of violations of particular provisions in the statutes. It has failed utterly in developing its true function as a department of education, for establishing closer and more friendly relations between worker and employer, and for enlisting their active co-operation not only in the enforcement of the law but in the steady and constant improvement of working conditions.

THE PRESENT LABOR LAW

The ineffectiveness of the administration of the labor law in the state of New York is due, in large measure, to defects in the law itself. Many provisions of the labor law now in force are so imperfect, inadequate or antiquated as to preclude the possibility of successful administration.

The labor law is framed on what we believe to be a mistaken theory, that the requirements for the protection of the health and safety of workers should all be expressed within the four corners of the statute itself. The attempt to carry out this theory has led to the enactment of provisions, so specific and rigid in their requirements as to make their enforcement in many cases, unjust, or even impossible. They fail to take into account the varying conditions in different industries. In some instances where the impossibility of setting a rigid standard for all cases was manifest, the provisions of the law were made so vague and indefinite that their meaning or application could not be determined at all, or had to depend upon the exercise of an administrative discretion, a one-man discretion, so arbitrary in character and so calculated to work injustice, that it was either not exercised at all, or, when exercised, became a natural subject of distrust on the part of the courts. We believe that the only way of obtaining a labor law which can be enforced, is to abandon the theory underlying the labor law as it now stands; namely, that it is possible in any statute to provide specifically, the measures to be taken for the protection of the lives, health and safety of workers in each industry and under all conditions.

This theory of factory legislation we believe to be entirely erroneous. It is at variance with the systems in use in Wisconsin and in those European countries where the administration of labor laws has been a decided success.

These systems of labor legislation are based upon the theory that it is impossible to regulate factory sanitation and safety solely by statute.

The Commission, as a result of investigations and study of the subject, is convinced that it is impossible to legislate definitely by statute so as to cover the details of all industries. These details are too many and various to be safely enumerated in a statute which is difficult to change. Stringent regulations which are perfectly proper for one class of factories are often unnecessary and even injurious for others.

Conditions vary in different industries. New methods of manufacture, and new types of machinery present new and troublesome questions to be solved. Our labor laws should have reasonable elasticity and flexibility so as to permit of special requirements that may be adjusted to the progress of industry and its varying conditions. It should not be necessary to have to resort to the tedious process of amending an old law or enacting a new one whenever a remedy is needed for some condition overlooked in the old statute, or newly discovered.

We are of opinion that the legislature should make broad and general requirements for safety and sanitation, setting forth where practicable minimum requirements, and delegating to some responsible authority the power to make special rules and regulations to carry the provisions of the statute into effect in the different industries and under varying conditions. These rules and regulations should be collected in an industrial code that could be enlarged or changed with comparative ease from time to time as occasion might require. Such a principle is approved by all those who have given thought and study to this important subject.

In Europe the futility of regulating labor conditions by specific statutes, was recognized a long time ago. There the statutes are very broad and general and power is given to administrative boards to make rules and regulations for their application under varying circumstances and conditions.

The question of how to render these principles most effective and yet to secure a proper enforcement of the labor law as well as the rules and regulations adopted thereunder, has proved a very difficult problem.

To give one man, namely, the Commissioner of Labor, the power to make rules and regulations, would be entirely out of the question. This power is too great to entrust safely to any one individual. Two other methods were suggested: (1) to create a commission at the head of the Department of Labor in place of the present single commissioner, with power to make rules and regulations and to enforce them; and (2) to create a board within the Department of Labor to make rules and regulations, and to leave the Commissioner of Labor at the head of the department, as at present, with full power to enforce the provisions of the statute and the rules and regulations adopted by the board, and with full responsibility for their enforcement.

The Commission has carefully considered the advantages and disadvantages of each plan. We have found that there are advantages and disadvantages in each, but after careful study we have decided that the second alternative is the one likely to produce better results to the state. In reaching that conclusion, we were guided by the following principles:

1. Responsibility for enforcement of law must be definitely located.

2. Administrative work can best be done by one man.

3. Questions involving discretion and requiring deliberation are best decided by a body of men.

The plan we propose has the deliberative advantages of commission government, and the administrative advantages of a single head. The formation of a board to make, with due deliberation, regulations that shall carry into effect the intent and purposes of the law, will secure for the department all the benefits of a commission; and the retention at the head of the department, of a single commissioner to enforce the law and the regulations adopted thereunder, will prevent any shifting of responsibility.

The question has arisen, whether this board shall be merely advisory and its conclusions subject to veto by the Commissioner of Labor. We believe, however, that such veto power would not produce good results. Nevertheless, the Commissioner of Labor should not be placed in a subordinate capacity, but should be chairman of this board and thus have an important voice in framing the rules and regulations upon which the successful administration of his department so largely depends.

INDUSTRIAL BOARD

We therefore recommend that an industrial board to the Department of Labor be created, to consist of the Commissioner of Labor as chairman of the board, and four associate members to be appointed by the Governor with the advice and consent of the Senate. The first appointees are to serve for a period of one, two, three, and four years respectively, and subsequent appointees are to serve for a period of four years. The Commissioner of Labor shall have an equal vote in all proceedings of the board.

We strongly urge that the membership of this board be made up of a representative of labor, a representative of employers, a woman, and a scientist. The associate members shall each receive an annual salary of $3,000 and necessary traveling and other expenses.

The board may appoint a secretary and the commissioner shall detail from time to time to its assistance such employees of the Department of Labor as the board may require. The board may employ outside experts for special and occasional service and may form voluntary committees representing different interests concerned in any special subject that it has under consideration.

Meetings of the Board

The board shall meet at least once a month and at such other times as the public service may require. It is our opinion that the members of the board will never be giving less than one-third of their time to this work and that for the first year more than half of their time will have to be thus devoted.

The Commissioner of Labor or any two associate members of the board may call meetings. Counsel to the department shall act as counsel to the board without additional compensation. All meetings are to be public.

Powers of the Board

We recommend that the industrial board be given the following powers:

1. To make investigations concerning all matters which relate to the enforcement and effect of the provisions of the labor law; to subpœna and require the attendance of witnesses and the production of books and papers pertinent to the investigations and for that purpose to have all of the powers of a legislative committee. Each member of the board and the secretary shall have the power to make personal inspections of all factories, mercantile establishments, and premises affected by the labor law.

There will thus be in the Department of Labor itself the machinery for special investigations whenever the conditions warrant them, so that it will not be necessary to appeal to the legislature for the appointment of a commission, whenever a situation arises which, in the opinion of the people, requires study and investigation.

2. To make, alter, amend, and repeal rules and regulations for carrying into effect the provisions of the labor law and to apply such provisions to specific conditions and to prescribe specific means, methods, or practices to make such provisions effective. Such rules and regulations may apply in whole or in part to particular kinds of factories or workshops or to particular machines, apparatus, or articles; or to particular processes, industries, trades or occupations; or they may be limited in their application to factories or workshops hereafter established or to machines, or apparatus installed in the future.

The present provision in the law, for example, requiring adequate ventilation has been a dead letter. The industrial board would have the power to fix standards of ventilation, temperature and humidity, to be applied to different industries, under different conditions, and these standards could be changed or modified as circumstances required.

We also recommend that a provision be inserted in the labor law that all factory buildings and mercantile establishments shall be so constructed, equipped, arranged, operated, and conducted in all respects as to provide reasonable and adequate protection to the lives, health and safety, of all persons employed and that the industrial board shall be empowered to make rules and regulations to carry into effect the purpose and intent of the labor law for protecting the health and safety, and promoting the well-being of workers in industrial establishments. These rules and regulations should of course be consistent with such minimum or maximum requirements as may be specified in the statute.

Procedure of the Board

Before any rule or regulation is adopted, altered, amended or repealed, a public hearing must be held thereon, notice of which shall be published not less than ten days in the bulletins of the department or in such newspapers as may be prescribed.

Employers, workers and all others interested would thus be given an opportunity to make recommendations and to submit criticisms concerning proposed regulations. The board could at any time consult the experts of the department and in special cases outside experts could be retained. The formation of voluntary committees to advise the board concerning matters under consideration would be encouraged. Regulations would be adopted or modified, only after a full hearing of all interested parties and with the advice and suggestions of experts.

INDUSTRIAL CODE

The rules and regulations adopted by the board in force on the first day of January, 1914, and the amendments thereof and additions thereto shall constitute the Industrial Code and shall be certified and filed with the Secretary of State.

DELEGATION OF LEGISLATIVE POWER

We are convinced that this delegation of power to make rules and regulations is valid and constitutional. Chief Justice MARSHALL declared, in 1825:

> " The difference between the departments undoubtedly is, that the legislature makes, the executive executes, and the

> judiciary construes the law; but the maker of the law may commit something to the discretion of the other departments, and the precise boundary of this power is a subject of delicate and difficult inquiry, into which a court will not enter unnecessarily." *

The constitutionality of such delegation of power turns upon this question: Has the legislature laid down general rules determining the policy of the law and leaving the details to an administrative body, or has the legislature left it to the discretion of this administrative body to determine whether there shall be any legislation on the subject at all? A delegation of power to enunciate new policies in addition to those declared by the legislature would be unconstitutional; but the power to be conferred upon the Industrial Board is not to enunciate new policies, but merely to establish regulations for the purpose of carrying out effectively the policy declared by the law, which provides clearly and unequivocally that factories and manufacturing establishments shall be constructed, operated and maintained so as to ensure the health, safety and well-being of all employees.

A number of recent decisions have sustained legislation that permitted full power of regulation by an administrative body. The most notable recent instance of such a holding in this state is the case of *Saratoga Springs* v. *Saratoga Co.,* 191 N. Y., 123. There the court sustained a statute which established a commission with power to determine the maximum price to be charged for service by gas and electric light companies. The validity of the act was challenged on the ground that it delegated legislative powers to an administrative body. The court said that the legislature could not delegate legislative powers, adding, however:

> "But if it is intended to go further and deny the power of the legislature to confer by general laws upon other branches of the government, the duty not only of executing the law, but of determining its application to particular cases and *formulating rules for its exercise,* then in my judgment it is not true" (page 134).

* Wayman v. Southard, 10 Wheaton, 1.

The Court considered the difficulty of establishing in advance, by statute, rates for all cases, saying, at page 144:

> "It is plain that no uniform rate of charges could be established that would be just or reasonable. * * * While no consideration of convenience or of supposed necessity would justify us in ignoring any constitutional mandate or limitation, it must be remembered that we have no express constitutional provision on the subject, and that it is sought to condemn the legislation before us solely by extending the principle that the legislature cannot delegate legislative powers (a principle which, though unquestionably true, is, as we have seen, true only within limits), to a point that would render efficient legislation on the subject impracticable."

These considerations seem no less applicable to the safeguarding of employees than to the fixing of rates. In either case it is impossible to formulate in advance a rule to provide reasonable and adequate safeguards for every contingency.

In the case cited it was contended that the statute laid down no rule, but allowed the commission to legislate. The court answered at page 145:

> "The statute is complete. The legislature, not the commission, has enacted that there shall be maximum rates for the charges of the gas and electric light companies, that light shall be furnished to consumers at those rates, and has provided the penalty for extorting greater charges for service. What is entrusted to the commission is the duty of investigating the facts, and, after a public hearing, of ascertaining and determining what is a reasonable maximum rate."

So here the legislature announces its policy of providing adequate and reasonable safeguards for employees and leaves it to the Industrial Board to determine what are reasonable and adequate safeguards.

The court quotes, with approval, the following from Mr. Justice Brewer's opinion in *Chicago Co.* v. *Dey,* 35 Fed. 866:

> "The law books are full of statutes unquestionably valid, in which the legislation has been content simply to establish

> rules and principles, leaving execution and details to other officers."

The policy declared by the legislature need not be set forth in detail, but may be stated in general terms. In the case cited (191 N. Y., 123), it was contended that in order to justify delegation of legislative power to a commission, the statute must prescribe some standard to govern the action of the commission, and that the statute prescribed no such standard. But it was held that a provision allowing the commission to fix the rates " within the limits prescribed by law " was sufficient, because

> " The common law prescribes the rule that the rate shall be reasonable, and, I think, even without special mention, the statute would necessarily imply the same limitation."

This sole standard that the rates should be reasonable read into the statute by implication was held to be a sufficient declaration of policy, the court saying, at page 147:

> " Indeed, if the statute assumed to fix any other standard for rates than that they should be reasonable, we think it would be much more open to attack than in its present form. The law maker might exhaust reflection and ingenuity in the attempt to state all the elements which affect the reasonableness of a rate only to find that in a particular case he had omitted the factor which controlled the disposition of that case."

It is no easier task to prescribe in advance the standard of safety for the health and welfare of employees under all circumstances than to declare the reasonable rate in all cases.

The court quoted, with approval, the following from the opinion of Mr. Justice White in *Atlantic Coast Line* v. *North Carolina,* 206 U. S., 1:

> " The elementary proposition that railroads, from the public nature of the business by them carried on and the interest which the public have in their operation, are subject, as to their state business, to state regulation *which may be exerted, either directly by the legislative authority or by administrative bodies endowed with power to that end,* is not and could not be successfully questioned in view of the long line of authorities sustaining that doctrine."

In principle it would seem that this is equally true of any kind of business of sufficient public concern to call for detailed statutory regulation.

Perhaps the most recent declaration of the United States Supreme Court on this point is contained in *Interstate Commission* vs. *Goodrich,* 224 U. S., 194, where the Court says at pages 214-215:

> "The Congress may not delegate its purely legislative power to a commission, but, having laid down the general rules of action under which a commission shall proceed, it may require of that commission the application of such rules to particular situations and the investigation of facts, with a view to making orders in a particular matter within the rules laid down by Congress. This rule has been frequently stated and illustrated in recent cases in this court and needs no amplification here."

The court there sustained a provision of the Interstate Commerce Act empowering the Interstate Commerce Commission to prescribe the forms of accounts and records to be kept by common carriers.

The basis of the proposed enactment may be thus summed up: The protection of the health and safety of workers is one of the highest concerns of the state; it is impossible to prepare a statute which shall provide in advance rules for such protection in every industry and under all circumstances; such rules can be formulated only as necessity therefor is manifested, by a body competent to investigate each situation and to establish the requirements necessary to meet it. Under these circumstances the legislature is not powerless to remedy the many existing evils, but may write into the statute its policy of protecting persons employed at labor in every industry by reasonable and adequate means, and may leave to an administrative board to determine, after inquiry, the necessary and adequate means in each case.

THE ORGANIZATION OF THE DEPARTMENT OF LABOR

We have thus provided for the adoption of rules and regulations and for a flexible and elastic industrial code readily adaptable to the varying conditions in the different industries so that the Department of Labor will be able to keep pace with the changes that are constantly taking place in industry. It is necessary in addition to give the department an adequate number of field inspectors, and to increase its trained and expert staff so that the law may be effectively and intelligently enforced.

SALARY OF COMMISSIONER OF LABOR

As stated, we believe that the Commissioner of Labor should be the head of the department and solely responsible for the enforcement of the labor law and the industrial code. The present salary of the commissioner is $5,500 a year. This we believe to be inadequate compensation for the important and arduous duties performed by him. The salary of the commissioner should be enough to attract to the position one who has the ability, experience, executive control, and board outlook which this responsible office demands. At the same time, however, we must take into consideration the fact that the office carries with it honor and distinction, and opportunity for public service.

In fixing the amount that we believe the commissioner ought to receive, we have carefully considered the salaries paid in the federal and state service and have concluded that he should receive at least $8,000 a year. A New York public service commissioner receives $15,000 a year. It cannot be questioned, therefore, that the head of a department so important as this is to the state, should receive about half that amount.

BUREAUS

The Department of Labor has now five bureaus: factory inspection; labor statistics; mediation and arbitration; industries and immigration, and mercantile inspection. We believe it unwise to have separate bureaus of factory and mercantile inspection. All inspection work should be centralized in one bureau, under one head.

We therefore recommend that instead of separate bureaus of factory and mercantile inspection, there be one bureau of inspection. The other bureaus mentioned should be continued and provision should be made for the creation of such additional bureaus as the commissioner deems advisable.

BUREAU OF INSPECTION

The bureau of inspection, subject to the supervision and direction of the commissioner should have charge of all inspections. The first deputy commissioner should be the inspector general of the state in charge of the bureau of inspection and should receive a salary of $5,000 a year. The chief factory inspector now in charge of factory inspection only, receives $4,000 a year.

The bureau of inspection should have four divisions: factory inspection; homework inspection; mercantile inspection, and industrial hygiene. The division of industrial hygiene referred to in detail hereafter should be under the immediate charge of the commissioner himself.

Division of Factory Inspection

There is now a chief factory inspector in charge of the inspection of factories for the entire state. The majority of wage earners are in New York City. The census of 1910 showed that more than one-half of the state's population was located in that city.

Many appearing before us urged a separate department of labor for New York City. We believe, however, that uniformity in the administration of the labor law is essential and that it is the best to have the Department of Labor exercise jurisdiction over the entire state. We believe that factory inspection both in New York City and in the remainder of the state will be considerably improved if, for the purposes of such inspection, the state is divided into two inspection districts to be known as the first factory inspection district and the second factory inspection district. The first district should include New York City and the counties of the Bronx, Nassau and Suffolk, and the second district all other counties. Each inspection district should be in charge of a chief factory inspector who should receive a $4,000 salary. The creation of two factory inspection districts will tend to greater concentration in the work of inspection and consequently to beneficial results.

Number of Inspectors

The present force of field inspectors engaged in the inspection of factories is inadequate; this is the opinion of all appearing before the Commission. There are at present 81 factory inspectors who may be called field inspectors, 21 of whom receive $1,500 a year salary and the remainder $1,200 each annually. A number of these 81 field inspectors are assigned to home work inspection; that is, to the supervision of manufacturing carried on in tenement homes in the larger cities.

It need not occasion surprise that with a force of inspectors so plainly inadequate, inspections of factories are infrequent, and that the law dealing with the health and safety of employees in factories is not enforced as effectively as it should be. The suggestions received by the Commission as to an increase in the number of field inspectors vary greatly. It has been urged that we recommend as many as 300 field inspectors.

The present law provides for not more than 125 factory inspectors, including supervising inspectors and inspectors of technical and scientific experience. We recommend that there shall be *not less* than 125 factory inspectors of all grades in the division of factory inspection, of whom not more than 30 shall be women. This would leave 110 inspectors of the first, second, third and fourth grades for actual field work. Of these at least 15 should be assigned to the division of homework inspection, leaving 95 field inspectors for factory inspection exclusively. The present law provides for only two grades* of field inspectors, those receiving annual salaries of $1,200 and $1,500 respectively. Such salaries do not induce any man with technical training to enter the department or to remain there for any length of time. There should be opportunity for promotion based upon merit solely, that is, upon the length and character of service rendered, and ability as evidenced by a comprehensive written and oral examination, not the mere perfunctory promotion examination now resorted to.

We recommend the following grades of inspectors to do field work:

Grade.	*Number of Inspectors*	*Salary.*
First.	Not more than 95	$1,200
Second.	" " " 50	1,500
Third.	" " " 25	1,800
Fourth.	" " " 10	2,000

* There is a $1,000 grade, but that has been abandoned in actual practice.

An opportunity thus will be given for advancement and men of ability and experience will be attracted to the work.

Division of Homework Inspection

The conditions under which manufacturing is carried on in the tenement homes in New York City and other large cities is of vital concern, not only to those directly engaged in it, but to the public generally which uses the goods thus manufactured. We shall refer to this subject in detail later in our report.* In this connection however, we recommend that a separate division of homework inspection be created and that not less than 15 factory inspectors be detailed to this division, so that the law prohibiting manufacturing in an unsanitary tenement house, and whatever measures the legislature may adopt to prohibit the employment of young children in that work, may be effectively enforced.

Division of Mercantile Inspection

The jurisdiction of the department over mercantile establishments and the employment of women and children in them in now limited to the cities of the first class, New York, Buffalo, and Rochester. Elsewhere in the state the mercantile law (article 11 of the labor law) is enforced by the local departments of health. In cities of the first class the bureau of mercantile inspection is charged with the duty of enforcing this law.

The bureau is in charge of a mercantile inspector who has 9 deputy mercantile inspectors under his supervision. The mercantile inspector receives $3,000 salary and the deputy mercantile inspectors each receive $1,200 salary. This force is inadequate to inspect the many mercantile establishments in cities of the first class alone. Inspections are very infrequent. The mercantile inspector testified that many stores in cities of the first class had not been inspected in four years. The percentage of illegal child labor is as a result much greater in mercantile establishments than in factories. Since most of the employees in mercantile establishments are women, the necessity is apparent for frequent inspection to determine whether the laws relating to sanitary conditions and hours of labor are being

* See Manufacturing in Tenements, Appendix IV, Volume II.

observed. Factory work is carried on in most of the department stores. Formerly where this was done a separate inspection was made by a factory inspector but now a mercantile inspector must cover the entire ground.

Conditions in Second Class Cities

The jurisdiction over mercantile establishments in second-class cities is conferred by law upon the local boards of health. The mercantile law applies to every town having a population of more than 3,000, and theoretically mercantile inspection ought to be state-wide as is factory inspection. But the enormous expenditure this would involve makes it inadvisable to extend the jurisdiction of the department, over the entire state. We believe, however, that it is imperative for the department to assume jurisdiction over mercantile establishments in cities of the second class where thousands of women and children are employed in department and other stores. These establishments now receive practically no supervision.

The Commission's investigation into this subject showed that the local health departments in second class cities were very lax in their inspection of mercantile establishments. In not one of the second class cities has this subject been considered of sufficient importance to have a single inspector devote all of his time to that work. The usual plan seems to be to assign to the regular sanitary inspectors in the employ of the department of health, the duty of inspecting mercantile establishments in addition to all their other duties relating to contagious diseases, sanitation and plumbing. As might be expected, the actual amount of time devoted to mercantile establishments is very small. The statement of one official that inspectors visit mercantile establishments "when they haven't anything else to do," probaly represents actual conditions in more than one of these cities. In half of the second-class cities, mercantile establishments are visited only when a specific complaint comes to the health officer. As a result of this practice no one can tell how many violations of law actually exist. Even more surprising is the following statement made to the Commission by the health officer in one of the large second-class cities of the state:

> " I would say that this department has made no inspections of mercantile establishments as to the employment of women and children. I had supposed that such inspections were under the supervision of the mercantile and factory inspectors. The health officers who have preceded me have not made such inspections and were like myself not aware of section 172 of the labor law."

A striking indication of the failure to give serious attention to this subject is the fact that prosecutions are very rarely instituted in any of the second-class cities against employers found violating the mercantile law, while in Buffalo and Rochester the mercantile inspectors of the labor department presented to the courts 136 cases for prosecution during the year ending September 30, 1911.

We recommend therefore:

1. That there be a division of mercantile inspection in the bureau of inspection of the department as heretofore suggested, instead of a separate bureau.

2. That the division be in charge of a chief mercantile inspector who shall receive as at present a salary of $3,000. That the number of mercantile inspectors be increased from 10 to 20, of whom not less than 4 shall be women. The mercantile inspectors shall be divided into three grades, but not more than five shall be of the third grade. Each mercantile inspector of the first grade shall receive an annual salary of $1,000; each of the second grade an annual salary of $1,200, and each of the third grade an annual salary of $1,500.

3. That the jurisdiction of the department over mercantile establishments be extended to cities of the second class.

DIVISION OF INDUSTRIAL HYGIENE

The lack of a staff of trained scientific inspectors has always been a drawback in the enforcement of the labor law. It was not until very recently that a mechanical engineer was appointed, who is also an expert on accident prevention. He receives a salary of $3,500.

For some years past there has been a medical inspector of factories who has devoted himself to an investigation of various forms of industrial poisoning and has made special inspections, but has obviously been unable to cover the ground alone. He receives a salary of $2,400, which in our opinion is too low for the work expected of him.

We recommend that there be not less than four inspectors of the seventh grade, one of whom shall be a physician who shall be the chief medical inspector, one a mechanical engineer who shall be an expert on accident prevention and ventilation, one a chemical engineer, and one a civil engineer who shall be an expert on fire prevention and building construction. Each of these inspectors should receive an annual salary of $3,500. In order to work effectively, this expert group of inspectors should be placed in one division to be known as the division of industrial hygiene, to be under the immediate charge of the commissioner who may, however, select one of the group to act as director of the division. This director shall receive additional compensation of $500 annually while performing the duties of that office.

There will thus be created within the department an expert group of inspectors of scientific training who will perform the following duties:

1. Make inspections, highly technical in character, of factories, mercantile establishments, and other places subject to the labor law.

2. Conduct special investigations of industrial processes and conditions with a view to recommending the adoption or modification of standards, rules, and regulations by the industrial board.

3. Prepare material for leaflets and bulletins calling attention to dangers in particular industries and precautions to be taken to avoid them.

This division will act as an expert investigating body on the subjects of industrial poisioning and diseases, dangerous trades, prevention of accidents, ventilation, lighting and have charge of many other problems of sanitation and safety, which for their proper solution require the careful, scientific study of experts. To leave such important matters to the ordinary field inspector as has been done heretofore, is a waste of time and money and is productive of no results. Neither the manufacturer nor the employee is benefited thereby. It should be borne in mind also that the necessity for careful supervision is greatest in those very trades and occupations in which conditions are presented that are beyond the comprehension of an ordinary inspector.

Section of Medical Inspection

It is essential that a study be made of the effects of different occupations upon the health of workers. The subject of occupational diseases, although one of much importance, has been entirely neglected in this state.

We would therefore recommend that there be attached to the division of industrial hygiene a section of medical inspection, to be made up of the chief medical inspector, in charge, and three inspectors of the 6th grade, at least one of whom shall be a woman and each of whom shall receive $2,500 salary annually. Such inspectors shall be physicians duly licensed to practice medicine in this state.

The section of medical inspection shall inspect factories, mercantile establishments, and other places subject to the provisions of the labor law with respect to conditions of work affecting the health of persons employed, and shall have charge of the physical examination and medical supervision of children employed.

BUREAU OF STATISTICS AND INFORMATION

The bureau of labor statistics was founded as an independent office in 1883 to

> "collect, assort, systematize, and present in annual reports to the legislature, statistical details in relation to all departments of labor in the state, especially in relation to the commercial, industrial, social, and sanitary condition of workingmen and to the productive industries of the state." *

In actual practice, however, the work of the bureau was never confined to strictly statistical work. The bureau published all

* Labor Law, § 55.

kinds of information concerning labor and acted as a general information bureau on everything relating to labor conditions. As long as it remained an independent department, its information was collected entirely by its own research and investigations. In 1901 the bureau of labor statistics was consolidated with the office of factory inspector and the bureau of mediation and arbitration, then in existence, to form the present Department of Labor. Since it became a branch of the department of labor, the bureau of statistics has acted in a dual capacity; (1) as an independent investigator and (2) as the statistical and publication office for the other bureaus of the department. In its first capacity as an independent investigator the bureau has conducted investigations and gathered information and data on its own account from time to time and published the results in its annual report to the legislature and in the quarterly bulletin of the department. In its second capacity it has taken care of the following matters:

1. The preparation and publication of information and statistics received through the other bureaus.

2. The preparation and publication of statistics concerning the work done by the different bureaus and published in their reports.

3. The supervision of the printing and distribution of all of the reports issued at different times by the department.

This statistical and publication work for the other bureaus has grown so constantly during the past few years that it has practically absorbed all the resources of this bureau. The result has been that the bureau has been unable to do very much independent work in a very wide field of economic and social research not connected with the functions of the other bureaus, but concerning which there is constant demand for public information frequently with a view to legislation. An important example of this need for research is the question of the extent of seven-day labor in this state, and the effect of a one-day rest in seven requirement, which is now being much advocated.

The recommendations which we have made for reorganizing the other bureaus of the department, the extension of inspection work, and the broadening of such work in the direction of special investigations by the division of industrial hygiene, will enormously increase the work of the bureau of statistics. This bureau will be a most important one, since it is to be the publicity bureau of the department, that is, the bureau which shall disseminate among the employers and employees the information gathered from investigations made by the other bureaus and divisions. The bureau will have charge of the printing and distribution of the many bulletins and pamphlets to be issued from time to time concerning the prevention of accidents and industrial diseases. It will have to prepare many of these bulletins or collaborate with officals in other bureaus in their preparation. It will be the bureau of information and education.

As a foundation for the increased and important work this bureau will have to perform we recommend the following changes in the present law relating to it:

1. The title of the bureau should be changed from the bureau of labor statistics to the bureau of statistics and information. The proposed title indicates its true function.

2. There shall be the following divisions in the bureau of statistics and information:

(1) The division of general labor statistics which shall collect and prepare statistics and general information in relation to conditions of labor and the industries of the state.

(2) The division of industrial directory which shall prepare the industrial directory provided for in section forty-nine of the labor law.

(3) The division of industrial accidents and diseases which shall collect, and prepare statistical details and general information regarding industrial accidents and occupational diseases, their causes and effects, and methods of preventing, curing, and remedying them, and of providing compensation therefor.

(4) The division of investigations which shall have charge of all investigations and research work relating to economic and social conditions of labor conducted by the bureau.

(5) The division of printing and publication which shall print, publish and disseminate such information and statistics as the Commissioner of Labor may direct for the purpose of promoting the health, safety, and well-being of industrial workers.

Prompt Publication of Reports

The only publication now required by law from the bureau of labor statistics is an annual report to the legislature. The law should be amended so as to provide for the publication of special reports, bulletins, and leaflets directly by the bureau. Annual reports, owing to the time required for their preparation at the close of the year, are practically useless for prompt publication of information, and are valuable mainly as the means of printing detailed information for future reference.

With the exception of an annual report by the head of the bureau to the Commissioner of Labor on the administration of the bureau, the stereotyped form of annual reports should be replaced by the publication of special reports, bulletins or pamphlets on particular subjects. That is being done with success in the Federal Bureau of Labor.

COUNSEL TO THE DEPARTMENT OF LABOR

The counsel to the department now receives an annual salary of $3,000. His work will be largely increased because of duties connected with the Industrial Board for which he is to act as counsel without any additional compensation. We therefore recommend that his salary be increased to $4,000 a year. We also recommend that there be at least one assistant to the counsel assigned for up-state work. There is at present no counsel to represent the department in prosecutions instituted in cities up-state for violation of the provisions of the labor law. The counsel now confines his activities practically to New York City alone. The result has been that in other parts of the state prosecutions are not instituted so often and are not pushed so effectively and vigorously as they should be. This is particularly true in cases involving violations of the child labor law.*

MISCELLANEOUS RECOMMENDATIONS

Pensions for Inspectors

The work of an inspector is arduous. It involves physical and mental strain and we believe that the state ought to establish a system of disability and old-age pensions for the inspectors in

* See Bill 1, Appendix I, for provisions dealing with the reorganization of the Labor Department.

the department. We have not had sufficient opportunity to examine this subject as fully as is necessary in order to present detailed recommendations, but we suggest that it be carefully investigated by the Commissioner with a view to remedial legislation.

The necessity for such pensions is strikingly emphasized by the fact that there are in the department 5 veterans of the civil war between 60 and 75 years of age acting as factory inspectors. These men should not be allowed to continue at work which is beyond their physical strength, but should be taken care of by the state.

Examinations for Inspectors

The present civil service examinations for the position of factory inspector are in our opinion inadequate. The examination should be made more practical. The written examination should be supplemented by an oral examination to be conducted before a group of examiners and taken down in shorthand. Only those, however, who have successfully passed the written test should be permitted to take the oral examination.

Methods of Inspection

We shall not go into details in connection with the methods of inspection but simply point out some objectionable features that may be readily eliminated by the administrative head of the department. The first is the practice of assigning an inspector to the city or locality in which he lives and where he has been in many cases a life-long resident and of keeping him there permamently. Our investigations have shown that this practice has led to many abuses. It simply adds another embarrassment to the many difficulties an inspector must overcome. We believe that whenever it is practicable, inspectors should be shifted from one district to another. At any rate it is unwise and also injurious to the service to keep one inspector in his home town for years at a time unless an outside inspector checks up his work.

One of the most troublesome features in connection with a factory inspector's duties is the vast amount of clerical work he is called upon to do. Testimony showed that this clerical work took up about one-half of the working day of the average field inspector, naturally curtailing the activities of the inspector in his true sphere, namely, that of inspection. We do not wish to detract from the value of accurate and comprehensive statistics. We realize that in order to make the departmental records complete some clerical work must be done by the inspectors; but that they should be obliged to fill out and often recopy the multifarious cards and notices brought to our attention, we believe unnecessary, a waste of the inspector's working powers and an impairment of the efficiency of the entire department.

Offices for the Department of Labor

The Commission has personally visited the offices of the department in Albany and New York City. Both officies, particularly the one in Albany are entirely inadequate for the required work. For the greater efficiency of the office force and of the department as a whole, we urge that the department be given at an early date improved and suitable office facilities.

The Posting of Abstracts of the Labor Law

At present abstracts of the labor law are posted in the English language. In that form they are of no value to foreigners, who are employed in large numbers in our factories, and are unable to read the language. We therefore recommend that digests of the labor law and of the rules and regulations of the industrial board applicable to any particular establishment be posted in English and in such other languages as the commissioner may direct.

Penalties for Violation of the Labor Law

We have no recommendations to make at this time for any change in the present penalties for violation of the provisions of the labor law prescribed in section 1275 of the penal law. We do suggest, however, that this section of the penal law be amended so as to provide a penalty for the violation of any provision of the labor law instead of referring in detail to the different portions of the law. We submit a bill for that purpose.*

* Bill , Appendix I.

SUMMARY

The changes we have recommended in the organization of the labor department include the following:

1. The creation of an industrial board to prescribe regulations which shall make effectual the provisions of the labor law for the protection of the lives, health and safety of workers, and to act as a permanent investigating board.

2. An increase in the commissioner's salary from $5,500 to $8,000 a year.

3. The creation of a bureau of inspection in charge of an inspector general so that all inspection work may be centralized in one bureau under one head.

4. The creation of two factory inspection districts, one for New York City and its vicinity and the other for the remainder of the State, so that there may be greater concentration in inspection work, and so that each district may receive the undivided attention of a chief factory inspector.

5. An increase in the number of factory inspectors for field work from 81 to 110. The establishment of $1,800 and $2,000 grades for inspectors so that there may be an opportunity for promotion and men of technical training induced to enter the service.

6. A division of homework inspection to which fifteen factory inspectors shall be detailed, in charge of manufacturing in tenement houses.

7. The extension of the jurisdiction of the department over mercantile establishments to cities of the second class and an increase in mercantile inspectors from 10 to 20.

8. A division of industrial hygiene composed of an expert staff of inspectors to be a permanent expert investigating body within the department.

9. A section of medical inspection to have charge of the physical examination and medical supervision of children employed in factories and mercantile establishments and to inspect such establishments as to conditions affecting the health of the workers.

10. An enlargement of the functions of the bureau of statistics and information.

We have confined our recommendations to minimum requirements for a well-organized and efficient department of labor such as the State of New York should have; a department affording to the working people the protection and supervision they have failed to receive in the past and to which they are entitled. We believe that the measures recommended will result in the establishment of a department adequately equipped to cope with the complex problems of sanitation and safety in industry; one that will wield a strong educational influence and secure a closer co-operation and more friendly relation between employers and employees, and, finally, one that will be an important factor in conserving life in industry and in preventing and minimizing industrial accidents and disease.

II.

THE FIRE PROBLEM

Among the important problems this country must solve, and to which but scant attention has been paid in recent years, are those of " fire prevention " and " fire protection."

The annual fire losses in this country are large, and increasing at such a rate, that action should be taken at once to cause material reduction in this heavy charge imposed upon the country's resources.

During the thirty-five years between 1875 and 1909, the total value of property destroyed in the United States by fire amounted to $4,904,619,235. In 1910 the aggregate property loss was about $211,000,000, and in 1911 approximately $217,000,000.

Fire losses have increased steadily year after year in greater proportion than the growth of population.

Hon. Walter L. Fisher, Secretary of the Interior, states the situation admirably:*

> " If the Government should suddenly lay an annual tax of $2.51 on every man, woman and child in the United States on a promise of spending the money for some useful purpose, that promise would not avail against the storm of protest which would be aroused. Nevertheless, a tax which in the aggregate amounts to that is being paid by the people of this country. It is the annual fire loss of the nation upon buildings and their contents alone. It is expended not in productive enterprise, but in death and destruction, and an even larger sum is annually expended upon fire protection and insurance premiums. Not only is this property loss paid by our people, but, in addition, annually 1,500 persons give up their lives and nearly 6,000 are injured in fires.
>
> Possibly in no other direction is the national habit of waste more clearly exemplified than in the comparative indifference with which we permit such a sacrifice. In no other civilized country are conditions so bad as here.
>
> It seems ridiculous that a people so apt and so eager to seek out and destroy the mysterious and hidden enemies of

* Address before the Fifteenth Annual Meeting of the National Fire Protection Association.

mankind, should be so slow and sluggish in fighting a foe so plainly in sight and so readily vanquished. We have led the world in seeking out the causes of pestilence and removing them. We are in the vanguard of the battle against tuberculosis, typhoid and yellow fever, and still we stand apart and let the older nations lead the fight against an enemy much more easily conquered."

That this tremendous fire waste is preventable, is clearly shown by a comparsion of the statistics of fire losses in the United States with those of European countries:

> " The actual fire losses due to destruction of buildings and their contents amounted in 1907 to $215,084,709, a *per capita* loss for the United States of $2.51. The *per capita* losses in the cities of the six leading European countries amounted to but 33 cents or about one-eighth of the *per capita* loss sustained in the United States." *

A comparison of the fire losses sustained in European cities in 1904 and in cities of the United States having approximately the same population in 1907, shows how far behind we are in the solution of the fire problem. The comparison is a just one, although owing to the absence of accurate official statistics, the years selected are not the same for both countries.

EUROPEAN LOSSES FOR 1904

CITY.	Population.	Fire loss.	Per capita.
Paris, France	2,714,068	$1,266,282	$0.47
Frankfort, Germany	324,500	99,492	0.31
St. Petersburg, Russia	1,500,000	2,128,541	1.42
Birmingham, England	550,000	226,506	0.41
Sheffield, England	426,686	75,989	0.18
Toulon, France	101,602	55,391	0.55
Bremen, Germany	203,847	78,372	0.38
Molenbeek, Belgium	63,678	106,150	1.67
Laeken, Belgium	31,121	22,349	0.72
Etterbeek, Belgium	23,992	19,504	0.80

UNITED STATES LOSSES FOR 1907

CITY.	Population.	Fire loss.	Per capita.
Chicago, Illinois	2,049,185	$3,937,105	$1.43
Cincinnati, Ohio	345,230	1,971,217	5.70
Philadelphia, Pennsylvania	1,441,737	2,093,522	1.45
Baltimore, Maryland	558,669	916,603	1.66
Cleveland, Ohio	460,000	515,194	1.12
Atlanta, Georgia	104,984	225,237	2.15
St. Paul, Minnesota	204,000	522,447	2.56
Evansville, Indiana	63,957	196,702	3.08
Oshkosh, Wisconsin	31,033	80,500	2.59
Easton, Pennsylvania	25,238	32,078	1.27

* Bulletin 418 of the United States Geological Survey.

In 1911 New York City had 324 fires for every hundred thousand inhabitants. London had but 67 and Paris, 152. London in 1911 had 4,455 fires but its loss was only one-fifth of that in New York, while that of Paris was one-ninth.

This great difference between the fire loss in the United States and that in European countries is strikingly emphasized when we consider that in European cities the fire-fighting equipment and force is very inadequate in comparison with ours.

The average annual cost of maintaining fire departments in European cities is 20 cents *per capita,* while in cities of corresponding population in the United States, the cost is $1.53 *per capita,* or 7½ times as much.

The significant fact therefore remains that our losses by fire increase steadily every year despite our elaborate and expensive systems of fire-fighting and despite the fact that our city fire-fighting systems are the best in the world both as to equipment and personnel.

Not only does this wide difference exist in the property loss by fire, but the life hazard because of fire is greater in this country than in European countries. Rarely do we hear of a fire in a European city in which life is lost. Yet testimony has been given before the Commission that in New York City alone there is an average of one life lost daily because of fire.

In our building construction, although some attention has been paid to the property hazard, albeit with comparatively poor results as we have seen, practically no attention has been paid to the life hazard in factory buildings where large numbers of people congregate. Architects, engineers, and builders have designed and constructed buildings without giving due thought or consideration to the methods of escape available to the occupants in case of fire.

CAUSES FOR THE DIFFERENCE IN FIRE LOSS

The main causes for the difference between the fire losses in Europe and in the United States are the following:

1. BUILDING CONSTRUCTION: In European countries practically all buildings are constructed of fire resisting materials. Frame buildings are few in number owing to the high price and

scarcity of timber. In the United States the conditions have been exactly reversed. Lumber, at least until recently, has been the cheapest material besides being more easily worked than brick, stone, or steel.

> "The comparative immunity of Berlin from disastrous fires results not from the efficiency of its fire department—although it does promptly and well what work it has to do—but from the absence of wooden houses and the solid, careful construction of all kinds of stone and brick buildings under the rigid scrutiny of the building police." *

The buildings are so constructed that fire is confined in practically every case to a single floor and often to a single room.

In Vienna it was reported by the Consul General:

> "There is no cause known in this city where a fire has extended beyond the building in which it originated and cases are hardly ever known where a fire extended beyond the floor on which it originated."

2. HEIGHT OF THE BUILDINGS: In many European countries the height of buildings is restricted. There is no such restriction in most of the cities in the United States. In New York City particularly, the problem of fire hazard is complicated by the fact that manufacturing in which inflammable materials are used is permitted at eight, ten, and fifteen stories above the ground.

3. INDIVIDUAL RESPONSIBILITY FOR FIRES: In European countries the person on whose premises a fire occurs is held strictly to account.

In all parts of Europe where the Code Napoleon prevails, the law of voisinage holds the landlord responsible for his negligence to all concerned, whether tenants or neighbors, and if fire originates from the carelessness of a tenant, he is held responsible to all concerned, whether landlord or neighbors. This law places the responsibility where it properly belongs and makes every one maintain his premises in as safe a condition as is possible through human foresight.

* Frank H. Mason, U. S. Consul-General to the Bureau of Manufactures of the Department of Commerce and Labor.

In this country the average person pays little attention to fire loss, hardly realizing that insurance does not replace the property destroyed but merely equalizes the loss among all those whose property is insured.

The loose system of insurance in this country renders over-insurance prevalent and opens the door to incendiarism, which is here the cause of many fires. The careful investigation of the causes of fires in European countries and the more efficient system of inspection there maintained, also contribute to the difference in fire losses that has been pointed out.

SCOPE OF THE COMMISSION'S INVESTIGATIONS

The Commission has limited itself primarily to an investigation of the hazard to life in factory buildings, but throughout our investigations the fact has been repeatedly brought to our notice that matters affecting property hazard directly concern protection of human life and *vice versa.* Thus a fire wall in a building enables the occupants to reach a zone of safety with comparative ease, and at the same time prevents the spread of fire since it confines the destruction of the contents of the building to a limited area. The requirement that stairways be enclosed by fire-resisting materials results in affording to the occupants a temporary haven of refuge and also prevents the spread of fire from floor to floor. An automatic sprinkler system checks the fire in its incipient stages, saves property, and protects human life.

> "In the United States we are so prone to consider the rights of the individual that we are apt to overlook the rights of the aggregation of individuals. It is not denied that municipal building regulations adopted by any American city, requiring uniform fire-resistive building construction after any fixed date, would give rise to seeming injustices and hardships, but if laws requiring the remodeling of present risks were also rigidly enforced, in addition to laws covering the erection of new buildings, the hardships would soon be equalized, and benefit accrue to the community in the way of reduced fire losses, reduced insurance premiums, reduced expenses for maintaining fire-fighting equipments, and added security to life and property interests." *

* Freitag, Fire Prevention and Fire Protection, p. 17.

The consideration of the fire hazard problem is divided into two parts:

1. Investigation of conditions in existing factory buildings and the measures to be adopted to render those buildings safe for occupancy.

2. Requirements for the future construction of factory buildings.

THE EXISTING FIRE PROBLEM IN NEW YORK CITY

Five kinds of buildings are used for factory purposes in the city of New York:

1. The converted tenement or dwelling.
2. The non-fireproof loft building.
3. The fireproof loft building less than 150 feet in height.
4. The fireproof loft building over 150 feet in height.
5. The factory building proper, constructed for factory purposes and occupied by one establishment, which may be fireproof or non-fireproof.

Three of these types are especially dangerous when used as factory buildings. They are (1) the converted dwelling or tenement house, which was never intended to be used for business purposes above the ground floor; (2) the non-fireproof loft building, usually six or seven stories high; and (3) the fireproof loft building less than 150 feet in height.

1. THE CONVERTED DWELLING OR TENEMENT

Owing to increase in land values and to change in residence localities, many buildings formerly used for living purposes have been made over into factories. These buildings are from four to six stories in height and usually 25 feet wide by about 60 to 85 feet deep. The exterior walls are brick or stone, and the floors, interior trim, stairways, beams and doors are of wood. The stairways are usually from two to three feet in width with doors often opening inward. There are no automatic sprinkler systems, no fire prevention or extinguishing appliances except fire pails, which are not always reserved for fire purposes. The work rooms, divided by wooden partitions, are crowded with employees, and the machines are placed as close together as space will permit, without regard to means of exit. There are exterior fire-escapes with balconies on each floor, connected by vertical ladders (those of later construction by inclined stairways), which usually lead to a yard in the rear of the premises or to some blind alley, from which there is no means of escape. There is ordinarily a ladder from the lowest balcony to the ground, but it is generally not in place, or very difficult to use in case of fire, because of its weight. There is usually but one door leading from the street. In buildings of this sort we have a type constructed for dwelling purposes only, in which the number of occupants is multiplied many times beyond the capacity originally intended without any addition to the exit facilities.

2. THE LOFT BUILDING

The loft building marks an evolution in the construction of factory buildings in the city of New York. The first lofts were built about twenty-five years ago for the storing and sale of merchandise, but the manufacturer soon found it desirable to have his goods manufactured in workrooms adjacent to his salesroom and directly under his supervision.

Increase in land values, morever, forced the manufacturer to extend upwards instead of spreading out horizontally. The availability of the loft for manufacturing purposes was soon appreciated, and to-day this type of building is generally used for factory purposes.

(A) The Non-Fireproof Loft Buildings

The non-fireproof loft building is usually six or seven stories in height, 25 feet wide by 80 feet in depth, with brick, stone, or iron fronts and rears, brick side walls, wooden floors and wooden trim. There is usually one unenclosed wooden stairway, varying in width from two to three and one-half feet, and often winding around the elevator shaft. Wooden doors lead to the stairways and very often these doors open inward. The buildings, as a rule, have exterior fire-escapes similar to those found on the converted tenement described above. Usually every floor in these buildings is occupied by a different tenant and in some cases there are two or more tenants on each floor. The tenant uses the floor, or his portion of it, as salesroom, office, and factory, dividing one from the other by wooden partitions. In the manufacturing part there are usually a number of machines placed together as closely as possible with little aisle space. These buildings are to be found in great numbers on the lower east and west side of New York City. The number of people permitted to work on any one floor is restricted only by a provision of the labor law which requires a minimum of 250 cubic feet of air space per person, with no specific requirement for the floor area. As the distance between floor and ceiling is at least ten feet and often more, this cubic air space is easily obtained without any appreciable diminution of overcrowding and congestion. The present law does not require the posting of the number of people allowed even by this standard, and so prosecutions for violations are practically unknown. These buildings usually contain no automatic sprinklers. They have fire pails, which are rarely kept for the purpose intended. A few of them have standpipes with hose which is often useless.

(B) The Fireproof Loft Building Less than 150 Feet High

The fireproof loft building less than 150 feet in height, that is. about 12 stories or under, has brick, stone, or metal exterior walls, wooden floors and trim, stairways of metal or stone, and elevators. The stairways are generally about three feet wide, enclosed by fireproof walls. These buildings are either 25, 50, 75, or 100 feet wide by 85 to 200 feet in depth, the usual size being 50 by 80 or 90 feet.

The conditions of occupancy are similiar to those in the non-fireproof loft buildings just described. The Triangle Waist Company occupied a building of this type at 23-29 Washington Place, New York City. That building, in its construction and interior, is typical of the so-called fireproof loft buildings, and indeed much better than hundreds of buildings used for similar purposes in New York City to-day. Some of these buildings have automatic sprinkler systems. They are usually provided with standpipes, connected with the city water supply, and have on each floor a hose of required length, and some are provided with exterior fire escapes. It is to be noted that in these buildings elevators are used for passage from the street to the upper floors not only by the employers and others but also by the employees. For this reason the latter are in most cases quite unaware of the location of the stairways. Auxiliary fire appliances are usually provided, but their existence is unknown to the workers and no care is given to their preservation. The interior arrangements are similar to those existing in the non-fireproof loft building; that is to say, there are wooden partitions, great congestion, and doors opening inward.

Testimony shows that the danger in these so-called fireproof buildings comes from the use of wood for floors, doors, and trim. The buildings are usually of such height that the ladders and extensions of the fire department, and even the water towers, do not have standpipes, with which hose is connected on each floor, and reach the upper stories. Fire occurring in these places under the conditions of manufacture hereafter described, usually results in the destruction of the entire contents of the building although walls and floors remain substantially intact.

(C) The Fireproof Loft Building More than 150 Feet in Height

This type of building is more than twelve stories in height. The walls are of brick, stone, or metal; the floors of cement or stone; the trim and doors of metal or fire-resisting material; and the stairways of stone or metal, enclosed by fireproof walls There are usually several stairways and elevators. The buildings are sometimes supplied with automatic sprinkler systems and other appliances for extinguishing fires. In addition, these buildings sometimes have exterior stairways leading either to the street or to the ground in the rear. The buildings are usually 50, 75, or 100 feet or more in width and are from 75 to 200 feet deep. They are used for manufacturing and other purposes, and sometimes one tenant is found to occupy more than one floor. In these buildings, if a fire occurs, it is usually confined to the floor on which it starts, since it cannot burn up or down except through the windows the sashes of which are fireproof.

Above the sixth floor these buildings are open to the same objection as are fireproof buildings less than 150 feet high, namely, the upper floors cannot be reached by the firemen. The exit facilities are usually well constructed, but the number of people who occupy these buildings is not determined by exits, width of stairways, or floor space. The only restriction is, as in all other buildings, the provision for 250 cubic feet of air space for each employee. The distance between the floors is usually 10 to 15 feet, so that the cubic air space may fulfil the legal requirements although the floor is in a congested condition.

Danger to Life in Fireproof Buildings

Particular investigation was made of the so-called fireproof building, which is generally believed on account of its construction to be safer for the occupants than the non-fireproof building and to require few if any precautions either to prevent fire or to preserve the safety of the occupants when it occurs. The testimony disclosed the weakness of this fancied security. Although the fireproof building itself will not burn, the merchandise, wooden partitions, and other inflammable material burn as readily in a fireproof building as in any other. It is assumed by all fire insurance experts that when a fire occurs on any one floor, the contents of that entire floor will be destroyed. It is like placing paper in a fireproof box; the fire is confined to a specific locality, but the fire is no less hot and destructive within its given bounds. Therefore, unless means are provided for automatically extinguishing fires and for the rapid escape of the occupants, loss of life may occur even in fireproof buildings.

The Triangle Waist Company fire is illustrative of this fact. There the building was practically left intact, yet the fire was severe enough to cause the death of a large number of the occupants. In a fireproof building the fire is confined to a limited area and for this reason is more easily controlled. The occupants of floors over eighty feet from the ground cannot, however, be reached by the fire department's ladders, and must trust for escape to the stairways or to exterior fire-escapes.

In many of these buildings the occupants manufacture garments and other inflammable articles. The floors are littered with quantities of cuttings, waste material, and rubbish, and are often soaked with oil and grease. Seldom is regular effort made to clear the floors. Fireproof receptacles are not usually provided for accumulated waste, which in some cases is not removed from the floor for many days. Many of the workmen, foremen, and employers smoke during business hours and at meal times. Lighted gas jets unprotected by globes or wire netting are placed near inflammable material. Very often quantities of made-up garments and inflammable raw material are stored in these lofts. Fire drills are held only at rare intervals, exits are unmarked, and the location of the stairways and exterior fire-escapes is often unknown. Access to the stairway and the outside fire-escapes is obstructed by machinery, wooden partitions, and piled-up merchandise, and in some cases the fire-escape balcony is at such distance from the floor as to make it almost impossible for women employees to reach it without assistance. Wired glass is not used in the windows facing the balconies of the fire-escapes except in fireproof buildings over 150 feet high. In some cases the windows leading to fire-escapes are not large enough to permit the easy passage of adults. Automatic or manual fire alarms are hardly ever provided, except in the larger fireproof buildings.

> "Under the majority of the present building codes the so-called fireproof buildings are fireproof only in the sense that a conflagration does not seriously damage the structure. A fire may rage from room to room and floor to floor, partitions and all interior fittings may be charred and consumed, the contents may be destroyed, but the four walls and framework, the organic structure of the building, usually come through the ordeal intact. It is the damage to the contents far more than to the buildings themselves that makes the fire loss of the United States so heavy. In the matter of new laws, therefore, it is not so much the buildings which should receive added attention but the contents and inmates thereof. We must add to the term 'fireproof,' the terms 'deathproof' and 'conflagration proof.'" *

So far as the safety of the occupants of the building is concerned, the term "fireproof" is misleading and a misnomer. In the Iroquois Theatre fire, in the Triangle Waist Company fire and in many others in which the loss of life was great, the buildings were fire-resisting so far as the structure was concerned, but the

* Fire Prevention by Edward F. Croker, Former Chief of the Fire Department of New York City, p. 9.

character of the building did not lessen the danger to the occupants.

THE EXISTING FIRE PROBLEM IN OTHER CITIES OF THE STATE

In the cities of Buffalo, Rochester, and Syracuse, although there are loft buildings in which manufacturing is carried on, comparatively few are of great height, so that this problem is far from being so complicated and extensive in those cities as in New York. In these cities manufacturing is usually conducted in special factory buildings which vary from three to six stories in height. Such buildings, save those recently constructed, are almost always non-fireproof. The walls are of brick, stone, or metal; the floors, trim, doors, and stairways are wooden, the latter are in an open well or surrounded by wooden partitions. Sometimes there are exterior fire-escapes. These buildings do not have, as a rule, any automatic sprinklers, or appliances for extinguishing fires, except fire pails, which are frequently in a useless condition.

A feature of some of these buildings is the "gas-pipe" fire-escape. These fire-escapes consist of vertical, iron or metal ladders, affixed to the wall of the building and adjacent to the windows. The ladders usually run from the top floor of the buildings to the first floor and afford no means of reaching the ground; only an acrobat could safely descend them. The chief of the fire department of one of these cities testified that he could not use these ladders but that if it came to a question of being burned alive or using the fire-escape, he supposed he would try it.

The lack of precautions to prevent fire is marked throughout the state as well as in New York City. Smoking goes on in just the same way, rubbish is piled upon fire-escapes, overcrowding and congestion prevail, and no attempt is made to keep clear and unobstructed passageways to exits. Access to exterior fire-escapes in many cases is impossible because of obstructions in front of doors and windows. Wooden partitions exist in most of the buildings, doors open inward, inflammable material used in manufacturing is kept on hand in quantities, gas jets are unprotected, and there are no means provided in the building for giving an alarm of fire either to the occupants or to fire headquarters. Little attention is paid to the regular cleaning of buildings. Fire drills are practically unknown.

RECOMMENDATIONS

At the outset the Commission recommends that the following definition of a factory building be incorporated in section two of the labor law:

> "The term 'factory building' when used in this chapter means any building, shed or structure which or any part of which is occupied by or used for a factory." *

PREVENTION OF FIRE

The old adage that an ounce of prevention is better than a pound of cure applies with special force to the prevention of fires. Expert testimony given before the Commission was to the effect that at least 50% of the fires occuring in this state could be prevented if simple and inexpensive precautions were taken.

The prevention of fire is nothing more than a matter of "good housekeeping." Cleanliness of the workroom and of the factory building, the removal of rubbish, the collection of waste cuttings and inflammable material in fireproof receptacles, the prohibition of smoking, and the protection of gas jets are most effective aids to this end.

The enlightened manufacturer realizes that the calamity of fire, hitherto characterized as an act of God, is often due simply to carelessness and usually preventable.

In its preliminary report to the legislature, the Commission submitted a bill containing the following provisions:

1. The provision of fireproof receptacles in which all inflammable waste materials, cuttings, and rubbish were to be placed.

2. The removal of waste materials, rubbish, and cuttings of a manufacturing establishment at least twice a day, and the removal of such cuttings and waste materials from the factory building at least once a day.

3. Gas jets in factories to be enclosed by globes or wired cages or otherwise properly protected.

4. Smoking in factories prohibited and to be punishable as a violation of the labor law.

---

* Bill 8, Appendix I.

The bill containing these requirements was passed by the Legislature and is now embodied in section 83b of the labor law.

The prohibition of smoking has been productive of excellent results according to the testimony of the Fire Commissioner of New York City. Since the law went into effect last October, more than 200 prosecutions for violation were successfully instituted in that city.

The only change that we recommend in this law is one relating to the requirement that all waste materials be removed from a factory at least once a day. We believe that if such materials and cuttings are baled they may be safely stored in fireproof enclosures and removed therefrom once a month. We therefore recommend the following change in the provision referred to:

> " All such waste materials, cuttings and rubbish shall be entirely removed from a factory building at least once in each day, *except that baled waste material may be stored in fireproof enclosures, provided that all such baled waste material shall be removed from such building at least once in each month.*" *

We also recommend the following change in the form of the provision relating to the prohibition of smoking:

> " [Smoking in a] No *person shall smoke in any factory* [factory is prohibited]. A notice of such prohibition, stating the penalty for violation thereof, shall be posted *in every entrance hall and in every elevator car, stairhall and room* on every floor of such factory in English, and also in such other language or languages as the fire commissioner of the city of New York, in such city, and elsewhere, the state fire marshal shall direct."†

FIRE ALARM SIGNAL SYSTEMS

After careful consideration the Commission has come to the conclusion that a fire alarm signal system is necessary in every factory building over two stories in height in which more than 25 persons are employed, to notify the occupants promptly of the occurrence of fire. In the Triangle Waist Company fire the em-

* Matter in *italics* is new; matter in brackets [ ] is old law to be omitted.
† Bill 3, Appendix I.

ployees on the 9th and 10th stories were not promptly notified of the outbreak of fire on the 8th story. That delay, short as it was, undoubtedly contributed greatly to the loss of life.

We do not believe that there should be any hard and fast requirements in the statute itself as to the kind and number of signals. The provision of the statute should be general, leaving it to the fire commissioner in the city of New York and the state fire marshal elsewhere, to determine what methods shall be used in the different types of factories throughout the state. Requirements that would be necessary in a high loft building in New York City would be superfluous in a small country factory. We therefore recommend the following provision:

> "*Every factory building over two stories in height in which more than twenty-five persons are employed above the ground floor shall be equipped with a fire alarm system with a sufficient number of signals clearly audible to all occupants thereof. The industrial board may make rules and regulations prescribing the number, kind and location of such signals. Such system shall be installed by the owner or lessee of the building and shall permit the sounding of all the alarms within the building whenever the alarm is sounded in any portion thereof. Such system shall be maintained in good working order. No person shall tamper with, or render ineffective any portion of said system except to repair the same. It shall be the duty of whoever discovers a fire to cause an alarm to be sounded immediately.*"*

FIRE DRILLS

In our last report we referred very fully to the necessity for fire drills in factories. The greatest danger in a factory fire is the panic and pandemonium that arise when the cry of fire rings through the workroom, and the operatives rush madly to the exit that they generally use. This exit is often the elevator which in most fires is soon rendered useless.

In many of the larger buildings where occupants use the elevators for passage to and from their work, the location of the stairs or exterior fire-escapes, as has been said, is unknown. A fire drill conducted periodically under competent supervision would give the employees in case of fire a sense of security now entirely

* Bill 4, Appendix I.

lacking; it would show them the location of all the exits, the quickest way to reach them and how to use them; it would emphasize clearly the necessity for keeping passageways to exits unobstructed and constantly bring to the minds of employer and employee alike the possibility of fire and the necessity for using every precaution to prevent it.

It is our belief that regular fire drills are the best means of preventing panic when fire occurs. Although the good discipline resulting from them cannot be made so effective in a factory as in a school, it undoubtedly would go far in preventing a mad rush toward the exits. We therefore recommend that in every factory building over two stories in height in which more than twenty-five persons are employed above the ground floor a fire drill shall take place at least once a month, which will conduct all the occupants of the building to a place of safety and in which all the occupants in the building shall participate simultaneously. In New York City the fire commissioner and in the rest of the state the state fire marshal shall supervise such drills and shall make regulations therefor.

It is particularly important that in a loft building where different floors are occupied by different tenants there should be a co-operative fire drill, that is, a drill participated in simultaneously by all of the occupants of the building, including the employees of its different establishments. Only in this way can it be determined whether the exit facilities furnished are adequate to enable the occupants to escape at a time of fire.

Fire drills participated in only by the employees of one floor of a factory building are not of any great value because the probable conditions of a fire are not in this way reproduced.

We therefore recommend that in case of buildings containing more than one tenant, the fire commissioner and the state fire marshal as the case may be, shall make rules and regulations suitable for the adequate co-operation of all the tenants of the building. Such rules should also prescribe upon whom shall rest the duty of carrying them out.

AUTOMATIC SPRINKLERS

The necessity is very apparent of an efficient means of extinguishing fire in its incipient stages, particularly in high buildings. Fire departments are unable to reach with their ladders any point above the seventh story of a building, or higher than ninety feet above the ground. Ordinary precautions are therefore insufficient above that height.

The automatic sprinkler system consists of a tank usually upon the roof of the building, containing an independent supply of water, communicating with pipes which run along the ceilings of each floor. At regular intervals in these pipes are placed what is known as "sprinkler heads," fastened with fusible nuts, which when exposed to a certain degree of heat automatically melt and discharge a flow of water. The chiefs of various fire departments testified that one of the best means of preserving life, especially in high buildings and in those where wooden trim is used, is an automatic sprinkler system. The fire chief of the city of New York and the fire commissioner then in office testified after the fire in the building of the Triangle Waist Company that if an automatic sprinkler system had been installed in that building, the fire would have been checked at its beginning or would have been confined to a very small area, and not a single life would have been lost.

The Superintendent of Buildings of the city of New York, in a memorandum submitted to the Commission last year said:*

> "Of greater importance than fireproof construction as a safeguard is an efficient means of extinguishing fire in its incipiency. For this purpose there is nothing better than a well designed automatic sprinkler system."

The advisory expert to the Commission in 1911 in his report stated as follows:†

> "It is believed that the sprinkler system where properly installed will, in many cases extinguish fire in its incipiency and in most cases will retard its spread affording more time for the escape of persons to safety and preventing the fire from gaining material headway until the arrival of the firemen. They should be required in all non-fireproof factory buildings occupied by more than 200 persons above the first

* Volume I, Preliminary Report New York State Factory Investigating Commission, p. 699.

† Volume I, Preliminary Report New York State Factory Investigating Commission, p. 153.

story and exceeding three stories or forty feet in height. In fireproof buildings with window openings protected with approved fireproof frames, sash, and glass, sprinkler systems are more useful and valuable as a protection of property than to life."

The advisory expert to the Commission in 1912, in his report, said:

> " Sprinkler systems are quite as effective in fireproof as in non-fireproof buildings especially in preventing the spread of fire and giving the occupants more time to make their safe exit from the building."

The Efficiency of the System

The Superintendent of Buildings in New York City in his memorandum quoted above, said that fully 90% of the fires in buildings equipped with automatic sprinklers have been extinguished in their incipient stages or effectively held in check.

Testimony as to the efficacy of sprinkler systems varies, but the lowest estimate of their successful operation is 75%, and the highest, 95%. Proof was given that in New England mills where sprinkler systems have been in use for many years, there was only one loss of life where the sprinkler system was installed, and in that case the water supply for the system was cut off just before the fire.

The installation of an automatic sprinkler system eventually pays for itself by the reduction of fire insurance premiums granted where the system is installed. The reduction varies from 35% to 50% in insurance premiums on building and contents. The reduction of premiums is allowed, however, only if the system is one approved by the National Board of Fire Underwriters, consisting of representatives of most of the fire insurance companies in the United States. Anyone desiring to obtain the benefit of a reduction in insurance rate must install one of these approved systems. Some testimony was offered indicating that there was or had been an arrangement or understanding by which high prices were charged for these systems, but this statement was declared to be without foundation by many witnesses, including architects and engineers. Testimony was given that any competent plumber could install a sprinkler system which would be effective in case of fire.

The Commission has had no opportunity to conduct the thorough investigation into this subject that is necessary to ascertain the full facts, but recommends that such an investigation be made.

Recommendations for Existing Buildings

The Commission, although desiring in view of the circumstances to make no drastic recommendations on this subject, is nevertheless convinced that in buildings over seven stories or 90 feet in height in which wooden flooring or wooden trim is used and in which manufacturing is carried on above the seventh story and more than 200 persons are employed above that story, the only safe means to prevent the spread of fire and the loss of life incidental thereto, would be the installation of an automatic sprinkler system.

The danger to life is just as great in a fireproof building where wooden trim and wooden floor finish are used, as it is in a non-fireproof building, particularly where manufacturing is carried on at a height which is beyond the reach of the fire fighting and life saving equipment of the fire department and where a large number of persons are employed above that height. It will be found also that in practically all of the manufacturing carried on above this height the materials of manufacture are of a more or less inflammable character. We therefore recommend that in existing buildings an automatic sprinkler system be required under the conditions mentioned.

Recommendations for Future Buildings

In the case of buildings hereafter constructed, the Commission recommends that an automatic sprinkler system be installed in all buildings over seven stories or ninety feet in height with wooden floor or wooden trim in which any manufacturing is carried on above the seventh story, irrespective of the number of persons employed above that story. In most buildings of this kind now being constructed automatic sprinkler systems are installed.

Recommendations for Both Existing and Future Buildings

In addition to the minimum requirements set forth above for existing buildings and buildings hereafter erected, the Commission recommends that the industrial board be authorized to make rules and regulations for the installation of automatic sprinkler systems in every case in which they are needed because of the hazardous character of the business carried on, to ensure the safety of the occupants of the factory building.*

FIRE ESCAPES AND EXITS IN EXISTING BUILDINGS

We make the following recommendations for exits and fire-escape facilities in existing factory buildings.

Required Exits

Every building over two stories in height should be provided on each floor with at least two means of exit or escape from fire and these exits should be remote from each other. One of the exits should lead to or open on an interior stairway or to an exterior enclosed fireproof stairway, the other to one of such stairways or to a horizontal exit or to an exterior screened stairway, or when, in the opinion of the Industrial Board the safety of the occupants of the building would not be endangered thereby, to fire-escapes on the outside of the building. No portion of any floor of such factory should be more than 100 feet distant from one such means of exit.

A horizontal exit is an opening through a fire wall in a building, or through a party wall between two buildings, or through exterior balconies connecting a building with an adjoining or nearby structure.

* A conference including representatives of the following bodies, in a memorandum submitted to the Commission, recommended that an automatic sprinkler system be required in all factory buildings over fifty feet in height:

Allied Real Estate Interests; American Institute of Consulting Engineers; Brooklyn Chapter American Institute of Architects; Brooklyn League; Citizens' Union; City Club of New York; Committee on Safety; National Board of Fire Underwriters; New York Board of Fire Underwriters; N. Y. Chapter American Institute of Architects; N. Y. Society of Architects; Joint Labor Conference on Workmen's Compensation.

The memorandum stated as follows: "In the opinion of this conference the automatic sprinkler is so valuable a means of fire prevention that it should be required in more buildings than those specified in this (the Commission's) Bill."

Inadequacy of Outside Fire-Escapes

Even in the case of existing buildings, we have hesitated to recommend that an outside fire-escape be under all circumstances accepted as a required means of exit. Such fire-escapes are as a general rule totally inadequate in case of fire. The objections to the use of such fire-escapes as a means of exit have been ably summed up in a brief submitted to the Commission as follows:*

> "All outside fire-escapes are open to the following objections: Inmates are not accustomed to their use and do not generally seek them except as a last resort. They do not allow of a quick and ready means of escape, as persons are unaccustomed to them and will move along slowly, thus delaying those who are following. In wintry weather they are liable to be obstructed by snow and ice, and when covered with sleet or ice become unsafe and dangerous. Very often they are rendered useless becase of smoke and flame issuing from the windows at which they are placed. The means of getting from the lowest balcony is generally the least satisfactory of the entire equipment, and being at a point where it is most needed greatly delays quick egress. They are liable to be blocked by being used as storage platforms, and no amount of inspection can entirely prevent this in crowded districts. Numerous instances may be found in the public press in which inmates seeking fire-escapes have failed to know what to do and have waited for the fire department to come and take them down. On account of the contracted dimensions of these fire-escapes large persons have sometimes found difficulty in making proper use of them. The fire department has generally advocated their use, but it will be found that this advocacy is based on a desire to have a means of getting into the building; but if desirable for this purpose, then they should be provided as such and not offered to the inmates as a satisfactory means of egress."

Only under conditions prescribed by the Industrial Board should outside fire-escapes be accepted as one of the required means of exit in existing buildings. In the case of buildings hereafter erected we unhesitatingly recommend that the construction of out-

* Brief submitted by Rudolph P. Miller, Volume I of the Preliminary Report of the New York State Factory Investigating Commission, p. 699.

side fire-escapes be discouraged and that under no circumstances should they be allowed as a required exit from a factory.

Stairways to the Roof

Wherever it is found that egress may be had from the roof of a factory building to an adjoining or neighboring structure, we believe that it is necessary that stairways extending to the top floor of the building be continued to the roof to enable the occupants of the building to escape in case of fire. Of course where egress may not be had from the roof it would be an unnecessary expense to require the stairways to be continued to the roof. All stairways that constitute required means of exit from the building should be extended to the roof.

Stairway Enclosures

There are very many buildings throughout the state with wooden stairways which are unenclosed or which are enclosed by non-fireproof partitions. In many cases such stairways wind around hoistways and elevator shafts. When a fire occurs it spreads through these stairways like a flame through a chimney, and renders escape impossible by means of the stairs. The rapidity with which a fire spreads in buildings in this country as compared with European countries, is undoubtedly due to the fact that we have here neglected properly to protect vertical openings.

In the opinion of every expert on the subject, the vertical hazard constitutes a very grave danger. The unenclosed wooden stairway in a factory building is a menace to property and to life. A number of great fires occuring in this country has plainly shown this fact. To require the wooden stairs to be removed and fireproof ones erected would in our opinion be too great a hardship. Reasonable safety will be afforded if these stairways are enclosed by partitions or walls of fire-resisting material. The occupants of the building will thus be permitted to descend the stairs in safety, since the fire will be checked at the entrance to the stairs. We therefore make the following recommendation:

> All interior stairways serving as required means of exit in buildings more than four stories in height and the landings, platforms and passageways connected therewith shall be en-

closed on all sides by partitions of fire-resisting material extending continuously from the basement.

Doors

The present labor law (section 80) provides that doors leading to exits shall open outward wherever practicable. Up to the time of the Triangle Waist Company fire this provision was liberally construed and there were but few orders requiring changes in existing doors. That fire showed, however, the grave danger to life caused by doors opening inward in a factory building, particularly where large numbers of persons are employed. The fact that the doors opened inward undoubtedly contributed to the great loss of life occurring in that fire. We therefore recommend that where five or more persons are employed on any one floor of a factory building, every door on such floor shall open outward or slide freely and that all exit doors in the first story including the doors of the vestibule, shall open outward. All doors that open outward, however, shall be so constructed as not to obstruct the passageway.

Outside Fire-Escapes

As previously mentioned, the Commission places little reliance on an outside fire-escape as a means of escape during fire. In existing buildings we have recommended that such fire-escapes be accepted as a required exit only where the safety of the employees in the building would not be jeopardized thereby. We are submitting, however, to the legislature detailed specifications for the construction of fire-escapes to be placed hereafter upon existing buildings.*

Existing Outside Fire-Escapes

As they are at present constructed, many existing outside fire-escapes are nothing but fire traps. Often there is no stairway leading to the roof, no proper stairway leading to a landing place and a fire-escape often ends in a blind alley or cul-de-sac from which no escape is possible.

Under no circumstances should the so-called vertical ladder type of fire-escape be permitted and no existing outside fire-escape should be accepted unless it has stairways placed at an angle of

* Bill 6, Appendix I.

not more than 60°. We recommend the following requirements for fire-escapes now in existence on factory buildings:

1. A stairway leading from the top floor balcony to the roof except where the fire-escapes are located on the front of the building.

2. A "counter-balanced" stairway from the lowest balcony to a safe landing place beneath.

3. Safe and unobstructed exit should be provided to the street from the foot of the fire-escape either by a fireproof passageway leading to the street and adequately lighted, or into an open area having communication with the street.

4. Where the distance from the floor of a work-room to the sill of the window opening upon a fire-escape is more than three feet, suitable steps should be provided to reduce such distance.

5. The windows of all openings leading to fire-escapes should have metal frames and sash, and wired glass. Doors leading to fire-escapes should be of fireproof construction.

REQUIREMENTS FOR NEW BUILDINGS

Fireproof Construction

The Commission is of the opinion that all buildings hereafter erected over four stories in height should be of fireproof construction if used for factory purposes. The difference in cost between a building of fireproof construction and a building of mill or slow burning construction is rapidly decreasing owing to the increasing cost of lumber.

Experience in European countries has shown that the construction of buildings of fire-resisting materials has resulted in confining a fire to a limited area, and as a consequence in those countries the fire loss is, as has been pointed out, much less than in the United States. A building hereafter erected should be deemed of fireproof construction if it conforms to the following requirements:

> All walls constructed of brick, stone, concrete or terra-cotta; all floors and roofs of brick, terra-cotta or reinforced concrete placed between steel or reinforced concrete beams and girders; all the steel entering into the structural

parts encased in at least two inches of fireproof material, excepting the wall columns, which must be encased in at least eight inches of masonry on the outside and four inches on the inside; all stair-wells, elevator wells, public hallways and corridors enclosed by fireproof partitions with metal-covered doors, trim and sash; all stairways, landings, hallways, and other floor surfaces of incombustible material; no woodwork or other combustible material used in any partition, furring, ceiling or floor; and all window frames, doors and sash, trim and other interior finish of incombustible material; all windows shall be fireproof windows except that in buildings under seventy feet in height, fireproof windows are required only when within thirty feet of another building; except that in buildings under one hundred feet in height there may be wooden sleepers and floor finish and wooden trim.

CONSTRUCTION OF FACTORY BUILDINGS OVER ONE STORY IN HEIGHT

We make the following recommendations for the construction of factory buildings hereafter erected over one story in height.

Roofs and Cornices

The roofs of all buildings should be covered with incombustible material and their cornices should be constructed of such material. The necessity for a fire-resisting roof covering to serve as a protection from heat, sparks or embers from a neighboring fire or from more distant sources, was directly emphasized in the fire of 1902 at Paterson, N. J., where several fires broke out in different parts of the city at one time from flying embers falling on wooden roofs. Likewise, in order to prevent the rapid spread of fire from one building to another, all exterior walls of a non-fireproof building within twenty-five feet of any other non-fireproof building should be not less than eight inches thick and should extend to three feet above the roof.

Floor Area and Required Exits

There should be from every floor area not less than two means of exit remote from each other, one of which should be an interior enclosed fireproof stairway or an exterior enclosed fireproof stairway and the other should be one of such stairways or a horizontal exit. The term "floor area" signifies the entire floor area between fire walls or between a fire wall and an exterior wall of a building or between the exterior walls of a building where there is no intervening fire wall.

The Commission is of the opinion that the present type of outside fire-escapes consisting of inclined stairways should not be permitted as required means of exit in factory buildings hereafter constructed.

No point in any floor area should be more than 100 feet distant from one such exit. Whenever any floor area exceeds 5,000 square feet there should be provided at least one additional exit as before described for each 5,000 square feet or part thereof in excess of 5,000 square feet.

Smoke-proof Towers

Undoubtedly the best type of fire-escape for a factory building is the so-called Philadelphia fire tower which consists of a stairway enclosed by fire-resisting material, separated from the interior of the building, except for an exterior balcony at each floor level which forms a means of communication through the outer air between the tower and the interior of the building. Such fire-escapes have no direct communication with the interior and the danger from smoke is reduced to a minimum. Interior or covered vestibules may take the place of the exterior balconies. Such vestibules should open to the outer air by means of openings in the exterior wall extending from floor to ceiling. Any smoke that may chance to enter the tower from the interior of the building thus escapes directly to the outer air.

We therefore recommend that in every new factory building over 100 feet in height there shall be at least one such tower stairway to which access can readily be had from any point in the building.

Construction of Stairways

All stairways should be constructed of incombustible material and should be not less than 44 inches wide. The stairways should be wide enough to permit two persons to go down abreast comfortably. The treads should be not less than 10 inches wide exclusive of nosing and the rise not more than 7¾ inches, and the sum of the rise and tread should be not less than 17¾ inches. The treads should be constructed and maintained in such a manner as to prevent persons from slipping thereon. Every stairway should have proper and substantial hand-rails. All stairways serving as required means of exit should lead continuously to the street or to a fireproof passageway independent of other means of exit from the building, opening on a road or street, or to an open area affording unobstructed passage to a road or street. All stairways that extend to the top story should be continued to the roof. Provision should be made for the adequate lighting of all stairways by artificial light.

Winders

No stairway with winders should be permitted except as a connection from one floor to another. Winders are a source of great danger in case of fire, causing congestion and consequent panic. They are forbidden in New York City in theatres and public buildings, and there is every reason to prohibit them in the future in factory buildings where the fire hazard is far greater.

Enclosure of Stairways and Elevator Shafts

Every stairway and elevator shaft should be enclosed on all sides by fireproof partitions extending continuously from the basement to three feet above the roof.

We have already discussed the necessity for the enclosure of stairways in existing factory buildings. There can be no doubt about the necessity for this requirement in factory buildings over one story in height hereafter constructed.

Enclosure of Vertical Openings

The principal aim in the future construction of factory buildings is to confine a fire to a limited area and to prevent its spread from one floor to another. All vertical openings leading from one floor to another, including elevator and dumbwaiter shafts, vent and light shafts, pipe and duct shafts, and hoistways should be enclosed throughout their height on all sides by enclosures of fireproof material.

> " San Francisco's experience indicates that wells and elevator shafts, running up through many stories, should be guarded by brick or reinforced concrete walls, fitted with double metal rolling doors, bolted to the walls to allow for expansion, or with automatic sliding doors and wire glass partitions. There was little or no provision for cutting off the draught of air that will ascend through such a shaft during a fire, and great destruction resulted in consequence."*

Doors and Doorways

All doors should open outward. We have already discussed the necessity for this provision in the case of existing buildings. The width of hallways and exit doors leading to the street, at the street level, should be not less than the aggregate width of all stairways leading to them. Every door leading to or opening on a stairway should be of at least the same width as such stairway.

Partitions

To permit the use of wooden partitions in buildings of fireproof construction hereafter erected is highly illogical, and defeats the purpose of making the interior of the building as fireproof as possible. We therefore recommend that all partitions in the interior of buildings of fireproof construction hereafter erected shall be of incombustible material.

REQUIREMENTS COMMON TO BUILDINGS HERETOFORE AND HEREAFTER ERECTED

The Commission makes the following recommendation for requirements that shall apply to all factory buildings, those now in existence and those hereafter erected.

Doors and Windows

No door, window or other opening on any floor of a factory building should be obstructed by stationary metal bars, grating or

* " The San Francisco Earthquake and Fire "—Bulletin No. 324, United States Geological Survey.

wire mesh. Metal bars, grating or wire mesh provided for any such door, window or other opening should be so constructed as to be readily movable or removable from both sides in such manner as to afford the free and unobstructed use of such door, window, or other opening as means of egress in case of need, and they should be left unlocked during working hours. No door leading into or out of any factory on any floor thereof should be locked or bolted during working hours.

Exit Signs

The Commission ascertained, by investigation and testimony, that exits to outside fire escapes and interior stairways were often unknown to many of the operatives. It is essential that the location of these exits be clearly indicated. We recommend, therefore, that a clearly painted sign marked "EXIT" in letters not less than eight inches in height shall be placed over all exits leading to stairways, elevators and other means of egress, and, in addition, a red light shall be placed over such means of egress for use in time of darkness.

Access to Exits

A contributing cause to the loss of life in the Triangle Waist Co. fire was the lack of clear passageways leading either to the outside fire-escapes or to the stairways or elevators. The operatives were crowded together, seated at machine tables with chairs back to back, so that, when a great number of them attempted to leave at the same time, there was panic and confusion.

The tables containing the sewing machines on the 9th floor were placed so close to the south wall of the building that the only convenient way for the operatives seated near that wall to reach the elevators and stairways at the southwest corner, was to walk the entire length of the crowded space between the tables, to the north side of the building and then use the aisles which extended along the north and west sides of the building. As a result twenty dead bodies were found near the machines, the operatives being "apparently overcome before they could extricate themselves from the crowded aisles." *

* Report of the New York Board of Fire Underwriters.

The Coroner's jury which investigated the fire made the following report on this subject:

> "We find that one of the tables to which the machines were attached and at which the employees worked, was 75 feet long, and that it extended along one side of the room to within 16 inches of a partition at another end, thus leaving only 2 passageways, one of about 13¼ inches and one of 16 inches, which the employees, working at that table, were obliged to pass to reach the stairways and elevators. The condition which prevailed in this building obtains in many similar buildings."

The Commission's investigators found that in many buildings the work tables, merchandise, stock, and even the workers were crowded together so as to make it impossible for the employees to move about with freedom. The aisles in many cases were found to be too small or narrow to admit of easy passage. Exits were often found to be obstructed by the erection of temporary partitions put up indiscriminately by tenants without any consideration of the obstruction of exits and passageways.

We therefore recommend that there shall at all times be maintained continuous, safe, unobstructed passageways on each floor of the building, with an unobstructed width of at least three feet throughout their length leading directly to every exit including outside fire-escapes and passenger elevators and that all exits shall be maintained in an unobstructed condition.

INDUSTRIAL BOARD TO MAKE RULES AND REGULATIONS FOR SAFETY

The foregoing are simply minimum requirements for the safety of the occupants of factory buildings in case of fire. It is obviously impossible to provide for every contingency in a statute. We would recommend, therefore, that in addition to these minimum requirements the statute contain a provision that no factory shall be conducted in any building whether heretofore or hereafter erected, unless such building shall be so constructed, equipped and maintained in all respects as to afford adequate protection against fire to all persons employed therein, and that the Industrial Board shall have the power to adopt rules and regulations, establishing requirements and standards for the construction, maintenance, and equipment of factory buildings or of particular classes of factory buildings and the means and adequacy of exits therefrom, in order to ensure the safety of all of the occupants in factory buildings, in addition to the specific requirements of the statute and not inconsistent therewith.

LIMITATION OF THE NUMBER OF OCCUPANTS

That every factory building should have exit facilities sufficient to enable all of the occupants thereof to escape in safety in case a fire occurs seems open to no question. Yet in actual practice, that requirement has been entirely disregarded. Employees are crowdod into our tall loft buildings and our converted tenement houses with no provision for escape in case of fire. This condition is permitted by law. The number of stairways required in a building under the present provisions of the building code of New York City (and those provisions are substantially followed in other cities of the state) is based not upon the number of occupants or even upon the height of the building but upon its area. The present provision of the labor law simply provides that there shall be 250 cubic feet of air space in a factory for each occupant. As the ceilings in most cases are high, this provision does not prevent overcrowding. The theatre law for several years past has limited the number of occupants in theatres in accordance with exit facilities provided. This same provision we believe should be extended at once to factories where the fire hazard is so much greater and where the height at which manufacturing is carried on involves increased danger to life.

The problem in existing buildings which have been permitted by law to be erected without regard to the safety of the occupants, is a very difficult one. It has been urged that requirements for added exit facilities would work hardship upon the owners; but the duty of the state in this regard is a plain one and should not be shirked. No requirement necessary for the preservation of the lives of the employees in these factory buildings in case of fire is unreasonable. That we have been indifferent and neglectful in the past is no reason why we should continue to disregard the fundamental laws of safety.

Limitation of Number of Occupants According to Stairways

We recommend therefore that the number of persons permitted to be employed on any one floor of a factory building shall be limited in accordance with the size and number of exits provided and that such number of persons be allowed to increase in proportion to the additional exits or means of extinguishing or preventing the spread of fire provided by the owner or tenant.

For that purpose we recommend certain minimum requirements that may however be increased and made more stringent when and where in the opinion of the Industrial Board such a course is necessary for the safety of the occupants in different classes of factory buildings.

The ordinary means of exit in case of fire are interior stairways, elevators, and outside fire-escapes. The Commission believes that in determining the number of persons to be permitted to work on a floor no allowance should be made for elevators and outside fire-escapes. Their availability in case of fire is always more or less uncertain. In this view we are supported by all of the experts who have appeared before us.

Capacity of Stairways in Existing Buildings

The capacity of the stairway as an exit is limited by its height and width. It is manifest therefore that the number of persons occupying the building must bear some relation to the capacity of stairways in the building.

After careful consideration of the testimony of experts and parties in interest appearing before the Commission and of the briefs submitted by them, we recommend that in existing buildings, no more than 14 persons shall be employed or permitted to work on any one floor of a factory building for every 18 inches in width of stairway provided for such floor and that for any excess in width of less than 18 inches a proportionate increase in the number of occupants shall be allowed. For every additional 16 inches over 10 feet in height of any floor, one additional person shall be permitted to be employed thereon for every 18 inches in width of stairway provided for such floor.

Occasions may arise, however, where this requirement might work hardship. For example, one floor of a building may have a great may occupants on it while the floor below may be used as a show-room and have but few employees on it. In that event an additional allowance may safely be made in present buildings. We recommend, therefore, that the Industrial Board be given power to make rules and regulations allowing an increase in the number of occupants on any floor of a factory building heretofore erected, but not exceeding the rate of 20 persons for every 18 inches in width of stairway, where the conditions are such as to warrant such increase and where the safety of the employees in the building would not be endangered thereby.

The limitation of the number of occupants in existing factory buildings is a very drastic innovation, and it is only just and proper that the Industrial Board be given some discretionary power to afford relief in cases where the minimum requirement outlined in the statute would work hardship and would be unnecessary to secure the safety of the occupants of the building.

Reduction for Winders

If any stairway has winders the capacity of the stairway should be counted as 10 per cent. less than the capacity of a straight stairway of the same width. Winders are a source of danger in case of fire and cause congestion and consequent inability to escape rapidly. A stairway with winders can accommodate fewer persons than a straight stairway.

Capacity of Stairways in Future Buildings

In the case of buildings hereafter constructed we recommend that not more than 14 persons shall be employed or permitted to work on any one floor for every full 22 inches in width of stairway provided for such floor and that no allowance be made for any excess in width of less than 22 inches. We have already recommended that in case of buildings hereafter constructed all stairways shall be not less than 44 inches wide and shall have no winders.

Enclosed Stairhalls

Where the stairways and stairhalls are enclosed in fireproof partitions properly constructed, and the openings in such partitions are provided with fireproof doors, so many additional persons may be employed on any floor as can occupy the enclosed stairhall or halls on that floor allowing 3 square feet of unobstructed floor space per person. This allowance is based upon the assumption that the additional number of persons permitted on a floor will, when they enter the enclosed stairhall, reach a zone of safety, within a comparatively short period of time. The partition wall separating the stairhall from the loft in which the fire occurs, will resist the fire long enough to enable the employees to escape from the building.

Horizontal Exits

Horizontal exits are afforded when there is provided in the building one of the following:

1. A fire wall extending from cellar to roof constructed of brick, porous terra-cotta blocks, or reinforced stone concrete, and having at each floor level one or more openings protected by fireproof doors so constructed as to prevent the spread of fire or smoke through the openings. The openings shall be unobstructed and unlocked whenever any person is employed on either side.

2. Openings in the party wall separating two buildings protected by fireproof doors constructed as described in the preceding paragraph.

3. Exterior balconies or bridges not less than 44 inches in width connected with an adjoining or nearby building; the doors opening out upon such balconies or bridges to be fireproof doors level with the floor of the balcony; the doors in the connected buildings opening on such balconies and bridges to be continuously kept unlocked and unobstructed whenever any person is employed on either side of the exit; the balconies to be enclosed on all sides and at top and bottom by fireproof material unless all windows or openings upon such balconies or directly below them or within 30 feet of them in the connected buildings shall be provided with metal frames and sash, and shall have wired glass where glass is used.

The occupants on one side of a horizontal exit in case of fire simply pass through the doorways in the fire wall, party wall, or exterior balcony as the case may be. These doorways are self-closing and the employees thus find themselves in what is practically an independent structure so far as the danger from the fire is concerned.

Where a horizontal exit is properly constructed and maintained, we recommend that such additional number of persons may be employed on any one floor as can occupy the smaller of the two spaces on either side of the fireproof partitions or fire walls or as can occupy the floor of an adjoining or nearby building which is connected with such floor by openings in the party wall or by exterior balconies or bridges, allowing 3 square feet of unobstructed floor space per person. There shall in every case be on each side of the wall, partition or exterior balconies forming the horizontal exit, at least one stairway conforming to the requirements of required means of exit.

Fire Division Partitions on one Floor

A number of cases have been called to the attention of the Commission, where in fireproof buildings only one floor of the building would have more employees on it than could be safely accommodated on the stairways provided for that floor. These buildings had all been erected recently and it was urged that it would be a hardship to compel in such cases the construction of a fire wall extending from the cellar to the roof. We believe that in the case of buildings of fireproof construction, heretofore erected where a floor is sub-divided by partitions of brick, terra-cotta, or concrete not less than 4 inches thick, extending continuously from the fire proofing of the floor to the under side of the fire proofing of the floor above, with all openings protected by fireproof doors, such additional number of persons may be employed on the floor so bisected as can occupy the smaller of the two spaces on either side of such division partitions allowing 3 square feet of unobstructed floor space per person. There must, however, be on each side of said partitions at least one stairway conforming to the requirements for required means of exit and the doorways in the partitions shall be kept open and unobstructed during working hours. The windows on the floor on which the division partition is constructed and on the two floors directly underneath shall be fireproof windows.

Automatic Sprinklers

Where automatic sprinklers are provided, we recommend that the number of persons permitted to work on any one floor based upon the capacity of the stairways provided for that floor, be increased fifty per cent. In other words, where automatic sprinkler systems are installed in existing buildings there may be 21 persons for every 18 inches in width of stairway on any one floor instead of 14 persons, and in the case of buildings hereafter constructed, 21 persons for every 22 inches in width of stairway instead of 14 persons.

The sprinkler system is conceded to be the most efficient means of rapidly checking the spread of fire. Although it does not in itself afford an additional means of escape, yet by keeping the fire in check and confining it to a small space it is recognized as one of the best indirect means of assisting escape when a fire occurs. It is for this reason that we believe the number of persons on a floor may safely be increased fifty per cent., if a sprinkler system is installed.

Prevention of Congestion

The Commission is of the opinion that in order to prevent congestion it is necessary to limit the number of persons permitted to occupy any floor, irrespective of the exits provided for that floor. The Commission believes that there shall be not less than 36 square feet of floor space per person in a building of non-fireproof construction and 32 square feet of floor space in a building of fireproof construction. This limitation is to apply generally to all factory buildings and to take the place of the provision requiring 250 cubic feet of air space per person, which is now in force. That the present provision is inadequate even for the purpose for which it was designed, namely, to furnish sufficient ventilation, is generally conceded.

The recommendation we are making will not only prevent congestion but it will also insure better ventilation.

Posting

We recommend that in every factory building over two stories in height the Commissioner of Labor shall cause to be posted notices specifying the number of persons that may occupy each floor in accordance with the exit facilities provided as previously recommended. Every such notice shall be posted in every stair-hall and in every workroom. No more persons shall be permitted to work on any one floor of a factory than are specified in such posted notices.

FILING OF PLANS WITH DEPARTMENT OF LABOR

We recommend that provision be made for the filing of plans for the construction or alteration of factory buildings with the Commissioner of Labor, for the approval of such plans by him if they comply with the provisions of the statute and the rules and regulations of the Industrial Board, and for the issuance of a certificate of compliance if the building is constructed or the alteration made in conformity with the plans and specifications filed.

The Department of Labor will not be equipped with facilities for making the necessary inspection in the course of the construction or alteration of all buildings and the commissioner should be given the right to call upon the local building department to certify to him whether or not the building has been constructed or altered in accordance with legal requirements.

EFFECT OF THE FOREGOING REQUIREMENTS AS TO EXITS AND OCCUPANCY

The requirements recommended by the Commission in this section should be additional to and not in substitution for the requirements of any special law or local ordinance relating to the construction, equipment or maintenance of buildings but should supersede all provisions inconsistent therewith in any special law or local ordinance.

DETAILED SPECIFICATIONS

The detailed recommendations and specifications for construction, relating to this subject will be found in Bill No. 6 in Appendix I of this report.

III.

MANUFACTURING IN TENEMENTS

For almost thirty years the legislature has attempted to regulate the system of giving out factory products to be manufactured in tenement homes. In 1884 an act was passed prohibiting the manufacture of cigars and cigarettes in tenement houses in cities having over 500,000 inhabitants. This act was declared unconstitutional by the Court of Appeals in the case of *In re* Jacobs (98 N. Y., p. 98), referred to hereafter.

From 1885, when the Jacobs case was decided, down to 1892, practically nothing was done to regulate or control manufacturing in tenement houses. The unsanitary conditions found in tenement workrooms made it necessary for the state to take some action, and in 1892 the system of licensing homework was established. The law passed in that year provided that a home worker engaged in finishing certain articles must obtain a license for the apartment in which he lived and worked. From time to time this law has been amended, but licensing is still its essential provision. It is no longer the apartment or the worker, but the entire tenement which must now be licensed before any manufacturing on forty-one specified articles can legally be done by any tenant. To-day more than twelve thousand tenements* in the state are thus licensed and all the families living in them may legally secure work to do at home. Articles not mentioned in the law may be manufactured in any dwelling. The Department of Labor is charged with the enforcement of this law. (Article VII, sections 100-105 of the labor law.)

While the legislature has been amending the statute designed to regulate the vast overflow of work from factories to tenement homes, and while the state's funds have been spent in the increasingly elaborate task of attempting to supervise home workrooms, the legislature at the same time has been seeking to develop an adequate plan of protection for women and child workers in factories. But so complex has been the problem presented to the

* New York State Department of Labor, Bulletin No. 52, September, 1912, p. 338.

lawmakers by the home-work system, that regulation of home workrooms has been limited merely to an attempted supervision of sanitary conditions. The laws passed to protect women and children in factories by shortening hours and preventing employment at too early an age have never been extended to the home workers employed by factories. Furthermore, the unregulated condition of employees who work at home as compared with their fellow-employees who work in the shop, is an anomaly which tends to nullify the effect of every provision of the labor law in its application to trades employing home-workers. Thus the home-work system challenges the attention of the legislature.

The important phases of the subject are comprehended in these questions:

Does the present law adequately protect the public health, including not only the physical well-being of the workers, but also the health of consumers? If not, what further action should be taken by the state?

SOURCES OF INFORMATION

To answer these questions the Commission not only called witnesses at public hearings, but also caused an independent investigation to be made in order to ascertain (1) in what industries and in what localities home-work prevails, and to what extent manufacturers keep informed as to the actual conditions under which their work is done in the homes; and (2) what conditions commonly prevail in the homes of the workers; what guarantee of sanitation the license provides, and how the labor conditions compare in general with the standards within the factories as to wages, hours of work, and the employment of children. Between May 20th and August 1st, 1912, agents of the Commission visited factories and workers' homes in Auburn, Buffalo, Lockport, Niagara Falls, Tonawanda, Rochester, Syracuse, Utica, Troy, Yonkers, Little Falls, Dolgeville, Herkimer, Gloversville, and Cohoes. The investigation in New York City was made between October 10th and November 25th, 1912. A preliminary investigation of this subject was made in 1911.*

* Preliminary Report of New York State Factory Investigating Commission, p. 33.

The method of inquiry was to secure names of factories giving out home work by following newspaper advertisements for home workers and by seeking information from persons who have first-hand knowledge of industrial conditions in these communities. These factories were visited and the employers were asked to give names and addresses of the home workers on their payrolls. A fair proportion of these workers were visited at home.* In New York City the information secured by first-hand investigation was further substantiated by the testimony of witnesses at public hearings.

INDUSTRIES IN WHICH HOME WORK IS FOUND

The list of articles named in the law, for the manufacture of which a house must be licensed, has been extended from time to time as home work in other industries happened to be brought to the attention of the legislature. The following is a list of the various articles manufactured in whole or in part in tenement homes. Those which by law can be made only in a licensed house are given in *italics*.†

I. Clothing, millinery.

Coats, vests, trousers, overalls, knee pants, play suits, *shirts, blouses, waistbands, suspenders,* hose supporters.

Dresses, waists, skirts, cloaks, kimonos, wrappers, jackets.

Underwear, aprons, handkerchiefs, pillow-cases, bolster cases, sheets, napkins, tablecloths, roll covers.

Infants' wear—bonnets, bibs.

Jabots, *neckwear,* neck ornaments.

Leggings.

Hats, caps.

---

* In New York City, 193 factories were visited, of which 147 stated that they employed home workers. Of these, 75 gave names and addresses of their home workers. The total number of addresses at which inquiries were made was 1,020. Records of nearly 400 families were secured with detailed information concerning 306 of those households. In addition, 148 families were visited in other cities of the state. Miss Elizabeth C. Watson was in charge of this investigation.

† Some information was secured by the Commission concerning home work in each of these groups of manufactures. Although it is well known that the men's ready-made clothing trade employs large numbers of home workers, no special investigation of this occupation was made, in view of the fact that the United States government has recently published a comprehensive report on that industry. U. S. Government Report on Condition of Women and Child Wage-earners in the United States (Vol. II), Men's Ready Made Clothing; Senate Document No. 645. Washington: Government Printing Office, 1911. A number of clothing manufacturers, however, appeared before the Commission.

Artificial flowers and feathers.
Millinery.
Embroideries, laces, doilies.
Bed spreads, bed covers, pillow tops, center pieces, laundry bags, dolls' clothing.

II. Textiles.

Blankets, carriage robes.
Bath robes.
Hosiery, sweaters, *jerseys,* mufflers, scarfs, afgans, shawls, booties, passementerie, millinery ornaments.

III. Fur and Leather goods.

Furs, fur trimming, fur garments, gloves and mittens, *purses,* hand bags, *pocketbooks, slippers.*

IV. Paper goods.

Paper boxes, collar boxes, *paper bags,* sacks, calendars, tags, toy novelties, pin-wheels, balloons, kites, sample cards.

V. Miscellaneous.

Rubber goods, umbrellas, buttons, pin trays, broom holders, hair ornaments, hair-dressing articles, brushes, pincushions, stuffed toys, human hair, mesh bags, carding jewelry, fly-swatters.

VI. Foods and Tobacco.

Preserves, nuts, macaroni, spaghetti, icecream, ices, candy, confectionery, cigars, cigarettes.

Homework has been discovered in some process of manufacture in each of these large divisions. The extent of it cannot be stated, but it is of the utmost significance to realize that the system has found its way into so many industries.

The Commission's investigators reported that in 193 factories investigated the total number of factory employees was 4,330. In addition these establishments gave work to 3,113 home-workers or 42 per cent of the entire number. In a report on the men's ready-made clothing trade issued by the United States government,* it is stated that 88 factories investigated reported 561 home workers.

> "Nowhere are there accurate statistics to indicate the extent of home finishing or other home work," says the report.† "It is resorted to more extensively in New York and less proportionately in Chicago than elsewhere. * * * There are solid blocks in New York where, by actual count, more than three-fourths of the apartments contain home finishers."

The number of finishers working at home as compared with those working in the shops in this branch of the garment trades in New York City is stated to be 44.7 per cent.‡ The report continues:

> "The foregoing figures, it should be remembered, are not representative of the real proportion of home workers. If a manufacturer with a large inside shop says that he employs no home workers, that statement may be literally true, as he refers only to the inside shop directly operated by him. But, on the other hand, he may manufacture only about one-fifth of his product in his own inside shop, while four-fifths of it may be scattered among a number of contractors, who in turn may give out all the garments they make to be finished in the homes."

Thus, even after an intensive investigation of an entire industry has been made, it is impossible to state with any degree of accuracy what proportion of firms give out home work or how many home workers they employ. Nevertheless, the fact that the work is sent out to homes by such large industries indicates its probable extent.

COMMUNITIES IN WHICH HOME WORK IS FOUND

A very large proportion of the licenses issued for home work are in New York City, that is, 11,691, as compared with 520 outstanding in the remainder of the state on June 30, 1912.§ The reports of our investigators show, however, that homework is

* United States Government Report on Condition of Woman and Child Wage-earners in the United States, Vol. II, Men's Ready-Made Clothing, p. 260.
† *Ibid*, p. 218.
‡ *Ibid*, p. 219.
§ New York State Department of Labor, Bulletin No. 52, September, 1912, p. 338.

by no means confined to New York City. They found home workers engaged in rope-splicing and button-carding in Auburn; finishing men's clothing in Buffalo; carding buttons in Lockport; carding hooks and eyes in Niagara Falls; making paper boxes and cigars, sewing buttons on shirts, and mending maltsters' bags in Tonawanda; finishing men's clothing, carding buttons, hooks, and eyes, working on children's moccasins, women's neckwear, paper boxes, novelties, sanitary belts, and druggists' specialties, making seedsmen's paper bags, fringe and passementerie in Rochester; finishing men's clothing, making willow baskets, sewing fancy trimmings on waists, and crocheting infants' jackets and women's shawls in Syracuse; finishing men's clothing and crocheting edges of knit underwear in Utica; trimming felt slippers and stitching gloves in Little Falls; trimming felt slippers in Dolgeville; running tapes in knit underwear in Herkimer; making and trimming gloves in Gloversville; making brushes and working on collars and shirts in Troy and Cohoes; and making willow plumes in Yonkers.

Long as is this list, it probably is not long enough to show actual conditions. As the investigation was made between May and August, the slack season in many of these trades, comprehensive data could not be secured. The significant fact, however, was that home workers in the up-state cities live in dwellings which house one or two families, thus not coming within the scope of the law regulating "tenement" manufacture, since a tenement is legally defined as the dwelling-place of three or more families.

Thus, the law designed to regulate homework does not even apply to a large number of homeworkers, who work on products not named in the law, or who live in houses not legally tenements.

SANITARY CONDITIONS

A license is granted by the Department of Labor to the landlord or his agent for the entire house, not for a worker, or family, or apartment. It is issued only after examination by the Commissioner of Labor of the records of the local department of health and the tenement house department. If these records show any orders outstanding against the building or reveal any infectious or contagious disease among the tenants, the commissioner may withhold the license until the records show that the premises are in satisfactory sanitary condition. Before issuing the license, an inspector visits the premises, and reports in writing the result of his inspections.

In the effort to insure the continuance of satisfactory sanitary conditions after the granting of the license, the statute has been elaborated with an attention to detail which strikingly reveals the difficulty of enforcement. Licensed tenements are required to be inspected by the Commissioner of Labor once in six months (a task for the accomplishment of which the state has never yet provided even an approximately sufficient number of inspectors). A sanitary building may be occupied by tenants with low standards of cleanliness. The law therefore provides that if a room or apartment in a licensed tenement is found to be habitually filthy, a sign may be affixed to the entrance of that apartment forbidding its use for home work on any of the articles specified in the law. If an occupant of an apartment has contracted a contagious disease, no article mentioned in the law may be manufactured therein until the board of health certifies that the disease has terminated and that the rooms have been properly disinfected.

The Commissioner has power to revoke the license if it is brought to his attention that any licensed tenement is no longer sanitary. Articles manufactured in violation of the law may be labeled by the commissioner with a tag bearing the words "Tenement-made," or they may be seized and held by him until they have been disinfected or until the law has been otherwise complied with. Landlord, tenant, and manufacturer are each responsible for violations of the statute.

Reports of the Commission's investigators and the testimony reveal the great difficulties in the way, of enforcing this, the basic provision of the state's attempt to insure a minimum standard of sanitation in the dwellings of home workers. Investigators reported the following instances:

> One family was found running ribbons and sewing buttons on corset covers. The father has had tuberculosis for several years. He had just been sent away to the country. The house had not been fumigated, and the members of the family

were still working. Moreover, they were working all the time the father was ill.

In another house, where four members of the family had been sick with typhoid, and one was just convalescent, the family was working on feathers. Mary one member of the family had been doing the work all through her convalescence.

In another house, a young woman whose father was finally sent away to a tuberculosis hospital, was working on dolls' clothes in the same room where her sick father lay. A relief society had refused this young woman further assistance unless she also would go to a tuberculosis hospital. She refused to do this, and is working on dolls' clothes with tuberculosis progressing towards its final stages.

In another family which was visited the mother was out. The daughter went upstairs for her, followed by the investigator, who saw the mother come out of an apartment, on the door of which the Board of Health had posted "Diphtheria." When the mother had returned to her own apartment, she fell to work on the willow plumes which were lying on the table near a pile of clothing. After the interview she went upstairs again to the supposedly quarantined apartment. In the same house were four apartments in which there had been diphtheria since September, 1912. (This investigation was made November 9, 1912).

Among homeworking families, our investigators found many cases of impetigo, a loathsome skin trouble, which is contagious, and practically due to dirt. A child, whose face and head were sore with this eruption, was seen playing with a felt slipper just manufactured. In another instance, a child with this disease was lying on a bundle of finished clothes, while in a third case a little girl suffering with impetigo was picking nuts for a factory.

In one apartment visited a woman was found working on passementerie while her young son was lying in bed ill with measles.

Dr. Annie S. Daniels, who has been a practicing physician since 1876, and who is now in charge of the out-door practice of the New York Infirmary for Women and Children, testified that during the year ending October, 1912, she had found in her visits in tenements 182 families engaged in home manufacture of some description. Of these, 35 families were at work in unlicensed houses. Part of her testimony was as follows:

"I have found during this past year, 182 families, 79 with contagious diseases doing this tenement-house work. One family was embroidering monograms and three of the children were sick with measles. The woman was embroidering monograms on table napkins. I found sixteen cases of scarlet fever during the entire time. Where they had scarlet fever, most of the people were finishing men's clothing; that is doing all the hand sewing that is done on men's coats and trousers. The children had scarlet fever. The work was being done in the same room where they were sick, and during the convalescence of the child, by the child, sometimes while the child was peeling. The law requires us to report every one of those cases * * * the notice of the Board of Health of a contagious disease was on the door while the work was going on. I found nine cases of tuberculosis among the 182 families, all of them working. Tuberculosis can be carried. There was one family, where they were making buttons for women's clothes—that is covering buttons for women's clothes. One of these children was three years old; the mother had tuberculosis. The mother was working herself, and the children were working. I found two cases of poliomyelitis, an infectious paralytic disease of children. The exact nature of how that is carried is not known. It is contagious from child to child. It is a very horrible disease. I know one case where the child died and the woman hardly stopped her work while the child was dying. She was finishing trousers. I was present at that time.

Q. And the child was dying? A. The child was dying.

Q. And the woman did not stop work? A. She could not.

Q. She had to——A. She had to do it; her husband was a gambler. The woman was somewhere between 25 and 30 years old. The child was about—less than two years old; eighteen months. The woman was working in the same room where the child was sick; they had only two rooms.

The relation of the home-work system to the campaign for stamping out tuberculosis was thus defined by Dr. S. Adolphus Knopf, professor of diseases of the lungs at the New York Post Graduate Medical School:

"The work in the tenements by adults, as well as by children, I hold largely responsible for the great morbidity and mortality of tuberculosis in this city. The bad ventilation of the tenement house, added to the inhalation of dust by the workers, and the frequency of tuberculosis among them, causes the fearful condition which we are now trying to combat. I firmly believe that if we could do away with this one source of propagation of tuberculosis, we would reduce the mortality and morbidity very greatly.

"You know how tuberculosis spreads. One single individual in a family is capable of infecting a number of them within a very short time. Most of the tubercular workers are not trained and are not educated how to dispose of their sputum. They expectorate more or less, and when this carelessly expectorated material dries and is pulverized, and is inhaled with the dust in the so-called factory at home, it is inevitable that any number of them become infected.

"In the Gouverneur Hospital Dispensary for tuberculars, we have made very careful tabulations and found that 37 per cent. of all the tuberculars who applied there for relief were garment workers. It is among the workers in this trade that tuberculosis is most prevalent.

"We will never be able to eradicate this disease from our midst unless we take energetic steps and stop work at home. Every tenement home which is utilized for work predisposes the workers to tuberculosis. They inhale the bad air; they work long hours, and in addition, very often are underfed.

"In the children whom we put to work we have another type of tuberculosis, and these children later on invariably fall victims to the more serious type and become a burden to the community.

"We spend millions of dollars annually in this city and other cities for the cure of tuberculosis, and we spend that money in vain, because by our deficient laws regarding proper housing, regarding child labor, regarding labor in factories and homes, we produce consumptives every day anew, and all the millions of dollars spent for their cure and care is useless."

The danger to the consumer from conditions in the men's ready-made clothing trade is thus summarized in the United States government report to which reference has already been made:

"The results of this investigation show that men's ready-made clothing is often made, or at least finished, in the homes of a class of people whose under-nourished condition, due to poverty and lack of thrift and hygienic sense, general low standard of living, and dirty habits make them most susceptible to contagious diseases; hence it is asserted that the practice of giving out to workers garments to be finished or made up in their homes is to place the wearer in the way of contracting tuberculosis and other contagious or infectious diseases, or of catching vermin.

"As stated, in the two congested blocks of New York City, where a large proportion of the men's ready-made clothing sold all over the United States is sent to be finished, the death rates due to contagious diseases are abnormal.

"During this investigation it was learned that doctors who will agree to conceal diseases from the health department, are the most popular with garment workers. Agents of the bureau found women working on garments while children in the house were suffering from contagious diseases. They would put the garments down from time to time to minister to or fondle such children. To the inquiry as to why there was no 'sign on the house,' it was sometimes said that the doctor was 'nice,' 'had sorrow' for them, or knew they were 'poor women with lots of children,' so he 'wouldn't tell on them,' because if he did, the police wouldn't let them work. The home finishers could not understand why when disease was present they could not continue to work at the time of all times when they needed the money most." *

That the United States Government recognizes the danger of contagion through tenement manufacture is set forth in the following quotation, from a review of Professor Common's testimony before the industrial commission:

"'While neither the Federal Government nor any state government has undertaken to abolish tenement-house work where the work is sold to private purchasers, yet where the Federal Government is itself a purchaser of clothing it has undertaken to establish this condition. Since the Spanish-American war, when it seemed to be clearly demonstrated that the contagion of measles and other diseases in the army was owing directly to tenement-house manufacture, the War Department has inserted in its contracts with the manufac-

* Report on Condition of Woman and Child Wage-earners in the United States, Vol. II, pp. 306-307. For details of cases on which this statement is based, see pp. 307-309.

turers of military garments that all work must be done in a regularly organized factory, and no part of the work shall be sublet to contractors. In the several States clothing for the National Guard is usually purchased from the War Department, and is, therefore, protected by the specifications of that department; but in those States where clothing is purchased by the state authorities there exist at present but few restrictions.' "

LACK OF CARE TAKEN BY MANUFACTURERS TO PROTECT CONSUMERS

Special inquiry was made to discover whether the manufacturers took any precautions to ascertain conditions in the homes to which they gave out articles to be manufactured or finished. The investigators of the Commission reported that 80 per cent. of the addresses of home workers furnished them by manufacturers proved to be incorrect. Either the families had never lived at the addresses given or they had moved elsewhere without taking the trouble to change the record at the factory. The employers who appeared before the Commission testified as follows regarding their knowledge of conditions in the workers' homes:

1. *A manufacturer of crotcheted goods:* (Including bedroom slippers.)

> "I do not keep any track of their homes, or where they do their work. There is no inspection of any kind, as there is in my factory. In my factory I am amenable to the factory inspection law, and the Board of Health and the Fire Department, while the people who do the work at home, do it wherever they please and whenever they please."

2. *A manufacturer of dolls' toys:* (The dolls' dresses are made by home workers.)

> "I keep track partly of where the goods are made. I mean when we give out a gross of garments we give to the woman a ticket. On that ticket is her name and address. We keep one, she keeps one; that is all we know about it. We do not investigate the homes. We try to govern that by their addresses. I look at the addresses; if the address looks all right, and the woman looks all right, I give her the goods. I have never gone into any of the places myself, or sent any-

body to see under what conditions these dresses are made. These dolls, after they are made and dressed, are sold to the retail stores, and are used by the children of the city."

3. *An employer of hand-embroiderers:* (Monograms.)

This was the only employer who testified that he or his daughter always inspected the homes where his work was done, and that in case of sickness no work was given to the family. His reason was thus brought out:

"Q. Why are you so careful about the sickness part? A. Well, I will tell you. Three or four years ago, we had a child, my own child; she came in the factory, and she takes the diphtheria, and in three days she dies. After that we are very careful in the factory, too."

4. *Manufacturer of fancy leather goods.*

His work was given out to a contractor who in turn employed the home workers.

"I don't know where she has it done. I don't follow that up."

5. *Manufacturer of cigarettes:* (Hand-made with monograms.)

He testified that some of his shop employees took work home at night.

"I have never investigated to find out where they live. These men who do the work in their homes, do it wherever they live, and wherever there may be disease or sickness or anything. I don't know anything about that at all.

6. *Manufacturer of made-to-order cigarettes.*

"It (the home work) is done in pretty low-grade tenement houses, although the people make good money; they live in pretty filthy surroundings—that is not my fault, but that is a fact. I am afraid that is true."

7. *Manufacturer of cigarettes and tobacco:* (With gilt monograms, made to order.)

He stated that only the hand-made cigarettes were given to home-workers, and to only three of them:

"I do not know where this man (one of the home workers) lives. These two people I have mentioned live on the east side somewhere. I have never been in the place where they make these cigarettes."

8. *Manufacturer of confectionery.*

(Cracking pecan nuts and extracting meat is the task of home workers.)

"I never saw the places where the work is done. They do it in tenement houses. I do not know whether the people are sick or anything about them at all. If we find that there are some sick people in some houses, we would not give them any more work. Once in a while we find it out through other people. But I do not know whether or not people are sick where they do this work.

Q. How do they pick the meat out of the nuts? Do they have any instrument or do they pick it out with their fingers? A. They should pick it out with an instrument, a knife. We do not give them the knife.

Q. Do you know if they crack the nuts with their teeth? A. They should not do that. I do not know whether they do or not."

To sum up, these eight manufacturers who testified before the Commission all, with one exception, declared that they made no effort to find out the conditions under which their goods were made. The only employer who testified to having made any effort to inspect the homes of his outworkers was the one who, through the death of his own child by contagious disease contracted from one of his factory employees, had become convinced of the necessity for inspection.

It seems evident that home work is a danger to the health of the community, and that the effort to maintain proper sanitary conditions is so herculean a task as to be wholly illusory as a safeguard of public health.

CHILD LABOR IN TENEMENT MANUFACTURE

One of the most serious charges brought against the homework system is that it has made legally possible the work of little children in manufacturing pursuits at home, when the law rigidly excludes them from such occupations in the factories.

To determine the extent of child labor at home is difficult. The work of children is easily concealed and as a result factory inspectors find few children at work, whereas social workers, physicians, and teachers state that little children are often steadily employed in home work. In some of the occupations, like hand embroidery, the work is too highly skilled to be done by very little children. In several households visited, there were no children under sixteen. The investigators reported that 79 school children in 47 families were actually found at work after school. Fourteen others who were too young to attend school or who had dropped out as soon as they were fourteen admitted that they worked regularly. Of the 79 children, 7 were between five and eight years old, 14 eight to eleven, 33 eleven to fourteen, 25 fourteen or fifteen, while the ages of six obviously under sixteen were not recorded.

An investigation made in New York in the spring of 1912 and reported by the National Child Labor Committee in our Preliminary Report showed the following facts regarding child workers:

Nut-picking: 41 families visited, having 91 children, 77 of whom were found at work.

Making brushes: 41 families visited, having 72 children, of whom 69 were found at work.

Making dolls' clothes: 66 families visited and 35 children found at work.

Making artificial flowers: 33 families visited and 70 children found at work.

Thus, in these four occupations, 251 children under sixteen were found at work in 181 households.

In the men's ready-made clothing trade in New York the United States government investigators found 81 children at work, of whom 3 were five years old, 1 six, 3 seven, 5 eight, 7 nine, 5 ten, 8 eleven, 21 twelve, 8 thirteen, 14 fourteen, and 6 fifteen. The investigators believed that this number understated the extent of child labor.

> "Unless a child was caught working it was seldom admitted that such child did work." * "Sometimes upon a

* Government Report on Condition of Woman and Child Wage-earners in the United States, Vol. II, p. 230.

first visit they denied working, but were found at work when visited again. Often as an agent entered a house where children were at work, a sudden dropping and concealing of the work was noticed. It is the opinion of the agents on this investigation that all children of a household where home work is done are drafted into this work with more or less regularity, after school, at night, and on Sunday."

The following are a few instances of child labor reported by our inspectors:

It is no uncommon sight to find four and five year-old babies making flowers. Little Camilla only three years old was found in the afternoon of November 15th, 1912, running ribbons in corset covers. Rosie, her 11 year-old sister, was taking care of the baby, while Elsa, age 6, and Camilla helped mother.

Angelina says, "When I go home from school I help my mother to work—I help her earn the money—I do not play at all. I get up at six o'clock and I go to bed at ten o'clock."

Camilla, 9 years old, says, "I have no time for play, when I go home from school, I help my mother. Half hour I make my lessons. Every morning I get up at 6 o'clock—I go to bed at 11 o'clock."

Giovanna: "I get up at 5 o'clock in the morning. Then I work with my mother. At 9 o'clock I go to school. I have no time for play. I must work by feathers. At 10 o'clock I go to bed."

Maria: "I have no time to play when I work by my mother, but when I don't work, I mind the baby and clean the house."

Little 9-year old Antoinette: "I earn money for my mother after school, and on Saturday, and half day Sundays. No, I do not play, I must work; I get up to work at 4 o'clock in the morning, I go to bed at 9 o'clock."

Michaelina is not quite 14 years old. She crochets Irish lace. She gets up at 5:30 every morning, prepares her father's breakfast, crochets one hour before going to school, works again two hours after school, and takes care of the baby. Pasqualina, her sister, is 12 years old. She gets up at six o'clock and crochets an hour and a half every morning before going to school, and three hours every day after school. It takes two and a half hours to make one yoke for which the children receive nine cents, but as each yoke takes a spool of thread, two and a half cents is deducted from the profits. Working together the two children make 25 cents a day.

Francesca, 12 years old, works from 3:30 P. M. to 9:30 P. M. crocheting slippers. Even her little fingers can make eight or nine slippers in six hours. (These are children's slippers, and it takes from one-half to three-quarters of an hour to make one slipper).

Nicolina is 9 years old. She cuts embroidery four hours every day and two hours at night. Little Pasqualina, her 8 year-old sister, helps too, and together they can make $2 a week.

Two children, one nine and one seven years old, appeared before us with their mother and told of their work at home. Mary Piccolino, aged nine, denied at first that she had ever worked, then said that once she worked on corset covers, and then told how she actually helped every evening to run ribbons through the corset covers which her mother brought home after the day's work in the factory. Her sister, Camilla, aged seven, was a clear-headed little witness. She said that she helped to make corset covers every afternoon and that she worked until eight o'clock in the evening.

Dr. F. Josephine Baker, director of the Division of Child Hygiene of the Department of Health of New York, testified regarding the effect of home work on the health of school children. She explained that a large number of the children in the public schools suffer from some physical defect, and these defects are due very largely to the conditions of their home life—lack of proper ventilation, or of proper hygiene, overwork, lack of play and proper exercise. When asked why work after school hours might cause ill-health or physical defects in children, she replied:

"Because the children are just at the age when they are naturally developing and growing, and when they need a larger amount of free air and more freedom than adults do, and the effect of bad air, close confinement, and vitiated atmosphere, are very much worse for children than they possibly can be for grown people. These children go to school in the morning, are heavy, dull and tired. They are

> not able to study. They suffer from headaches and most of them have malnutrition—that is, they suffer from lack of proper nutrition, they are anemic."

This statement of the effect of home work on school children was confirmed by observations of a teacher and a principal in two public schools in New York. They pointed out also that home work prevented the children from keeping up with their classes and was a cause of truancy.

Testimony was given by the chairman of the Scholarship Committee of the New York Child Labor Committee that "when a child is unable to get its working papers at the proper time it is very often due to the fact that at some stage of school life it has been working at home and has been kept away from school," and that "a large part of truancy is due to the fact that the child starts working at home, at first after school hours. He finds that it is difficult or impossible to keep up in his studies to the required standard, and then gradually drops out of school."

Evidence of the relation of the early toil of these children to delinquency in adolescent years, was presented by Miss Maud E. Miner, secretary of the Probation Association:

> "I have seen girls from these homes, who have been leading lives of immorality and lives of prostitution. I have known of girls who have told me that they have become tired of work long before it was time for them to go to work; in other words, before they could go out into the factory, simply because they had to work in the home day after day, night after night, and on Sunday."

The labor law forbids the employment of any child under fourteen years of age in, or in connection with, any manufacturing establishment, and provides that no child between the ages of fourteen and sixteen shall be employed before 8 A. M. or after 5 P. M., or more than 8 hours in any one day. By means of home work a manufacturer may utilize the labor of children of any age for unlimited hours provided that the children of school age, 7 to 16 years, attend school between the hours of 9 A. M. and 3 P. M. Home work is a menace to the physical, mental, and moral well-being of children.

UNRESTRICTED HOURS OF LABOR FOR WOMEN IN THE HOME WORK SYSTEM

Section 77 of the labor law prohibits women from working more than 9 hours in any one day or more than 54 hours in a week in a factory. It further provides that if a woman is employed in two establishments consecutively within twenty-four hours, the total number of hours of labor in both places of employment must not exceed the total legally permitted in a single factory. A home in which manufacturing is carried on is not a factory in the eyes of the law. The 54-hour law, therefore, does not apply to work done in tenements where workers can be engaged in factory work to any hour of the night.

One of our inspectors reports the following interview with a home worker:

> "I saw her last Monday and asked whether she was doing any work. She said no, it was very quiet, but that on Friday she had received a special call to come for some beads because there was a rush order, and she had to work all night. She was given a gross of these beads to finish and sometimes she has a daughter of about twelve who helps her after school hours to help her at night with these beads. She said it took her all night. I didn't ask her whether she got any sleep that night, but she said she worked all night to get them at the factory the next morning at eight o'clock. She was compelled to work all night to get one gross finished."

In the investigators' report it was stated that some Italian girls were found who work downtown in a bathing-suit factory from 8 A. M. to 6 P. M. They return home for supper, and crochet slippers until 10 and 11 o'clock at night. Employers in the embroidery industry stated that 90 per cent. of their shop hands are obliged during the rush season to take work home at night.

That the hours of work of women employed only in homework are not limited by law is an obvious fact. That women and girls who toil in the factories by day may legally take work home at night shows how homework frustrates the intent of the 54-hour law.

EARNINGS OF HOME WORKERS

Accurate information regarding earnings is difficult to secure, owing to the chaotic conditions of the home-work system. Employers keep a record of the amounts paid to the workers who appear at the factory, but they have no accurate knowledge of the number of workers or the time required to earn these amounts. Statements regarding the hours of work and the number of workers and the prices paid for various kinds of work vary so that earnings per capita or per hour are not clear. Nevertheless, the records of our investigators' interviews with home workers and the testimony of witnesses furnish data.

Of 277* families visited, 258 gave information about wages, and of those only 18 reported that their usual weekly earnings from home work amounted to $6 or more.

Testimony was given by a neckwear manufacturer that women taking work from his factory to be made at home averaged from $6.67 to $8.15 a week for the entire year.

From the earnings of home workers certain factory expenses must be met by the home worker. The obvious costs of rent, light and heat are transferred to the home worker by the manufacturer. One woman did not work at night because she could not make enough to pay for the gas burned; another was found crocheting by the light from a street lamp.

Moreover, the home worker often must provide her own equipment, such as crochet needles, scissors and sewing machine needles, and sewing machines with special attachments when such are required.

In certain trades, materials also must in many cases be paid for out of the home worker's wages. For example, workers in Irish crochet must buy their own crochet cotton. An Irish crochet yoke for which the worker received 9 cents required an outlay of 2½ cents for thread.

In nut picking, there are always some broken nuts which must be separated from the whole nuts and returned to the employer. The pay, 4c. or 4½c. per pound, covers only the unbroken nuts. For broken nuts, the worker receives nothing, although the breaking comes less often from careless picking than from the quality

* This does not include 29 families working on tobacco.

of the nut itself or from the machine cracking done by the factory.

Mandalino Vitrani, a home worker 28 years old, whose husband earns sometimes ten and sometimes twelve dollars a week in a candy factory, told the Commission about the pay which she receives for running in ribbons and sewing buttons on corset covers.

> "For sewing buttons and one line of ribbons on a dozen six cents; if there is two lines of ribbons, nine cents for a dozen. Q. How many dozen do you make a day, or how many dozen do you fix a day? A. It depends on as many as I get, sometimes ten dozen, and sometimes eleven, also depending upon the number of yards of ribbon I must sew." * * * "If I have plenty of work, a dollar, as a rule 50 or 75 cents I make in one day. I can't work all day, but I do as much as I can. I have other duties, household duties and so on. The day I made the dollar, I worked until eight or nine or ten o'clock at night."

Samples of goods which had been found in process of manufacture in tenements were shown, and the prices paid stated. For a dozen lace crocheted ornaments of fine quality the price was 60 cents, and a dozen was all that the worker could make in a day. For crocheting an edge, fine hand work, the price was 2 cents a yard for one row, 4 cents for a double row, with an output of three to five yards an hour. This lace was given out by sub-contractors, who secured it from manufacturers, thus saving the manufacturer the trouble of dealing with the individual workers. A pair of white gloves, finely stitched at home by a worker living on Macdougal street, was exhibited. These gloves are cut in the factory and the home worker stitches all the seams, receiving one dollar and forty cents per dozen pairs. The woman is an expert and can make from nine to twelve pairs a day. An imitation pearl necklace was shown; the manufacturer pays the worker 60 cents for stringing and putting the catch on a gross of strings (144). For a kind of beading used as an ornament the rate was 2 cents an hour. For a task demanding close attention and eye-strain,— pulling threads of men's linen handkerchiefs to prepare them for hemstitching,— the pay was 3 cents a dozen, and the worker, with an eleven-year old daughter to help her, could pull the threads in seven dozen handkerchiefs a day, earning 56 cents. The investigator had seen the book in which their weekly wages were recorded, and she testified that $2.50 was the largest sum she made in a week and that the usual earnings were $1.30, $1.87, or $2.00.

ECONOMIC STATUS OF HOME WORKERS' FAMILIES

"None was found living alone who could maintain herself by the amount she earned at home finishing,"* is the statement made in the Government report on the men's ready-made clothing trade, and it is not surprising to learn, therefore, that the widow with little children to support is not the typical home worker. In New York 87.3 per cent. of the home finishers were married women living with their husbands, while only 9.6 per cent., 47 of a total of 488, were widowed, divorced, separated, or deserted, and 3.1 per cent. unmarried women.

The findings of our investigators agree with these results. Of 306 families of home workers, the father was living and at home in 252 households, while in only 37 was the mother widowed or deserted. Twelve of the home workers were single women, and of five the conjugal condition was not reported. The low earnings or unemployment of the father, or in some cases his laziness or greed account for the necessity of supplementary income earned by the work of the mother and her children.†

Miss Lillian D. Wald, of the Nurses' Settlement, director of the work of 85 nurses who visit the sick in their homes throughout Greater New York, gave the following testimony: "In all these cases where there is no man in the family, or the man is sick and unable to work, the family even with the children working is not able to support itself. They have to be helped by charity anyhow. It is only a question of degree of help."

Few, if any, households are dependent solely, or even chiefly, upon home work for support.

SOLUTIONS ADVOCATED

None of the witnesses who testified before the Commission believed that the present method of regulating the home-work sys-

* 2 *Ibid*, p. 228.

† The great majority of home workers are Italians, 78 per cent in the families investigated by the Commission's agents, and 98.2 per cent of the home finishers interviewed by Federal investigators of the clothing trade.—Government Report on Condition of Woman and Child Wage-earners in the United States, Vol. II, page 221.

tem was adequate. The representative opinions appear as follows in the testimony:

Manufacturer of crocheted goods:

"My idea is that home labor should be permitted, but should be regulated. It should be carefully watched. It should be put under the factory law. And children under age should be prohibited from working as in factories. That I am very much in favor of, to cut out the very young children from working. That is shameful. That is a bad thing. If it was found impossible to regulate work in the homes, it would be hard to fully prohibit the matter, because we have to compete with the world. Germany and France and European countries are doing that same thing, and seem to be doing it with advantage to the consumers. It is a question in my mind whether it would be advisable to shut that out altogether."

Manufacturer of dolls and toys:

"If it is done right, I would permit people who live in a tenement house to do the home work. * * * I mean, when I say that if it is done right, the places where the work is done in tenements, should be inspected as is a factory. I do not know if that it is practicable. If it was not practicable to inspect places in tenements where work of this kind is done I would be in favor of abolishing it or of prohibiting it."

Manufacturer of embroidery:

"I think it would be very nice to permit the work in the homes, if somebody inspected it to see if the conditions were good.

"Q. Suppose it was not practicable,—you know we have got to take this thing from a practical standpoint. Suppose it was not practicable, it would not be possible, it would be too big a thing, to inspect every place in which work was done at home, as they inspect your factory, would you be in favor then of abolishing the work at home? A. I think it is no good for the factory, no good for the people, but it don't mean very much for me; just about the same thing. If I have a big factory I could have plenty of room, in my opinion, I think by giving out the home work sometimes I help a great deal some woman in my line of business."

Manufacturer of fancy leather goods:

"I believe, as an intelligent manufacturer, they (the home work rooms) ought to be inspected the same as my factory is. I think that home work should be done under certain restrictions. I think it would work a hardship with a great many people if it was abolished altogether. I dare say there are a great many articles manufactured at home that should be discontinued." (Naming foods and foodstuffs, and favoring absolute prohibition of their manufacture in tenements.)

Manufacture of cigarettes:

"I think it would be better if they were prohibited from doing it in their homes. I would be in favor of that."

Manufacturer of cigarettes:

"Having cigarette papers sent home to be made by Syrians in their homes is a bad feature. It should be prohibited; there is no question about that."

Manufacturer of cigars and cigarettes:

"I disapprove of home work. I do not think it should be done at home at all, any of this work. I think it would be better to have it all done in the factory."

Foreman of a confectionery company:

"I do not know what I would do for the cracking of nuts if this work was stopped in the tenement houses.

"Q. Would you employ people to come to your factory to do it? A. That is what we are trying to do all the time."

(No more definite expression of opinion could be secured from him.)

Dr. Annie S. Daniels:

"I approve of abolishing home work; all kinds of home work. I have approved of it since 1888. If home work was prohibited it would not be any great hardship on the women and children; I am sure it would not because these women are strong, able and capable of working in factories, and their children would be taken care of in kindergartens, and day nurseries. They always have room for children whenever they ask to go in. And the women would work in factories and get better pay. I am pretty sure it would result in making the husbands work in some cases."

Dr. F. Josephine Baker:

"In my opinion it is exceedingly difficult to regulate home work so children could be kept from working. I can't see any way of regulating it. I think the only possible way of regulating it is by making it absolutely illegal for any one to work in the home. Personally I would advise that.

"Q. Do you think that there is any hardship in the prohibiting of women from taking home work? A. There again I have nothing to base my statement upon except bare surmise; but we in the Department grant about 40,000 employment certificates to the children between the ages of fourteen and sixteen years to go to work each year. Investigation has shown that only approximately about 23 per cent. of these children go to work because there is any need of their money in the family. The remainder go because they are tired of school or because their families want them to leave school, and applying such a ratio to home work in general, it would seem to me that the greater good would be served by abolishing it."

Miss Lillian D. Wald:

"I would like to contribute a bit of the results of my observations. When I first went downtown I found that cloaks, ladies' cloaks, were frequently made in the tenement houses, and at that time I think the manufacturers and public sentiment wholly approved of it because it was considered essential. I remember one instance where the cloak that was being made was covering a child who was sick with scarlet fever, and we naturally stopped it and reported the case to the Board of Health, and in this instance paid the woman the amount of money she was earning. Now, the ladies' suit and cloak industry has practically been taken out of the tenement houses, and I do not believe that the trade suffers. The volume of that trade in the City is enormous, and nobody suffers. It is the centre of that trade in the whole United States. If my figures are right, the output is $250,000,000 a year. That trade has been taken out of the tenement houses altogether, and nobody has suffered. The wages have been standardized. It is practically impossible to standardize a wage in an industry that is carried on without supervision, but we have succeeded in doing that, in taking the work out of the tenement houses. And that was practically true of the cigar business, too. That has been practically taken out of the tenements, occasionally you will find a stripper. That has not hurt the people working in it ——"

"Q. Are you in favor of the prohibition of this work in tenements or of regulating it? A. I do not think it can be regulated; I think it must be abolished. I do not see how, without an enormously expensive set of investigators, it would be possible to protect the children from excessive hours of work; standardize the wages, supervise the sanitary conditions under which the manufacturing is done — I am afraid there is nothing to do but eliminate it."

Miss Rose Schneiderman, of the Women's Trade Union League:

"We urge the prohibition of home work. * * * If we can prohibit home work entirely, it would force employers to engage the amount of people that they need in their factories and not avoid the responsibilities of having employees and all that, and it would also perhaps give the employees a chance to get a living wage for the work that they do."

Professor Felix Adler:

"I can see no way, I must admit, of devising a system of inspection which will really control the sanitary conditions and labor conditions of work done out of sight, done in the homes of the workers, and the conclusion would seem to me that we must move forward through the prohibition of this kind of work altogether."

Miss Pauline Goldmark:

"I don't suppose there is any way of regulating or supervising homework or keeping the children out of it except getting it out of the homes by prohibiting it altogether. I do not see why any set of manufacturers should have the advantage of such savings on rent and on wages and then put the State to such great expense to regulate and inspect 10,000 homes. Also, we might add, to maintain these people when they break down. Naturally if the workers are not making a living wage somebody has got to pay the difference sooner or later."

Miss Mary F. Maguire, principal of Public School No. 3:

"I feel that the homework ought to be stamped out."

Mr. Marcus M. Marks:

"I am in favor of a much more careful supervision of work going on in homes than at present exists * * * I think it would be a crime to do what has been suggested — to eliminate the right to work in the home."

Mr. James R. Kaiser, manufacturer of neckwear:

"If a law were enacted prohibiting instead of regulating homework, without regard to the age of the worker, it would disastrously affect two classes of employees who figure very largely in our industry and many others. First, the married women who have children to take care of, and who have to prepare the meals of their husbands. It is difficult, if not impossible for those people to come to our factory or to the other factories, and it simply deprives them of their living. The other class is much more numerous, it represents workers who by reason of their limited incomes have to live at a distant point, Hoboken and other places at a distance, and they would lose at least two hours in transit, plus their car fare."

Miss Maud E. Miner:

"If it is simply a question of giving liberty — individual liberty — to the homes, to the family, to the children, which is urged as a reason for not taking this sweatshop work away from the homes, we cannot but believe that it is absolute slavery we are permitting instead of any kind of liberty. I would favor the absolute, immediate prohibition of all of it; there is nothing that can be done by inspection really to better the conditions."

RECOMMENDATIONS

Manufacturing in tenements under the conditions disclosed, is accompanied by certain grave evils. It is frequently carried on in unclean and unsanitary surroundings and in homes where there are infectious and contagious diseases; it enlists the services of little children both during and after schools hours; it nullifies the requirements of compulsory education because children who should be at school, work undetected at home; it permits the evasion of the child labor law because, although no child under 16 may work in any factory after 5 P. M., the manufacturer, by sending his goods to the home, may have young children of any age legally do his work there for any number of hours.

Furthermore, the fifty-four hour law is frustrated because women who have worked in the factory nine or ten hours take work home to do at night.

The wages paid to home-workers are low in comparison with those received by factory workers. The system of giving work from the factory to contractors who in turn distribute it among homeworkers has produced a "sweating system" that deprives the homeworkers of fair compensation.

The ramifications of home work are extensive, particularly in cities of the first class. Some of the most important industries resort to it extensively. There are, undoubtedly, thousands of families who rely upon work at home to a certain degree, but those households are few and rare for whom it is the sole or even chief source of income.

There can be no doubt that immediate legislation is needed to remedy the evils inevitably accompanying this work. Every manufacturer using home-work who appeared before us conceded that some change is desirable. But concerning the specific nature of these changes there have been divergent opinions.

On the one hand it has been urged that all manufacturing in tenement houses of goods for the open market be prohibited; that a manufacturer should no longer be permitted to make a tenement home a branch of his factory and in this way evade all the responsibility and expense of compliance with the requirements of the labor law. It has been argued that it is impossible to supervise and regulate homework sufficiently to correct its dangerous features, and that no system of inspection to which the state would be justified in resorting would effectually prevent manufacturing in homes which are unclean or in which there is disease.

Again it has been argued that since homework now affords employment to thousands who are more or less dependent upon it for support, the prohibition of manufacturing in tenements would injure many industries and deprive thousands of homeworkers of a livelihood. It has been maintained also that homework can be so regulated that work may not be done in unsanitary and unhealthful surroundings, or with the assistance of young children; that no adequate attempt has been made in this state to regulate homework and that until such an attempt has been made and has resulted in failure it is unfair and unjust to say that any regulation would be futile.

We have given careful consideration to these divergent views. We realize the manufacturing in tenement houses is a serious evil, that it is, in fact, a blot on our industrial system. It is to be condemned because it is injurious to the health of the women and children directly engaged in this work and because it unjustifiably invades their homes. Moreover, the health of the public using such products is endangered. From an economic point of view its continuance is unjustified; it undermines the wage scale of the factory workers; it is wasteful both of human labor and of material. Public welfare would be promoted by its eradication. In the long run the home-worker would gain precisely as the men working in the coal mines of Pennsylvania were benefited when their young children were prevented from working and thus from competing with their parents.

The Commission did not feel justified, however, in recommending that the whole system be rooted out at once. It is deeply entrenched in our industrial life and to overturn existing conditions too suddenly would, perhaps, cripple certain industries and would work great hardship to thousands of workers engaged in them. It is true that for more than twenty years there has been a statute regulating homework, but it is also true that no serious effort has been made to enforce this law in the spirit in which the legislature undoubtedly intended it to be carried out. The inadequate resources of the Depatment of Labor account in large measure for this failure. Licenses have been issued as a matter of form and prosecutions for violations of the law have rarely been instituted. Licenses, moreover, have not been revoked for unsanitary condition of premises as often as circumstances demanded.

The present law is in many respects entirely inadequate. It covers only tenement houses in which the 41 articles specified in the law are manufactured and leaves the manufacture in tenement homes of all other articles, without supervision of any kind.

Our recommendations are therefore embraced under the following heads:

1. Entire prohibition of the employment of children under 14 years of age in tenement house work;

2. Immediate prohibition of work in tenement houses on all articles likely to become contaminated and therefore injurious to public health; or on articles by which it is clear that disease may be communicated;

3. Extension of the present law to cover manufacturing in any tenement house of all articles and the strengthening of the administrative features of the law;

4. Adequate number of inspectors to enforce the law;

5. Further investigation and study by the Industrial Board.

PROHIBITION OF THE EMPLOYMENT OF CHILDREN

All witnesses appearing before the Commission, including manufacturers who send work to homes, have recognized the necessity of stopping immediately the employment of very young children in this work. We therefore recommend an amendment to the labor law prohibiting the employment in tenement houses of a child under fourteen in any work *for* a factory and that

> *"work shall be deemed to be done for a factory, whenever it is done at any place, upon the work of a factory or upon any of the materials entering into the product of the factory, whether under contract or arrangement with any person in charge of or connected with such factory, directly or indirectly, through the instrumentality of one or more contractors or third persons."*

The employment of a child in violation of this provision should be sufficient cause for revoking the license of the entire tenement in which the child lives. This sweeping prohibition of the work of young children will eliminate one of the most objectionable features of homework and one that the public especially condemns.

PROHIBITION OF MANUFACTURE OF FOOD PRODUCTS AND INFANTS' WEAR

We recommend the immediate prohibition of the manufacture in tenement houses of food products, dolls, and dolls' clothes and of infants' and children's wearing apparel. The investigations we conducted show that such restriction is plainly called for in the interests of public health. The classification is reasonable and one that may, under the decisions, properly be made by the legislature. Food products are much more liable to contamination than any others and their preparation under entirely sanitary and hygienic conditions is a matter absolutely necessary to the public health. Infants and children are more susceptible than adults to contagious diseases and it is intolerable that the manufacture of garments and other articles to be worn by them, or which they play with, should be permitted under circumstances that may tend to spread disease. The many reports of work done in homes in which there were cases of scarlet fever, diphtheria, and measles prove that this danger to children is a serious one.

We therefore recommend the following amendment to the labor law:

> *No article of food, no dolls or dolls' clothing and no article of children's or infants' wearing apparel shall be manufactured, altered, repaired or finished in whole or in part, by any person for a factory, either directly or through the instrumentality of one or more contractors or other third persons in a tenement house, in any portion of an apartment any part of which is used for living purposes.*

We are convinced that this measure is a valid exercise of the police power and that its constitutionality is not open to doubt. The Jacobs case (98 N. Y., p. 98) is not contrary authority. It held unconstitutional an act which forbade the manufacture of tobacco products in tenement houses in cities having a population of over 500,000. This decision was based upon the ground that the act was not a health measure and not passed in the interests of the public health. The court relied upon evidence which they claimed justified this finding. The Board of Health of the City of New York had officially declared, after careful investigation "that the health of the tenement population is not jeopardized by the manufacture of cigars in those houses; that this bill is not a sanitary measure, and that it has not been approved by this board."

Presiding Justice Davis said:

> "If the Act were general and aimed at all tenement houses and prohibited for sanitary reasons the manufacture of cigars and tobacco in all such buildings, or if it prohibited such manufacture in the living rooms of all tenants another case would be presented." (In re Jacobs, 33 Hun, 374, 382.)

The measure we recommend differs from the act as construed by the court in the Jacobs case in the following important particulars:

1st. It is to apply to *all* tenement houses throughout the state.

2nd. It is limited in its application to apartments used for *living purposes.*

3rd. It is essentially a health measure necessary for sanitary reasons and in the interests of the public health; that fact is proved convincingly by the testimony heard by the Commission and by the results of our own investigations.

4th. It is limited to work done *for* a factory; that is, it prohibits the use of a living room in a tenement house as a branch of a factory in the preparation and manufacture of products having an intimate relation to the public health.

Thus the measure we recommend meets all of the objections that the court raised in the *Jacobs'* case.

AMENDMENTS TO PRESENT LAW REGULATING TENEMENT HOUSE MANUFACTURE

There is no logical reason for limiting the application of the licensing law to certain specified articles (41), and we therefore recommend that its scope be extended to cover the manufacturing of any article in a tenement house.

To aid in the enforcement of the law we recommend the following:

1. Every employer in any factory sending goods to a tenement house to be manufactured shall issue with all such goods a label bearing the name and address of his factory. At present the inspectors complain that they are generally unable to ascertain from the home-workers, the names of the factory owner for whom the work is done.

2. The owner of every factory for which articles are manufactured in any tenement house shall secure a permit for that purpose from the Commissioner of Labor. This permit may be revoked or suspended by the commissioner whenever any provision of the law relating to the sanitary condition of tenement houses or their freedom from contagious diseases or the employment of children under fourteen years of age is violated in connection with any work for the factory. No factory shall send goods to be manufactured in a tenement home unless this permit has been issued.

We also recommend that there be published by the Department of Labor a complete list of all factories holding such permits, together with the names and business addresses of the owners of all such factories, and that there be also published, from time to time, a list of tenement houses licensed in accordance with the law.

DIVISION OF HOMEWORK INSPECTION

We have heretofore recommended the creation of a division of homework inspection in the Bureau of Inspection to be in charge of tenement homes in which manufacturing is carried on. Not less than fifteen inspectors should be assigned to this division and the number should be increased from time to time as circumstances demand. We believe that at least one-third of these inspectors should be women. The inspections should not be limited to the period between 9 A. M. and 3 P. M. as is the practice at present. It is highly important that inspections should also be in the late afternoon and at night.

CONCLUSION

We believe that the prohibition of the employment of young children in tenement house work, the prohibition of the manufacture of food products, dolls' dresses, and clothing and the wearing apparel of infants and children, together with the recommendations we have made for an improvement in the administrative features of the present law and the creation of a division in the department for its adequate enforcement will protect the public more effectively. It is probable, however, that in the future more radical action will be necessary.

We recommend, for the present that this entire subject receive the careful consideration of the Industrial Board, which should make investigations from time to time to ascertain the conditions under which manufacturing in tenement houses, is carried on. If, after two or three years, it is found that attempted regulation is unsuccessful and that the necessary control over unsanitary and unhealthy conditions of work in tenement houses cannot be secured by inspection and supervision, then all manufacturing in tenement houses should be prohibited in the interests of the home-workers, of the dwellers in tenement houses and of the public at large.

---

* Bills 8 and 9, Appendix I.

IV.

THE CANNERIES

The fruit and vegetable canning industry differs from all other manufacturing industries in New York State in the important respect that the canneries are geographically isolated. They are scattered over eighteen counties largely rural, in hamlets, villages, and little cities, and are usually situated in the farming region even when there are other industries in the same county.

Through their situation the canners are thus removed from the regular field of work of the state factory inspectors who must make special tours, expensive in time and money, to inspect them. They are also removed from the daily observation of the consuming public and of the workers in other industries.

The employees are either the native American neighbors of the canneries or foreigners imported from cities in family groups of men, women and children. These diverse elements separated by race, language, and religion have little in common with one another and form no organizations of any kind. They have, moreover, little communication with the outside public. Being scattered units they have no effective means of making public their opinions and wishes.

For these reasons little is known about the canning industry. It has therefore been difficult for legislators to weigh intelligently the claims made by canners for exemption from the provisions of the labor law relating to the employment of women and children.

With regard to these provisions the fruit and vegetable canning industry has always occupied a unique position. The industry has, as a whole, never obeyed them for it has never been compelled to do so. Officials who should properly assist in enforcing the law no less directly than the Commissioner of Labor seem to have contributed actually to its relaxation. This fact applies not only to local magistrates and juries but also to local school authorities and to state officials.

Ever since 1903, the canners have unweariedly sought for their industry both complete exemption through amendment of the statute relating to factories. and partial exemption, through interpretation of its provisions by the Attorney-General. The canners have achieved both these ends. The opinion rendered by a former Attorney-General which will be referred to more fully hereafter, declared that the factory law did not apply to cannery sheds. This opinion removed an ever increasing body of women and children from the protection of the factory law and has resulted in the enployment of children of a very tender age in the sheds.

In 1912 the legislature exempted the canning industry from the operation of the provisions of the factory law regulating the hours of labor for women. Subdivision two of section seventy-eight of the labor law as amended in 1912 provides that the provisions relating to the hours of labor of women in factories,

> "shall not apply to the employment of women and of minors sixteen years of age and upwards in canning and preserving perishable products in fruit and canning establishments between the fifteenth day of June and the fifteenth day of October each year."

This wide open exemption permits the employment of minors over 16 years of age and of women, for any number of hours during the canning season.

EXTENT OF THE INDUSTRY

The industry thus exempted from this very important provision of the labor law is growing in extent. There were, during the summer of 1912, 128 canneries engaged primarily in canning fruits and vegetables.

According to the United States Census of 1910, the canned goods packed in the state of New York in 1909 amounted to 4,356,861 cases of all products packed, valued at $8,454,359.

In its output of canned peas New York ranks second among the states of the Union; in its output of canned beans, third; and in its output of canned corn, sixth.

Our investigators report that there are employed in the canning factories, off and on, throughout the season approximately 14,000 men, women and children.* Of the children our investi-

* A memorandum submitted by the Canners' Association of New York places the number as high as 40,000. The Census Report for 1910 fixes it at 8,818.

gators found 1,355 under the age of sixteen, at work, but are of the opinion that the number actually employed was approximately 1,700.

The crops with which the canneries deal include peas, beans, corn, succotash, tomatoes, pumpkins, and other vegetables; apples, berries, cherries, peaches, pears, plums, and other fruits.

CLAIM OF THE CANNERIES TO EXEMPTION FROM THE FACTORY LAW

The canners rest their plea for exemption from the factory law upon the perishable nature of their material, the shortness and variability of their season, and the alleged healthfulness of the surroundings amid which women and children work. The nature of the material and the variability of the season are, they assert, conditions beyond their control. But these two peculiarities of the industry involve in themselves, according to the canners, certain mitigations for the workers; for, between the periods of maturity of the various crops, rest from employment usually follows a rush period. They further declare that since their factories are among the fields, work in them is more akin to agricultural than to factory labor. They point to the fact that "the Lord ripens the crops," and place upon Him all responsibility for the irregularities of their industry.

THE INVESTIGATION OF THE COMMISSION

The fact that most of the employees in the canneries are women and children made it very important for the Commission to devote a portion of its time to a careful study of conditions in this unregulated industry. Accordingly the Commission both through personal visits of its own members and through the assistance of investigators, made a thorough inspection of conditions in this industry during the canning season of 1912. The investigation covered the employment of women and children and their hours of labor, and general sanitary conditions both in the canneries themselves and also in the living quarters of the foreigners employed in the canneries.

The investigation was conducted by Mr. Zenas L. Potter, assisted by nine field inspectors. It was unusually thorough.

One hundred and twenty-one out of one hundred and twenty-eight canning factories of the state were inspected. The method generally employed was that of a regular official inspection by the Commission's investigators. Where, however, special information in regard to working conditions was needed several of these investigators would secure employment as workers in the canneries and in this way be able to describe in detail the working conditions of the women and children. Much information was also obtained from the official records and time books of the canners. Furthermore, the members of the Commission personally inspected a number of canneries and examined under oath the canners, their superintendents, and the women and children who were found there actually at work.

A public hearing to consider proposed legislation for the canneries was held by the Commission in Albany on November 26th, 1912, to which all of the canners of the state were invited. Twenty of the canners were present in person and the entire canning industry of the state was represented by counsel. Every opportunity was given to the representatives of the industry to present their side of the case. The Commission permitted counsel for the canners to cross-examine the investigators and inspectors called by the Commission. It also permitted the canners to call witnesses and to have their own counsel examine them. Many of the canners themselves testified to working conditions. At a later public hearing at Rochester, the Commission again allowed the counsel for the canners to call and examine several witnesses. The counsel for the canners regarded the proceedings and investigations of the Commission as most fair to all concerned. A memorandum submitted on behalf of the Canners' Association is set forth in Appendix X.

CHILD LABOR IN THE CANNERIES

Our investigators during the canning season of 1912 found 1,355 children under sixteen years of age at work in the canning factories proper and in the sheds of these factories. Of these, 96 were employed in the factories proper and 1,259 in the cannery sheds. Of the shed-workers 942 were under fourteen years of age; 141 under 10 years of age, of whom 30 were six years old or under.

Only 12 children under fourteen years of age were employed in the factory proper. The Commission itself in the tour of inspection of the canneries made in August, 1912, found a number of children under ten years of age at work in the sheds.

A canning factory is made up generally of a group of at least three buildings: a process building where the vegetables are sealed and cooked, a store house, and a shed where the vegetables and fruits are prepared, as for example, beans are snipped and corn is husked. It is in these sheds that nearly all of the children are employed.

ATTORNEY-GENERAL'S OPINION—CANNERY SHED NOT A FACTORY

For a clear understanding of the child labor situation in the canneries it is necessary to refer briefly to the laws of the state relating to the employment of children, to the interpretation placed upon those laws by state officials, and to the present status of such laws so far as their practical operation and enforcement are concerned.

The child labor law enacted in 1886 prohibited the employment in a factory of any child under fourteen years of age and prohibited the employment of children between fourteen and sixteen years unless an employment certificate was obtained. In 1903 this statute was amended by including in this prohibition the work of such children "in connection with any factory."

There is but little doubt that up to this time everyone concerned in the enforcement of the child labor law believed that it applied to the sheds maintained in connection with a canning factory. In 1905 a number of canners requested the Commissioner of Labor then holding office, to investigate conditions and to determine whether the factory law applied to the sheds. The Commissioner of Labor applied in turn to the Attorney-General for a ruling on the question. The latter delivered an opinion in which he held that under certain conditions work in the cannery sheds was agricultural in character and that the factory law did not apply to it; that is, that the child labor law relating to factories did not apply to children at work in the sheds.

In the concluding portion of his opinion the Attorney-General said:

> "If the employment is in sheds devoid of machinery, in the open air, unconnected with a factory, and not subject to the discipline and hours governing factory employment, I am of the opinion that such employment of children under fourteen is legal, providing it does not conflict with the provisions of the compulsory education law."

The correspondence between the Commissioner of Labor and the Attorney-General together with the latter's opinion are set forth in full in Appendix V., *Report on Industrial Conditions in the Canneries.*

Views differ as to the correctness of the opinion of the Attorney-General, as a legal document. In any event the opinion did not warrant the employment of children in the cannery sheds at any age, for any number of hours, and under any conditions as is the practice to-day. As a practical matter, however, the opinion was interpreted to mean that the factory law, irrespective of the conditions upon which the opinion was based, did not apply to work in cannery sheds. At any rate nothing was done by the Commissioner of Labor who asked for the opinion, to enforce the child labor law even as to work in such sheds as could not possibly come within the Attorney-General's classification as agricultural.

In the actual practice of enforcement it would as a matter of fact be virtually impossible to make the distinctions that the Attorney-General pointed out in his opinion. The result was that for several years after the opinion was rendered nothing at all was done to check the employment of young children in cannery sheds.

In 1907 when a later Commissioner of Labor, in response to popular demand, instituted proceedings for violation of the child labor law in the employment of children under fourteen in the sheds his efforts were successfully opposed in every case brought to trial, by the reliance of the defense solely on the opinion of the Attorney-General previously quoted. In practically every one of these cases the conditions were different from those assumed by the Attorney-General as the basis of his opinion. The verdicts in these cases showed, however, that not only the canners but the local courts, instead of construing the opinion strictly, stretched it to the utmost, without regard to the conditions mentioned therein, namely, that the sheds in which the children were employed should contain no machinery and should be structurally unconnected with a factory. The people, of course, cannot appeal from verdicts rendered for defendants in criminal cases so that there has been no ruling on the subject by any superior court.

THE SHEDS

Whether or not the Attorney-General's opinion is sound law and whether or not the interpretation placed upon that opinion by local courts is correct, is relatively unimportant at this time. We are no longer deeply concerned with what the law in the past has been theoretically or in practice, but we do deem it to be of vital importance that in the future it should be expressed so clearly and unequivocally as to leave no room for any doubt or speculation concerning its scope or applicability.

Anyone unacquainted with the arrangement of cannery buildings might assume that the shed is always out in the open fields away from the factory proper and unconnected with it in any way. That assumption, however, would be frequently an error. Of the 33 sheds that were inspected in which children were employed, 11 were contiguous with the factory proper, 2 were within one foot or less, 9 were within from nineteen to twenty-five feet, 2 were within from twenty-five to fifty feet. In twenty factories visited the passage between the shed and the factory was unobstructed.

The following facts show the character of the sheds where children worked:

Floors

Floored	24
Unfloored	9

Walls

Entirely enclosed	6
One side open	2
Two sides open	3
Three sides open	9
All sides open	13

Distance from Process Building

Contiguous with it	11
10 feet or less from it	2
11 to 25 feet	9
26 to 50 feet	2
125 to 300 feet	4
½ mile	4
2 miles	1

Connection with Process Building

No connection	15
Structural and power connection	5
Power and conveyor	7
Structural and by power and conveyor	6

Barrier to Free Passage of Workers Between Shed and Factory

Actual barrier	8
No barrier	20
Distance barrier	5

Artificial Light

Contain artificial light	24
No artificial light	9

Machinery

Sheds containing machinery		14
(Operated when children work	8)	
(Sheds containing machinery, "dead" when children work	6)	
Sheds containing no machinery		19

The sheds are, therefore, in most cases clearly a part of the general manufacturing plant since they are one of a group of buildings constituting the factory.

A significant point to be borne in mind is that 24 out of 33 of these sheds in which young children were found working have provision for artificial lighting by which work may be carried on after nightfall. This has made possible the abuses in the employment of children that have been called to the Commission's attention.

It is our conclusion from personal inspection, from the reports of the investigators, and from the testimony of witnesses given before us that the majority of the cannery sheds more nearly resemble factories than places in which agricultural labor is carried on.

AGES OF CHILDREN

Because the cannery sheds have been exempted from the factory law the canners have been permitted to employ in them children of any age. The ages of 1,259 children found at work in 33 sheds are as follows:

Ages	*Number of Children*
14 to 16 years,	317
10 to 14 "	801
Under 10 "	141

Of the children found at work, 141 were under ten years old, ranging from three years up, and 942 were under fourteen years.

Ages of Children in Sheds

The ages of 1,259 children found at work in 33 sheds are as follows:

Ages	*Number of Children*
3 years of age,	1
4 " " "	3
5 " " "	10
6 " " "	16
7 " " "	26
8 " " "	46
9 " " "	39
10 " " "	180
11 " " "	186
12 " " "	239

Ages.	Number of Children
13 years of age	196
14 " " "	188
15 " " "	129

For the following reasons these figures do not include all the children who were employed in the sheds:

(1) At several factories which were known to employ considerable numbers of children, only a few were found at work when the inspection was made.

(2) At four establishments which regularly employ children, none were found at work during our inspection.

(3) At one cannery, when the inspector appeared at 5:30 A. M. approximately two hundred children of all ages were hurried away, so that records of their ages could not be made. These children were apparently already working when the inspector arrived.

(4) At another factory, upon the inspector's arrival, fourteen children ran out at a command from the Italian "boss." All seemed to be and probably were under ten years of age. This factory pretended to employ no children under that age.

Taking into consideration those factories where we were unable to get facts, it is our opinion that if 450 children were added to the number found at work by the inspectors, the total of 1,700 would represent approximately the number of children under sixteen who found employment last summer in the cannery sheds of New York State.

TYPE OF WORK DONE BY CHILDREN

The work of the children in the sheds is confined to the snipping of beans and the husking of corn. The work of "snipping" is simple. At the end of the bean which has been next to the vine is a small collar and at the other end is a stringy point. To prepare the beans for canning, these collars and points must be snipped off. The beans are brittle when snipped and it requires only a quick twist to remove the collar and the stringy point. No great muscular effort is required, but after a day of snipping at the beginning of the season, it is usual for the wrist to become lame and the fingers sore. In children these effects are aggravated.

At a number of factories, including those where the largest number of children are employed, the children who snip the beans carry the full boxes to the weigher to be weighed, a distance sometimes of 100 to 200 feet and even farther. The majority of the boxes when full weigh from 19 to 21 pounds, and some as much as 29 pounds.

Corn husking requires more effort than bean snipping. It sometimes takes all the strength of a small child to tear the husks from the ear of corn and to break the stalk from the ear. This operation when it is performed for long hours becomes fatiguing even to an adult. The crates of corn are carried to the checker usually by two persons and weigh from 40 to 60 pounds. In many canneries children of all ages, both girls and boys, carry the crates. The strain is considerably greater than in carrying boxes of snipped beans. Small girls have been seen tugging at crates that they were hardly able to carry.

The seats provided for the shed workers are poor. In practically all of the cannery sheds which the Commission personally inspected, boxes without any backs were provided. These were often too high or too low and not properly adjusted for work. The light and ventilation in the sheds is good, but because one or more sides of the sheds are open, the workers are often exposed to dampness and cold.

HOURS OF LABOR

No record is kept of the hours of labor of children in the sheds, and so far as the canner is concerned they are free to come and go as they please. Children told the Commission that they often worked in the sheds from early in the morning till late at night. At one canning factory our inspector reported as follows:

> "Inspector stayed at factory till 9:30 P. M. Twenty-three children under fourteen years in shed till 9:15 P. M. Some left then, but about a dozen stayed later. When inspector first came, children were carrying boxes of beans weighing

> 15 to 25 pounds from shed to factory, a distance of about 150 feet, to be weighed. Later, however, a man with a wheelbarrow brought them to the factory. At 9:10 a girl of thirteen and a boy of eleven went to sleep at their work, bent over the boxes into which they had been snipping, their heads resting on their arms. Boys told the inspector that 'Boss' had said snipping would commence at 4 o'clock next morning. One-half of the shed was covered a foot deep with beans which were held over night."

Children as young as four and five were reported to be working at night, but they were with their parents. Many children ten years of age and over came alone. At some factories no snipping is carried on at night. At others the work goes on in the shed sometimes until eleven o'clock, according to the policy of each factory. The factories which employ children fall into two groups: those which use local American help for snipping and husking and those which employ foreigners to do the work. In the former, the conditions are usually much better than in the latter. The canner, to get his beans snipped, must either bring out a larger number of foreigners from the city, at increased expense, or work those he has for longer hours. For this reason the hours of shed work are generally longer in factories where foreigners are employed. It was in a factory where the workers were Italians and Poles that two hundred children were sent scampering away when an inspector appeared at 5:30 A. M.

CHILDREN FORCED TO WORK

When the snippers are foreigners, their exploitation is the rule and not the exception. Children are commonly driven by their parents to work for long hours. The canners keep the sheds open for labor, and supply the beans or corn to be snipped or husked. The parents see that the children are there to work. This fact is illustrated from the following paragraph taken from the report of a "working investigator":

> "The parents are continually driving children to work. One little boy, aged 11, who was throwing some bean snip-

pings at another had stopped work a second. His father hit him brutally across the face and set him to work again. Everywhere parents are forcing the 'kids' to work."

Again an investigator reports:

"Nellie V—— says she is 10, but she looks 8. She snipped from 4:30 A. M. to 7 A. M.; from 7:30 A. M. to 12 M.; from 12:30 P. M. to 5 P. M. She got up at 4 A. M. Liked to snip, but was 'awful tired.' Said her mother made her keep at it."

The following is a report of an investigator who worked in a factory employing Italians:

"Little Jack, aged 12, up from 3 A. M. and snipping from 4:30 A. M. to 10 P. M., with only a few minutes for supper, said: 'My fingers is broke.' He went to bed last night at 12 and got up at 3. He said he was 'awful tired,' but his mother made him work. He tried to go home several times. His hands were swollen. His sister, aged 10, could hardly keep her eyes open, and her mother scolded her constantly. Jack made $1.40. He said he couldn't keep any of it. He said work like this was nothing to peas when his mother and sister would come home every night at 1 and 2 A. M. and 'they was so sick they fell down and vomited.'" (August 20, 1912).

The next day the investigator reported:

"This morning when I got to the shed at 7, Jack was sitting wrapped up in a big shawl, very pale, with his black eyes just sagging out of his head. He had his fingers done up in a dirty rag. I asked him if he had to get up at 3 again. He said: 'They pulled me out of bed at 4 o'clock.' His sister cried, but they had to go 'or get a beating.'

Another little chap, about 11, who had snipped from 4 A. M. to 7 P. M. yesterday, and to-day from 6:30 A. M. to 10 P. M., told me he thought it was 'only 8 o'clock at night when they dragged him out this morning at 4.' He thought he had been asleep 'only a minute.'"

The following is from the evidence given at the Albany hearing by Miss Mary Chamberlain, one of the inspectors of the

Commission, concerning the hours of labor of some of the shed workers in the establishment in which she was employed:

Milly V——, aged 10, shed worker:

On August 15th she worked from 11 A. M. until 6:45 P. M.; 7 3/4 hours, and ate only a peach for lunch.

August 17th she worked from 7:30 A. M. until 10:30 A. M., picking; 10:30 A. M. until 3 P. M., snipping, and ate a little bread and butter for lunch; total 7 1/2 hours.

August 20th she worked from 4:30 A. M. until 7:30 A. M., snipping; 11 A. M. until 12:30 P. M., snipping; 1 P. M. until 6 P. M., snipping; 6:30 P. M. until 9:30 P. M., snipping; total 12 1/2 hours.

Q. That child went to work that day at what hour? A. 4:30 in the morning.

Q. And she stopped at what time? A. 9:30 P. M.

August 21st she worked from 4:30 A. M. until 7 A. M., snipping; 7:30 A. M. until 12 M., snipping; 12:30 P. M. until 5 P. M., snipping; total 11 1/2 hours.

August 24th she worked from 11:30 A. M. until 6 P. M., and she ate a little while she was snipping; she worked from 6:30 P. M. until 11 o'clock at night, snipping, a total of 11 hours.

August 26th she worked from 4 o'clock in the morning until 7:30, snipping; from 8 o'clock until 12:30, snipping; 1 until 6, snipping; 6:30 until 10, snipping; total 16 1/2 hours.

Q. From 4:30 in the morning until when? A. Until ten o'clock at night.

Where American help is used for snipping or husking, work seldom commences before 7 A. M. and never, to our knowledge, before 6 A. M. Where foreigners are used, it is not unusual for work to commence at 4 or 4:30 A. M. when the rush of beans or corn is on. Where Americans are employed the children seldom do other work during the day. The Italian children, however, when the crops are coming in, are frequently roused at dawn, snip till it becomes light, pick beans in the fields after they dry off from the night dew, and with nightfall go into the sheds and snip again.

Where American help is employed for snipping, the children are in some cases forced by their parents to do this work, as the following report of a "working investigator" indicates:

> "Lucy D., 11 years, came into the shed and said she didn't want to string. I asked her why she did it and she said, 'I've got to.'"

Cases in which American mothers force their children to work are, however, the exception and not the rule, and even then the children are not forced to work excessive hours. Many of the American children are eager to go to the sheds where there are many other children and where they can earn a little spending money.

There are nevertheless unquestionably some instances of child exploitation when the sheds are kept open for work up to 14 hours a day, even where American help is employed. Since, however, no records are kept of the hours during which the children work, these instances could be discovered only by careful study of such individual cases as we were able to trace. For instance, a "working investigator" reports:

> "Mrs. McG—— had a little girl aged ten in the factory. She did not use such stringent methods of forcing the child to work as the Italians did, but kept her constantly at work six or seven hours a day. She was not so brutal about this as the Italians were, and she did let the child go home to meals, and stop when she pleaded and pleaded with her mother that she was tired."

WORK IN SHEDS IS NOT PLAY

One investigator who worked in the sheds comments as follows on the difference in the attitude toward their work of the children at the beginning of the bean crop and later when the season is well under way:

> "The difference in the attitude of the children toward snipping is very noticeable. At first, when there were only a few hours of work and they had lots of time to 'help mother snip beans' they were full of play and acted like real children. Now they sit like little machines with their fingers tied up in rags, and snip away all day long. If they start

for home or evince any spirit of play, they are promptly whacked or supplied with more beans by their parents."

An incident which occurred at one factory where a rule was put into effect, that no child under ten is permitted to snip, illustrates the greed of parents for the earnings of children. Some boys under ten got into the shed and when the foreman attempted to put one out he fought to stay. His mother came to his rescue by throwing boxes and finally managed to bite the foreman viciously on the arm. If the mother would fight in this way to have the boy permitted to work, it may well be asked what she would do to the boy should he refuse to work.

Nor are the parents alone to blame. Their parental love is often dulled by the hard grind of necessity. Manifestly a canner who pays low wages to parents cannot argue convincingly that the children should be permitted to snip beans to increase the meager earnings of the family. If children should not be permitted to work, the cannery owner would still be under the necessity of obtaining the labor of their parents and unquestionably would soon have to pay the parents approximately what is now the total family income.

THE NECESSITY FOR THE EMPLOYMENT OF YOUNG CHILDREN

It has frequently been asserted that the employment of young children is indispensable in this industry. We have not found this to be the case. There are in the state 76 canneries in all, packing corn. Our investigators received information from 68 of these as to whether they employ children for husking. Of these 23 do so and 45 do not. In other words about two-thirds of the canners pack corn without employing children for husking. The following table shows for the 10 factories packing the largest number of cases of corn, set forth in the order of the number of cases packed, whether or not they employ children for husking:

Factory	No.	1	Employs children.
"	"	2	Employs no Children.
"	"	3	" " "
"	"	4	" " "

Factory No.	5	Employs no children.
" "	6	" " "
" "	7	" " "
" "	8	" " "
" "	9	" " "
" "	10	Employs children.

Only two of the ten employ children. One of these two factories has the largest output in the state, but the owner of this factory has stated to the inspector that he intends to have husking machines in 1913 and thus to eliminate child labor entirely.

It can hardly be maintained that the successful packing of corn demands the employment of young children. Within the last few years husking machines have been perfected which husk corn satisfactorily and they are rapidly being installed in the corn canneries of the state. The use of children for husking is becoming yearly more and more confined to the small canneries. It is only a matter of time when husking will be done entirely by machine. An important effect of a law prohibiting the employment of children for husking will be to hasten the substitution of machinery. In the long run this change will probably prove a benefit, not a detriment to the industry.

There are, in all, 61 factories in the state packing beans. Of these 30 use children for snipping; 6 send beans into the homes of the workers to be snipped, and 25 use no children. In other words, half of the factories canning beans employ no children. The following table shows for the 10 factories packing the largest number of cases of beans, set forth in the order of the number of cases packed, whether or not they employ children for snipping:

Factory No.	1	Employs children.
" "	2	" "
" "	3	Employs no children.
" "	4	Sends beans into homes.
" "	5	Employs children.
" "	6	" "
" "	7	Employs no children.
" "	8	Employs children.

Factory No. 9	Employs children.
" " 10	Employs no children. Part of snipping is done in homes.

The existence of the many canners who pack beans without employing children, proves that child labor is not necessary in that industry and that the problem of its elimination is simply a question of adjusting the size of the pack to the available adult labor supply, and of obtaining a larger supply of adult workers by increased wages.

EMPLOYMENT OF CHILDREN TO OBTAIN PARENTS' LABOR

A number of canners have disclaimed any desire to employ children, especially the younger ones, but contend that the labor of their parents is necessary and cannot be secured unless the children are allowed to accompany them to the factory. Our investigations proved, however, that this contention is without foundation. Of the 1,259 children under 16 years of age employed in the sheds, 754 came alone, and only 505 came with their parents.

Provision can readily be made, as has been shown in the case of several canning factories in this state, for places in which the children may remain with a caretaker while their parents are at work. This is an inexpensive method by which the canners may employ the parents without employing their children.

SUMMARY OF FINDINGS

The results of our investigation concerning the employment of children under fourteen in cannery sheds may briefly be summarized as follows:

1. That young children are employed in cannery sheds to an extent unknown in any other industry of the state.

2. That work in the cannery sheds is more closely akin to factory work than to agricultural labor.

3. That numerous children under ten years are employed at such work.

4. That children are in the sheds not for play but for work.

5. That children are kept in the sheds late at night and often, though not working, are deprived of necessary sleep.

6. That truancy is aggravated by child labor in canneries, and that children, particularly of foreign parents, are often deprived of weeks and months of schooling.

LAWS IN OTHER STATES

In Illinois, Ohio, Tennessee, Iowa, Maine, Michigan, Missouri, New Jersey, and Pennsylvania, nine of the fifteen leading canning states, no children under fourteen years of age are permitted to work either in the factory or in the sheds.

In four states, California, Indiana, Maryland, and Georgia, no child under 12 years may be employed in canneries. In the first two states such employment is permitted only during vacation time.

In but one of the leading canning states, Delaware, is there total exemption from a fourteen-year age limit applying to other industries.

In practically all of the large canning states, therefore, the employment of young children in or in connection with a canning factory is prohibited.

RECOMMENDATION

That young children should be allowed to work in cannery sheds under the conditions that have been described is a wrong against childhood and against the state. During vacation time they should be out in the sunshine at play, and not at work in a cannery shed. In our industrial life they should not be made to do the work of men and women. The state must not suffer the lives of its children to be blighted, their health impaired, and their education neglected by premature employment.

The solicitude of the canners lest the family income be reduced if children are prohibited from working, deceives no one. Experience in other industries in the past has shown the contrary to be the case. The employment of young children in the cannery sheds is an unnecessary evil. The industry can get along without it. Many of the canners themselves are opposed to such employment, and half of them do not resort to it to-day. In any event, the state of New York cannot countenance a plea by any industry that it is dependent for its prosperity upon the employment of young children.

We recommend therefore that the definition of the word "factory" in the labor law be amended so as to include "*all buildings, sheds, structures or other places used for or in connection with* any mill, workshop or other manufacturing or business establishment, and that children under fourteen years of age be prohibited from working in connection with any factory *or for any factory at any place in this state.*" This should not apply, however, to children working on their home farms for their parents.* Boys over the age of 12 years may be employed in gathering produce for not more than six hours.

The proposed bill recommended in the preceding section of the report to prohibit the employment of young children in tenement-house work has been drafted so as to cover the prohibition of the employment of children in the cannery sheds.

WOMEN'S WORK IN THE CANNERIES

The main purpose of this inquiry has been to furnish information on which the legislature may determine how many hours per day and week the state of New York should permit women to work in the canning industry. The needs of the worker and the demands of the industry must both be considered. The constitutional basis for all laws restricting women's hours of labor is the protection of their health by preventing exhausting labor.

CONDITIONS OF LABOR

According to our most careful estimate approximately 7,000 women were employed in the New York State fruit and vegetable canneries in 1912.† The conditions under which they worked varied from factory to factory and according to occupation.

An important part of the canners' plea for exemption of their industry from the application of the factory law, rests upon the rural surroundings of the factories and the nature of the work. The investigation of the Commission, however, shows that the

---

Bill 8, Appendix I.

This does not include shed workers or women employed in pickle factories, fruit drying establishments or fish canneries.

canneries, though differing occasionally from other factories in the matter of light and ventilation, nevertheless resemble them in certain essential respects.

In particular, the canneries, like other factories, are filled with machinery. Much of this machinery is noisy and some of it is dangerous. Projecting set-screws or power-driven machinery, unguarded bolts, chains, and pulleys are common. The work in the cannery factory is for the most part speeded to keep pace with the machines.

The accompaniment characteristic of all factory work of women is strain. All the causes that may contribute to strain in other industries are also present in the canneries; for example, heat and cold, glare (when work is done by artificial light), noise of machinery, sitting in uncomfortable positions or standing, wet floors, danger from machinery, heavy lifting, and monotony of toil. Nearly half of the women, 47%, work amid a steady grinding of machinery, sometimes so great as to prevent conversation. Indeed, great noise always attends the operation of certain indispensable machines at which large numbers of women are employed. This fact is especially significant in measuring strain in a working day of from twelve to twenty hours.

Even in the matters of temperature, ventilation and light, the conditions in the canneries were often found to resemble those in many other factories. For instance, the work is done in summer and in many cases the factory buildings are hot because of the cooking of products. There were found 11% of the women working where the heat was excessive and 19% where the ventilation was poor or only fair. Furthermore, 16% of the women were working in bad light. This circumstance caused eye strain day after day.

The floors were wet where 19% of the women worked, a condition due in many cases to carelessness, but in others to processes in which it is impossible to keep the floors dry. Such a simple precaution as the provision of a slat floor above the cement or wooden floor is rarely seen. In nine sheds in which women and children worked there was no artificial floor whatever.

For 5% of the women there were no seats; where seats were provided 77% were without backs. Boxes, stools, often uncomfortably high in relation to the work, and seats without backs, formed the equipment. In general, the height of these seats has no relation to the age, height, health, or comfort of the worker.

No conspicuous value, therefore, attaches to the claim that the rural surroundings of canneries offset the disadvantages of long and irregular working days for women.

VARIETIES OF WORK

Tomato Peeling

It seems to be the general opinion among the canners, and it is probably the fact, that women when standing can peel tomatoes more rapidly than when seated. Many canners accordingly do not provide seats. The tomatoes are first scalded and then carried in pails to the workers. Often they are steaming hot and fill the air with vapor. The whole process is extremely damp. The floors usually become wet and the workers themselves are soaked unless well protected by waterproof aprons, which are furnished by a few factories. At certain factories the women must carry from the scalder to their tables twelve-quart pails of tomatoes, and after peeling them, from the table to the "checker." A description follows of the process at one factory where the worst conditions prevail:

> "Sixty-eight women, and eight girls between 14 and 16 years of age, stand peeling tomatoes. Floors are damp and air is laden with steam, especially near the scalder. Women carry dish-pans of tomatoes to tables from the scalder, and pails from the tables to the checking place, a total distance of about 36 paces. The weight of the pans and pails was about 25 pounds each. The superintendent said at 4 cents a pail, women averaged $1.50 a day. This means carrying about four loads an hour or 37 1/2 a day. The owner said it did women good to stand and carry pans and pails: 'It gives them exercise,' he said. No seats were provided for the tomato peelers except for one very stout woman."

Other factories maintained better conditions. Several provide men or conveyors to carry loads, and a few have installed porcelain sorting tables with little basins at the places where women sit to peel tomatoes.

Sorting

Peas, beans, and corn, before being placed in the cans, go through various processes. Peas first come from the viner and go through a cleaner which, by an air current, blows out much foreign matter. They then pass through a grader which separates them according to size. There still remain in the peas thistles, pieces of pods, and broken particles. To remove these the peas are run over "sorting tables" or moving belts along the sides of which women sit and pick out foreign matter.

Pea graders are constructed of horizontal metal planes with holes for the peas to fall through. In bean graders wire frames are used instead. These planes or frames are shaken by power and the machines when operated emit a continuous roar. It is often almost impossible to carry on a conversation where the women sorters work. Two-thirds of the women bean sorters worked where the noise was excessive. Sometimes the sorting tables are located near the washers or blanchers, with the result that the floors are wet where the sorters work.

Sorting is partly "machine-paced." The women pick over products passed before them, and if they are conscientious, or if they are closely under the supervision of a forewoman or superintendent, they keep pace with the machine. Investigators describe women, when the conveyor has carried beans past faster than they could be handled properly, frantically pushing them back in the hope that the stream would soon slacken. If the employer tries to drive the machinery too fast, however, the quality of the pack suffers, for the women do not attempt to sort cleanly. An offset to speeding is the fact that in many smaller factories slack moments are frequent, due to breakdowns in machinery and changing of grades of beans on the tables.

The steady, ever-moving stream of peas and beans often produces nausea akin to sea-sickness, to such a degree that some women are unable to continue the work. Eye-strain, especially in picking out small foreign particles from peas, is often intense.

The following reports are from women investigators of the Commission who actually worked at sorting:

> "Mrs. P—— told me at lunch time that she had a very sick headache. Working at bean tables always makes her ill.

"Towards the close of the afternoon Dolly R——, who sorted peas, complained of headache. She said she had worn thin slippers and got her feet wet. She hopes that she can work inside at weighing beans, as working at the tables makes her ill.

"I went to work at 7 o'clock this morning (Sunday). I worked several hours at sorting peas and then became so dreadfully sick that I had to leave the factory. This work is simple enough and does not require great physical effort, but the factory was so insufferably hot, damp, and smelly, that I became sick in a very few hours. The floors are concrete and covered with water; the room is hot and full of steam; the noise of machinery is deafening, and the combination was more than I could stand. An American girl working in the warehouse told me that she too had been working at the sorting table on Saturday and that she could not stand it. The other two American women said that they worked at the sorting table last year and it made them dizzy and sick.

"Sorting is very hard on the eyes; all the women complain of this. One said that when she got home at night she took up the paper and tried to read, but 'the print kept flying by just like the peas.' The light is very good, however, and the electric lights are quite adequate. After eleven hours of work the eyes of all the women looked very tired.

"The bean tables are right under the combination grader and sorter, and the noise is terrific — simply ear splitting; my ears are still ringing. Combined with the jiggling of the grader the work is most unpleasant. It makes one quite seasick, though sorting beans is not so monotonous and trying on the eyes as sorting peas.

"Mrs. McA—— worked on the bean sorter this morning. It made her sick at her stomach (very!) and she could not work on it this afternoon. It gives one the same sensation as sea-sickness when the graders go up and down and the beans move forward on the tables."

Feeding Corn Cutters

Corn cutting machines are usually fed by women. The task of feeding the cutters is unpleasant, because, almost without exception, the workers must stand, and the sticky milk of the corn spatters over them. This is the most highly speeded work in any of the canneries. The accident reports of the labor department show that several fingers are lost in canneries every year. Undoubtedly most of these are caught in corn cutters, since the hands of operators come near the knives of the cutters and are likely to be drawn in, especially if a piece of cob gets lodged in the entrance to the knives and an attempt is made to remove it with the fingers. One large factory uses only men for work at the corn cutters.

Filling and Weighing

The next process is the filling and weighing. The cans are required by law to equal a certain weight. Those for peas and corn are usually filled by machines. Berries are sorted directly into cans. Beans are put into cans partly by machinery, but must be balanced by the proper weight. Cherries, tomatoes, pears, etc., are placed in cans by hand.

This work is usually paid by the piece and consequently is done at a high rate of speed. The products worked on are often steaming and the air is, therefore, filled with vapor. Workers at this task usually stand, for no seats are provided.* It is regarded as one of the most skilled tasks in the factory. Workers often get their fingers cut on the sides of the cans, and the acids, especially in tomato filling, irritate the sores. Here are reports of "working investigators" regarding this work:

> "Lizzie J—— complained in the morning that she did not feel at all well, so I was not surprised when she did not return in the afternoon. Her place was taken for a few minutes by a young girl called Emma, who is working at filling cans with peas. She said it was hard because they have to stand all the time.
>
> "Mr. J—— said I could probably arrange to get a job filling cans. The only trouble was that it is very hard on the hands as the can sometimes cuts the fingers which always have to be protected."

* At one plant seats were provided for the women "fillers" for the first time on the day of the Commission's visit to the factory.

On the Line

After cans have been filled they are passed to the "capping line," a series of machines which fill cans with syrup, stamp them to show variety and grade, and seal them. Women are largely employed in the four operations connected with this process.

The machine used for filling peas and corn often begins "the line." Into it cans are fed by a chute leading generally from the second floor. Here a woman — in some factories two women or a boy — feeds cans into the chute. The rate of work is determined absolutely by the speed of machinery that demands very rapid action when only one woman is employed. A machine has been invented which automatically rights cans at the "filler." Such a machine wherever installed greatly relieves the tension of work, for then cans need not be placed in the chute right side up as is otherwise the case. This machine, however, is not yet very extensively used.

Women also put caps on cans. The cans go over "the line" at the rate of 40 to 110 per minute. The capping machine in most general use has a capacity of about 72 cans per minute. As the cans go by, the women must place a small tin cap on each can. The speed is regulated absolutely by machinery and often women work at high tension. In 22 factories only one woman was used on a "line;" 35 factories used two. A machine greatly relieving this strain has been invented which automatically places caps on cans and the operator has only to feed them into it. Only a few factories, however, have installed this machine for it is a recent invention. The women who put on these caps always work close to a row of twelve red-hot soldering irons, and often the heat is excessive. Very commonly, too, the floors are wet.

Here are reports from "working investigators" regarding this capping machine work:

> "Lizzie J—— who works most of the time at the capping machine was transferred to the sorting tables and I sat next to her. She told me that a man had invented a machine to put on caps, so now there is only one girl who puts them on by hand. She said it was 'frightfully hot work.'
>
> "A girl who works at the capping machine said that she found it 'very hot.'"

Sixteen factories employ women for "inspecting." Unless cans are perfectly sealed the contents spoil. The capping machine does its work remarkably well, but a considerable number of cans come through with slight defects. The "inspector" sits by "the line," and as the cans go by examines each one. The eye strain of the work is intense and frequently aggravated by defective lighting. These inspectors suffer the same heat as the women who put on the caps, since each is placed at about an equal distance from the hot soldering irons. Floors where inspectors work are often wet.

The speed of tasks "on the line" is, as has been said, determined by the speed of the machinery, and women often work at high tension. This strain is partly offset by the fact that there are frequent interruptions in the work, due to changing the grade of product. In the larger canneries these interruptions are not so frequent because one line is devoted exclusively to one grade of goods. Even here, however, there are interruptions due to breaks in machinery and other causes, which partially relieve the high pressure.

Labeling

Before the cans are shipped they are labeled, and some of the fancier products are wrapped in tissue paper. This is usually done in the storehouse, though not always, apart from the noise and strain of most of the machinery. Sometimes labeling is done by hand, sometimes by a hand-operated machine, and sometimes by one driven by power. Hand labeling is usually piece work, so there is incentive to rapid work. Machine labeling is usually done at a high rate of speed. A description follows of this work at one factory:

> "Work on labeling machine keeps me at pretty high tension. I kept track of the speed of cans through the machine this afternoon. This is the speed per minute, ten different minutes, at which cans passed in front of the label inspector: 140, 141, 150, 112, 160, 20, 100, 148, 100, 140. She must take out any unlabeled can or one with a flaw. It keeps one busy and is trying on the eyes. One also uses the sense of feeling by keeping the hand running over the cans. The gilt of the can labels comes off and makes the hand smart.

To be fair in judging this high speed, one must consider the fact that now and then there is a stop of five or ten minutes when there is trouble with the machine or a new set of labels to be put in. When there are small orders, there are very frequently stops, but when there are big orders of five hundred or more cases, the high rate of speed continues quite a while. Also one must consider that there are two girls on each machine, one inspecting and one repairing, so that when one girl cannot stand the inspecting longer, the other can shift into her place. The noise is terrific, worse than at the pea sorting tables, and almost as bad as at the bean tables. The clap of the cans going into the machine, which sounds exactly like the capping machines, the roll of the trucks, the pounding of the machine which nails on the case covers, the clatter of the cases as the men thump them onto the carriers, tires one extremely."

Again the investigator reported:

"This afternoon we packed from our label machine 1,100 cases. Since I worked on the machine all the afternoon, I inspected 2,400 cans or 80 per minute. This was steady work for the orders were large."

From the labeling machine, goods are packed into cases ready for shipment.

The Packing of Cans in Cases

From the capping lines, cans are put into large iron crates in which they are immersed in great vats and cooked. Then they are cooled in tanks of water and after they are labeled are taken to the storehouse and packed in cases. Sometimes women do this work. One "working investigator" describes this process as follows:

"Ten hours in the warehouse to-day. All the women complained of being very tired before our work was over. They kept us more steadily at the packing of boxes, the pauses being less frequent and of shorter duration — about two minutes' pause every half hour or so. We work very fast and stoop constantly to get the cans out of the crates. I have aches and pains all over, and the other women complain of pains in their arms. The foreman told us that if the superintendent came and saw us resting, even for a minute, he would send some of the women away to the factory and make it so much harder for the rest."

CANNERY WORK ESSENTIALLY FACTORY WORK

It is manifest throughout this evidence that the work of women in canning factories is distinctly factory work. The machinery in the modern cannery is becoming more and more intricate and highly speeded. There is extreme nervous and physical strain in many of the occupations in which the women are engaged. These facts must be considered in judging the strain to which the women are subjected by excessively long hours of labor.

THE CANNERY SEASON

The length of the season varies from cannery to cannery according to the goods packed. As a rule, berries are canned in June, peas in July, beans in August and September, corn in September and October, apples and pumpkins in November. Some factories pack only one product. Many small establishments pack only corn, and three pack only peas. For these factories the season lasts only a few weeks. Two factories pack only peas and corn. Work is carried on in them a few weeks in the spring and early summer, and again a few weeks in the fall. Most factories, however, pack a larger number of products, and a few put up pork and beans or plum pudding, so that work in them lasts practically all the year round.

The length of the period of each crop varies from year to year in the different factories. Some years the weather is cold during the period when peas are ripening, and the packing is consequently spread over five or six weeks; in other years warm weather brings in the crop more quickly and the season is shorter. Weather conditions in certain parts of the canning region sometimes make crops last longer than in others.

The methods of planting, cultivating, and harvesting crops have much to do with determining the number days the crops last. If a canner planted all his beans on a single day, which is of course never the case, he might expect them to mature on a certain day.

If the planting is spread out over a number of days, the plantings do not mature all together. If then the canner plans to spread his plantings over many days or weeks the duration of the crop is necessarily longer than if such care were not taken.

A canner who puts up a large pack of any crop, drawing his products from an extended area and many different plots of ground, has a longer season than one who puts up a small pack drawn from a restricted area, since varying conditions on widely separated farms lead to early and late ripening.

The period when perishable products are canned lasts approximately from June 15th, when berries begin, until October 15th, when corn ends. It is true that strawberries often ripen the second week in June. But the period from June 15th to October 15th is fixed by the canners during which they wish an exemption from the law restricting the hours of women.

RUSH PERIODS

Every crop comes on slowly. At first there are a few days when work in the canneries is light and the hours few. Soon, however, the products begin to come in more rapidly, and almost invariably the hours of labor increase steadily until they reach a peak. Then they recede again until, at the end of the crop, there are only a few scattered days of work. Peas ripen more quickly than other crops and deteriorate faster after harvesting.

In factories where more than one variety of vegetable is canned there is often a rush of work for each variety with brief slack periods between. Early and late peas, for example, often result in two rush periods with about a week of slack work between.

Beans, tomatoes, and corn are not subject to such sudden ripening and are not so perishable as peas. Their rush periods are therefore not so extreme as the rush of peas and are longer sustained.

Between peas and beans there is very frequently a marked slackening of work, during which the factory operates but a few hours per day, or is sometimes shut down entirely. Not often is there a lapse between beans and corn. Generally the two crops run together so that there is sometimes a rush of work rather than a slackening.

Tomatoes generally ripen at about the same time as corn, and these two crops run together causing an unusual rush of work. For this reason some canners who pack one of these crops do not pack the other, although both may be grown profitably in their territory. The days and hours of work are most consecutive where the greatest variety of products are packed.

HOHRS OF LABOR OF WOMEN

The information of the Commission regarding working hours is based on complete transcripts for two years, 1910 and 1911, of official records of 70 different canneries.

The longest hours per week discovered were 119¾, worked by a woman in one factory during the pea season of 1912; and the longest hours per day discovered were 21½, worked by a woman in another factory during the cherry and berry season of 1911. These are extreme cases, but it is an indisputable fact that many canneries during the rush periods work women for excessive hours.

The following tables show the longest hours of labor per day and per week recorded in the canneries in 1911:

Hours Worked; Longest Day

13	canneries	worked	women	12 hours or less
20	"	"	"	12 to 14 hours
19	"	"	"	15 to 17 hours
13	"	"	"	18 hours or more.

Hours Worked; Longest Week

15	canneries	worked	women	under 60 hours
8	"	"	"	61 to 66 hours
6	"	"	"	67 to 72 hours
10	"	"	"	73 to 79 hours
11	"	"	"	80 to 89 hours
7	"	"	"	90 to 99 hours
3	"	"	"	over 100 hours.

These long hours did not occur in isolated cases. In one cannery on a certain day

40	women	worked	15 hours
51	"	"	15½ "
27	"	"	16 "

The actual hours worked by individual women, day after day and week after week, in the height of the rush season, disprove the assertion of the canners that a day or a week of extraordinary length is rare.

Miss J. H. worked:

Monday	15	hours.
Tuesday	20	"
Wednesday	21	"
Thursday	19	"
Friday	21½	"
Saturday	21	"
Total	117½	"

For this work the woman was paid at the rate of ten cents an hour. A photograph of this woman and of her time sheet will be found in Appendix V of the report.

The following list shows the number of hours that Mrs. D. worked in one week:

1912.				
July	7.	Sunday	16	hours.
	8.	Monday	16¼	"
	9.	Tuesday	19¼	"
	10.	Wednesday	19¾	"
	11.	Thursday	16	"
	12.	Friday	15½	"
	13.	Saturday	17	"
		Total	119¾	"

In Appendix V to this report will be found a photograph of the pay envelope of another woman in the same cannery who worked 115 hours in the same week, for which she received $11.50 or 10 cents an hour. This woman also worked 66 hours the following week.

In another cannery during five successive weeks one woman taken at random from the payroll was employed as follows:

1st week	54	hours
2nd "	77	"
3rd "	85	"
4th "	85½	"
5th "	60½	"

Another woman at the same plant:

1st week	51½	hours
2nd "	77	"
3rd "	88½	"
4th "	85½	"

The following cases show the extreme overtime for *successive* weeks in different canning factories:

CASE A.

1st week	88	hours
2nd "	94½	"
3rd "	62½	"

CASE B.

1st week	62	hours
2nd "	82½	"
3rd "	86½	"

CASE C.

1st week	74	hours
2nd "	74½	"
3rd "	105	"
4th "	61	"

In case after case testimony was given by the canners themselves before the Commission, that women work 100, 110, and 115 hours a week.

What do these hours of labor mean to the women who perform them? The following passages from diaries of investigators who worked in the factories give the answer:

> "At nine o'clock last night, Nellie —— complained that she 'got tired sitting as well as standing.'"
>
> "Another worker at our table is Miss R——, a beautifully built young woman of twenty-four. This morning at 8 she complained of 'aching everywhere' she was so tired."
>
> "I worked till 11:45 last night with the rest. To-day the heat was intense. Scalding liquids from the par-boiling is poured out at one end of the factory about 12 feet from the sorting tables. This condition added to fatigue, made awful inroads on the workers. Big strong young men sat down with heads in hands, waiting for the next job."
>
> "Mrs. T—— said yesterday, 'This sleepy feeling is more like pain than anything else.'"
>
> "Mrs. McG—— said that in 1910 after a spell of night work for several nights till midnight, the women were so exhausted they couldn't do anything more one night, and a whole batch of peas had to be thrown out."
>
> "Coming home at 9:30 Friday night Mrs. B—— complained that her knees were shaky and she felt as if she would fall together any moment. Her eyes ached and were red from the strain."
>
> "'I'm all in. I don't know what I'll do if they work us like this for another week.' Irma B——, aged about 20, made this statement twice to-day."
>
> "Many of the women complained of feeling very tired and sleepy this morning after the long hours last night. Emma C—— said she had been unable to sleep."
>
> "My place was under an electric light and a portly matron next to me said: 'Your eyes are better than mine, so you might change places.' I did this. She complained of being tired and sleepy, and a younger woman next to her said she was 'all in.'"

It should be noted that investigators who made these reports in no case worked in factories where women worked over 80 hours a week. Of the fatigue of women who worked 90 or 100 hours per week, we have no description.

HOUSE WORK

Nor are the women through with work when they leave the cannery. Many are housekeepers and have cooking, sweeping, bed-making, sewing, and washing to do, and often children to take care of before and after hours in the factories. Of 941 women, 671 or 71% did housework before or after their factory work. These cares must be added to the wear of factory life in measuring the strain under which these women live.

Moreover when the factory hours are long, the housework often suffers.

> "Mrs. McG—— said to one 'working investigator:' 'If we have a free Sunday, I'm going to cook and eat all day long. I'm so starved for something cooked.'"

Another report is:

> "Mrs. —— told me she was so tired and exhausted from lack of sleep she had to go home and go to bed. She commented on the lack of hot food for herself and daughter since work began. She thought this lack added to her fatigued condition."

Although women work extreme hours at certain times during the season these periods of rush alternate with periods of slackened work during which the hours are few or the factory is closed altogether.

AVERAGE HOURS NO MEASURE OF FATIGUE

The plea of the canners is that if the average number of hours per day worked in their factories during the canning season be taken, it is found to be less than the hours of labor fixed by law. They contend that the average number of hours between June 15th and October 15th, even of women who work the longest, generally falls below 10 hours per day. They have on this ground repeatedly sought an exemption from the labor law to allow them to employ women on an average of 10 hours a day during the season of four months. Such a concession, however, would make the provisions of the labor law utterly worthless, for by this device a factory packing only peas or corn and operating but a few weeks could legally work women 24 hours a day if it were physically possible, and still the average number of hours from June 15th to October 15th would fall far below 10 per day. Average hours cannot measure the strain on the worker. Few people believe that women can work to the limit of their endurance during successive days or weeks and then readily and fully recover from such fatigue by working short hours on the following weeks.

THE NECESSITY OF OVERTIME WORK

Observations made by investigators when employed as factory workers, and their conversations with many canners and official inspectors show that most canners have made but feeble attempts to prevent overtime work. They say repeatedly, "The Lord ripens the crops and the situation is beyond men's control." In this connection it may be noted that the men who have been the worst exploiters of women are those who have represented the industry most frequently at Albany in its fight against regulation of hours of women's labor in the factories.

The canners' plea that the hours of women in their industry should not be restricted is based on the fact that they are handling perishable products. But several canners were found to have worked women 13 and 14 hours a day on labeling cans, after the regular canning season was over. If the canners had really tried to restrict hours, there would have been no overtime on labeling, for in that case no perishable products were at stake.

Many canners have made no effort to distribute the hours of labor with any degree of equality among women in their employ. On the same day some women were found working in the same cannery 5 hours and others 16 hours. In answer to this criticism they say: "Some work requires particular skill and the workers cannot be shifted promiscuously from one task to another." This is more or less true, but neither the Commission's workers in the different factories nor our official investigators reported a single instance where an effort was made to prevent overtime by distributing work among workers who were actually employed on the same work in the same factory each day. Until the canners make such an attempt they cannot reasonably maintain that they have done all in their power to prevent overtime work.

Not all canners have been indifferent to the restricting of hours of women's labor, nor unwilling to consider a plan for reducing them, although such a course would mean an increase in their payrolls. Certain canners have at considerable trouble and expense, according to their statements, limited the working hours of women in their factories in spite of the fact that their competitors refused to do so. There are a few — very few — men who have had enough respect for the law, even though they were not altogether in sympathy with its provisions, to make an attempt to comply with it.

The ultimate cause of overtime work in the canneries is that an attempt is made to handle a varying supply of raw material with a fixed plant and labor force; and that during rush periods the capacity of the plant and labor force is exceeded. Overtime work necessarily results.

A solution of the overtime problem can be achieved either by adjusting the supply of raw material so as not to exceed, under any condition, or at any time, the capacity of the plant and labor force working within legal hours; or by increasing the capacity of the plant and labor force so that, under all conditions and at all times, they may be able to handle the product without overtime work. A combination of the two methods is of course possible.

Regulation of Planting and Harvesting

There is great disagreement as to the progress that can be made in the way of preventing "glut" periods by the regulation of planting and harvesting. Almost every pea canner can cite instances where peas planted days, or even a week or two weeks apart, have all matured on the same day. In some cases peas planted a week after others have matured first.

Rain or drought, hot or cold temperature, conditions of the soil and the situation of the land all tend to make the period from planting to maturity somewhat uncertain. There are conditions, too, which make the canners' control of planting difficult. Often several days of rain so delay planting that the canner, to make up for lost time, is tempted to plant a larger acreage per day than he might otherwise have done. Much of the acreage is grown under contract with farmers. The products which the farmers raise for canners are often but a small item of their total crop and they are unwilling to put aside other business to follow the exact orders of canners.

It seems to be true that no canner can plant with such scientific accuracy as absolutely to prevent "gluts." There is always the unknown quantity, weather conditions. As one old factory employee said to an investigator who worked in the factory, "You can't change the course of nature." This does not excuse the canners, however, as some of them seem to think it does, from making every effort so to control planting as to prevent these rush periods as far as possible. Most of them hire "road men" to look after planting and harvesting peas, but few hire them for any other crop. Often these men are quite unfitted for their work.

The control of planting calls for a scientific agriculturist who has capacity to grasp the factory problem of keeping the work within fixed hours. Until canners employ such men and set to work carefully to prevent gluts by regulating planting and harvesting, instead of making half-hearted efforts in that direction, the extent to which gluts can be minimized will not be known.

Cold Storage

The second possibility of adjusting the supply of raw material to the capacity of the plant is to hold goods after harvesting. Peas may be held unshelled twelve to fourteen hours under favorable conditions, without serious deterioration. Many canners hold them overnight, to be able to start the factory the first thing in the morning. No successful artificial means have been used as yet in New York State for preventing the rapid spoiling of peas after they are cut. In Wisconsin, however, the Federal Government investigator found in use large tanks of running water in which shelled peas were immersed and held over night.*

It is possible that such devices will come into use in New York and help to eliminate overtime work on peas. It is, however, Wisconsin, not New York, canners who have been experi-

* The Federal Government conducted an investigation into industrial conditions in the canning industry in Wisconsin in 1912.

menting with these devices. Wisconsin's fifty-five-hour law for women applies to the canneries and has been enforced.

Replacement of Women by Men

Workers employed on the earlier processes finish their work at night and go home before the others. Those on the "capping line," the can dropper, those who put on caps, the inspector and the syrup maker are among the last to leave, and women are often used for these tasks. The time books in many factories show that half a dozen or more women work half or three-quarters of an hour longer per day than the others. These are the women "on the line." Were these women replaced by men, as they might be at a small additional expense, the most extreme overtime would be eliminated.

Two large factories, one packing the largest number of different products canned in any New York State cannery, have been operated under a rule that women were not to work after 9 P. M. This has been strictly enforced, and as work has not started before 7 A. M., the hours of women have been limited to 12 per day and 72 per week. Occasionally products have remained at 9 P. M. which would spoil if left till morning. In these cases, most of the machinery has been shut down and men who have worked in the factory during the day have run through the remaining product. These men are paid more than 1½ times as much as women, so the payroll has been larger than it would have been had women been worked overtime.

One of these factories puts up 22 different products,— more than any other cannery in the state. The second plant, which never works women after 9 P. M., packs 15 different products, which are more than are packed in the majority of the canneries.

Another large factory among the first ten in the state in its pack of peas and beans, has endeavored to obey the law limiting working hours of women to 12 per day and 60 per week. In some cases it has exceeded those hours, but during the past two seasons has never worked a woman over 13 hours in a day and 67 hours in a week. This factory also has sent the women home when their hours were up, and, shutting down most of the machinery, has run through what product remained by using the men who work regularly in the factory.

Adjustment of Acreage to Capacity

One factory which, until recently, had worked overtime but not extreme hours, and had paid good profits, secured this year a new manager who, saying the factory was not operated up to its capacity, increased the acreage. This year the women in the factory worked much longer hours than they worked in 1910 and 1911. The manager boasts that next year he will again increase the pea acreage by 100 acres.

Evidently extreme overtime work is due not so much to the character of the industry as to the policy followed in the management of the business. The superintendent of one cannery which works women extreme hours thus described this policy to an investigator:

> "The way to make money in the canning business is to carry a little larger acreage than you can handle comfortably, so that you can run pretty steadily throughout the season and your plant won't be idle in slack periods."

How may overtime be eliminated? A canner's reply is here quoted:

> "In my opinion," said the superintendent of a large canning company, "the only way that the State can govern canning evils is to make the factories adhere to the rule of supply and capacity. Many factories contract for an acreage which the capacity of the factory could not turn out, making extra work and harrowing conditions for their employees inevitable. This is the root of the evil, to my mind."

Every vegetable canner contracts in the spring to purchase the product of a certain acreage. He cannot tell at that time whether a full crop will be returned; therefore he cannot figure on the size of the crop. He knows, however, from experience about how many cases each acre will yield when a full crop is returned. He knows exactly how many cases of each crop his factory is capable of canning in any given number of hours. Certain canners contract year after year for an acreage which they must know from repeated experience foredooms their employees to work overtime and, if the crop is a good one, extreme overtime. *"The Lord ripens the crop" truly, but every canner determines, to a certain extent, how much of a crop the Lord is to ripen for him.* The relation between the acreage contracted for and the capacity of the plant, more than any other thing, determines how much overtime will have to be worked.

Some canners, when asked on what basis they determined the size of the acreage they would carry, frankly testified that they contracted for all the acreage they could get the farmers to grow. Canners usually sell from 50 to 100 per cent, of their goods the winter before they are packed.* Some testified that they sold all the goods they could, and then contracted for an acreage to meet the sales.

REASONABLE HOURS IN SOME FACTORIES

The time records of canning factories show that the situation is not beyond the canners' control. A few factories have kept reasonable hours although others packing the same products have worked extremely long hours.

Factories which keep more reasonable hours have done so year after year, and on the other hand those which require extreme hours persist in that habitual practice.

Two companies operated 6 of the 13 factories which worked women over 18 hours on their longest day, and 5 of the 12 factories which worked women over 90 hours in their longest week. One of these companies, which operated factories from one end of the cannery region to the other, worked women extreme hours in all of them, regardless of local conditions.

WAGES AND RESTRICTION OF HOURS

Canners stated that one cause of overtime work was the difficulty they experienced in getting sufficient help. In spite of this difficulty the wages of both men and women in the industry are very low. One factory pays women as little as seven cents an hour. The supply of labor depends upon the wages paid. In cannery towns as elsewhere a high wage attracts many workers, a low wage attracts few. The wages of women in the canning industry is lower than in other industries in which large num-

* There is usually a clause in the contract which makes it unnecessary for the canner to deliver in full if short crops prevent the packing of the amount of goods expected.

bers of women are employed. Until women are paid more than seven or ten cents an hour for seasonable and intermittent work no canner can claim to have exhausted his labor supply.

The wages of men average $1.77 for a ten-hour day, but the wages of women average less than a dollar for the same time. The average pay per day for the canning season amounts, however, to much less, because of irregularity of work. This is true, in spite of the long hours of labor in some weeks.

At many tasks women are paid for the amount of work they turn out. Snipping beans, husking corn, peeling tomatoes, pears, peaches and beets, hulling strawberries, quartering and coring apples, stemming cherries, and labelling cans, are sometimes paid for by the piece. The rates vary from factory to factory, just as wages by the hour.

The average weekly earnings of cannery women are $4.53. No woman could maintain a decent standard of living, even were she able to have steady work the year round on such a wage. Room and board may be secured in the cannery towns for $3 to $5 a week. One of the "working investigators" secured them at $3 and reported that the food was so scant and poorly prepared that she could hardly live on it. But even if room and board are secured for that amount, it is obvious that there is little left for clothing, to say nothing of other necessary expenses. Clearly the industry may be considered parasitic in the sense that a woman working in it cannot make a living wage, but must find other means of support. True, many of the workers have fathers, husbands, and brothers able to help them, but the unmarried girl trying to make a living out of this work finds it hard. This fact does not pass unnoticed. The report follows of a young woman investigator who worked in the factories:

> "There are several very 'fresh' bosses at the factory and the youth who keeps time and has charge of the sorting tables has a good deal of influence over the girls he puts at the tables. The situation is much like that in a department store where the floor-walker has a lot of girls under him receiving low wages and all more or less at his mercy. Only up here night work makes the situation even more dangerous."

A few days later she reported again:

> "I find that the time-keeper who was objectionable to me the other day has been insulting several girls. He said to me, 'You can't make enough to pay you, but I will give you a chance to make 2 or 3 dollars on the side any time. If you come up here to work at night, we can go for a stroll.' I feel that this ought to be repeated to you by me to show what the effect of an 8-cent wage is in the canning industry."

The time-keeper of this factory was the superintendent's cousin, using the low wage as an inducement to immorality.

Nor is this the only effect of the low wage. We have seen that in some cases children are routed out of bed at 4 A. M. and forced to work until late at night, not by the canners, but by their parents. The canners supply the materials to work on, the parents do the driving. Clearly this is not alone due to the hard-heartedness of the parent. It is the necessary and logical outcome of a wage of $4.53 a week for women workers, and a correspondingly low wage for men. Yet certain canners argue that children should be allowed to work because of the poverty of the parents.

The willingness of the women to work long hours is also the logical outcome of so low a wage. One woman in 90 hours' work was able to make only $6.75. A canner argues against restricting women's hours by saying, "The longer the day the better, because then the more money can be made."* Of course the women want to work long hours. They must do so to make anywhere near a living wage.

That is not saying, however, that a restriction of hours will lower their wages. One "working investigator" reported:

> "I believe that were the 54-hour law enforced here the wage would have to be increased from 8 cents because the girls would leave rather than work for 72 cents in a 9-hour day. I have talked with many girls about the new 54-hour law and they all say, 'Believe me, if I've got to work here for 72 cents a day I ain't staying long.'"

Were the hours restricted, the canners, to keep their help, would have to raise the wages.

---

* See letter to "New York Sun, Dec. 3, 1912, by a canning factory 'Director.'"

The "working investigator" also makes the following interesting report:

> "All the Italian girls are sore at the low wage, but are afraid to quit on account of the Poles and the Americans. They would like to strike but say that these would take their places. The Syrians and the Poles are willing to accept the 8-cent wage. The Americans say it is too low and grumble, but would stick by the American employer rather than join the 'Eyetalians' in a strike."

SUMMARY OF FINDINGS

The following is a summary of the Commission's findings on the conditions of women's work in the canneries of the state:

I. Nature of Work

1. That work in canneries is not easy out-of-door work akin to agricultural labor, but is distinctly factory work.

2. That most of the occupations for which women are employed subject them to the same hardships as those found in other factories.

3. That much of the work is done at high speed paced by machines, or speeded by piece work at low wages.

4. That the constant noise of machinery close to the women workers entails nervous strain.

5. That many women stand at their work all day long.

6. That a number of occupations involve eye strain.

7. That many women are compelled to stand on wet floors all day, and in some cases are wet to the skin. Shed workers are exposed to rain and cold.

8. That women suffer in health from long and irregular hours, from the loss of proper rest at night and on Sunday, and from irregular meal hours.

9. That the harmful effects of excessive work in long continued rush periods cannot be counter-balanced by rest in slack seasons.

II. Hours of Labor

1. That women are constantly employed for excessively long hours.

2. That overtime work is not occasional but is often continuous for many successive weeks.

3. That the season in which overtime occurs is not short but often lasts for five months.

4. That women work frequently 15 and 16 hours a day, and that it is not uncommon for them to work 70 hours a week continuously for many weeks. One woman worked 119 3-4 in a week in 1912.

5. The days of rest do not as a rule follow days of excessive labor.

6. That many canners have made no intelligent effort to prevent women from working overtime by equalizing daily working hours for each employee, since one woman may be employed long hours on consecutive days while other women in the same plant work short hours or not at all.

7. That although women are rarely compelled to work overtime, their conpensation is, as a rule, so low that there is every incentive to work long hours.

8. That long hours of labor are often not related to the alleged perishable nature of the crops, since such work as the labeling of cans is done at night.

III. Labor Supply

That the canners' labor supply is not so limited as to necessitate excessive hours of labor for the available workers.

IV. Canners' Failure to Prevent Oversupply of Raw Materials

1. That few canners systematically attempt to regulate the planting and harvesting of the crops and the time of their delivery at the cannery.

2. That the canners have not sufficiently encouraged the growth of different varieties of crops, nor controlled closely enough different times of planting in order to lengthen the season.

3. That products are often not properly cared for at the canneries so that they may be held, if necessary, for short periods before canning.

4. That output is often not adjusted to capacity of plant, based on its present labor supply, and that overproduction is therefore chiefly responsible for excessive overtime work.

LAWS IN OTHER STATES

In Illinois the hours of labor of women in the canneries are limited to ten hours a day; in Tennessee, to 60 hours a week; in Pennsylvania, to 12 hours a day or 60 a week, and in Wisconsin, to 10 hours a day and not more than 55 hours a week. In Michigan and in California, two of the leading cannery states, in which no restrictions as to hours exist, the movement to limit the hours of labor of women in canneries has become widespread and the industry in this respect will in all probability be regulated very shortly by the legislatures of those states.

SUMMARY

Up to 1911 the law limiting the hours of labor of women in factories to 60 hours a week applied to canneries, but was never obeyed. Practically no attempt was made to enforce it and whenever, at rare intervals, such an attempt was made it was successfully opposed or evaded.

In 1912 the Legislature, convinced of the necessity of more adequate protection for women working in factories, passed the 54-hour law. This law prohibited the employment of women in factories for more than nine hours in any one day or 54 hours in any one week. At the same time, however, the canneries of the state were exempted from the operation of the provisions of the law relating to the hours of labor of women during the canning season between the fifteenth day of June and the fifteenth day of October in every year. The canning industry thus became legally what it had been for many years past illegally, an entirely unregulated industry.

The fifty-four hour law went into effect on the first of October, 1912, so that the 7,000 women working in the canning factories of the state have no protection during the next canning season so far as the length of their working day is concerned. There is no limitation, except that which is imposed by nature itself, on the number of hours that a woman may be employed in any one day or in any one week.

The investigation that we have made has convinced us that the plea of the canners that this wide open exemption is necessary because of the peculiar conditions in their industry, is entirely without foundation. We believe, moreover, that this exemption is a most improper one, is directly opposed to the best interests of the state, and has been granted because of a misapprehension of the true conditions which exist in the canning industry.

Work by women in canneries is distinctly factory work. The physical and nervous strain on the workers is just as great in a cannery as it is in any other factory.

The canning industry is a seasonable industry. During certain times of the year the goods handled are extremely perishable. Crops must be harvested, vegetables prepared and canned without delay. The industry is subject to rush and slack periods — periods when the hours are many and periods when the hours are few — alternating through the season. These conditions distinguish the canning industry from practically every other.

The conditions in the canning industry are not such as require the labor of women for 110, 115 and 119 hours a week. No words of ours can express too strongly our condemnation of the inhuman greed and avarice that permit women to be thus exploited.

We do not believe, however, that the 54-hour law should apply to the canneries during the canning season. That would be unfair and unreasonable to the industry and to the workers to which it gives employment. A wide-open exemption during this period is even more unfair and unreasonable. We do not claim that in the present state of our knowledge, overtime can be entirely eliminated in this industry, but we are certain that a proper and careful attention to the regulation of the planting and harvesting of crops, to the distribution of labor within the factory, to the possibilities of cold storage, to the obtaining of an increased labor supply by offering to the workers a living wage, and to the adjustment of acreage to the capacity of the plant, would reduce overtime in this industry to a minimum, and would do away entirely with the excessively long hours of labor of women for which the canners of this state deserve the censure and criticism to which they have been subjected.

The state cannot regard with indifference any system permitting women to work excessively long hours of labor. Even if this extreme overtime lasts only a few weeks, we believe it to be injurious to the health of women engaged therein. The estimate of the average number of hours worked per day by a woman does not constitute a fair test of reasonableness for this exemption of the canning industry from the factory law.

Few people will claim that a woman can recover from the fatigue of working fifteen hours a day for several weeks in succession by thereafter working only five hours a day. Average hours do not measure the strain on the worker. We recommend therefore that during the canning season, between the 15th day of June and the 15th day of October, the hours of labor of women should be limited to 10 hours a day and 60 hours a week. During the pea crop season, which extends from the 25th of June to the 5th of August, when the perishability of the product handled is extreme and the rush of work is very great, the Industrial Board on application of any canner may permit women in his establishment to work for not more than 12 hours in any one day and 66 hours in any one week if in the opinion of the Industrial Board such increased number of hours may be allowed without endangering the health of the women workers. This same principle has been adopted in England. There the Home Office has granted the canners the exemption allowed by law, but has accompanied the grant with special requirements which make it necessary for the canner, if he is to enjoy the right to work women longer hours than they are worked in other factories, to maintain unusually good sanitary conditions in his factory.

We believe that these limitations on the hours of labor of women in the canning industry are entirely fair to the industry and are calculated to protect the health and safety of the women employed therein.

This restriction on the hours of labor of women will stimulate the canners to more scientific management so that the necessity for overtime may be largely eliminated. Increased efficiency has always and everywhere resulted from improved labor conditions. Probably few industries reward good management and penalize bad management more than the canning industry. It needs careful estimating in advance of the season and a cool head under trying conditions when the rush periods occur.

It has been urged that if the hours of labor were reduced the women employed in the canneries would be deprived of a livelihood. But we do not believe this to be so. No woman works 10, 12, 15, or 20 hours a day for pleasure. She does it for money. The lower the wages the greater is the incentive to long hours of labor. The very low wages paid in the canning industry largely explain the desire of the women to work long hours. It has been the experience all over the world that low wages and long hours go together hand in hand; that the lowest paid industries are the industries in which the longest hours of labor prevail. A reduction in the hours of labor in this industry will soon result in a compensating increase in the wages of the women workers, which we believe the industry can well afford.

The interests of the state demand that extreme overtime by women be prohibited and that women workers be surrounded with every protection and safeguard to enable them to perpetuate a race of strong, sturdy citizens. There are no words that express the necessity for such protection more clearly and forcibly than those used by Mr. Justice Brewer of the United States Supreme Court in the case of *Muller* v. *Oregon,* reported in 208 U. S., 412:

> "* * * her physical structure and a proper discharge of her maternal functions — having in view not merely her own health, but the well-being of the race — justify legislation to protect her from the greed as well as the passion of man. The limitations which this statute places upon her contractual powers, upon her right to agree with her employer as to the time she shall labor, are not imposed solely for her benefit, but also largely for the benefit of all. Many words cannot make this plainer. The two sexes differ in structure of body, in the functions to be performed by each, in the amount of physical strength, in the capacity for long-continued labor, particularly when done standing, the influence of vigorous health upon the future well-being of the race, the self-reliance which enables one to assert full rights, and in the capacity to maintain the struggle for subsistence."

Furthermore, in January, 1913, in the case of *People* v. *Kane* (New York Law Journal, January 30, 1913), Mr. Justice Blackmar, sitting at Special Term of the Supreme Court in the Second Judicial District, in sustaining the constitutionality of the 54-hour law for women in factories, passed at the last session of the Legislature, said:

> "An act of the Legislature in the interest of the health, morals or safety of the community operates within the field of the surrendered rights and does not abridge civil liberty. * * * The development of the industrial life of the nation, the pressure of women and children entering the industrial field in competition with men physically better qualified for the struggle, has compelled them to submit to conditions and terms of service which it cannot be presumed they would freely choose. Their liberty to contract to sell their labor may be but another name for involuntary service created by existing industrial conditions. A law which restrains the liberty to contract may tend to emancipate them by enabling them to act as they choose and not as competitive conditions compel. All these considerations are for the Legislature, and for the Legislature alone."

RECOMMENDATIONS

We therefore recommend that the following provision be adopted exempting the canneries from the operation of the fifty-four hour law for women (Subdivision 3 of § 77):

> *3. A female eighteen years of age and upwards may, notwithstanding the provisions of subdivision three of section seventy-seven of this chapter, be employed in canning or preserving perishable products in fruit and canning establishments between the fifteenth day of June and the fifteenth day of October in each year not more than six days or sixty hours in any one week nor more than ten hours in any one day; and the industrial board shall have power to adopt rules and regulations permitting the employment of women eighteen years of age and upwards on such work in such establishments between the twenty-fifth day of June and the fifth day of August in each year not more than six days or sixty-six hours in any one week or more than twelve hours in any*

*one day, if said board shall find that such employment is required by the needs of such industry and can be permitted without serious injury to the health of women so employed.**

This act is to apply to all parts of the canning establishments, including the canning sheds.

SPECIAL INSPECTION OF CANNERIES

We have no fear that the measures we recommend for the hours of labor of women in the canneries will be impossible of enforcement. We believe that our recommendations are fair to the industry and that if enacted into law will be observed. We do not believe that since conditions have been fully disclosed, any local court or jury will lightly disregard the laws the legislature will enact. Public sentiment all over the state will demand that such laws be enforced promptly and effectively.

To secure such enforcement we recommend that during the canning season a special squad of inspectors be organized in the Department of Labor, to investigate conditions in the canneries, with special regard to the employment of women and children and to their hours of labor.

A few prosecutions promptly instituted and vigorously pushed to a successful termination will quickly dispel from the minds of the recalcitrant few the idea that laws regulating the employment of women and children in canneries are "dead letters" and need not be obeyed.

The present system of inspecting a cannery once a year can hardly be productive of results. One of our investigators visited a canning factory that had been in operation for six years and had never been officially inspected. Another small cannery was inspected which had operated for ten years without a visit from the factory inspector.

It is small wonder that under these circumstances the labor law should have been so lightly regarded in the cannery regions.

SANITARY CONDITIONS

To the credit of the canning industry of this state it must be said that sanitary conditions in the canning processes are usu-

* Bill 10, Appendix I.

ally excellent. Most canners take every reasonable precaution to guard their products from contamination. The pure food law provisions against the use of artificial preservatives make it impossible to can products that have begun to decay.

Two conditions however that affect the workers in several canneries should be noted, namely, inadequate washing facilities and uncleanliness of water closet accommodations. There can be no excuse of such conditions in any cannery and they should be promptly corrected.

HOUSING CONDITIONS

When foreigners are brought from different cities to be employed in rural canning factories, housing facilities are provided for them by the canners. Usually no rent is charged for these living quarters, though sometimes a very nominal sum is paid by the workers.

The types of buildings found in use were tenement-buildings in which three or more families keep house independently, barracks-buildings in which three or more families live with a common cooking place, and shacks, separate houses in which not more than two families are housed.

These tenements, barracks and shacks are often overcrowded, no provision is made for the separation of the sexes, there is no proper privacy and they are kept in a decidedly unsanitary condition.

At present the labor department has no jurisdiction over conditions in these labor camps and the local health department pays little if any attention to them. We recommend that the labor department be given jurisdiction over the conditions in labor camps attached to factories in the state, including those maintained in connection with canneries, and that certain minimum requirements as to sanitary conditions in such camps, and the healthfulness of their surroundings be incorporated in the labor law or the Industrial Code.*

* Bill No. 11, Appendix I.

V.

CHILD LABOR

Two of the greatest evils of child labor in this state, namely, the employment of young children in cannery sheds and in tenement houses, have already been discussed under *Manufacturing in Tenements* and *The Canneries.* This section of the report, therefore, will be confined to the subject of the employment and necessary protection of children in factories.

In this matter the state has a vital concern, for there are now employed in its factories nearly 14,000 children between the ages of fourteen and sixteen years. There can be no question that these children should be so guarded and protected by the state that they may grow up into strong and efficient men and women.

Under the present law no child under fourteen years of age is permitted to work in a factory; and no child between fourteen and sixteen years is permitted to be employed in a factory unless an employment certificate is obtained and filed in the office of the employer at the place of the employment of the child. This certificate is granted if the child satisfies the requirements as to age, physical condition, and education.

THE PHYSICAL REQUIREMENTS

Before 1912 that portion of the law requiring a physical examination of the child before a working certificate was issued, provided for such examination only in doubtful cases. As a result the Commission found many sickly children working in the factories of the state.

The commission therefore recommended that the law should be so amended that the physical fitness of every child applying for an employment certificate must be determined by a medical officer of the local department or board of health. That physician was to make a thorough physical examination of the child, to record the result of this examination on a blank to be furnished for the purpose by the Commissioner of Labor, and there to set forth such facts concerning the physical condition and history of the child as the Commissioner of Labor might require. The local health department or officer was also required to transmit to the state department of labor a duplicate record of the physicial examination of all those children to whom employment certificates were issued.

This law became effective on October 1st, 1912. Health officers throughout the state are of the opinion that much good will be accomplished by it. The percentage of rejections for physical unfitness has already increased largely since the law became operative. No longer will weak, puny, and sickly children be permitted to engage in work that over-taxes their strength and so weakens them as to render them easy victims to the many diseases that find their prey among factory workers. The proper enforcement of this law by excluding from factory work all young children whose family history shows a predisposition to tuberculosis, should also play an effective part in the war that is now being waged for the eradication of that disease.

Although much has been accomplished by the foregoing amendment, it is the opinion of the Commission that the requirement for the physical examination of children should be still further strengthened in these two particulars.

1. It should be made to apply to mercantile establishments as well as to factories.

2. The local health department or officer should be required to transmit to the Department of Labor duplicate records of the physical examinations of children whose applications for working certificates are denied because of physical unfitness. This record would be of great value for statistical purposes and should result in directing attention to physical ailments of children seeking to work in factories and stores.*

THE EDUCATIONAL REQUIREMENT

Testimony has been presented showing the meagerness of the educational requirements of our present law. The statutes provide that a child under sixteen years of age who desires to leave school to work must be able to read and write simple sentences

* Bill 13, Appendix I.

in the English language, must have received instruction in reading, spelling, writing, English grammar, and geography, and must be familiar with the fundamental operations of arithmetic up to and including fractions.

According to statements made to the Commission this provision is variously construed throughout the state because of the lack of any definite standard in matters of school grading. It is left to each local school authority to determine at just what point in the school curriculum a child has fulfilled the requirements of the law.

In view of this condition it has been urged that great good would come from the establishment of a uniform and state wide standard. This practice has been adopted in Ohio, Wisconsin, Minnesota, and other states, and has been found very satisfactory. The standard proposed for this state is the completion of the work of the first six years of the public elementary school or school equivalent thereto, or of the parochial school. Children who begin school at seven years of age and are promoted at the normal rate, complete the sixth year of regular school work between their twelfth and thirteenth birthdays. Thus, if this standard were to be adopted for a fourteen-year-old child, the state would be requiring only what is being regularly accomplished by thousands of children two years under that age. Several cities in our state already interpret the law as requiring this standard.

A further argument in favor of the prolongation of school life for children is the reduction in juvenile delinquency which this extension may be expected to bring about. The recent investigation of the federal government into conditions surrounding wage earners in the United States included a special study of the relation between working children and juvenile delinquency. One chapter of this report concludes with the following statement:

> "Summing up the results of the discussion to this point, it is found that the working children contribute to the ranks of delinquency a slightly larger number and a much larger proportion than do the non-workers, that this excess appears in offenses of every kind, whether trivial or serious, and

among recidivists even more markedly than among first offenders."

When one realizes that attendance upon our elementary schools constitutes all the education that the majority of our wage earners receive, the Commission believes that the minimum of six years — of the eight years of work which these schools offer — is not too high a standard for the state of New York.

Accordingly, amendments to the labor law and to the compulsory education law are recommended to accomplish this object. It is suggested also that the date when these changes are to become effective shall be deferred two years to allow school authorities to make necessary adjustments.*

SUPERVISION OF THE ISSUANCE OF EMPLOYMENT CERTIFICATES

Another administrative feature brought to the Commission's attention is the need for supervision in the issuance of employment certificates by health officers throughout the state. Under the law, children who desire to work must obtain an employment certificate from the health officer of the city or town in which they reside. The law prescribes the age of the children, and the educational and physical qualifications which they must meet to receive such a certificate. It is evident that the good the law seeks to accomplish through these safeguards may be nullified by the carelessness or indifference of the official issuing the certificate. In view of the many communities in which these certificates are issued it is not surprising that a great difference has resulted in the thoroughness of the attention given to this matter. In some towns the health of the children who apply has received little or no attention; in others improper kinds of proof of the children's ages have been accepted; and still in others the test as to their educational proficiency has been entirely neglected.

Furthermore, the announcements of changes made by the legislature in the law frequently reach health officers by mere chance notice of them in the newspapers. Another result of the lack of supervision is the great variety of forms in use by different officials. Some of these forms are excellent and carefully prepared; while others are out of date because of changes in the

* Bills 13 and 14, Appendix I.

law, or fail to satisfy fully the legal requirements. In order to protect children in the manner in which the law-makers intended, the Commission feels that to the Department of Labor, the agency most closely connected with working children, should be assigned the definite duty of supervising the issuance of employment certificates by the local health officers, and at least for smaller places the duty of preparing and furnishing the necessary blanks and forms needed by them in that work. To the inspectors of the Department of Labor should also be given the right to examine the records of any local health department pertaining to the issuance of employment certificates.

THE PHYSICAL EXAMINATION OF CHILDREN IN FACTORIES

The Commission has previously recommended the creation of a section of medical inspection in the state department of labor, to be composed of four medical inspectors, all duly licensed physicians. With this machinery it is now possible for the Commission to make definite recommendations concerning the medical supervision of children between 14 and 16 years of age, after they have been granted employment certificates and are actually engaged in factory work.

The necessity for this continued supervision of the child after it has entered the ranks of industrial workers has been clearly emphasized in our preliminary report. It can hardly be said that the state has performed its full duty by issuing an employment certificate permitting a young child of fourteen to work in a factory, if after that it entirely disregards the child's physical condition.

Under the present law, after an employment certificate has once been issued, the medical inspector is powerless to act when he finds a child who is physically unfit working in a factory.

Dr. Rogers, the medical inspector of the Department of Labor, called attention to the following striking case:

> "I found a boy of fifteen years old in a pottery factory who had not recovered from an attack of typhoid fever. He was in what should have been the convalescent stage of typhoid fever and should have been at home. That boy was running slips in the pottery, a very dirty occupation, and

> putting handles on to the cups. The boy was anemic and absolutely unfit to continue at work. Yet that boy was legally employed and we had no power under the law to order the boy to go home."

The health officer of the city of Buffalo testified before the Commission:

> "Our experience shows that a great number of children who receive employment certificates between the ages of 14 and 16 are just about inside the line of being healthy, but perhaps a few days or a few weeks of work will place them in the subnormal class again so that they should not be permitted to work. We believe children of that kind should be stopped from working."

The doctor also testified that he examined a number of children in factories within a few weeks after they had been granted employment certificates, and found that ten per cent. of these children were physically unfit for any kind of factory work. To permit these children to continue at work in a factory means the undermining of their health and in many cases causes early death.

Of course, four inspectors with their many other duties could not attempt to make a physical examination even once a year of every one of the 14,000 children employed in factories. We would not, therefore, recommend that the physical examination of all such children be made mandatory. We believe that the desired results would be accomplished if the medical inspectors of the department were given power to examine any child between fourteen and sixteen years employed in a factory, and to cancel the working certificate of any child found physically unfit for factory work. The medical inspector on entering the factory could use his discretion as to what children he thought should be examined. The trained eye of a physician can often tell at a glance whether or not a child is ill. The appearance of the child, the nature of the work in which he was engaged, the sanitary condition of the workshop would all be factors in determining what children should be examined. In the course of a year there is no doubt but that several thousand of these young factory workers would be examined and that a great many of them who were found physically unfit would be prevented from continuing at work that overtaxed their strength.

OCCUPATIONS DANGEROUS TO HEALTH

Closely related to the physical examination of young children in factories is the power of dismissing a child from employment deemed dangerous to his health. There are very many cases where the child is physically fit for general factory work, but where the particular occupation in which he is engaged is dangerous to his health.

Our statute sets forth a number of occupations deemed injurious to health in which the employment of children is prohibited. This list is inadequate, for it fails to cover many dangerous occupations and overlooks the fact that there may be certain processes or methods of manufacturing within a given industry not on the prohibited list which are so injurious to the health of minors as to demand their exclusion therefrom.

New cases are constantly coming up where the medical inspector is powerless to act, because power is not specifically granted in the statute. The medical inspector called the following cases to the attention of the Commission in his testimony:

> "I have seen several boys in the glass blowing industry legally employed and yet in my opinion and the opinion of any good medical man, they had no business to be in that place at all. Large quantities of fine glass dust were blowing around in the air. Yet these boys were working there legally. We could not force the employer to remove that glass dust; it was not created by machinery and we could not force the dismissal of the boys because they had working certificates and were legally employed."
>
> "In an incandescent mantle factory children were sitting in a frame probably 20 x 30 feet long, lighted with gas flames. The frame is probably 6 or 7 feet wide and these children were sitting right in the midst of escaping illuminating gas which contains large quantities of carbon monoxide gas, a most dangerous poison because it destroys the blood cells.

> The children were legally employed because they had working certificates, yet it is an occupation I would very much hesitate to put a robust man in to work at."

In addition to the occupations specifically prohibited in the statute, power should be given to the Industrial Board of the Department of Labor to specify as dangerous to health particular trades, occupations, and processes of manufacture, or particular methods of conducting the same, and to prohibit or regulate the employment of minors under the age of eighteen in these occupations and processes of manufacture. The practical result would be that if a medical inspector found a minor under sixteen working under unhealthful conditions he could demand either that the improper conditions be remedied, or the process of manufacturing changed. Failing in both attempts, he would report the case to the Industrial Board, who, within a very short time, would adopt a regulation placing that occupation or process of manufacture on the list of prohibited employments.

In most cases the knowledge that the Industrial Board had this power would, on demand, bring about an immediate improvement in the unhealthful conditions and the removal of the dangerous elements complained of. In any event, it would not be necessary to go to the legislature every time a new case of an unhealthful occupation was called to the attention of the medical inspector.*

DANGEROUS MACHINERY

What is true of prohibited employments deemed injurious to the health of minors applies with equal force to the prohibition of minors from operating or assisting in operating dangerous machinery.

The law now specifies in detail the machines which a child under 16 years shall not be permitted to operate; but when a child is found working at a dangerous machine not specified in the statute, the Department of Labor is powerless to stop that employment. The result is that we find many cases of accidents

* Bill 26, Appendix I.

that occur to children while operating machines not specified in the statute. A number of such cases reported to the Department of Labor within the past six months follows:

F. S——, male, 15, roller boy, earning $5.70 a week, working on French drawing frame. Tried to fix broken end on drawing frame and index finger, right hand, was caught in the porcupine roller. Flesh on finger torn away by porcupine teeth. Will probably have to have finger amputated.

J. S——, male, 14, nail sticker, earning $4 a week, operating American Lightning Heeling Machine. A nail flew out of loader as nails were released. Injured boy attempted to brush it off with his finger. He was caught by descending drivers. Bone broken in forefinger of left hand between 1st and 2nd joints. Flesh cut and torn.

F. K.——, male, 15, earning $3.50 a week, operating Baling Press. Gearing wheels carefully guarded. Notwithstanding, he stooped and placed his hands under the guard to the gearing wheels. Lacerated first finger, amputation 2nd and 3rd finger at first joint, lacerated middle finger.

E. M——, male, 16, earning $5.00 a week, operating Filling Machine. Cover on guard over revolving cylinder was removed while machine was in motion and the operator caught his hands on the pins of the cylinder. Severe laceration of two fingers of left hand and of wrist; one finger was partly amputated.

M. C——, female, 14, earning $3.00 a week, operating Automatic Cutting Machine. Was waiting for work to be given her and took up a screw driver and was scraping around with it; she put her foot on starting lever and drew in the screw driver, also her finger. First finger of left hand was smashed and apparently broken and was later taken off at the first joint.

These cases are but typical of many annually reported to the labor department, of accidents to children while they were operating machines not specified in the statute. The remedy is plain. In addition to naming specific machines that a child shall not be permitted to operate, the statute should contain a broad provision forbidding any child under sixteen years to operate or to assist in operating any dangerous machine or machinery, and permitting the Industrial Board to determine by rules and regulations what machines are dangerous. In a very short time there would be a comprehensive set of rules and regulations on the subject which could from time to time be readily augmented or altered.

If, for instance, an inspector should find a child under sixteen years operating a dangerous machine not specified in the statute he would immediately report the fact to the Industrial Board. In the meantime the inspector by calling attention to the board's powers would probably secure an immediate dismissal of the child from the dangerous employment or in any event, the board in a very short time would add that machine to the list of those at which the employment of a child is prohibited. As the law is to-day, no one cares to go to the legislature for an amendment to the statute every time a new type of dangerous machine is discovered.*

JURISDICTION OVER PROSECUTIONS FOR VIOLATION OF CHILD LABOR AND COMPULSORY EDUCATION LAWS

The Commission has been urged to recommend the extension of the jurisdiction of the Children's Court in cities of the first class, to include prosecutions for violation of the child labor law and compulsory education law of the state.

At present such prosecutions must be begun in the Magistrates' Court and continued in the Court of Special Sessions if the magistrate finds the evidence sufficient to hold the defendant for trial in the higher court.

By the proposed arrangement all such cases would be heard immediately in the Children's Court. In favor of this change it is argued that since the children are frequently witnesses in trials they are now subject to the contaminating influences of a court room in which criminal cases of all kinds are heard. It is urged also that it is altogether logical that a Children's Court should hear cases where children are sinned against as well as the cases in which they are sinners.

* Bill 26, Appendix I.

This extension of the jurisdiction of the Children's Court has been opposed by many, because that court would then cease to be what its name implies. They argue that such an extension of jurisdiction is utterly inconsistent with the theory upon which these courts have been created, which is that they shall deal exclusively with youthful misconduct; and that it would bring questions of criminality into the Children's Court, which legislation has in the past sought zealously to exclude.

In the opinion of the Commission such a proposed extension of jurisdiction would not be wise at this time. The Children's Court in this state is yet in an experimental stage. It is still struggling against too many difficulties, to perform the additional work that would be thrust upon it by the proposed measure. Even now it is unable to do properly the work which it is called upon to do. The Manhattan court has about 10,000 children each year arraigned before it; and even with the improvements that have recently been made in the way of building facilities and in the number of probation officers, the court will still be handicapped in its work for some time to come. No extension of the court's work, even assuming that it is desirable, could wisely be made for at least three or four years.

We wish to emphasize, however, the necessity of protecting the child witnesses from any contaminating influences in the court room. It is simple to do this both in the Magistrates' Court and in the Court of Special Sessions by keeping the children in a separate room until they are called as witnesses. We recommend that this step be taken at once. It could also be arranged that the cases in which children are witnesses be tried on a special day.

THE ENFORCEMENT OF THE CHILD LABOR LAW

To the effective enforcement of the child labor law throughout the state, all the energies of the Department of Labor should be directed. Much has already been accomplished by the department in the city of New York; but a great deal still remains to be done through the rest of the state. Prosecutions for violation of the child labor law in cities up-state are not as frequent as the conditions demand.

A table is attached of prosecutions instituted by the Department of Labor for violation of the child labor law from October 1st, 1911, to September 30th, 1912. This table shows the difference in results between the city of New York and the rest of the state.

STATEMENT OF THE PROSECUTIONS FOR VIOLATION OF THE LABOR LAW WITH REFERENCE TO CHILDREN.

OCTOBER 1, 1911, TO SEPTEMBER 30, 1912

Offense [With reference to section of Labor Law violated.]	No. of Cases.	Results to September 30, 1912. Pending.	Dismissed or Acquitted.	Withdrawn.	Convicted. Sentence Suspended.	Convicted. Fined.	Fines.
(A) PROCEEDINGS INSTITUTED BEFORE OCTOBER 1, 1911.							
New York City:							
Employing child under 14, § 70	25	......	2	......	7	16	$425 00
Employing child under 16 without Board of Health Certificate, § 70	40	......	3	1	20	16	340 00
Employing child under 16 over 8 hours a day, or before 8 A. M. or after 5 P. M., § 77	21	......	......	......	9	12	245 00
Total, New York City	86	......	5	1	36	44	$1,010 00
Up State:							
Employing child under 16 without Board of Health certificate, § 70	2	......	......	2	......	......	....
Total New York State	88	......	5	3	36	44	$1,010 00

(B) PROCEEDINGS INSTITUTED IN CURRENT YEAR.

New York City:							
Employing child under 14, § 70	40	21	2	......	5	12	$280 00
Employing child under 16, without Board of Health Certificate, § 70	152	49	13	......	36	54	1,125 00
Employing child under 16 over 8 hours a day, or before 8 A. M. or after 5 P. M., § 77	618	124	20	......	234	240	6,145 00
Employing child at prohibited occupation, § 93	6	......	1	......	2	3	105 00
Total, New York City	816	194	36	......	277	309	$7,655 00
Up State:							
Employing child under 14, § 70	21	......	......	......	14	7	*$103 00
Employing child under 16, without Board of Health certificate, § 70	34	......	†5	......	20	9	‡167 00
Employing child under 16 over 8 hours a day, or before 8 A. M. or after 5 P. M., § 77	39	......	°3	......	20	16	325 00
Employing child at prohibited occupation, § 93	6	......	......	......	3	3	60 00
Total, Up State	100	......	8	......	57	35	$655 00
Total, New York State	916	194	44	......	334	344	$8,310 00
Grand total	1,004	194	49	3	370	388	$9,320 00

* Includes 3 cases in which fines of $20 were imposed, $15 of which was remitted in each case; and the one case in which fine of $20 was imposed, $17 of which was remitted.

† Includes 2 cases in which Grand Jury failed to find indictment.

‡ Includes 1 case in which fine of $20 was imposed, $18 of which was remitted.

° Grand Jury failed to find indictment in each case.

The Commission is of the opinion that the inspectors in cities up-state are not doing their full duty in connection with the enforcement of this law. Only recently a factory inspector in Syracuse gave us the astounding information that if he found a child between fourteen and sixteen employed in a factory after 5 o'clock in the evening in violation of law, he would not prosecute the employer, but would simply notify the Albany office of the Labor Department. A notice would then be sent directing the owner to cease the illegal employment. The inspector would visit the premises a few days later and unless he found that same child again employed after 5 o'clock in violation of the law, no proceedings would be instituted against the employer.

Of course such procedure is absurd. It simply fosters contempt and indifference for the law. That is not the procedure adopted by the labor department in New York City, and it should not be countenanced anywhere in the state.

This condition of affairs is due in a measure to the fact that there is no special counsel assigned for the prosecution of such cases in cities up-state, whereas there is one in the city of New York.

To remedy this situation the Commission has recommended the appointment of an additional assistant counsel to the Department of Labor whose headquarters shall be in the city of Buffalo or in such other city as the Commissioner of Labor may direct.

Continuation Schools

Owing to the limitation of time placed upon our work we have necessarily been obliged to confine ourselves to matters that are directly concerned with health and safety. We feel, however, that it would not be fitting to close this portion of our report without referring briefly to what we consider one of the most crying needs in our present industrial system, the continued education of children who are obliged to go to work at an early age. In our preliminary report we said:

> "Under our present economic system, children often begin their life of toil at an early age, but this evil certainly does not lessen the obligation of the State to provide for their education. Modern factory conditions undoubtedly deaden

in the great majority of cases whatever intellectual interest the child may have. It is for these young workers that we must plan, and provide with even greater care than for those who are fortunate enough to continue at school."

If we are to keep pace with the progress of European countries we must provide as they are doing for this continued education. We strongly commend this subject to the attention of the various departments of education, state and local, and hope that continuation-schools for children who have gone to work, will soon be a reality.

SUMMARY

For protecting the health and safety of young children employed in the factories of the state we make the following suggestions for remedial legislation:

1. That the present requirement for a thorough physical examination before an employment certificate is issued, which now applies only to factories, be extended also to mercantile establishments.

2. That every local health board be required to transmit to the Department of Labor duplicate records of all physical examinations, including the records of children whose applications for employment certificates were rejected because of physical unfitness.

3. That instead of the present vague and indefinite educational requirement for employment certificates, there be adopted a uniform standard; that is, the completion of the first six years of the public elementary school, or school equivalent thereto, or of the parochial school.

4. That the Department of Labor shall have supervision over the issuance of employment certificates by health departments in the different cities and that the department shall furnish uniform blanks and forms to be used by each local health department.

5. That power be given to the medical inspectors of the Department of Labor to examine any child between fourteen and sixteen years of age employed in a factory and to cause the cancellation of the employment certificate of any such child who is found to be physically unfit for factory work.

6. That the Industrial Board shall have power to make rules and regulations specifying from time to time trades, processes of manufacture, and occupations deemed injurious to health, and to prohibit the employment of minors under the age of eighteen in all such occupations.

7. That there be added to the present statute specifying dangerous machines which children are not permitted to operate, a broad provision prohibiting any child from operating any dangerous machine, and leaving power to the Industrial Board from time to time to specify such machines.

We also recommend:

1. A more effective enforcement of the child labor law in all the cities of the state as well as in New York City.

2. That children who attend as witnesses in criminal courts on the trials of cases involving prosecution for violation of the child labor law and of the compulsory education law be kept in a separate room until their cases are called and, if practicable, that their cases be heard on special days.

3. That the entire matter of the continued education of young children, after they begin work, be thoroughly investigated by the various departments of education both of the state and of its individual communities.

VI.

NIGHT WORK OF WOMEN IN FACTORIES

None of the investigations carried on by the Commission has shown conditions more dangerous to health and public welfare than the employment of women at night in the factories of the State. Conditions of life were revealed which seemed certain not only to destroy the health of the women employed at night, but to threaten the very existence of the young children dependent upon them for nourishment and care.

For instance, in one large industrial plant in the central part of the state, from 130 to 140 women were found at work on night shift. They were employed for ten hours on five nights of each week, from 7 P. M. to 5:30 A. M., with a break of half an hour at midnight. The output of this factory is twine made from hemp and the work involves exposure to much dust, great noise, and, in some rooms, great heat. The married women who worked at night had on an average about four and one-half hours of sleep in the day time; they prepared three meals each day, including breakfast which had to be made ready immediately after the night's work. They also did all the washing for their families. Many of them returned to their homes after ten hours of work at night in the dust and roar of the twine factory, to nurse their babies in the morning and during the day time.

The lack of detailed information in regard to the night work of women of the United States in general, and in the factories of New York State in particular gives special value to this investigation by the Commission, and makes it desirable to set forth the facts in some detail.

The Danger to Health from Night Work

The twine works were repeatedly visited by agents of the Commission, both at night and during the day and individual reports were secured, giving the personal histories of one hundred of the women who worked on night shift.

The general appearance of the night workers is thus described:

> "Most of the women on the night shift are married," says the investigator. "The appearance of the women workers is very disheartening. They are stolid, worn looking, and pale. Their clothes, faces, and hands are covered with oil and hemp dust."

And again:

> "The women as a whole were a disheartening group, in their oily, dust laden clothes, with drawn white faces and stooping gait."

The special investigators report that of the one hundred women, whose personal histories were secured, 95 were Polish. There were 80 women between twenty and thirty years of age. Of these one hundred women 62 were anemic, 57 complained of backache, and 53 of headache. In 77 cases menstrual periods were regular; in 24 not regular (8 pregnant). All operatives worked standing.

These observations agree with the findings of all previous investigators who have studied the industrial night work of women.* The publication of the results of these studies by the International Association for Labor Legislation in 1903 was so convincing as to the injurious effect of night work, that three years later an international treaty prohibiting the employment of women at night was signed by fourteen European nations,—an epoch making event which will be described more fully later in this report.

The authorities all agree that after a shorter or longer period women who are employed at night or until late evening hours suffer from all those symptoms which mark lowered vitality, if not actual disease, such as loss of appetite, headache, anemia, and weakness of the female functions.

Experimentation upon animals has shown that in extreme cases death results far more quickly from continuous loss of sleep than from starvation. Thus a special investigation shows that though puppies can live without food for twenty days and recover after careful feeding, the loss of four to five days' sleep results in death.† It has also been shown that animals kept in the dark without sunlight suffer a loss of the red coloring matter in the

---

* Night Work of Women in Industry, Reports on its importance and legal regulation. Preface by Prof. E. Bauer, Jena, 1903.

† Sleep, by M. de Manaceine, London, 1897.

blood. The same is found true of night-workers who are deprived of sunlight; impoverished blood is one of the main symptoms. This fact was confirmed by an examination of 800 bakers by the investigators of the Commission, described in its Preliminary Report. Night work was found to increase their morbidity and mortality, as well as to upset all the normal habits of social life.*

The chief danger of health from night work is thus due to the inevitable lack of sleep and sunlight. Recuperation from fatigue takes place fully only in sleep, and best, in sleep at night. Hence, night work is, in a word, *against nature.* When exhausting factory work fills the night, and household work most of the day, health must inevitably be sacrificed.

This injury to health is all the greater, because sleep lost at night by working women is never fully made up by day. For in the first place, sleep in the day time is not equal in recuperative power to sleep at night. Dr. Epstein says, in his work on the "Diseases of Bakers": "Doctors and experts on hygiene are unanimous in declaring that sleep at night can in nowise be replaced by sleep in the day time."† Various other medical authorities confirm this opinion. Morover, quiet and privacy for sleep by day is almost impossible to secure. Upon returning home in the middle of the night or at dawn the workers can snatch at most only a few hours' rest.

We have seen that the married women who worked on night shift had on an average only about four and one-half hours of sleep in the day time.

> "The hours of sleep varied with the individual," continues the investigator. "Some slept an hour or two in the morning, and for a time in the afternoon; others slept at intervals of about an hour each during the day. They all slept in bedrooms which had been occupied during the night by husband and children."

Forty-eight of the women worked at night in the spinning room of the mill, thirty in the balling room, twenty-two in the preparing room. Of the conditions of work the investigators say:

> "Dust is the predominating evil." Again: "There is considerable dust in nearly all parts of the mill. This dust

* Preliminary Report of the Commission, 1912, Appendix III. Report on Bakeries and Bakers in New York City.

Epstein. Handbuch der Arbeiterkrankheiten, 1908.

> is caused by the nature of the raw product, hemp. It fills the preparing room where the hemp bales are opened and the hemp prepared. * * * The dust in this department is so thick that the clothes and caps of the women are completely covered with it." *

Of the noise in which the women work, the investigator says:

> "The clatter of the machinery here is so frightful that a voice can hardly be heard below a shriek. * * * The intense noise of the machinery must have some effect on hearing and the nervous system. The investigator had ringing in her ears and was somewhat deafened when she went from the spinning room into the office. * * * The night matron said she could not stay as long as the investigators did in the spinning room because she couldn't stand the noise, but that the Poles were used to it."

Besides noise and dust, some of the workers are subjected while at work to great heat. "The spinning room in the basement is eight or nine feet high. On hot days it must be a veritable inferno." "The watchman says that on very hot nights, the temperature on the top floor is 108 degrees F.," writes the investigator quoted above.

The wages earned were as follows:

One-third of the women earned from $7 to $7.99 a week, another third earned from $8 to $10 (28 earned from $8 to $8.99, and 6 from $9 to $10). Only one woman made $12 a week; 11 women made as little as from $6 to $7. The remaining 23 received varying wages, so that an average could not be accurately taken.

Most of the 100 women specially investigated were married. There were 18 unmarried and 5 widowed. Of the 82 married or widowed nightworkers, 75 had children. Of the children 24 were infants under one year, 19 between one and two years, 18 between two and three years, 17 between three and four years and 19 between four and five years. There were 43 children between five and ten years of age. In many cases the mothers explained that they worked at night though they found the labor exhausting, in

* Since the visit of the Commission, we are informed that a contract has been closed by the management to install dust-removing apparatus for the various machines.

order that they might nurse or take care of their children in the day time. "N. W. wants to work at night on account of her baby which she is nursing." "N. D. wants to do night work on account of baby." "N. T. is nursing her baby now and would rather work nights so that she can feed the baby in the day time;" such are the repeated reports of the investigators. Only a few of the women seemed to realize that this combination might prove disastrous.

> "Mrs. M. N—— changed from night to day work, because it took all her strength to stay up all day besides. Now working days she gets up and dresses, and cares for all the children before she goes to work.
>
> "Another woman says she did not like night work. It was too hard. Quit three weeks ago. 'I used to be cross to my children when I worked nights, because I was so tired all the time.'"

Even without night work it has been shown that the return of married women to factory work after childbirth increases the mortality of infants. Indeed, owing to complex causes a much higher death rate of infants exists in such manufacturing towns as Fall River, Massachusetts, and Biddeford, Maine, than in non-manufacturing towns. The following table shows this fact:

The number of deaths of infants under one year per 100 deaths at all ages was, in the year 1910 as follows:*

Boston	19
Chicago	21
New York City	21
Biddeford	27
Lowell	29
Lawrence	35
Holyoke	35
Fall River	39

In 1910 the number of deaths of infants under one year per 1,000 births in the selected cities, was as follows:†

New York City	125
Boston	126

* Bureau of the Census. Department of Commerce and Labor, Bulletin 109. Mortality Statistics, 1910, p. 14, Washington, 1912.
† *Ibid*, p. 18.

Philadelphia	138
Lawrence	167
New Bedford	177
Holyoke	213
Lowell	231

What must be the result when in addition to the ordinary labor of mothers, the factory night work of mothers is added?

Ignorant women can scarcely be expected to realize the dangers not only to their own health but to that of the next generation from such inhuman usage. But it is precisely to prevent such conditions of toil as threaten the welfare of society that labor laws are designed. These instances show the urgent need of providing by law an adequate period of rest at night for women who work in factories.

The twine factory is not the only establishment in New York State that employs women on regular night shift. It has been here described at some length both because it shows the practices which obtain without a legal prohibition of night work, and also because no such detailed information regarding women's night work in other establishments is available.

The Commission heard evidence also as to the custom of employing women on night shifts in other industries. Thus, for instance, in certain textile mills in the central part of the state, women work from 7:00 P. M. until 6:00 A. M. on five nights in the week. In New York City certain candy factories employ regular night shifts of women on five nights of the week during December.

THE DANGER TO HEALTH FROM LATE OVERTIME EVENING WORK

The preceding examples illustrate the dangers of a regular night shift. But far more usual than the all-night shift is employment "overtime" until late at night. In many trades employees are required to work many hours after and in addition to the regular day's work, a practice which subjects women already fatigued to the added strain of night employment. A detailed study of bookbinding in New York City carried on during the last few years has just been published.* The hours of labor were reported of women working in 208 binderies employing 5,689 women.

> "Few binderies (not more than two or three)," says the report, "have regular night shifts for women who begin work in the evening without having worked during the day. In a far greater number, girls who work during the day stay on through the night hours. * * * Some of the actual instances of overtime work demonstrate that the prescribing of a definite rest period during definite hours of the night is essential to prevent the joining together of two working days at the stroke of midnight."

Thus, for instance, one girl of 23 worked from 8.30 A. M. until 5:30 the next morning.

> "She was employed to fill the boxes of a gathering machine in a magazine bindery. She worked from 8:30 A. M. until 5:30 P. M., with a half hour at noon. She began again at 6:30 P. M. and worked until midnight. After a recess of thirty minutes she continued her day's task until 5:30 A. M. At the time of this employment the New York law permitted a twelve-hour day, and since the employment of women at night was not prohibited, a working day of twenty-four hours was legal, for with the stroke of the clock at midnight a twelve-hour day ended and another twelve-hour day night began. In the case of this girl, not the long hours of work, but the fact that fourteen hours instead of twelve preceded midnight was a violation of the law."

Under the present fifty-four hour law, which allows a working day of only ten hours, the lack of a legal closing hour would presumably allow the employment of a woman ten hours before and ten hours after midnight. This is a stretch of twenty working hours, practically continuous, but falling on two calender days.

In 152 cases, instances of illegal overtime were found among the bindery workers in 42 binderies. In eighteen per cent. of these cases—almost one in every five—work continued until 10 P. M. or much later at night, in addition to the day's work.

> "Several flagrant cases were included in this last group. One reported work until 12:30 A. M.; three until 1:00 A. M.;

* Women in the Bookbinding Trade, Chap. VI; by Mary Van Kleeck, Secretary of Committee on Women's Work, Russell Sage Foundation, published by The Survey Associates, Inc., New York, 1913.

two until 3:00 A. M.; one until 5:30 A. M.; one until 8:00 A. M.; and one until 9:00 A. M. In every one of these cases the girl had gone to work in the morning, had worked through the day and evening until after midnight.

"The detailed reports of working days longer than twelve hours," says the report, "show appalling conditions. These hours represent actual working time, after deducting the length of noon hours and the time allowed for supper. In four positions the day was 12¼ hours long; in seven, 12½; in three, 12¾; in nine, 13; in one, 13½; in two 14; in two, 15½; in two 16; in two 18; in one, 19½; in one, 21½; and in one, 22."

The United States Bureau of Labor in its report upon wage-earning women* confirms our foregoing assertion of the existence of these excessive hours of labor for women in bookbinderies. In one bookbinding establishment in New York City agents of the government found girls employed overtime from 16 to 24¼ continuous hours, once and sometimes twice a week, during a period of from sixteen to twenty-four weeks.

The Commission found instances of extreme overtime work by women in the canneries. Here the employment of many women from the morning of one day until after midnight, or even until dawn of the next day is proved by the employer's written records.

The time sheets of one factory for July 11th, 12th, and 13th, were put in evidence at a hearing held by the Commission at Auburn, N. Y., on August 14th, 1912. This establishment packs fruits and vegetables and on the busiest pack employs from 150 to 200 people. About 75 are women. One of these women was a Mrs. D.—— The overtime hours, incredibly long, which she worked were clearly proved.

The counsel for the Commission examined the manager of the factory:

"Q. According to your time sheet which you have produced of July 10th, 1912, which is Wednesday, Mrs. D—— began work at 6:45 in the morning that day; is that right? A. Yes.

Q. And she finished at 2:30 the following morning? A. Yes.

---

* Report on Condition of Woman and Child Wage-earners in the United States. Vol. V, p. 205. Senate Document No. 645, 61st Congress, 2nd Session, 1910.

Q. Working 19¾ hours? A. Of course she had ½ hour out for lunch and supper that we gave her."

* * * * * * *

"Q. You produce the time sheet for the date of July 11, 1912, and I find the same Mrs. D——, that is the same one, is it? A. Yes; 16 hours.

"And she began that morning at a quarter of seven and stopped at 12 o'clock, and she began at 1 o'clock — that was her lunch hour? A. Yes; she had an hour out.

Q. You didn't pay for that hour? A. No.

Q. Then she stopped at 6 and started at 7; you didn't pay for that hour? A. No.

Q. She stopped at a quarter of one in the morning? A. Yes, sir.

Q. And she worked 16 hours that day? A. Yes."

* * * * * * *

"Have you got July 13, Mrs. D—— ? She began that morning, according to your sheet, at a quarter to seven, stopped at 12, began at one in the afternoon and stopped work at 6, stopped at 6 and began at 7 and worked until a quarter of two the following morning; 17 hours during the day, actual work, taking out at her own expense one hour for lunch and one hour for supper? A. Yes."

Other women were employed in the same factory for hours equally long. This fact was shown by the employer's own time sheets. From these it was found that on July 11th, from among 55 women workers, one-half (27) worked until after 11 P. M., most of them continuously from 6 or 7 A. M., with an hour out for dinner and supper at their own expense. Of the 27 women who worked until late at night,

15 worked until after 11 P. M.,
2 worked until midnight or 12:30 A. M.,
4 worked until between 1 and 2 A. M.,
6 worked until 2 A. M. or later.

The women who did not finish until 1 or 2 A. M., were employed from 16 to 17 hours out of the 24.

The time sheets show that on the next day, July 12th, the night work dropped off somewhat, yet 12 women out of the 55 worked later than 10 P. M.

On the third day, July 13th, 32 or almost two-thirds of the women worked late at night again. 23 of them worked until between 1 and 2 A. M.; 5 of them worked until between 2 and 3 A. M. On this day again these women were employed from 16 to 17 hours.

Instances may be further cited showing also the duration of night work done overtime in the laundries of New York City. In February, 1912, an inquiry was made by the Bureau of Mediation and Arbitration of the New York State Department of Labor into the causes of a strike of laundry employees. At a number of hearings, these employees testified under oath in regard to their hours of labor. Testimony was given showing that work often continued until midnight and occasionally until 1 A. M. The three schedules following, of long weeks reported in the stenographic minutes of evidence, while not necessarily typical, nevertheless illustrate to what extremes the night work of women in laundries may be carried when there is no legal closing hour:

Day of week.	Woman who has worked two yrs. in laundries.	Woman who has worked five yrs. in laundries.	Woman who has worked eleven yrs. in laundries.
	A. M. P. M.	A. M. P. M.	A. M. P. M.
Monday	12—12	12—12	?— 9
Tuesday	9—11.30	9—11.30	9—11
Wednesday	9— 9.30	9— 9	9— 8
Thursday	9— 7	9— 7	9— 7.30
Friday	9— 6.30	9— 6	9— 6
Saturday			

In many other occupations also employment overtime often occurs until late at night. This is especially the case, although to a less degree than in the binderies and laundries, during the fall months in factories that supply the Christmas market, notably in candy and paper box manufactories. Overtime is usual too, through the wide ramifications of the clothing and stitching trades, and also in dressmaking and millinery establishments.

THE DANGER TO MORALS

Besides the injuries to health from the all night shift and the late overtime night work of women, it has universally been found that such work renders women liable to unusual moral dangers and temptations. When women are dismissed in the middle of the night or at dawn, they face the possibility of insult or attack on the streets. Those, moreover, who are living away from home find it difficult to obtain respectable boarding places to which they may return after midnight.

THE PROPOSED LAW

The Commission recommends that night work of women in the factories and workshops of this state be at once prohibited. It finds that such work is unnecessary from an economic point of view and indefensible from the standpoint of public welfare; for it is dangerous to health, inimical to good morals, and destructive of the vitality of women as wives and mothers. We, therefore, recommend the enactment of a new section of the labor law as follows:

§ 93-b. Period of rest at night for women. In order to protect the health and morals of females employed in factories by providing an adequate period of rest at night, no woman shall be employed or permitted to work in any factory in this state before six o'clock in the morning or after ten o'clock in the evening of any day.*

We believe that this bill meets the objections raised by the Court of Appeals in declaring unconstitutional that portion of Section 77 of the Labor Law (Laws of 1899, Chapter 192) which prohibited the employment of women in factories between 9 P. M. and 6 A. M. (*People* vs. *Williams,* 189 *New York,* 131, *decided* 1907). The bill submitted by the Commission fixes 10 P. M. as the closing hour and specifically states that its purpose is to promote health.

CONSTITUTIONALITY OF THE PROPOSED BILL

Two considerations of the utmost importance seem to the Commission to differentiate the proposed bill from the law of 1899 which was held to be unconstitutional.

First, the decision of the United States Supreme Court in *Muller* vs. *Oregon*† upholding the constitutionality of a ten-hour law for women as a legitimate exercise of the police power, decided in 1908, one year after the decision of the New York Court of Appeals in the *Williams* case.

---

* Bill 15, Appendix I.
† 208 U. S., 412.

Second, the existence of many facts of common knowledge regarding the necessity for the prohibition of night work on physical, moral and administrative grounds,— arguments which were not brought to the attention of the New York court for its judicial notice when it considered the act of 1899.

1. *The Change in Judicial Opinion*

The decision in *People* vs. *Williams* was the first and remains the only decision of any superior court in the United States to pass upon the constitutionality of an act prohibiting the night work of women.

The decision in *Muller* vs. *Oregon,* it is true, concerned solely an act limiting the number of hours of labor to be performed by a woman in one day. The decision in *People* vs. *Williams* dealt with a statute prohibiting employment of women before and after certain specified hours. But the opinion in the *Muller* case lays down certain broad considerations of public health and welfare which apply with equal justice to all limitations upon women's labor, be they by night or by day. In rendering its decision in the *Williams* case, the New York court did not have the benefit of the reasoning in *Muller* vs. *Oregon.* On the contrary, the Court of Appeals followed closely the reasoning of a previous decision of the United States Supreme Court in *Lochner* vs. *New York,* decided in 1905.*

In this well known case the Federal Supreme Court held invalid the New York bake shop law, which limited the employment of men in bakeries to 60 hours in one week. The court declared this law to be an unwarranted interference with the freedom of contract guaranteed by the federal constitution. This reasoning was relied upon by the New York Court of Appeals in *People* vs. *Williams.*

> "I need only refer," wrote GRAY, *J.,* for that Court *(p. 136),* "to the recent case of *Lochner* vs. *State of New York (198 U. S., 145),* where the Supreme Court of the United States had before it a case arising in this State under a provision of the Labor Law, which restricted the hours of labor for the employees of bakeries."

* 198 U. S., 145.

> "The argument there was, and it had prevailed in this Court, that the legislation was valid as a health law under the police power; but the Federal Supreme Court refused to recognize the force of the argument, and held, if such legislation should be justified, that the constitutional protection against interference with the liberty of person and the freedom of contract was a visionary thing. *It was held that bakers 'are in no sense wards of the State' * * * so I think in this case we should say * * * an adult female is in no sense a ward of the State.*"

And again GRAY, *J.*, says even more specifically (p. 135):

> "* * * *An adult female is not to be regarded as a ward of the State, nor in any other light than the man is regarded, when the question relates to the business pursuit or calling.*" *

But since the decision of the *Lochner* case, upon which Judge GRAY'S argument was based, the current of judicial opinion has flowed in another channel, and in 1908 the United States Supreme Court, taking cognizance of the "world's experience on which the legislation limiting the women's hours of labor is based," said in the case of *Muller* vs. *Oregon,* cited above:

> "That women's physical structure and the performance of maternal functions places her at a disadvantage in the struggle for subsistence is obvious," said the Court (p. 421).
>
> "The two sexes differ in structure of body, in the functions to be performed by each, in the amount of physical strength, in the capacity for long continued labor, particularly when done standing, the influence of vigorous health upon the future well-being of the race, the self reliance which enables one to assert full rights, and in the capacity to maintain the struggle for subsistence. This difference justifies a difference in legislation and upholds that which is designed to compensate for some of the burdens which rest upon her" (p. 422).

This, then, is the decision of the highest tribunal of the country concerning the relation between the employment of women and the public welfare. It is fair to presume that this reasoning would be followed by the New York Court of Appeals if it again

* *Italics* are ours.

had an opportunity to pass upon the constitutionality of any law affecting hours of women by night or by day.

It is significant that since *Muller* vs. *Oregon* was decided, the Supreme Courts of five great states, Illinois, Michigan, Ohio, Washington and California, have upheld laws limiting a woman's hours of labor.* Indeed, the Supreme Court of Illinois, in *Ritchie* vs. *Wayman,* decided in 1910, completely reversed a prior decision overthrowing the validity of an Illinois eight-hour law. The court, in sustaining a new ten-hour law, was not deterred, as the same court had been fourteen years before (*Ritchie* vs. *The People,* 155 *Ill.,* 198 *decided* 1895) by the theory of freedom of contract.

All that body of "general knowledge" concerning the ill effects of the overwork of women, of which the Federal Supreme Court had taken judicial cognizance, was again admitted to carry its due weight, the Illinois court remarking:

> "What we know as men we cannot profess to be ignorant of as judges."

The "Facts of Common Knowledge" Concerning Night Work.

The Commission supports the proposed bill not only by this convincing array of judicial decisions, without a single adverse opinion since the decision of *Muller* vs. *Oregon,* but also by "facts of common knowledge" regarding night work, proving its ill effects to working women, and to the community of which they are a part. These facts are physical, moral, and administrative.

The dangers to health and morals have already been recounted in connection with the cases of night work discovered by agents of the Commission and other investigators. These facts seem to the Commission to meet the criticism of Judge GRAY, who said of the previous night work law, in his opinion in the *Williams* case (p. 134):

> "I find nothing in the language of the section which suggests the purpose of promoting health, except as it might be inferred that for a woman to work through the forbidden hours of the night would be unhealthful."

* Ill. act of 1909 held constitutional, Ritchie vs. Wayman, 244 Ill., 509; the Ill. act of 1911 held constitutional, People vs. Eldering, 98 Northeastern Rep., 982; Withey vs. Bloem, 163 Mich., 419; ex parte Hawley, 98 N. E. Rep., 1126; State vs. Somerville, 122 Pacific Rep., 324; Matter of Miller, 124 Pacific Rep., 427.

The law proposed by the Commission explicitly states that it is designed to protect the health and morals of women employed in factories, by providing an adequate period of rest at night. That the closing hour has been fixed at ten o'clock instead of at nine o'clock as in the old law, clearly shows that the purpose of the proposed law is to promote health. Moreover, the facts referred to in this report prove that it is unhealthful for a woman to work during the forbidden hours of the night, and make plain the need of prohibiting night work, as a health measure.

The prohibition of night work by women is not a new subject of discussion. In fact, the United States is the only great country having labor laws for women in which the prohibition of night work is not an important part of such laws. In the very first legislation to protect women from overwork, enacted in England in 1844, fixed opening and closing hours were set, before and after which work was prohibited. Through nearly a century which has since elapsed, the prohibition of women's night work has gone hand in hand in all European countries with the reduction of the length of the day's work, and a legal closing hour has been found an essential part of effective laws, necessary not only to protect health and morals, but also to assist in the enforcement of the daily limitation of hours of work.*

For many years international action was urged to secure a uniform prohibition for women's night work. After twenty-five years of effort, representatives of fourteen European powers assembled at Berne, Switzerland, December 26, 1906, in response to an invitation from the Swiss Federal Council. These countries were Austria-Hungary, Belgium, Denmark, France, Germany, Great Britain, Italy, Luxemberg, Portugal, Spain, Sweden, Switzerland, and the Netherlands. An international agreement or convention was submitted to this conference. This was to bind the contracting states to prohibit the industrial night work of women without distinction of age. A minimum period of eleven consecutive hours was set for the duration of the night rest, to include the time between 10 P. M. and 5 A. M. in all cases. Only two exceptions permitting night work were admitted: first, in case of the interruption of work by causes beyond the employer's con-

* Fatigue and Efficiency: A Study in Industry. By Josephine Goldmark, pp. 216-222; Charities Publication Committee N. Y., 1912.

trol, frequently described as " the act of God "; second, to save raw material* liable to rapid deterioration. A slight modification in favor of the seasonal industries was made by reserving the right to reduce the length of the night rest from eleven to ten hours during sixty days of the year. No other concessions were made.

By January 14, 1910, all the participating states, excepting Spain and Denmark had ratified the convention.

The United States could not take part in the Berne convention since the federal government cannot bind the separate states to enact legislation restricting hours of labor. Hence the initiative is left solely to the action of the states themselves.

THE NEED OF LEGAL CLOSING AND OPENING HOURS TO ASSIST ENFORCEMENT

The examples of work, after and in addition to the day's employment, given above, show that the legal closing hour is necessary not only to provide an adequate rest period at night to protect the health and morals of working women, but also to control overtime work and thus to make possible the enforcement of the limitation of hours per day. The two things are practically inseparable. Unless the inspectors remain on the premises from start to finish, which is practically impossible, they cannot know the number of hours worked; and for various obvious reasons, when the law has been violated, the statements of neither employers nor employees can be relied on. But when definite hours are set before and after which work is illegal, a single inspection suffices to prove a violation.

The Report of the Federal Government states after detailed study of the question:†

> " The indications are strong enough to warrant the conclusion that overtime runs to dangerous limits in * * * manufacturing establishments in the absence of restrictive laws not only setting definitely a limit to the hours of labor per day and per week, but *fixing the closing hours.*"

* This contingency has been regulated by special acts in various European countries. Thus in England, since 1907, work is prohibited after 10 P. M. on such perishable material.

† Report on Condition of Woman and Child Wage Earners in the United States. Senate Document No. 645, 61st Congress, 2nd Session, 1910. Vol. V, p. 215.

It appears from the opinion of Judge GRAY in *People* vs. *Williams,* that the Court might have considered the night work law valid if it had seemed to them to prohibit overtime work, after and in addition to the regular day's work.

The prohibition of *all* work between 9 P. M. and 6 A. M. did not seem to them a legitimate exercise of the police power, because under such prohibition:

> "An adult woman * * * cannot be employed, or contract to work, in any period for any length of time, no matter how short, if it is within the prohibited hours."

But universal experience, the facts of which have in great part been recorded and published since the decision in the *Williams* case, proves that the fixed closing hour, after which all employment is prohibited, is the only known device to check late overtime work continued into the night. The Court of Appeals specifically said, in the *Williams* case, that if the intention to check such late overtime work had been clear the Court might consider this more properly "a matter of legislative concern." Indeed, before the *Williams* case reached the highest court of New York, the Justices of the Appellate Division of the Supreme Court had been divided in opinion (116 App. Div., 379). Two of the five judges handed down minority opinions, expressing their belief that the entire provision of the labor law relating to the hours of labor for women, including the prohibition of nightwork, was within the police power of the state, and therefore valid. They apparently saw no reason for differentiating the provision which prohibited night work from the other provisions establishing a ten-hour day and sixty-hour week, the constitutionality of which was not questioned. In his minority opinion, Mr. Justice HOUGHTON said:*

> "I think the act limiting the *hours and times of day* in which women may work in factories * * * is a valid exercise of the police power for the preservation of the public health." * * * *(p. 381).*
>
> "The purpose of the statute is to prohibit women working in factories *more than 60 hours in any one week,* and *presumably unhealthful hours,* and to that end it prescribes that they shall not work before six o'clock in the morning, and

* *Italics* ours.

14

after nine o'clock at night, and no more than ten hours in any one day." * * * *(p. 381).*

"Constant night work is unhealthful for men and more so for women. * * * Excessive labor of an automatic character such as most factory work finally assumes, tends to dull the mental and moral perceptions and leads to degrading recreations, *especially when work ceases at any unseemly hour of the night." (p. 384).*

"The legislature has deemed that if she (a woman) be continuously employed in the same service in a factory *more than a certain number of hours per day or week, or during the night time,* her health would be likely to be injured." *(p. 384).*

In this opinion Mr. Justice INGRAHAM concurred, saying of the provision in its entirety:

"Regulation by the legislature as to the hours of labor by women when engaged in such work as would have a tendency to impair their health is, I think, within the power of the legislature and comes fairly within the police power of the State as relating to 'the safety, health, morals and general welfare of the public.'" *(p. 386).*

That the state has the right to fix closing hours in order to enforce its requirement for the limitation of the hours of labor for women seems clearly established by a recent decision of the United States Supreme Court in *Purity Co.* vs. *Lynch* (226 U. S., 192). In that case Mr. Justice Hughes, delivering the opinion said:

"It is also well established that, when a state exerting its recognized authority, undertakes to suppress what it is free to regard as a public evil, it may adopt such measures having reasonable relation to that end as it may deem necessary in order to make its action effective. It does not follow that because a transaction separately considered, is innocuous, it may not be included in a prohibition the scope of which is regarded as essential in the legislative judgment to accomplish a purpose within the admitted power of the government. With the wisdom of the exercise of that judgment the court has no concern; and unless it clearly appears that the enactment has no substantial relation to a proper purpose, it cannot be said that the limit of legislative power has been

> transcended. To hold otherwise would be to substitute judicial opinion of expediency for the will of the legislature — a notion foreign to our constitutional system."

The history of the night work law in New York State shows that thirty-five years ago the legal closing hour and the prohibition of night work was thought imperative to assist in the enforcement of the ten-hour day by those most conversant with the circumstances,—the factory inspectors.

In 1886 the Legislature of New York State had passed its first factory law providing that no women under twenty-one years might be employed more than sixty hours in any one week, unless for the purpose of making necessary repairs. The employment of any child under thirteen years was prohibited.

In their annual report for 1887 the factory inspectors pointed out the dangers to health and to output from excessive overtime work and urged the establishment of a legal closing hour.

> "An inquiry among those females above the statutory age, who worked twelve and fifteen hours a day in printing offices, candy factories, woolen mills and other manufacturing establishments," said the factory inspector's report, "elicited the information that the women who labor these long hours were more subject to fits of nervous prostration and debility than those who worked the normal day of ten hours, and as a rule they would not have so much working time to their credit as those who were not so over-worked."

To remedy these evils the factory inspectors recommended that the employment of women at night, irrespective of age, be prohibited after 9 P. M. The recommendation was not, however, followed.

In 1889 a first step in this direction was taken by prohibiting the night work of women under twenty-one years between 9 P. M. and 6 A. M. Employment of women under twenty-one years was also prohibited for more than ten hours in one day, except for the purpose of shortening the hours of work on Saturday.

Ten years later, in 1899, by a single act, all of these provisions of the law were extended to all women, irrespective of age.

The enforcement of the night work law remained more or less of a dead-letter for the following seven years. In 1907 the decision in the *Williams* case removed the law from the statute books.

Now, after the lapse of five years, the Commission believes that the time has come to enact a new law. The decision of the United States Supreme Court in the *Muller* case has changed the whole trend of judicial opinion regarding legislation limiting women's hours of labor.

SUMMARY

The available facts, in the opinion of the Commission justify the enactment of a new law for the two reasons emphasized above:

> *First,* because an adequate period of rest at night is essential for the health of women employed in manufacture.
>
> *Second,* because the provision of legal closing and opening hours is the only effective method of enforcing the limitation of hours.

The proposed law is a moderate measure. It is most fair and reasonable to all concerned. It provides that women employed in factories shall have a period of rest at night between 10 P. M. and 6 A. M. It thus allows a stretch of 16 hours—from 6 o'clock in the morning until 10 o'clock at night—during which the 10 hours of daily labor permissible by law may be performed. Early evening work is not curtailed, but the excessive overtime, extending as has been shown, until long after 10 P. M. is confined to more reasonable limits. The dangerous all night shift is prohibited.

No legitimate industry will suffer from this measure, urgently needed to protect the health of the workers and to assist the factory inspectors in the difficult task of enforcement.

No objections to the proposed measure have been received from any source although the bill has been widely distributed. On the contrary the purpose of the bill has been commended by physicians, by manufacturers and by all those having the best interests of the state at heart.

In enacting the proposed bill, the state of New York will not be taking a new and untried step. It will be taking its place among the enlightened nations of the world, and will join the other three states, Massachusetts, Indiana, and Nebraska, which now provide by law a period of rest at night for working women.

WOMEN'S WORK GENERALLY

SEATS

The continual standing of women in factories and manufacturing establishments is one of the worst features of a large part of their work. Women are required to stand in candy factories, laundries, textile mills and printing shops for hours at a time and often for the entire day. The effects of continual standing upon the female organism are grave. Much of this standing is unnecessary. A great deal of the work could very readily be carried on in a sitting posture. We therefore recommend the following amendment to section 17 of the labor law:

> *Where females are engaged in work which can be properly performed in a sitting posture, suitable seats, with backs where practicable, shall be supplied in every factory for the use of all such female employees and permitted to be used at such work. The industrial board may make rules and regulations prescribing the number and kind of seats that shall be provided and the use thereof.**

TIME BOOK

The keeping of correct time books showing the hours of labor of women employees, is of considerable aid in the enforcement of the law. Since 1907 the New York law has required that under certain circumstances the employers shall keep a time book showing the hours worked daily by each woman employee.†

Our investigations showed that such time books were not correctly kept. In one cannery the Commission visited, the time books were so kept as to show an apparent compliance with the requirements of the Labor Law. All hours worked beyond the

---

* Bill 16, Appendix I.

† N. Y. Labor Law, Section 77, Subdivision 5. In a factory wherein, owing to the nature of the work, it is practically impossible to fix the hours of labor weekly in advance the commissioner of labor, upon a proper application stating facts showing the necessity therefor, shall grant a permit dispensing with the notice hereinbefore required, upon condition that the daily hours of labor be posted for the information of employees and that a time book in a form to be approved by him, giving the names and addresses of all female employees, and the hours worked by each in each day, shall be properly and correctly kept, and shall be exhibited to him or any of his subordinates promptly upon demand. Such permit shall be kept posted in such place in such factory as such commissioner may prescribe, and may be revoked by such commissioner at any time for failure to post it or the daily hours of labor or to keep or exhibit such time book as herein provided.

legal 60 hours were separately and privately kept, and were not supposed to be seen by the factory inspectors. The Commission learned the real hours worked from what the employer at the hearing called, "The daily time sheets, or a sort of a cash book * * * that shows the total payroll for each week." Thus on the day that Mrs. D, according to the actual payroll or time sheets, worked 19¾ hours, her time was set down in the official time book as 8½ hours.

The following is from the testimony taken by the Commission at the cannery:

> "Q. Why does it appear in your time book, Mr. ———, that she only worked 8½ hours on Wednesday when, as a matter of fact, your time sheet shows she worked 19¾ hours?"

With interesting frankness, the manager answered:

> "That is for the reason of keeping our record as near as possible to the sixty hours law.
>
> Q. That shows that you could only add 8½ hours to what she had already done in the preceding three days to make up sixty hours for the week? A. That is the idea."

And again:

> "Q. These time sheets you have produced, Mr. ———, of July 10th, 11th, and 12th and 13th, those sheets show the actual number of hours of each one of the employees named therein who worked? A. Yes; that is all there is to it; that is all.
>
> Q. And the time book proper which you have shown me is an incorrect book. A. The time book proper shows they only worked 60 hours, and on that page shows the overtime.
>
> *By Senator Wagner:*
>
> Q. Purposely so arranged, wasn't it? A. It was; yes, it was.
>
> Q. To show an apparent observance of the law; is that right? A. That is the idea."
>
> * * * * *
>
> "Q. Don't you know you are breaking the law by that? A. I admit it was an infringement of the strict meaning of that law, the intention of that law.

Q. Wasn't it meant to fool the factory inspector? A. Yes, it was."

This striking example shows that the law should be amended so that such false entries may be punishable by law. If the time book is to be of value in assisting the factory inspectors to enforce the law, it must be reliable and give the actual hours worked.

We therefore recommend that the making of any false entries or statements in a time book kept pursuant to sub. 5 of Section 77 (quoted, *supra*), shall be punishable as a misdemeanor.

HOURS OF LABOR

In investigating the conditions under which women work in the state, the Commission has found that the intensity of the work is ever increasing. The complexity of modern machinery, with the development of the system of paying by the piece, has added a special strain upon all workers who are forced to a tremendous speed. This strain is physical as well as nervous and an especial burden upon women, the large majority of whom are young and have not reached their maturity.

How this strain is to be lightened and the most effective way is still a problem. The goal of working people themselves throughout the world is the eight-hour day. Eight hours is a daily period which many communities — city, state or national, as model employers — set for the labor of adult men in their employ. It may not be feasible at this time to put this limit in practice for women in private employment, yet it is the recognized goal for ordinary industrial occupations. Even the eight-hour day involves, with the noon hour and the journey to and from work in most instances, ten hours' absence from home. The Commission believes, however, that the manufacturers of the state should be given an opportunity to readjust their work on the basis of the 54-hour law before any further legislation is had.

VII.

BAKERIES

The Commission conducted in 1911 a special investigation into conditions in bakeries, the results of which are set forth in detail in Appendix III of the Commission's Preliminary Report.

Under the supervision of Dr. George M. Price who was assisted by a corps of inspectors, 485 bakeries were inspected in New York City and Yonkers.

Of the bakeries inspected 479 were cellar bakeries. In conjunction with the sanitary investigation the Commission engaged a staff of physicians who made physical examinations of 800 bakers.

In 1912 about 125 bakeries were inspected in different cities of the state.

GENERAL CONDITIONS

There are few industries so closely related to the public health as is that of bread making. This industry, therefore, should be carried on under the most sanitary conditions and with the highest regard for cleanliness. We were surprised by the results of the investigations conducted.

In the majority of the bakeries, the walls, ceilings, and floors were unclean. In 109 of the bakeries inspected, toilets were immediately in the bakeshop, and eighty-six of these toilets were characterized by the inspectors as very "filthy." The utensils found in the bakeries such as vats, pans, and mixing-boards, were in a very dirty condition; they invariably looked as if they had never been cleansed. The ventilation in most cases was poor, and the lighting inadequate. There were 171 bakeries which had no windows at all.

In most of the bakeries no provision was made for the disposal of the street clothes of the bakers. Their clothing was placed upon tables and walls in close proximity to the bread and pastry products. Many bakers were found working in their ordinary clothes or underwear. Personal cleanliness of the bakers was the exception rather than the rule. The practice of sleeping in the bakeries was found to be very prevalent among the workers.

The results of the physical examination of bakers were equally surprising. Of the 800 bakers, 19 were found suffering from tuberculosis (including suspected cases), 177 from bronchial diseases, 3 from venereal disease, and 45 from skin diseases.

It is inconceivable that such conditions should be permitted to exist in an industry in which the public is so directly concerned. These filthy conditions are not only a menace to public health, but their existence is manifestly unfair to the proprietors of numerous other bakeries in which every effort is made to maintain cleanliness and purity. It has well been said that a dirty bakery is a menace to the entire trade.

THE EXTENT OF THE INDUSTRY

The bakery industry in New York State is an important one. The census of 1910 showed that in 1909 there were 2,962 bakeries in the state of New York employing 13,676 workers. That number has since then been increased considerably. Of these bakeries 2,498 were in New York City.

PRESENT JURISDICTION OVER BAKERIES

The Department of Labor by Article VIII of the labor law is given power to inspect bakeries and to enforce certain sanitary requirements therein. The sanitary codes in all of the larger cities of the state confer jurisdiction over bakeries expressly or by implication upon the local boards of health. The result is that we often have in one city, two departments, one a city department and the other a state department exercising concurrent jurisdiction over conditions in bakeries. There is in this way a confusion of duties with the usual result — a shifting of responsibility. This, in our opinion, accounts for many of the unsanitary conditions that we found. There is no co-operation between these two departments in any city. Neither department is sufficiently equipped to make frequently a systematic inspection of the bakeries under its charge or promptly and effectively to enforce the prohibition of unclean and unsanitary conditions. The Department of Labor, working with an inadequate force of inspectors, can inspect a bakery only about once a year.

PROPOSED CHANGE IN JURISDICTION

The cities of the first class of the state, New York, Buffalo, and Rochester, have well organized departments of health with special divisions for food inspection. Sole jurisdiction over bakeries, in our opinion, should be given to these departments and they alone should be held responsible for conditions in them.

This change would in every case fix definitely in one department the responsibility for sanitary conditions in bakeries; that is, in the local departments of heath in cities of the first class and in the Department of Labor throughout the rest of the state.

Arguments for making the local health department in cities of the first class solely responsible for conditions in bakeries are many. The change will obviate dual jurisdiction and dual responsibility. It will do away with the double inspection that results so frequently in conflicting orders, and no results. The departments of health in the larger cities are already doing part of this work but have practically no responsibility. There is no reason why they should not do all of the work and be made strictly accountable for sanitary conditions. The Department of Labor relieved by this transfer of duties will then be able to devote all its energies to general factory inspection in those cities. Although the state department would still have jurisdiction over the safeguarding of machinery in bakeries and the employment of women and minors therein, its supervision would be confined mainly to the larger establishments which are very few in number.

The law should specify for sanitary and structural conditions in bakeries the minimum requirements which the local departments of health in cities of the first class must enforce, and should give to those cities power to incorporate detailed rules and regulations in their sanitary codes.

SANITARY CERTIFICATE

Having definitely fixed the responsibility for sanitary conditions in bakeries, in one department, we must then determine by what method conditions in bakeries can best be controlled by the responsible authority.

Experience has shown that conditions in establishments which are liable to become a public nuisance in one way or another can best be controlled if those establishments are required to obtain some kind of permit before they are allowed to operate.

There are a number of industries to which the principle of state or municipal licensing has already been applied. These industries have features which make their control necessary in the interest of public health and safety. They are either dangerous to life because of intrinsic perils in materials and processes, as for example in the manufacture of explosives, or they are such as may become a nuisance to neighbors, as in the keeping of stables, or they are occupations that bear directly on the public health, as is true of the plumbing trade, the dairy industry, and slaughter houses.

In this class of licensed occupations the bread-making industry clearly belongs, for it is closely related to public health. To apply this principle to all of the bakeries in the state is the immediate step in remedial legislation. It is a public health measure for which the trade, the workers, and the entire public are ready, and which they are anxious to see an accomplished fact.

There has been much discussion as to what form the licensing should take and what name should be applied to a permit to allow a bakery to operate. Questions of form, however, are of very little consequence provided that the required results be obtained.

We believe that the desired control over conditions in bakeries can be secured if a bakery before it is permitted to operate, shall be required to obtain a sanitary certificate, in cities of the first class from the local health department, and in the rest of the state from the Department of Labor. This sanitary certificate should be granted only after a thorough inspection showed that the bakeshop conformed in all respects to the requirements of the statute and to the rules and regulations adopted under it, and the certificate should be revoked in case of failure to observe these requirements.

This recommendation meets with the approval of all of the employers and workers in the industry who appeared before the Commission.

PHYSICAL EXAMINATION OF BAKERS

The necessity for a physical examination of those engaged at work in the baking industry is strikingly emphasized by the results of the examination previously mentioned of 800 bakers made by the Commission.

The following are cases taken from the records of the physical examination of bakers made for the Commission last December:

> *Case 1.* G. E.———, Italian, 24 years of age; 6 years in the trade and is married. His general appearance is good but his personal cleanliness is poor; had anemia in a marked degree. We found on his body a rash mostly due to scratching. On careful examination we found that the rash was due to body lice. He had a slight bronchitis.
>
> *Case 2.* J. G.———, Russian, baker 16 years. General appearance poor and cleanliness bad. His lungs on one side showed signs of tubercular infection.
>
> *Case 3. J. P———*, Italian, 28 years. General appearance fair, personal cleanliness poor. His skin showed what is commonly known as pimples and technically, acne. The acne extended all over the body and even on his arms, so that the part that necessarily makes the dough was also infected. An examination of this man's lungs revealed that he had an infection which looked very much to be tubercular, but a positive diagnosis could not be made.
>
> *Case 4.* F. W———, Austrian. In general, his appearance was anemic. An examination of his skin showed that he had eczema in patches on his arms and various parts of the body.

The bakers handle the bread both before and after it is baked and the food product is therefore twice subject to contamination. It has furthermore been definitely determined that the baking process which is supposed to sterilize the product, does not necessarily destroy all the infectious agents in the bread.

In the investigation made for the Lancet Commission in England,* numerous experiments are mentioned which show that the temperature which reaches the center of the baked loaves does not exceed 180 degrees and that pathogenic bacteria may not be destroyed, and that spore-bearing bacteria are certainly not destroyed. ' We can see no reason," say Drs. Waldo and Walsh, "why the origin of so many mysterious septic invasions of the human body may not eventually be traced to the agency of infected bread," * * * "baking does not necessarily destroy the vitality of the micro-organisms contained in the dough."*†

The Retail Bakers' Association of New York City, an organization that has taken a most enlightened attitude on the subject, warmly approves any requirement that will keep from the baking industry anyone suffering from a communicable disease. We believe that no person suffering from tuberculosis, venereal disease, skin disease, or any other communicable disease should be permitted to work in a bakery.

It is unwise, however, to make rigid specifications in the law as to this matter. We believe that it would be more effective to provide in the statute that no person suffering from any communicable disease should be permitted to work in a bakery, leaving it to the local departments of health in the cities of the first class and to the Department of Labor in the rest of the state to make detailed rules and regulations on the subject. The term "communicable disease" is a very broad one, covering both infectious and contagious diseases, so that the proposed provision would result in excluding from the bakeshop any person whose health or physical condition was such as possibly to contaminate the food product.

To aid in the enforcement of this law we recommend that whenever it is required by a medical inspector of the local department of health, or of the State Department of Labor as the case may be, any bakery employee must submit to a physical examination by such inspector, and that no person refusing to be examined shall be permitted to continue work in any bakery. We believe this requirement to be necessary in the interests of the public health.

CELLAR BAKERIES

The majority of bakeries throughout the state are situated in cellars in tenements and other dwellings, or in buildings partly used for manufacturing purposes. The location of bakeries in cellars has been common throughout the world but within the

* Report of the Lancet Special Commission on Bakeries and Bread Making. London, 1889-1890.

† F. J. Waldo and D. Walsh. Bread, Bakehouses and Bacteria, London, 1895.

last few years steps have been taken in foreign countries, especially in England, to bring about a prohibition of bread making in such places. In England new bakeries have for several years past been forbidden to occupy cellars.

In Chicago there has been a very active campaign against the cellar bakery by the board of health with the result that by ordinance in that city no new bakeries are permitted to be located in cellars. In Buffalo too the board of health has been especially active, and by its own regulation has been instrumental in causing the use of cellars for bakeries to be discontinued. There are practically no bakeries in cellars in that city to-day.

Exceptionally bad conditions in the cellar bakeries in New York State were disclosed by the Commission's investigations. Most of the witnesses ascribed the bad sanitary conditions found in them to the fact that the bakeries were situated in cellars.

A cellar is unfit both for the manufacture of food stuffs and for the habitation of workers. There can be no natural light under the most favorable conditions in a cellar. They are also very difficult places to ventilate unless a mechanical system is installed, which is out of the question in the ordinary small bakery. The ovens and the heated atmosphere needed for dough raising, make it impossible for cellar bakeries to have a proper temperature. They cannot be kept as clean as other parts of the house for they are semi-dark, and contain most of the plumbing pipes and fixtures. They are also the natural habitation of insects and rodents.

Testimony was given by Raymond B. Fosdick, Commissioner of Accounts of the City of New York, that of the 145 cellar bakeries examined by him in 1911 in New York City, not one could be put in a sanitary condition and that this fact was due in each case to the situation of the bakery in a cellar without proper light and ventilation.

That a cellar bakery is more difficult to keep clean than one situated above ground, is the testimony of every expert appearing before the Commission. The question propounded by several representatives of the master bakers, "If a person is unsanitary in a cellar bakery, is he not just as apt to be unsanitary in a bakery located above ground?" has been answered in the negative in every case.

The complete correction of all these unsanitary conditions in cellar bakeries we do not believe possible by any system of inspection to which the state or municipality can justly resort. The Commissioner of Health of the city of New York made the statement, in referring to these cellar bakeries: "I have not yet been shown that the bakers of the city can and will keep their bakeries in a sanitary condition." Nowhere in the United States or in foreign countries has it been proved that the cellar bakery can as a general rule be regularly maintained in a clean and sanitary condition. In Buffalo and many other cities of the state, in Chicago, and in England, it has been clearly shown that cellar bakeries cannot be adequately supervised and controlled by inspection.

Nor yet would it be just to recommend the immediate prohibition of all cellar bakeries now in existence. The hardship to proprietors of these bakeries and to the owners of buildings in which they are situated, through such legislation would obviously be too great.

PROHIBITION OF NEW CELLAR BAKERIES

What, then, may be done to remedy these conditions that evidently are quite intolerable to all concerned for the public welfare?

The Commission is of the opinion that the most just and effective legislation would (*a*) provide at once for all possible improvement of the sanitary conditions in existing cellar bakeries; and (*b*) prohibit the location of any new bakery in a cellar.

The standards for proper sanitation of the bakeshop and for the cleanliness of its utensils should be raised in the case of existing cellar bakeries. Those able to comply with these requirements should be permitted to operate under close inspection. Those unable to comply should be closed at once in the interest of the public, of the employees and of the baking industry itself.

To abolish cellar bakeries gradually, without inflicting too great hardship upon those engaged in the industry (a result that will be brought about if new bakeries are prohibited from locating in cellars), is not only practicable, but is imperatively demanded by the conditions that have been disclosed. This course of gradual elimination should work hardship neither to the bakers nor to the owners of buildings in which cellar bakeries are now located. Buildings hereafter constructed, in which it is desired to maintain bakeries should have basements instead of cellars,—that is, the bakery should be more than one-half above the level of the street.

There are undoubtedly a few cellars not now used as bakeries in which a sanitary bakery might well be established in the future, but these few cases are so rare as to be negligible, and should not be permitted to stand in the way of the enactment of legislation that is for the greatest good of the greatest number.

Whenever it is sought to abolish a serious evil the plea is always made that it would work hardship on some individuals if the proposed change were made. This argument has been urged against every progressive step in civilization, and the same plea has been offered whenever any legislation has been introduced for the improvement of conditions for the human race, from the time of the enactment of the first child labor law in England over a century ago, to the passage of the 54-hour law in this state at the last session of the legislature. But this apparent hardship to the few is inevitable in the march of progress.

The Commission therefore recommends that no new bakery shall hereafter be located in a cellar and that no sanitary certificate be issued for any bakery so located hereafter. This prohibition should not apply, however, to any cellar used and operated as a bakery on the fifteenth day of January, 1913, or to any cellar so used or operated within a year prior thereto. No such cellar shall be entitled to this exemption unless satisfactory proof of its use as a bakery as specified, is furnished to the local health department or to the Commissioner of Labor as the case may be, in such form as may be required within six months after this act shall take effect. Upon receipt of such proof the Commissioner of Labor or the local health department shall issue a certificate of exemption.

ADDITIONAL MINIMUM REQUIREMENTS FOR BAKESHOPS

Our attention has been called to a number of matters not now specified in the law dealing with sanitary conditions in bakeshops that should properly be included in it in order to bring about an improvement of conditions. Accordingly, we recommend the following additions to sections 111 *et seq.* of the labor law:

1. Mechanical means of ventilation when provided shall be effectively used and operated at all times during working hours.

2. Windows and other openings in the bakery shall be provided with proper screens.

3. All workmen and employees while engaged in the manufacture and handling of bread shall wear slippers or shoes, and a suit of washable material which shall be used for that work only, and these garments shall be kept clean at all times.

SANITARY CODE FOR BAKERIES

In addition to the minimum requirements contained in the statute, we recommend that the local health department in cities of the first class and the Industrial Board of the Department of Labor for the rest of the state shall also adopt detailed rules and regulations for the construction of bakeshops, their maintenance, the cleanliness of their utensils, and the health and personal cleanliness of the workers therein, to be formulated as a sanitary code for bakeries so that the master bakers may know just what is required of them and may not, as they are to-day, be in a position to plead ignorance of the law because of the vagueness and indefiniteness of many of its requirements.

SUMMARY

We have outlined some of the evil conditions that were found by our investigators in the bakeries of the state. We do not wish, however, to give the impression that all or nearly all of the bakeries of this state are unsanitary. There are many men operating small bakeshops which are models of cleanliness. But unfortunately this is not generally true.

We have recommended as changes which we believe will result in improved conditions, (a) that the jurisdiction over bakeries and responsibility for conditions therein be placed, in cities of the first class, in the local department of health, and for the rest of the state in the Department of Labor; (b) that every bakery be required to obtain a sanitary certificate in order to operate; (c) that the employment of diseased bakers be prohibited; (d) that new bakeries be prohibited from locating in cellars; and (e) that certain additions be made to the minimum requirements of the present bakery law; and (f) that sanitary codes for bakeries be enacted which shall specify in detail standards of cleanliness and sanitation.*

After the responsibility for the enforcement of the law has been definitely fixed in one department, that department should be given adequate means to perform its full duty. This duty should involve a thorough inspection of every bakeshop not less than once in every two weeks, and oftener when necessary. Nowhere is frequent, periodical, and efficient inspection more needed than in bakeries.

---

* Bill 17, Appendix I.

VII.

GENERAL SANITARY CONDITIONS

The Commission conducted an extensive investigation of the general sanitary conditions under which manufacture is carried on throughout the state. In 1911, 1,838 establishments were inspected in which 63,374 wage earners were employed. In 1912, 1,338 establishments were inspected in which 125,961 wage earners were employed. Altogether 3,176 establishments with 189,335 employees were inspected. The investigation covered 45 cities in the state and 88 industries. This list does not take into account the special investigations that were made in relation to canneries, lead poisoning, and wood alcohol. Particular attention was devoted to the following industries: clothing, textiles, metal, foods, furs, tobacco, printing, and chemical establishments.

The following table shows the general scope of the sanitary investigations conducted in 1911 and 1912:

	Industrial Establishments.	Shops.	Wage-Earners.
Clothing	341	623	2,822
Textiles	132	490	35,173
Metal	130	415	25,840
Foods	729	1,123	15,447
Furs	253	284	4,764
Tobacco	251	472	15,594
Printing	348	523	9,047
Chemical Industry	127	344	4,764
Miscellaneous	865	1,901	51,264
	3,176	6,075	189,335

The following general conditions were investigated: construction of factories, safeguarding of machinery, light and illumination, ventilation and heating, sanitary conveniences and comforts.

GENERAL RESULTS

To the credit of New York State and its many enlightened manufacturers it may be said that the Commission found in various cities many industrial establishments, some of small size, which were models in all or in most respects. In these the working conditions were excellent. Ample provision was made for the health and comfort of the employees and a proper regard for their safety was manifest. High standards of industrial efficiency were maintained in these establishments, and the owners in their desire to protect their employees went far beyond the minimum requirements of the labor law. These factories should serve as example for other manufacturers to follow. They are concrete proofs that industrial efficiency, progress, and business success are not incompatible with a high regard for the health and comfort of the workers.

The Commission found that more than half of the manufacturing establishments in the state were in a fair sanitary condition. The majority of the manufacturers have endeavored to obey the law. That they have occasionally failed to do so is largely due to the vague and indefinite requirements of many of our labor laws. Compulsory methods need not be used in the case of these employers. They are in accord with the general principles of the labor law and if any defective condition is brought to their attention they are willing to remedy it at once. What is needed in these cases is intelligent inspection, not from a "police" but from a friendly standpoint.

The investigations, however, have also disclosed in this state a large number of industrial establishments where the general sanitary conditions under which manufacture is carried on are deplorable and where there is apparent disregard for the health and comfort of the employees. These manufacturers represent the old "laissez faire" attitude in our industrial life. They maintain, as some have stated openly at public hearings of the Commission, that the working conditions in their establishments are of no concern to anyone but themselves and that the state has no right to interfere with them in the conduct of their business. This class of manufacturers, who fortunately are in a small minority, must be shown that the health of the workers is of paramount importance to the state, which not only has the right but is bound to take measures that workers be properly safeguarded in the course of their employment. Manufacturers must be reminded of their duty by frequent inspections and prompt and effective punishment of wilful disregard of any of the provisions of the statute.

UNCLEAN WORKROOMS

The Commission found distinct improvement in the cleanliness of workrooms in factories throughout the state. The conditions that existed in 1911 led to the enactment of a law recommended by the Commission (sec. 95 of the labor law), giving the Commissioner of Labor power to affix the unclean tag to articles manufactured in any workroom kept in an unclean and unsanitary condition. This new law has had a most salutary effect. Factory inspectors informed the Commission that they now get immediate results in attempting to remedy unclean conditions where formerly they had to wait weeks and months.

The Commission recommends that the present provisions of the labor law dealing, with cleanliness of workrooms and factory buildings be made more definite and certain, and submits bills for that purpose.*

LIGHT AND ILLUMINATION

The lack of proper light in our factories has long been recognized as a serious evil. Inadequate lighting in industrial establishments affects not only the eyesight and general health of the workers, but it also impairs the efficiency of their work and is responsible for many of the accidents that occur every year in our factories. The enlightened employer recognizes that it is to his commercial interest to secure adequate illumination, because of the improved output and quality of work.

There can be no hard and fast requirements, however, to regulate lighting in factories. The requirements for proper illumination must be adapted to the varying conditions of the different industries. In the present state of the science and art of illumination we believe that it would be impracticable to specify explicitly in any statute the precise methods of installation, arrangement, and use of lights to secure the results desired. The language of the statute should be made broad enough to give the Industrial Board power to make rules and regulations for light and illumination, both natural and artificial in the different industries. In formulating such rules the Industrial Board would have the power to call in illuminating engineers as experts and it could form voluntary committees of those interested in the subject.

* Bills 18, 19, Appendix I.

We therefore recommend the following amendment to Sec. 81 of the Labor Law:*

> *"All workrooms shall be properly and adequately lighted during working hours. Artificial illuminants in every workroom shall be installed, arranged and used so that the light furnished will, at all times, be sufficient and adequate for the work carried on therein, due regard being given to the prevention of strain on the vision and glare in the eyes of the workers. The industrial board, pursuant to the provisions of this chapter, may make and from time to time change or modify rules and regulations to provide adequate and sufficient natural and artificial lighting facilities in all factories."*

VENTILATION

In our preliminary report we emphasized the importance in factories of proper ventilation. Further investigation merely confirms the total disregard of this subject in most of our factories. Nearly all of the factories inspected were found to rely solely on window ventilation. It is clear that such ventilation is inadequate and in the majority of cases practically useless.

We do not believe that it is practicable to lay down in the statute specific requirements for the general ventilation of factories to be applied to all industries. Conditions in the different industries vary and, as in the case of illumination, we believe that the matter is one that should be left to the Industrial Board, to which should be given the power to make rules and regulations for proper ventilation of factories in the different industries.†

The subject of special ventilation for the removal of dust, gases, and fumes will be considered hereafter in the section of the report dealing with dangerous trades.

WASHING FACILITIES

To secure more adequate washing facilities in factories we would recommend the following amendment to subdivision two of section 88 of the labor law:

> "2. In every factory there shall be provided and maintained for the use of the employees suitable and convenient

* Bill 22, Appendix I.
† Bill 20, Appendix I.

washrooms, *separate for each sex,* adequately equipped with [sinks and proper water service; and] *washing facilities consisting of sinks or stationary basins provided with running water or with tanks holding an adequate supply of clean water. Every washroom shall be provided with means for artificial illumination and with adequate means of ventilation. All washrooms shall be constructed, lighted, ventilated, arranged and maintained according to rules and regulations adopted with reference thereto by the industrial board.**

WATER CLOSET ACCOMMODATIONS

No feature of industrial establishments is so neglected as the toilet accommodations. Their location in a large number of factories is inaccessible. In many cases the toilets are located outside of the buildings and the employees to reach them are required to walk a considerable distance. This condition may in winter and inclement weather result in seriously affecting the health of the employees.

In 186 of the establishments inspected the toilets were located in the yard. In some chemical establishments they were found at a distance of over 150 feet from the central portions of the establishments. In 795 shops the toilets were found in the halls, where, owing to this poor location, they are generally kept in an unsanitary condition.

The type of water closet in use is usually fair although there are still many establishments in which the plumbing was found unfit for use. A number of privies, school sinks, and trough closets were found. In a certain shoddy mill that the Commission visited we found that the owner, a member of the local board of health, had neglected to provide any water closets at all for his employees. The substitute for proper toilet accommodations in that establishment was a wooden barrel located in the sub-cellar.

The light and ventilation of the toilet compartments were found to be inadequate; 26.4% of the water closets were found to have "poor light" and in 16.4% the light was reported as "bad;" 28% of the water closet compartments had poor ventilation and in 17.8% the ventilation was bad.

* Bill 21, Appendix I.

Cleanliness of the water closet compartments was reported as "poor" in 34.2% and as "bad" in 19.2% of the cases.

We found a number of water closet compartments located in the workroom proper with no window opening to the outer air and with no vent duct provided. In many of the factories visited, the number of water closets was entirely inadequate. We therefore make the following provisions for water closets in factories to be incorporated in a new section, section eighty-eight-a of the labor law: *

SEC. 88-a. Water closets. 1. In every factory there shall be provided suitable and convenient water closets separate for each sex, located in such number and in such place or places as required by the rules and regulations of the Industrial Board. All water closets shall be maintained inside of the factory except where, in the opinion of the Commissioner of Labor, it is impracticable to do so.

2. There shall be separate water closet compartments for females, to be used by them exclusively, and notice to that effect shall be painted on the outside of such compartments. The entrance to every water closet used by females shall be effectively screened by a partition or vestibule. Where water closets for males and females are in adjoining compartments, there shall be solid plastered or metal covered partitions between the compartments extending from the floor to the ceiling. Whenever any water closet compartments open directly into the workroom exposing the interior, they shall be screened from view by a partition or a vestibule. The use of curtains for screening purposes is prohibited.

3. The use of any form of trough water closet, latrine or school sink within the factory is prohibited. All such trough water closets, latrines or school sinks shall, before the first day of October, nineteen hundred and fourteen, be completely removed and the place where they were located properly disinfected under the direction of the department of labor. Such appliances shall be replaced by proper individual water closets, placed in water closet compartments, all of which shall be con-

* Bill 21, Appendix I.

structed and installed in accordance with rules and regulations adopted by the industrial board.

4. Every existing water closet and urinal inside the factory shall have a basin of enamelled iron or earthenware, and every such water closet and urinal shall be flushed from a separate water supplied cistern or through a flushometer valve connected in such manner as to keep the water supply of the factory free from contamination. The woodwork enclosing all water closet fixtures shall be removed from the front of the closet and the space underneath the seat shall be left open. The floor or other surface beneath and around the closet shall be maintained in good order and repair, and all the woodwork shall be kept well painted with paint of a light color. All existing water closet compartments shall have windows leading to the outer air and shall be otherwise ventilated in accordance with the rules and regulations adopted for the purpose by the industrial board to the Department of Labor. Such compartments shall be provided with means for artificial illumination, and the enclosure of each compartment shall be kept free from all obscene writing or marking.

5. All water closets, urinals, and water closet compartments hereafter installed in a factory, including those provided to replace existing fixtures, shall be properly constructed, installed, ventilated, lighted and maintained in accordance with such rules and regulations as may be adopted by the industrial board.

6. All water closet compartments, and the floors, walls, ceilings and surface thereof, and all fixtures therein, and all water closets and urinals shall at all times be kept and maintained in a clean and sanitary condition. Where the water supply to water closets or urinals is liable to freeze, the water closet compartment shall be properly heated so as to prevent freezing, or the supply and flush pipes, cisterns and traps and valves shall be effectively covered with wool felt or hair felt, or other adequate covering.

7. All water closets shall be constructed, lighted, ventilated, arranged and maintained according to rules and regulations adopted with reference thereto by the industrial board.

DRESSING ROOMS

The provision of some private room for women is one of the essentials of decency in all occupations where women have to change their clothes, and becomes indispensable in case of sudden illness. Many of the dressing rooms that we inspected were small, dark, and badly ventilated. We recommend the following addition to subdivision three, section eighty-eight of the labor law:*

> *In every factory in which more than ten women are employed, there shall be provided one or more separate dressing rooms in such numbers as required by the rules and regulations of the industrial board and located in such place or places as required by such rules and regulations, having an adequate floor space in proportion to the number of employees, to be fixed by the rules and regulations of the industrial board, but the floor space of every such dressing room shall in no event be less than sixty square feet; each dressing room shall be completely separated from any water closet compartment and shall be provided with adequate means for artificial illumination; each dressing room shall be provided with suitable means for hanging clothes and with a suitable number of seats. All dressing rooms shall be enclosed by means of solid partitions or walls, and shall be constructed, ventilated, lighted and maintained in accordance with such rules and regulations as may be adopted by the industrial board with reference thereto.*

---

* Bill 21, Appendix I.

IX.

ACCIDENT PREVENTION

The table attached of accidents reported to the Labor Department for the year ending September 30, 1912, emphasizes more forcibly than words how much remains to be accomplished by the State, in what is perhaps the most important branch of factory regulation,— the prevention of industrial accidents.*

* Accidents in the chemical industry will be referred to in the next section of the report.

6.—ACCIDENTS REPORTED IN FACTORIES, MINES, QUARRIES AND CONSTRUCTION WORK IN YEAR ENDED SEPTEMBER 30, 1912.

	Industry.	Accident before October 1, 1911, Reported after Nov 1, 1911. Total.	Thereof Fatal.*	Accidents During Year Ending Sept. 30, 1912, Reported Prior to Nov. 1, 1912. Total.	Women.	Thereof. Children under 16.	Fatal cases.*
	(A) FACTORIES.						
I	Stone, clay and glass products	18	....	1,690	46	2	18
II	Metals, machines and conveyances	141	8	30,308	699	53	57
III	Wood manufacturers	32	3	2,470	47	12	8
IV	Leather and rubber goods	12	....	1,864	134	14	4
V	Chemicals, oils, paints, etc	9	....	2,136	73	5	13
VI	Pulp and paper	5	....	1,740	8	1	12
VII	Printing and paper goods	41	....	1,706	444	29	4
VIII	Textiles	10	....	2,413	539	34	13
IX	Clothing, millinery, laundry, etc	12	2	957	355	12	5
X	Food, liquors and tobacco	49	3	3,480	306	13	15
XI	Water, light and power	....	....	1,958	....	3	15
XII	Building industry (shops)	1	....	19	....	....	....
XIII	Miscellaneous	2	2	11	....	....	3
	Total, 1912	332	18	50,752	2,651	178	167
	(B) MINES AND QUARRIES.						
I	Mines	16	....	397	....	....	14
II	Quarries	3	....	337	....	....	13
	Total	19	....	734	....	....	27
	(C) BUILDING AND ENGINEERING.						
I	Excavating	65	8	9,172	....	2	148
	Thereof shafts and tunnels	*8*	....	*4,895*	....	....	*69*
II	Erecting and structural work	81	11	6,680	....	7	75
III	Finishing and furnishing	48	9	2,719	....	1	66
IV	Wrecking	4	2	128	....	....	2
V	Other or miscellaneous	29	3	2,536	....	1	48
	Total	227	33	21,235	....	11	339
	Grand total	578	51	72,721	2,651	189	533

* That is known to be fatal at time of report.

There were 50,752 accidents reported to the Department of Labor in one year for factories alone, 167 resulting in death, and the rest of a more or less serious nature involving loss of time and often permanent injury. Besides these there are many accidents occurring in factories every year that are never reported to the Department of Labor.

How cruel and unnecessary is this yearly waste of human life is clearly demonstrated by experts on the subject, who show that not less than one-third of all the accidents that occur in factories to-day could be avoided if simple, and for the most part inexpensive precautions were taken.

The entire subject of accident prevention was thoroughly discussed by the Employers' Liability Commission of this state in its report to the legislature on April 20, 1911. We shall, therefore, confine ourselves to a number of recommendations for improvements in the existing law, the necessity for which was called to our attention at public hearings and private conferences. These recommendations have practically all received the approval of manufacturers, representatives of labor organizations, and others interested in the subject who appeared before the Commission.

RECOMMENDED CHANGES IN EXISTING LAW FOR THE SAFEGUARDING OF MACHINERY

Every dangerous part of a prime mover whether in motion or not shall be securely safeguarded.

All hydro-extractors shall be covered or otherwise properly guarded when in motion.

All saws shall be provided with a proper and effective guard.

All planers or surfacers shall be protected by a substantial hood or covering.

All hand planers or jointers shall be provided with a proper and effective guard.

All cogs and gearing shall be boxed or encased either with metal or wood.

All belting within seven feet of the floor shall be properly guarded.

All revolving shafting within seven feet of the floors shall be protected on its exposed surface by being encased in such manner as effectively to prevent any part of the body, hair, or clothing of the operators or other persons from coming in contact with such shafting.

All set-screws, keys, bolts, and all parts projecting beyond the surface of revolving shafting shall be countersunk or provided with suitable covering, and machinery of every description shall be properly guarded and provided with proper safety appliances or devices.

All machines, machinery, apparatus, furniture, and fixtures shall be so placed and guarded in relation to one another as to be safe for all persons employed thereabouts.

Lighting of Passageways and Moving Parts of Machinery

Inadequate lighting of passageways in factories and of dangerous moving parts of machinery is a frequent cause of accident. We therefore recommend that all passageways and other portions of a factory, and all moving parts of machinery unless properly and sufficiently guarded, on which or about which persons work or pass or may have to work or pass in emergencies shall be kept properly and sufficiently lighted during working hours.

Industrial Board to Make Rules and Regulations

In addition to the foregoing minimum requirements to be specified in the law itself we recommend that the Industrial Board be given the power to make rules and regulations to govern the installation, position, operation, guarding, and use of machines, and machinery in operation in factories; the furnishing and use of safety devices and safety appliances for machines and machinery, of special clothing and of guards to be worn upon the person; and for any other purpose in order to provide for the prevention of accidents in factories.

In the field of accident prevention the Industrial Board must necessarily play a most important role. There can be no hard and fast legal requirements for the safeguarding of machinery. Each industry has its peculiar problems. The Industrial Board, acting as we have previously outlined in this report, would have the power to make the requirements for the safeguarding of machinery flexible and elastic, so that they might be adapted to the varying conditions in the different industries, and the new types of machines and machinery that are constantly being installed. The method of safeguarding a machine would no longer be left to the whim and caprice of an individual inspector. There would be uniformity of requirements. The manufacturer would know exactly what to do to protect his machinery and the inspector would know definitely what requirements he had the right to insist upon.*

ELEVATORS

A great many elevator accidents occur in factories every year. In the period from 1907 to 1910 the following elevator accidents were reported to the Department of Labor:

Falling down stairs....................	200	Killed	43
Factory elevator accidents...............	1,108	"	106
	1,308		149

The present provisions of the law relating to elevators and elevator shafts are entirely inadequate. We therefore make the following recommendations for the substantial enclosure of hatchways used for freight and passenger elevator purposes, for the protection of employees operating freight elevators, for the enclosure of passenger elevator cars, and for the lighting of all openings leading to elevators.

§ 79. *1. Inclosure of shafts. Every hoistway, hatchway or well-hole used for carrying passengers or employees, or for freight elevators, hoisting or other purpose, shall be protected on all sides at each floor including the basement by substantial vertical inclosures. All openings in such inclosures shall be provided with self-closing gates not less than six feet high or with properly constructed sliding doors. In the case of elevators used for carrying passengers or employees, such inclosures shall be flush with the hatchway and shall extend from floor to ceiling on every open side of the car and on every other side shall be at least six feet high, and such inclosures shall be free from fixed obstructions on every open side of the car. In the case of freight elevators the in-*

* For detailed recommendations on this subject, see Bill 22, Appendix I.

closures shall be flush with the hoistway on every open side of the car. In place of the inclosures herein required for freight elevators, every hatchway used for freight elevator purposes may be provided with trap doors so constructed as to form a substantial floor surface when closed and so arranged as to open and close by the action of the car in its passage both ascending and descending; provided that in addition to such trap doors, the hatchway shall be adequately protected on all sides at all floors, including the basement, by a substantial railing or other vertical inclosure at least three feet in height.

2. Guarding of elevators and hoistways. All counter-weights of every elevator shall be adequately protected by proper inclosures at the top and bottom of the run. The car of all elevators used for carrying passengers or employees shall be substantially enclosed on all sides, including the top, and such cars shall at all times be properly lighted, artificial illuminants to be provided and used when necessary. The entire top of every freight elevator car or platform shall be provided with a substantial grating or covering for the protection of the operator thereof.

3. Elevators and hoistways in factory buildings hereafter erected. The provisions of subdivisions one and two of this section shall apply only to factory buildings heretofore erected. In all factory buildings hereafter erected every elevator and every part thereof and all machinery connected therewith and every hoistway, hatchway and well-hole shall be so constructed, guarded, equipped, maintained and operated as to be safe for all persons using the same.

4. Maintenance of elevators and hoistways in all factory buildings. In every factory building heretofore erected or hereafter erected, all inclosures, doors and gates of hoistways, hatchways or well-holes, and all elevators therein used for the carrying of passengers or employees or freight and the gates and doors thereof shall at all times be kept in good repair and in a safe condition. All openings leading to elevators shall be kept well lighted at all times during working hours, with artificial illumination when necessary. The cable gearing and other apparatus of elevators used for carrying passengers or employees or freight shall be kept in a safe condition.

*5. Powers of industrial board. The industrial board shall have power to make rules and regulations not inconsistent with the provisions of this chapter regulating the construction, guarding, equipment, maintenance and operation of elevators and all parts thereof and all machinery connected therewith and hoistways, hatchways and well-holes in order to carry out the purpose and intention of this section.**

ENFORCEMENT OF LAW

The mere enactment of better laws, and the mere formulation of rules and regulations will not, however, solve the important problem of safety in our factories. We must have an intelligent and efficient administration of those laws and regulations. This involves not only their prompt and effective enforcement but the education of manufacturer and employee to an understanding of the benefits to be derived from compliance with the law and the encouragement of a higher standard of safety than any law can create.

Our inspectors have, for the most part, been woefully inefficient in the enforcement of the law relating to the safeguarding of machinery. In our inspections of factories in different cities of the state we found any number of cases of unguarded dangerous machines and machinery. The inspectors when they enter the service are not trained technical men, and until very recently there has been no safety expert in the Department of Labor to give the field inspectors the benefit of his knowledge and experience.

We believe that the recommendations we have previously made for an increase in the number of inspectors, for the grading and increased salaries of inspectors, for the creation of two inspection districts in the state, and for the formulation of definite rules and regulations by the Industrial Board will soon bring about a marked improvement in the enforcement of this branch of the law.

We urge that after inspectors have entered the department, they receive detailed instruction from time to time in the principles of the safeguarding of machinery, from the mechanical en-

* Bill 23, Appendix I.

gineer of the department in the form of lectures, illustrated bulletins, and manuals.

EDUCATION OF EMPLOYER AND EMPLOYEE

Education more than anything else will bring about the desired results in this field. The true function of the Department of Labor in this most important branch of its work should be that of teacher and guide. It should certainly not be limited to that of police officer. Bulletins should be issued for distribution among the manufacturers and employees showing the methods of safeguarding machinery and illustrating the different safety devices and appliances. Reports of serious accidents, their causes and methods of prevention should be sent out from time to time.

We do not wish to underestimate the value of complete and accurate statistics, but statistics in themselves are of little value to the average manufacturer. He wants those statistics interpreted for him, preferably in the form of concrete cases. Manufacturers and employees should be encouraged to make to the Department of Labor suggestions for the safeguarding of machinery and these suggestions should be incorporated in the department's bulletin. The experts of the department may very easily in the course of their visits to different cities give lectures on accident prevention and safety devices, and be consulted by manufacturers.

The department should make it clear that the prevention of accidents is not only a humanitarian instinct but is a sound business method. It pays both employer and employee in dollars and cents.

There is a great deal for the department to do in this branch of its activities. The people of the state in return for the increased facilities they have given the department will demand immediate results in the matter of the prevention of industrial accidents and we hope that the department will prove equal to the task.

WORKMEN'S COMPENSATION LAW

We have made no special study of this subject but we feel that the report of any commission which has investigated general factory conditions is not complete without a strong and earnest plea for the enactment of a proper and just workmen's compensation law, that will place the burden of an industrial accident on the industry as represented by the employer rather than on the unfortunate victim of the industry, and that will provide just and fair compensation to workers or their families for death or injury caused by accident in the course of employment.

X.

DANGEROUS TRADES

One of the most important industrial problems of the day is the protection of factory workers from industrial poisoning and occupational diseases. There are in many industries specific dangers connected with the trade which create certain pathological conditions to which much of the ill-health and premature death of workers are due. Investigations made in European countries show the large variety and number of diseases directly attributable to occupational hazards.

From the beginning of its inquiry the Commission has made a special study of industrial poisoning. In 1911 an investigation was made into lead and arsenic poisoning in New York City in which one hundred cases of lead poisoning were described and their origin in nearly every instance traced to industrial establishments. As a result of this investigation the Commission submitted to the last legislature a bill providing for hot and cold water washing facilities where poisonous substances were used or generated in the process of manufacture, prohibiting the eating of meals in workrooms in which such poisonous substances were generated, and providing for separate lunch rooms in such establishments. This bill was passed and has become a law.

In 1912 the Commission conducted the following investigations:

1. General conditions in the chemical industry.

2. Dangers to workers in the manufacture and use of commercial acids.

3. Further study of lead poisoning in various up-state factories.

4. The production, refining and use of wood alcohol and its dangers.

5. Study of diseases of the ear and upper respiratory tract among workers in the ostrich feather, fur, and cordage industries.

THE CHEMICAL INDUSTRY

The investigations in the chemical industry covered 142 establishments in which there were 359 separate factories, and in which 11,087 wage earners were employed.

In no other industry are perils to the body and dangers to the health of the workers so many, so insidious, and so deadly as in the chemical industry. The workers come in direct, close, and daily contact with lead, arsenic, mercury, phosphorus, and other powerful poisons. Injurious gases and harmful fumes are generated in many of the various processes. Irritating dusts, excessively high temperatures and burning or spurting liquids are to be found in most of the factories. Yet there is hardly an industry in the United States in which there is less protection to the health and welfare of the workers. In European countries the chemical industry is carefully regulated. There they have special rules and regulations for the control of working conditions in the industry that are designed to safeguard the lives of the workers; but in this country we are just awakening to the dangers of this industry and to the necessity for resorting to every possible safe guard to protect the lives of the workers in it.

The general sanitary conditions in the establishments inspected were found to be poor. The washing facilities were inadequate, toilets unclean, and in many cases located a considerable distance from the factory building proper.

The special dangers to the workers found in the chemical trade may be summed up as follows: Gases, fumes, poisonous dusts, and accidental injuries. Where in other trades a poisonous ingredient is used occasionally and poisonous gas and fumes are generated at intervals, in the chemical trade they are regularly present in most of the working processes.

In no other industry is a knowledge of the poisonous substances which are handled, so necessary to the worker; but in no other industry is the ignorance of the worker as to the character of daily substances with which he works, so complete.

Constant contact with dangerous elements in the trade and daily familiarity with them breeds a consequent contempt on the part of the employers and workers, and a recklessness and carelessness which result yearly in countless numbers of cases of disease, accident, and death.

Repeatedly our inspectors found men handling poisonous materials such as paris green and carbonate of lead with less thought than if these dangerous substances were sand or flour. In some of the factories visited, although the faces and clothes of the workers and all exposed parts of their bodies were thickly covered with poisonous dusts or colors, they took not the least precaution against ingesting or inhaling these materials. In one plant that manufactured paris green, workers were found handling and packing this poisonous material, some without gloves and all without respirators. The manufacture of bleaches and bleach powders is fraught with many dangers to the workers, but it is without any official supervision or protection of the workers. The English alkali act makes special and detailed provisions for the control of this industry and the protection of its workers; the amount of free chlorine gas in the air of the bleach chamber, the time a worker may stay therein and many other details of this branch of the trade are minutely described and the strictest supervision is maintained.

Dust

Dusty processes are common to many industries and the dangers of dust as a predisposing cause to tuberculosis and other respiratory diseases are not confined to the chemical trade. The problem of dust elimination is one of the most important in industrial hygiene. The dust in chemical works is especially dangerous, owing to the fact that it is mostly of mineral origin; it is often poisonous and produces not only the irritating effects of ordinary dusts but also the toxic effects of the poison. In almost all chemical establishments a profusion of dust is created in the various grinding and packing departments.

The Commission personally visited one of the principal carborundum factories in the state. Although the manufacture of carborundum is not strictly a chemical process, the dust in some of the rooms was so great as to hide even the form of the workers from view.*

* Since the visit of the Commission this plant has installed a ventilating system at the cost of several thousands of dollars.

Temperature

In many of the chemical establishments, extremely high temperatures are created and the furnaces are in constant use. The work in front of the furnaces and at short distances from them is, therefore, very exhausting. The temperature in one place near the furnace was said by the superintendent of the factory to be between 120° and 140° F., and the heat and glare were so overpowering that the men had to kneel and stoop and hold something over their eyes in order to continue their work.

COMMERCIAL ACIDS

Under the direction of Dr. Charles F. McKenna a special study was made for the Commission of the dangers to workers in the manufacture and use of commercial acids. The general conditions in acid works were examined and the manufacture of the principal acids such as sulphuric, nitric, acetic, hydrochloric, hydrofluoric, and hydrocyanic was investigated.

The manufacture of acids is associated in the mind of the general public with notions of great hazard to life and health. This idea is due largely to the mystery surrounding the processes and substances involved. In many acid works the conditions and often the substances themselves are incapable of causing serious dangers or producing any special disease. Yet it is true that this industry when viewed generally presents hazards for its workmen which are terrifying and unnecessarily numerous. Workmen in these trades are still to-day too lightly exposed to danger, too carelessly supervised, and hence, far too often injured. Particularly is this true where the influences are insidious and noticeable only as the result of careful observation. In these situations, occupational diseases come slowly but none the less surely.

Classified statistics in the chemical industries furnishing data to expose the hygienic state of acid works, are entirely wanting. Mortality from insidious cases cannot be traced. Accidents are not all reported and investigations of reported cases are rarely made, and, if made, do not find their way into the public printed records.

ACCIDENTS

In this state there are no special regulations for the chemical trades, with their peculiar hazards. The result is that the accident rate in this industry is much greater in New York State than in England, Germany, and France. Most of these accidents are the result of carelessness. It is almost impossible to go into any acid plant without finding that risks exist from half-concealed openings, unguarded stairways, slippery floors, uncovered and improperly guarded vats, improperly supported conduits used for carrying corrosive liquids. A striking example was witnessed by the Commission while inspecting a manufactory of caustic potash. Liquid caustic was being sent through several sections of a shallow, iron trough, these sections being supported by several wooden blocks at the junctions. The process was carried on in a dimly lighted place. The workmen frequently passed under the trough without any thought apparently that the dislodgment of one of these blocks might mean instant death by downpour of the burning liquid. The man in charge, when asked why this was permitted, simply shrugged his shoulders and said that the men knew that it was dangerous — so he made no effort to stop them.

LEAD POISONING

The investigation of lead poisoning commenced in 1911 was supplemented in 1912 by a study of conditions in up-state plants in which lead was used in the process of manufacture, by Dr. Charles T. Graham-Rogers of the Department of Labor.

Dr. Rogers' investigations showed that there was the same lack of precautions to prevent lead poisoning as had been found in New York City. In a number of plants which the Commission inspected, practically no precautions were taken to prevent this disease. In a large lead battery plant most of the workers in the foundry were seen handling the lead without gloves or other protection from the dust. Among the workers were a number of boys between 16 and 18 years. Upon inquiry they asserted that they had received no instructions as to the dangers involved. There was no hot water for washing the hands, nor any special lunch room for their use. One pot in which lead was being heated was without any hood and discharged its poisonous fumes into the workroom. Many cases of acute and chronic lead poisoning were traced to this plant by our investigators.

Lead poisoning can be prevented in nearly every case if very simple precautions are taken to guard against the disease. Yet case after case of lead poisoning has been called to the attention of the Commission due to a disregard of the most elementary principles of personal hygiene.

Dr. Rogers in his report has made some valuable suggestions for requirements in industries in which lead is prepared or used. We do not believe, however, that it is advisable to incorporate these in a statute but recommend that they be used by the Industrial Board as the basis of detailed and comprehensive rules and regulations for the prevention of lead poisoning in the various affected industries.

WOOD ALCOHOL

The steadily increasing number of cases of poisoning by wood alcohol reported in recent years made it advisable for the Commission to investigate the conditions under which wood alcohol is prepared, refined, and used in different industries and the dangers to which workers coming in contact with it in its different forms are subjected.

There are two main aspects of the wood alcohol problem.

1. The drinking of wood alcohol and its use in liquors, extracts, and drugs.

2. The inhalation of its vapors when it is prepared and refined and used in various processes in different industries, and the inhalation of its fumes in varnish preparations.

With the first aspect of the problem this Commission is not directly concerned. The only solution of it is the education of the public to a fuller appreciation of the dangers involved in the use of wood alcohol in any form for internal purposes and the more effective enforcement of the present provisions of the law prohibiting the use of wood alcohol in any food, flavoring, extract, or liquid capable of being used in whole or in part as a beverage or internally as a medicine (Sec. 201 of the Agricultural Law of N. Y.).

The Commission is deeply interested, however, in the second aspect of the problem, *i. e.,* the danger of wood alcohol in industry. Within the past year four deaths and four cases of blindness have been reported to the state labor department caused by the inhalation of wood alcohol fumes from varnish used to shellac the interior of beer vats and for coating lead pencils.

Scope of the Commission's Investigation

The investigation into this subject was carried on under the direction of Dr. Charles Baskerville, Professor of Chemistry of The College of the City of New York, who rendered his services without compensation and whose detailed and comprehensive report is set forth in Appendix VI.

Forty-five establishments were inspected covering three general types: (1) Those in which crude wood alcohol is produced by the destructive distillation of wood. (2) Those in which the crude product is refined. (3) Those in which wood alcohol is used generally as a solvent.

The dangers to the workmen engaged either in the production or refinement of crude wood alcohol are not very great. Many of the processes are carried on in closed chambers and proper ventilation is invariably provided. In such establishments the dangers are clearly recognized and are guarded against.

Wood alcohol is used also in different forms and quantities in a large number of industries, the most important being the manufacture of hats, electrical apparatus, furniture, pianos, organs, and in the painting industry.

The workers in many places where wood alcohol was used were found to be affected with eye trouble, headaches, and affections of the skin.

The dangers to the workers are due to exposure to the vapor of the alcohol and to constant contact of the liquid with the skin. Such dangers are not inherent in the nature of the processes involved and could be avoided by the application of comparatively simple precautionary methods. Through neglect and indifference and in many cases because of ignorance of the injurious effects of wood alcohol no precautions are taken to protect the workers from its toxic influences.

Girls are employed in processes in which wood alcohol is used and it is essential that they be properly protected from these injurious effects. Practically all of the dangers connected with the use of wood alcohol in industry could be obviated by the provision and maintenance of ample ventilation and by giving instructions to the workers of the dangers connected with its use.

RECOMMENDATIONS

Laws for the protection of workers in dangerous trades, and for the prevention of industrial poisoning and diseases should be drawn recognizing that conditions in the industries affected are constantly changing, that long-settled practices are being abandoned and new processes and new substances are constantly coming into use.

A state legislature can hardly be expected to take up and thoroughly test at each session the new problems of the year in the hygienic control of dangerous trades. The conditions in many industries vary so greatly and the factors affecting the health and safety of the workers are so dissimilar not only in these industries, but in different parts of the same establishment that no general laws can be enacted which would be applicable to all industries and all establishments and which would cover adequately the many elements of danger and hazardous processes in them. Each industry and each process must be studied separately in order to determine its danger. Any law enacted on this subject should be general in application and the Industrial Board should be empowered to make specific rules and regulations. Great Britain has adopted this plan successfully. The Industrial Board would have the power to consult experts and to form voluntary committees. Very soon a comprehensive set of rules and regulations covering dangerous trades and the prevention of occupational diseases would be enacted which could be augmented or modified as conditions required.

The division of industrial hygiene and the section of medical inspection recommended in the first portion of this report will make the necessary technical inspections in these trades and as a result of their investigations, will be able to submit to the Industrial Board recommendations for rules and regulations to be adopted for the protection of the health and safety of the workers.

Industrial Board to Make Rules and Regulations for Dangerous Trades

We recommend therefore the enactment of the following law:

§ 97. Dangerous trades. Whenever the industrial board shall find, as a result of its investigations, that any industry, trade or occupation by reason of the nature of the materials used therein or the products thereof or by reason of the methods or processes or machinery or apparatus employed therein or by reason of any other matter or thing connected with such industry, trade or occupation, contains such elements of danger to the lives, health or safety of persons employed therein as to require special regulation for the protection of such persons, said board shall have power to make such special rules and regulations as it may deem necessary to guard against such elements of danger by establishing requirements as to temperature, humidity, the removal of dusts, gases or fumes and requiring licenses to be applied for and issued by the commissioner of labor as a condition of carrying on any such industry, trade or occupation and requiring medical inspection and supervision of persons employed and applying for employment and by other appropriate means.*

This proposed bill would give the Industrial Board full power over the licensing of dangerous trades, the medical supervision of the employees, the removal of dust, gases, and fumes and would enable the board to make special rules and regulations based upon expert investigation and opinion, for the different industries involved.

Special Ventilation

The importance of special ventilation in these industries can hardly be overestimated. Ample provision should be made at all times for the removal of dust, gases, and fumes injurious to the health of the workers so as to prevent their inhalation by the workers. We therefore recommend that the following subdivisions be added to section eighty-six of the labor law:

2. *If dust, gases, fumes, vapors, fibers or other impurities are generated or released in the course of the business carried*

* Bill 24, Appendix I.

on in any workroom of a factory, in quantities tending to injure the health of the operatives, the person, persons, company or corporation operating the factory, whether as owner or lessee of the whole or of a part of the building in which the same is situated, or otherwise, shall provide suction devices that shall remove said impurities from the workroom, at their point of origin where practicable, by means of proper hoods connected to conduits and exhaust fans of sufficient capacity to remove such impurities, and such fans shall be kept running constantly while such impurities are being generated or released. If, owing to the nature of the manufacturing process carried on in a factory workroom, excessive heat be created therein the person or persons operating the factory as aforesaid shall provide, maintain, use and operate such special means or appliances as may be required to reduce such excessive heat.

3. *The industrial board shall have power to make rules and regulations not inconsistent with the provisions of this chapter regulating ventilation, temperature and humidity in factories and the special means, if any, required for removing impurities or for reducing excessive heat, and the machinery, apparatus or appliances to be used for any of said purposes, and the construction, equipment, maintenance and operation thereof in order to effectuate the purposes of this section.**

Covering of Vats

For the prevention of accidents due to uncovered and unguarded vats we recommend that the following provision be inserted in § 81 of the labor law:

"Every vat and pan wherever set so that the opening or top thereof is at a lower level than the elbow of the operator or operators at work about the same shall be protected by a cover which shall be maintained over the same while in use in such manner as to effectually prevent such operators or other persons falling therein or coming in contact therewith, except that where it is necessary to remove such cover while any such vat or pan is in use, such vat or pan shall be protected by an adequate railing around the same."†

* Bill 20, Appendix I.
† Bill 22, Appendix I.

Labeling of Containers of Wood Alcohol

We recommend an amendment to the public health law to the effect that all bottles or vessels used for transporting or selling products containing wood alcohol shall be required to bear a prominent display label stating that they contain poison and calling attention to the danger of working with the material without ample ventilation.*

Educational Work

The opportunities for educational work in this field are unlimited. In most cases the employees and in very many cases the employers are ignorant of the dangers involved in their industries. The Department of Labor should issue bulletins calling attention to the injurious elements in an industry and the precautions to be taken to guard against them. Such bulletins should be printed in the language of the employees and distributed among them.

---

* Bill 27, Appendix I.

XI.

FOUNDRIES AND EMPLOYMENT OF WOMEN IN CORE ROOMS

FOUNDRIES

The necessity for marked improvement in sanitary conditions in the iron, steel, and brass foundries of the state is unquestioned. The occupation is an arduous one. The workers are subjected in the course of the day to extremes of temperature. They are constantly exposed to the inhalation of mineral and metallic dust. The result is that the workers in this industry are peculiarly susceptible to all forms of respiratory diseases, kidney trouble, and rheumatism.

There are no official vital statistics of foundry workers in this country. The recorded industrial insurance mortality statistics show, however, an excessive mortality rate from consumption among foundry workers, which becomes marked between the ages of twenty-five and thirty-four,— a time when the workers are in the very prime of life. Moreover, the liability to accident in a foundry is great.

The statistical data available, considered in conjunction with careful observation of working conditions, show that employment in this industry is more or less injurious to health. All reasonable measures calculated to promote greater safety and health for employees in foundries should not only be insisted upon by the state, but should be welcomed by the foundry owners themselves.

Legislation for the improvement of conditions in foundries is not special or class legislation. We have on the statute books to-day special requirements for bakeries, laundries, mercantile establishments, and places where poisonous materials are used in the process of manufacture.

A foundry is in many respects unlike the ordinary factory. It presents different conditions for which special provision should be made.

The measures to be enacted for the improvement of working conditions in foundries have received the Commission's careful consideration. We visited a number of foundries and took the testimony of foundry owners and representatives of molders' organizations in the different cities of the state in which we held public hearings. Some of the employees in foundries testified before the Commission in executive session. The Commission then incorporated in a tentative bill the recommendations that had been received from different sources and copies of the proposed bill were sent to foundry owners and representatives of molders' organizations throughout the state for their suggestions and criticisms.

On November 25th, 1912, a public hearing was held in Albany to consider the proposed foundry bill and to receive suggestions for remedial legislation from all those interested. The hearing was largely attended. The Commissioner of the National Founders' Association appeared not only on behalf of the seventy-eight members of his organization in the state of New York, but as the authorized representative of a large number of other foundry owners in the state who did not belong to that organization. There were also present about twenty foundry owners and the same number of representatives of molders' unions.

We were impressed by the attitude taken by the foundry owners as a whole, concerning the advantages of improvement in working conditions in their establishments. The Commissioner of the National Association of Founders said:

> "I have been devoting considerable of my time in endeavoring to get the foundry owners throughout the country to bring about better working conditions which go far beyond anything you have suggested in these measures * * * It is a business proposition cutting out the philanthropy and all that sort of thing."

A very conservative foundry owner who was present stated:

> "We believe the most efficiency is obtained by men who are surrounded by good conditions and who are in well heated rooms free from gas, dust, and smoke, and furnished with water, good washing and bathing facilities."

These statements reflect a new attitude on the part of manufacturers that is everywhere appearing in the state of New York, and one that is full of promise for the future. We have carefully considered all of the suggestions and criticisms that were made at the hearings in Albany and in other cities of the state and as a result submit the following recommendations.

HEATING OF FOUNDRIES AND PREVENTION OF DRAFTS

In a great many of the foundries no provision is made for heating the foundry in cold weather. The result is that the worker is subjected to extremes of temperature and is exposed to cold often while in a perspiring condition.

Anyone who has ever been in a foundry will recognize the necessity for the requirement that entrances to the foundry shall be so constructed and maintained as to minimize drafts. Doors should be kept vestibuled so that cold outer air will not blow upon the overheated molder.

It is recommended, therefore, that all foundries shall be properly and sufficiently heated during cold weather and that entrances to foundries shall be so constructed and maintained as to minimize drafts and that all windows therein shall be maintained in proper condition and repair.

PROPER VENTILATION

From the nature of the business there must be smoke and dust and gases in a foundry. This fact only emphasizes, however, the necessity for a prompt and effective removal of these deleterious substances. Where necessary, a forced system of ventilation with exhaust fans of sufficient capacity and power should be required.

Conditions so far as ventilation is concerned can never be ideal in a foundry, but every possible precaution should be taken to minimize the danger from dust which, as statistics show, renders the foundry worker very susceptible to pulmonary troubles.

The milling and cleaning of castings in a foundry will be considered later in this report.

MEASURES TO PREVENT ACCIDENTS

Accidents in foundries are of frequent occurrence. They are caused mainly by the following conditions:

1. Inadequate lighting.
2. Narrow and obstructed gangways.

During casting time when the molder is carrying the ladles of heated molten lead these narrow and obstructed gangways constitute an element of special danger and are the cause of many serious burns.

3. Defective ladles, tongs, chains, and other lifting devices.

For the prevention of accidents the Commission therefore makes the following recommendations:

1. All foundries shall be properly lighted during working hours.

2. The gangways in foundries shall be constructed and maintained of sufficient width to make the use thereof by employees reasonably safe, and such gangways during the progress of casting shall not be obstructed in any way.

3. The flasks, molding machines, ladles, cranes, and apparatus for transporting molten metal in foundries shall be maintained in proper condition and repair.

WASHING FACILITIES

Workers in foundries are exposed to a great deal of dust. The cores and molds are made of sand and after a day's toil, health and decency require that the worker be afforded every opportunity to cleanse himself and to change his working clothes.

Although recognizing the advisability of having adequate washing facilities in a foundry, many foundry owners have called attention to the fact that installation of these often involves useless expense, because the men will not use them. In some cases this is undoubtedly true, but it will often be found that the failure to use the washing facilities is due to the fact that those furnished are inadequate or that they are placed in remote or inaccessible parts of the building. Sometimes they consist of troughs to be used by the workmen in common, an arrangement that is plainly objectionable and not conducive to habits of cleanliness. But simply because some workers will not use the washing facilities is no reason for saying that they should not be supplied. The workers should be encouraged to use them by the manufacturer and by the factory inspector. The education of the worker will soon bring him to an understanding of the benefits coming from habits of personal cleanliness.

Special requirements for washing facilities, it was felt, should not apply to small foundries in which less than ten persons are employed, since the expense of their installation in such cases would practically be prohibitive. These small foundries are, however, subject to the general requirements of the factory law.

PASSAGEWAYS TO OUTSIDE WATER CLOSETS

In many foundries the water closets are some distance from the foundries, and the workers, in order to use them, are obliged to go out in the cold and often inclement weather while they are perspiring and overheated.

The Commissioner of Labor testified before the Commission:

> "I have never been in a foundry yet where the men do not perspire rather freely and it is a very serious thing to require these men to go out into the open air while in the heat of their work. The condition of their bodies is such as to make it very hazardous to go out into the open air, though they cover themselves with a coat."

The workers in such cases should be protected against the elements. Where water closets or privy accommodations are permitted by the Commissioner of Labor to remain outside of the foundry, the passageway leading from the foundry to the water closets should be so protected and constructed that the employees in passing back and forth should not be exposed to the outdoor atmosphere, and the water closets themselves should be properly heated during cold weather.

MILLING AND CLEANING OF CASTINGS

The foregoing requirements were practically all approved by the foundry owners as a whole. The tentative bill contained a provision that the milling and cleaning of castings should be done in rooms that were not used for any other purpose. To this requirement serious objections were offered. It was asserted that in many cases this would require a substantial change in structural conditions and that the requirement would work hardship, particularly where the foundry owner had provided a system of tumbling mills for the cleaning of castings, with a connecting exhaust system. It was also asserted that it would be impossible to clean large castings in a separate room.

Devices such as canvas curtains, and temporary partitions were called to the attention of the Commission as easy and inexpensive means of complying with the requirement. We believe, therefore, that no hard and fast rule should be made and that in a great many cases a mandatory requirement for the milling and cleaning of castings in a separate room irrespective of conditions, would work unnecessary hardship.

The matter should be left to the Industrial Board to make rules and regulations that would meet the varying conditions in different foundries. We wish to emphasize, however, the necessity for providing every possible device for the removal of dust during the cleaning process, so as to prevent its inhalation by the worker. The constant inhalation of this dust is a predisposing cause to tuberculosis and accounts to a great degree for the high death rate in that disease among foundry workers.*

EMPLOYMENT OF WOMEN IN CORE ROOMS

There are about 300 women employed in core rooms of foundries in this state. They have been drawn into the industry to take the place of boys under eighteen who had previously done this work and in some cases they have supplanted men also. The work that the women do at present is limited to the making of small cores. The women stand for the most part all day long. Although seats are provided they are rarely used because the work is not adapted to a sitting posture.

The core makers are exposed to dust, both metallic and mineral. The core ovens are generally located in the same room in which the women make the cores. The heat from the ovens is

* Bill 25, Appendix I.

enervating and the women inhale the core gas which arises from the ovens and the baked cores.

Even where there are exhaust systems over the ovens, considerable gas escapes into the room as the Commission noticed in one of the foundries visited. Core gas irritates the mucous membranes of the eyes, nose, throat, and bronchial passages, and causes nausea and headache.

The cores are placed in the ovens by men. In some places they are carried to the ovens, from the place in which they are made, by the women. In others, men or boys do this carrying.

The wages that women receive are on an average about $8 a week. Most of these women are piece workers. It was testified that men would receive almost three times as much for the work.

There are no satisfactory vital statistics for women core makers. No official statistics exist, but very limited industrial insurance statistics show an excessive death rate from consumption among core makers between fifteen and forty-four years of age.

The injurious effects of the work are minimized because of the fact that the women do not as general rule continue to work in the industry for more than four or five years.

Most of the women are of foreign birth though a fair number, principally in the smaller cities, are American. According to the testimony given by the foundry owners, women are employed on small cores, because first, it is difficult to secure the services of boys for that purpose; and second, the women are handier, more skillful, and more regular in their work on small cores.

FOUNDRY NO PLACE FOR WOMEN

The foundry is no place for women. The work is arduous and the surroundings are bad. We believe that it would have been far better if women had never been originally allowed to enter this employment.

There are to-day, however, about three hundred women earning a livelihood from this work upon which they are dependent for their support. Many of these have appealed to the Commission not to deprive them of what they, in small country towns, consider their only means of earning a living.

We cannot say that work in a core room as such, is under all circumstances and conditions absolutely detrimental to a woman's health. Although we should like to see this work stopped, and believe that its suppression would be beneficial to the race, and although we know that such a course of action would in no way injure the foundry industry of the state, nevertheless we cannot at this time recommend an entire prohibition of work that would result in throwing the three hundred women now in the industry out of employment. We believe that work by women in core rooms should be strictly confined to its present limits, and should be gradually eliminated. It should be discouraged and ultimately suppressed. Every obstacle should be thrown in the way of its increase and expansion.

For the present, the law should require this work by women to be done under the most sanitary conditions. No woman should be permitted to make cores in the same room in which cores are made by men. No woman should be permitted to make cores in the same room in which the core oven is located. The partition separating the room in which the women are employed from the core oven should be a substantial structure extending to the ceiling and the openings in the partition should be so arranged as to prevent any gas from the ovens from escaping into the room in which the women work.

The Industrial Board should be given the power to regulate the size of the cores that women shall be permitted to make and the weights that they shall be permitted to carry, and generally to make rules and regulations to safeguard the health of the women in this employment. If it is impracticable, as some of the foundry owners have testified, to separate the room in which the women are employed from the core oven by a substantial partition, so as prevent the core-gas from escaping into the room in which the women work, these owners should cease to employ women in work never intended for them. We have no sympathy for the foundry owner who appeared before us and said that so far as work in the core room was concerned, there should be no distinction as to sex.

In this enlightened age very few will be deceived by any such fallacy. Nature itself has made the distinction which the foundry owner has said should not be made. Instincts of chivalry and decency as well as concern for the preservation of the race, demand that we should not permit women to engage in work detrimental to their health, that overtaxes their strength, and impairs their vitality as wives and mothers.

The Commission has received descriptions of the abuses that the employment of women in core rooms has led to in other states. We have been told that the cores on which women originally began to work were of a small size but that to-day the women are making cores with a rammer and the size of these cores is such that they have to be hoisted by a derrick.

We believe if our recommendations are carried into effect and are enforced in the spirit which we intend, that not only will the work by women in the core rooms be confined to what it is to-day and that too under improved sanitary conditions, but that in a few years such work will be completely done away with.

We have gone into the matter very fully because we believe that our views on this subject represent the sentiment of the times. We believe that these opinions are shared generally by the people of the state who do not wish to see their women employed at manual labor in foundries.

We recommend that such work be restricted, and that where it does take place, it be conducted under the most sanitary conditions. We hope that ultimately, with the co-operation of enlightened foundry owners, it will be entirely done away with.

We therefore make the following recommendations for remedial legislation:*

1. The prohibition of the employment of women and men core makers in the same room.

2. The prohibition of the employment of women at making cores in the same room in which the core ovens are located.

3. Authority to the Industrial Board to make rules and regulations governing the size of the cores that women shall be permitted to make, and the weights that they shall carry.

4. Authority to the Industrial Board to make rules and regulations generally that shall safeguard the health of the women employed in the core rooms.

* Bill 26, Appendix I.

XII.

EMPLOYMENT OF WOMEN AND CHILDREN IN MERCANTILE ESTABLISHMENTS

When the Commission was continued by the legislature in 1912, its powers were broadened to include an investigation of mercantile establishments. Attention had been drawn to the fact that thousands of women and children were employed in these establishments and that no study had been made by the state of their conditions of labor. The Commission therefore undertook a special inquiry into the department stores and five and ten cent stores of the state, which was carried on during the months of November and December, 1912. Four investigators were engaged in the field work. Practically all department stores employing ten or more women and children were covered in Greater New York, and as far as possible in Buffalo and Rochester, and in the six cities of the second class: Yonkers, Albany, Troy, Utica, Syracuse, and Schenectady. Owing to the need of limiting the study to stores employing at least ten persons, a very large number of small neighborhood stores with fewer than ten employees was necessarily omitted.

Two hundred and sixteen (216) establishments in all, were inspected. They vary in size from the largest New York City department stores each employing several thousand employees to the chain of small five and ten-cent stores which extends across the whole state. One-third of the entire number of establishments visited were five and ten-cent stores. Most of these employ less than fifty persons and none have more than two hundred (200) employees. The department stores proper have a far larger labor force under their roofs; thirty employ more than five hundred (500) persons, eighteen have over one thousand (1,000) employees, and nine have over two thousand (2,000).

NUMBER OF STORES AND NUMBER OF EMPLOYEES

	Department Stores.			Five and Ten-Cent. Stores.			Grand
	New York.	Up State.	Total.	New York.	Up State.	Total.	Total.
No. of stores	83	62	145	48	23	71	216
No. of employees	47,280	12,278	59,558	1,195	964	2,159	61,717
No. of women	29,067	7,583	36,650	980	755	1,735	38,385
No. of children	2,655	1,070	3,725	17	4	21	3,746
Percentage of total employees:							
Women	61.5	61.8	61.5	82	78.3	80.3	62.2
Children	5.6	8.7	6.3	1.4	.4	1.0	6.1

The total number of workers concerned in both groups is far greater than the number of establishments would lead one to expect, for it amounts to the significant figure of 61,717. The women number 38,385 or 62%, and the children number only 3,746 or 6% of the total. Since these figures were collected during the "rush" season before Christmas, they represent approximately the maximum number employed in these establishments at any time of the year.

On account of the short time available and the wide field of the inquiry it was necessary to confine this brief investigation to a few specific points. They were, in general: 1. Physical conditions of work; 2. Length of hours; 3. Wages and earnings. It should be noted that a large majority of the employees — 68% — were women and children. It was therefore appropriate that this preliminary investigation should concern itself exclusively with them. By limiting the study to this scope, we have been able to collect information immediately concerning the physical welfare of over 40,000 workers.

Unfortunately these cannot be enumerated according to their ages. The children (14 to 16 years) form a class by themselves. But the records of most of the stores do not enable us to classify the female employees above 16 years of age, even to differentiate those below from those above 21 years of age. It is known, however, from other sources that workers in department stores are very young. The United States Census of 1900 states that "three-fifths of the total number of saleswomen 16 years of age and over are under 25 years of age." These data were collected in 1900, over a decade ago, and the figures of the last census are not yet published. In the present inquiry time did not suffice to make a detailed enumeration of all female employees by age groups. But there is every reason to believe that the same large proportion of youthful workers still persists.

THE ORGANIZATION OF THE DEPARTMENT STORE

The organization of the modern department store is highly complex. No inquiries were made as to the store officials such as managers, buyers, etc. According to a rough classification, the rank and file of the women and children employees were, for the purpose of our inquiry, subdivided into five classes: 1. The saleswomen and floor help (including floor cashiers and wrappers); 2. Office and audit help; 3. Stock girls; 4. Packers and shippers; 5. Mail order clerks.

NUMBER AND PER CENT OF WOMEN AND CHILDREN ACCORDING TO DEPARTMENTS

	No.	% of all women
1. Saleswomen	24,234	66.1
2. Office help	5,757	15.7
3. Stock girls	4,386	12.
4. Packers and Shippers	1,382	3.8
5. Mail Order Clerks	891	2.4
Total in Department Stores	36,650	100.

Although these subdivisions may not be sharply defined in every store, for all practical purposes they correspond to the divisions of the work.

The largest percentage, 66% of all women employed, are saleswomen. The office help is next in numbers, namely, 16%. It includes audit girls, bookkeepers and cashiers, also the pneumatic tube girls who act as change makers. The stock girls constitute 12%. They bring stock to the counters and keep it in order. They are later advanced to be saleswomen. The packers and shippers make up nearly 4% of all women employed. There are only 2% of mail order clerks.

The proportion of children, 6% of all employees, is decreasing from year to year owing to the introduction of mechanical substitutes, such as the pneumatic tube systems. Nearly half of the stores employ no children at all, but they are still retained in some of the largest stores for messenger service and the like. Eleven stores were found to employ more than one hundred (100) children each.

CONDITIONS OF WORK

The girl who works in a department store has, in some respects, more attention paid to her physical welfare than any other class of employees. In the large establishments of the first-class cities, for instance, the sanitary conveniences, such as toilets and wash-rooms, are generally clean, adequate and kept in good repair. Our inspectors reported that 85% in all stores were in excellent or fair condition. Lunch and recreation rooms are supplied, and, besides medical care, a hospital room in charge of a nurse is often provided, where the girls are treated free of charge.

But such expensive care is given only to the employees of the largest establishments. The women and children in the smaller stores are not so well provided.

Merchants realize that any illness or even physical discomfort interferes at once with the efficiency of a saleswoman. It is therefore to their interest to supply these women with as comfortable surroundings as possible. Though these provisions are made, the physical and nervous strain of the work is often overlooked or minimized. Rest rooms, medical care, and other elaborate welfare features can at best only repair the damage done in the course of the work. They should not obscure the need for avoiding rather than relieving the effects of the fundamental hardships of the occupation.

Employment in a department store is commonly supposed to be light and easy work compared with that in a factory. But according to the workers themselves it is far more exhausting than seems to be the case. The girl behind the counter is subjected to peculiar strain; she must always be neat in appearance and on her best behavior; she is always on duty and has to preserve an even temper in meeting the tastes and whims of customers of all kinds.

Long hours of standing, close attention to customers, and poor ventilation are characteristic of the occupation for the main body of employees, the saleswomen. Constant standing is the greatest hardship. A saleswoman has to be on her feet practically the whole day. She is able to sit down for only a few moments at infrequent intervals. In the busiest hours of the day, in the rush season preceding Christmas, and whenever special sales are held, there is almost no opportunity to rest. In fact, the testimony of many girls proves that on some days they are unable to sit down at all.

When a girl works behind a counter, she can occasionally lean against the stock case for rest. But the girl who stands at an aisle counter or at a table, must endure the continued strain practically unrelieved all day. Almost without exception they complain of the extreme discomfort and fatigue that results from continuous standing. Swollen and aching feet and broken arches result. The pain at times is acute and reaches up to the thighs.

Evidence published in the brief in defense of the Illinois 10 hour law (in the Supreme Court of the State of Illinois: *People vs. Elerding,* Feb., 1912) regulating the employment of women in department stores quotes physicians whose practice brought them in contact with girls and women employed as saleswomen. They are unanimous in the opinion that long hours of standing are unquestionably injurious to the female organs and reproductive system. Moreover the effect on young and physically undeveloped girls is even more serious than on older women, for injuries to these organs during girlhood may affect a woman for the rest of her life.

The consensus of opinion seems to be that "It has a very grave effect upon the generative organs of women, entailing a great deal of suffering and also injuring a very large body of them permanently. * * * It is the prolonged hours and not being allowed to sit down." (Appendix to brief, p. 27).

The question naturally arises whether the mercantile law does not provide a remedy in that it requires one seat for every three women employed. The law is usually obeyed and seats or stools are provided in the correct proportion. But in practice the law is almost useless. The use of the seats is for the most part forbidden either by unwritten law or by explicit directions from floorwalkers or managers. Even if the use of seats is permitted in the rush seasons the girls have literally no time to sit down. Then, too, a girl who is placed at an aisle counter or at a table may have no seat accessible, her third of a seat may be behind a neighboring counter; or again, if an aisle manager sees that a girl has leisure to sit down, he will move her to another busier counter in order to make better use of her time.

There is, of course, no doubt that the employer must be free to use his employees where they are needed. The points at issue are whether it is not for the best interest of both alike to avoid the over-fatigue and consequent inefficiency that comes to an employee from standing too long; and whether "reliefs" at certain definite hours, for each individual are not as essential to the welfare of saleswomen as, for instance, of telephone operators. In most stores girls can obtain permission from the aisle manager to leave their counters for ten or fifteen minutes in the morning and in the afternoon. But during rush seasons permission is often given grudgingly or not at all, and it is understood that a girl must go back to her counter at the first possible moment. In no store was any system of "reliefs" described to our investigators which was invariably followed.

Aside from the physical injuries due to constant standing, saleswomen are subjected to unquestionable nervous strain. The rush and speeding of factory work has often been described, but little notice has been given to the tax upon the attention and watchfulness of the saleswomen. They are compelled to work with rapidity and accuracy. When there is a string of impatient customers, they sometimes wait on three persons at the same time.

The saleswoman is required not only to handle goods, but also to do accurate clerical work at each purchase and to handle money whenever cash sales are made. In case of error, no matter what the rush of work, the loss is usually deducted from her earnings. She must be constantly alert to avoid such "dockings."

Another hardship is the bad air in most department stores due to defective ventilation. Complaints are frequent even from the shopping public, who remain within the store only a few hours at most. The proper ventilation of rooms holding such masses of people, often thousands at a time, is admittedly a complex engineering problem, comparable in difficulty only to the ventilation of schools and theatres.

The vitiated air has a depressing effect upon the employees. Especially in basements the failure to provide enough fresh air is unmistakable even without scientific tests of the quality of the air. Though fresh air is pumped into some basements from shafts reaching to the roof, it is often not distributed evenly throughout the basement, and certain parts of the room may be entirely unaffected. Again basements are ventilated by openings at the street level and the dust and dirt from the thoroughfare sift down into the store. The goods which are sold in the basement are usually of such a kind, (kitchenware, china, hardware, etc.) that they are not injured by the dust. But it is injurious to human beings who in addition are obliged to spend their daylight hours wholly in artificially illuminated basements. In our inquiry we found that 5,409 persons were working in basements, 543 persons in sub-basements. Incidently it may be remarked that although these premises are by courtesy called basements, they are entirely below street level and therefore really cellars.

HOURS OF WORK

All the hardships of the conditions of work are intensified by long hours of toil. The injury caused by standing, for instance, is more than proportionately increased by overtime work that is frequently prolonged beyond the normal working day by 2 to 4 extra hours.

In the discussion of hours which follows, no extreme or exaggerated instances are quoted. No isolated cases of overtime have been selected for special mention. The data on hours refer either to the whole store or to certain specified departments of the store. By omitting inspections of small neighborhood stores, we have reason to believe that the most extreme overtime has not been detected. For it is in the stores where only a few women are employed that the demands on their time are greatest. On the other hand, overtime in large stores brings strain to a far larger number of persons. Employment in the huge department stores is in itself more taxing on account of the contact with multitudes of people.

Of the 216 establishments investigated, only 35 closed throughout the year at 6 P. M. or shortly thereafter. These included most of the large department stores in New York City. The usual hours of labor that prevail, except for special rush seasons, are not excessive. Of the 27,212 women employees, approximately one-half worked less than 54 hours and one-half less than 57 hours. However, it will later be shown that at certain seasons of the year the hours of all these workers are much lengthened by overtime.

Number of women working in 216 stores according to weekly hours of work.

Number Stores	50-54 hrs.	54-57 hrs.	57-60 hrs.	Over 60 hrs.	Total
		Stores close at 6 P. M.			
35	13,802	13,410			27,212
		Stores close after 6 P. M.			
181	2,750	3,577	4,732	114	11,173
216					38,385

Of the 181 stores which were regularly kept open after 6 P. M., 100 were open only one night a week, usually on Saturday; 54 were open 2 nights a week and 27 were open to the public 3 to 6 nights a week. Moreover, women employed in such night work were not dismissed until at least 9 P. M. and in a majority of establishments not until 10 or 11 P. M. on Saturdays. These late closing hours are usual in the five and ten cent stores, and prevail also in the regular department stores outside of New York City. In fact, of the stores investigated there are only two outside New York City that habitually close at 6 P. M.

Number of women working in 181 stores which are open after 6 p. m. on Saturday nights.

Closing Hours.	50 to 54 hrs.	54 to 57 hrs.	57 to 60 hrs.	Over 60 hrs.	Total No. Women.
		Weekly Hours of Work.			
9 to 10 P. M......	1,877	826	23	......	2,726
10 to 11 P. M......	873	2,724	4,632	89	8,318
After 11 P. M.....	......	27	77	25	129
	2,750	3,577	4,732	114	11,173

A glance at the table above reveals the large proportion of women who work until a very late hour on one night a week, generally Saturday.

Ten hours a day or 60 hours a week are the legal hours for women under 21 years employed in stores. The law, however, is inoperative for six days preceding Christmas, and in consequence at that time many stores keep their doors open long past the usual closing hour. To meet the great demands of the Christmas trade, the merchants greatly increase their labor supply, but only in a comparatively few instances do they institute regular shifts of employees, who replace each other at stated hours.

In the course of this inquiry the amount of overtime required at Christmas could be ascertained in New York City stores alone.

In sixty-six large department stores the employees worked the following hours during the 6 days preceding Christmas (Dec. 18 to 24, excluding Sunday).

In 16 stores there was no overtime (*i. e.*, store closed at 6 P. M.), or a double was employed.
In 3 stores the hours were from 60-65.
In 5 stores the hours were from 65-70.
In 4 stores the hours were from 70-75.
In 20 stores the hours were from 75-80.
In 18 stores the hours were from 80-85.

66

These are actual working hours as the time off for luncheon and supper has been deducted. In addition to these excessive hours during the week, girls in certain departments worked also on Sunday, December 22nd, varying from 5 to 8 hours.

In 28 five and ten cent stores the hours (from Dec. 18 to 24) were as follows:

In 3 stores there was no overtime.
" 1 store the hours were from 65-70
" 12 stores " " " " 75-80
" 12 " " " " " 85-90

28

These are, in brief, our findings on the hours of work during the exempted period (Dec. 18 to 24). What this rush work means to the girl behind the counter, who may have to stand for 80 to 90 hours a week, is revealed in the words of one of the employees of a large department store:

> "You feel terribly driven, all day. The girls pull out all the stock in the hurry and then you can't find the things that are asked for. The standing is the worst, the pain stretches up into the calves of the legs. I had to stand in line 15 minutes one day in the crowd trying to get lunch. You ache all over by 6 o'clock. I was not relieved at night for supper till nearly 8 P. M., after demonstrating dolls all day. I was so exhausted that I finally broke down and cried."
>
> * * * * * * *
>
> The work after supper takes it out of you worst of all. I got so tired and worried that I slept badly and dreamt a

> great deal about the store. In the morning when I woke up I felt as tired as the night before. Many girls had to go far uptown, and some to Astoria, and didn't get home till after 11 P. M. I didn't see how they could get back to the store on time the next morning. But they had a sense of honor and wouldn't throw all the work on the other girls."

It is generally understood that the saleswomen must be on time for beginning work every morning, however late they may have been dismissed the night before. Otherwise the work of the store would be entirely disorganized. At this time fines for a few moments' lateness are more often remitted if the girls have been required to work late for successive nights.

An employee of another store described the condition as follows:

> "In the toy department 6 girls out of 12 at the counter were forced to take a day off during the week of December 16th to 21st on account of extreme fatigue. Four others were so tired and sick that they complained constantly and declared they would have to be absent some day before Christmas in order to stand the strain of the work. Two only were not tired to death. The girls, of course, lose pay when they are absent but everyone of them said they 'just couldn't stand it' without taking a day off, although none of them could afford this rest. Moreover when girls are absent, the burden of their work falls on the remaining salesgirls. Thus one day with 3 girls away there was such a constant rush that one girl said, 'I didn't have a chance to sit down from 9:15 till 6:45 except at lunch, and I didn't see any other girl at the counter sitting down either.' "

There is scarcely a salesgirl who does not complain of the extreme lassitude and lessened power of work experienced as a result of this exhausting toil. From Thanksgiving to Christmas the pressure of work is cumulative. From day to day the crush in the store increases, and the demands upon a girl's time and attention grow more insistent and unremitting. The air of the store is vitiated. There is rarely a moment to sit down and relax. At lunch time comes the only break, and in the over-crowded condition of most stores, a girl may have to stand in line 10 minutes out of 45 before she can get her luncheon, though her feet may be aching cruelly from long hours of standing. She may thus lose part of her short noon period for recuperation. Moreover, she

18

must return to her counter strictly on time under pain of fine for lateness, no matter what the delay in the lunch room.

At 6 P. M. nervous endurance has ebbed and the tension of added evening work strains the physical and nervous powers almost to the breaking point. Girls ordinarily in good health complain that after the late return home their sleep is broken and unrefreshing. If a girl lives at any distance from the store her night rest is cut down, since she may reach home after 11 P. M. and yet have to return to her post at 8 or 8:30 the following day. Finally, when the rush is over, Christmas Day is often spent in bed, and for weeks thereafter the ill-effects to health are still felt. According to the testimony of physicians subsequent slack time can not repair the inroads upon health due to such extreme overfatigue.

It should not be thought that overtime work is limited to December only. Though it is most excessive in that month, there are many occasions, such as special sales, stock taking and rearrangement of departments, as well as auditing and bookkeeping, which keep the employees for many extra hours. At Christmas the overtime is for the purpose of arranging stock and replacing it for the demands of the next day, since the counters have to be constantly replenished. Such preparations are necessary in many departments of a large store, especially at the handkerchief, toy, candy, silverware and book counters where the goods are most quickly sold.

In discussing overtime, it is not sufficient to deal with the length of hours during which the stores are open for customers. The practice is well nigh universal of keeping employees after the day's work or on Sundays to work behind closed doors. This work is irregular. The girls may be called upon to stay any night without previous notice. Sometimes they are not notified until late in the afternoon that they are expected to work that night. The irregularity and failure to receive advance notice are distinct grievances. Some of the testimony given before the Commission by department store employees bears directly on this point:

> "Q. When you have to work overtime do they give you any notice in advance, or do they notify you at any time during the day? A. On Saturday we did not know until half past five that we were going to stay.

* * * * * * *

> A. The boss would tell you you should not make any plans about going out and that you should tell the people at home that if you are not at home at a certain hour not to expect you."

Mercantile establishments are not, like factories, required by law to post their employees' hours of work. Hence it was exceedingly difficult for our investigators to ascertain the exact hours of work. In some establishments it is true that automatic time-clocks are used and each employee registers his time of arriving and leaving. But in no case did our investigators find the time records so kept that they could tell at a glance the total daily or weekly hours of work for any department of the establishment.

A limited study of the duration of hours was undertaken for certain classes of workers in two large stores. It revealed two facts of importance, first the difficulty of obtaining this information, owing to the failure to keep adequate records, and second, the amount of overtime required in a few selected departments of the stores during November and December, 1912.

In the first store, the overtime hours could only be obtained from the daily overtime sheet which is made up and sent to the office every afternoon. It gives the names of all the employees who are required to stay overtime. They are entitled to supper, which the firm provides, but they must obtain supper passes from the timekeeper. If the employees prefer to finish their work without stopping for supper, their names are not put on the daily overtime sheet, since they do not need to obtain supper passes. There is no record of their hours except that the watchman, in order to prevent unauthorized persons from entering the store, takes down their names as they leave the building. It was from this list that the hours of this particular set of supperless workers was ascertained. These girls are seldom informed as to the hours when they are to be dismissed. They understand that they must stay until the work is finished.

There were 197 women who worked overtime in the five departments whose records were compiled. During the period from November 6th to December 26th (42 working days) there was overtime on 32 evenings and on 6 Sundays. On no two days and in no two departments were the hours of work exactly the same. Nor were the same women always employed. As a rule, the permanent employees rather than the "Christmas specials" were expected to remain.

The number of women who worked and their hours of leaving on these 32 evenings are shown below:

Date.	No. Workers.	No. Leaving.			
		7-8 P. M.	8-9 P. M.	9-10 P. M.	10-11 P. M.
Nov. 6	11		11		
" 7	9		9		
" 11	10		10		
" 12	14		14		
" 13	6		6		
" 16	10		10		
" 18	16		16		
" 19	5		5		
" 23	12		2	10	
" 25	24		24		
" 26	33		28	5	
" 27	7	7			
" 29	21		21		
Dec. 2	11		11		
" 3	29		23	6	
" 4	22		22		
" 5	26	1	25		
" 7	10	2	1	7	
" 9	11	1	10		
" 10	20		15	5	
" 11	30	1	12	7	10
" 12	29		8	15	6
" 13	14		12		2
" 14	38		9	23	6
" 16	28		10	4	14
" 17	37	4	13	17	3
" 18	50		23	24	3
" 19	41		6	14	21
" 20	37		11	13	13
" 21	34			31	3
" 23	38		16	4	18
" 26	13		13		

More than one-half of the women stayed till 9 P. M. or later. More than one-fourth stayed till 10 P. M. or later. A small proportion was kept till 11 P. M. or later. It will be noticed that 50 women constituted the maximum number employed any one evening (Dec. 18).

In this last week before Christmas 88 women were kept overtime. Their individual records have been separately compiled and show that 16 worked 3 evenings, 15 worked 4 evenings and 10 worked 5 evenings. It is important to note that 48 of these 88 women were at their tasks successive evenings, for example, 21 were employed 2 consecutive evenings, 11 worked 3 consecutive evenings, 3 remained 4 consecutive evenings, 10 worked 5 evenings on a stretch.

Sunday work is given for each of the six Sundays, viz.:

Dates.	No. Women.
Nov. 17th	39
Nov. 24th	14
Dec. 1st	7
Dec. 8th	10
Dec. 15th	54
Dec. 22nd	37

Although 54 was the maximum number employed on any one Sunday, 77 different women took turns in returning to the store for Sunday labor. Moreover, some of the 77 worked consecutive Sundays, thus 24 worked two Sundays or 14 days without break, 3 were employed 3 Sundays or 21 days without break, and 4 women worked 5 Sundays or 35 days on a stretch without a day's rest. Many of these 77 workers added evenings of toil when they were late in returning to their homes and their rest and leisure were seriously curtailed.

In the second store the overtime hours were obtained from the individual time cards which give the daily hours of arriving and leaving. The Christmas rush began later than in the first store. More overtime was concentrated into a shorter time, because a larger force was kept at work. Overtime did not begin until December 2d. During the weeks until December 27th, twenty-two working days, there was evening work on twenty-one days.

In the five departments investigated a force of 425 women was employed, compared with 197 women employed in five departments of the first store.

Moreover, in the week preceding Christmas (Dec. 16-21), when the rush was greatest, 273 women, in four departments, worked consecutive evenings as follows:

Week of December 16-21.

15	women	working	2	consecutive	evenings.
41	"	"	3	"	"
28	"	"	4	"	"
41	"	"	5	"	"
128	"	"	6	"	"

Such continuous night work is acknowledged to be a great strain. When the night's rest is cut down for six nights without break there is no opportunity to recover from the accumulated fatigue.

There was, however, comparatively little Sunday work in the second store. Only one department kept 32 of its employees busy on two Sundays before Christmas. It is the intensity of work from Sunday to Sunday that is especially striking.

The 51 packers, constituting 12% of the total number of women who worked overtime, remained in the store on 16 different evenings, or every evening between December 5th and 23rd. The latest hour of leaving for these employees was between 11 and 12 at night, but most of them worked until 10 P. M. Of these 51 women, 40 who worked on fifteen different evenings, between December 6th and 23rd, quit their work between 9 and 10; 28 women who worked on 14 evenings during the same period left the store between 10 and 11 P. M., and 14 who worked on 5 nights between December 11th and 23rd, left after 11 P. M.

The majority of the packers were young girls under 21 years of age. They stood at their work and had little opportunity to sit down. These girls were not required to report when the store opened in the morning, as there was no urgent call for their service until sales had accumulated for an hour or more. Except for the packers, there is little leeway allowed even during the Christmas rush. A great many saleswomen who were interviewed, stated that they must be at their posts on time ready for the day's work, whatever the hour of dismissal the night before.

In this preliminary investigation it was not possible to obtain the exact hours of labor of all employees in even one large store. The facts just recited concern 622 girls and women employed respectively in five departments of two large stores. We have no information about other departments in the same stores on account of the clerical work necessary to compile the figures. Nor could we have secured the information more easily from any other store.

The amount of overtime is striking, but equally significant in the opinion of the Commission is the difficulty in obtaining the facts. In the absence of readily accessible records the mercantile inspector faces almost insuperable obstacles in enforcing the law regulating hours of labor. Far simpler in comparison is the task of the factory inspector. For the owner of a factory must keep the time book of all employment outside the posted hours of work and enter therein the weekly hours of every individual worker. He must exhibit the time book to the factory inspector. In other words, his records must show at a glance the exact working hours of every employee.

If the mercantile law also required the employer to post hours of work and keep a time book, it would not only simplify inspection but would relieve the merchants of the repeated visits of inspectors who, under present conditions, are obliged to return many times to make their observations and obtain the facts.

WAGES

In response to the growing public interest in the wages paid to working women and to concern at the lowness of the wage scale in many industries and occupations, the Commission includes in its report of retail stores the result of an initial inquiry into wages.

The Commission's investigation of women's employment in canneries, and in certain textile mills, showed the hourly or piece work rates of pay for women and children, and their weekly earnings. A more detailed study of the level of wages paid in department stores is here presented. Girls prefer employment in the stores because the social standing of mercantile employees is considered higher than that of factory girls. They have been willing to accept practically any pay that is offered, knowing that there is never scarcity of labor and that there are always other girls eager to replace them.

The wage tables given below have been compiled from one source only, namely, copies of store payrolls giving the actual wages paid to employees, for the flat weekly wage obviously does not represent the real compensation which a girl receives for her labor. The actual amount contained in her pay envelope is the flat rate of pay with sundry deductions for fines or absence and with the addition of possible commissions and bonuses. The wage figures taken from payroll entries are therefore the only accurate measure of earnings.

In the short time at its disposal the Commission was unable to secure payroll data covering a whole year. We believe that the data for five weeks are representative of average earnings of the employees since, on the whole, department store work is not seasonal in character and the majority of the employees are permanently engaged. We are without specific information and can therefore make no comment concerning enforced holidays and vacations without pay imposed during the summer. The "specials" who are taken on for special sales, the half timers, and those who work only at night or on Saturdays are not included in our inquiry, because time did not suffice to study these wages in relation to hours and permanency of employment. Finally, no one under 16 years of age is included.

Copies were made of payroll entries for five consecutive weeks beginning October 1st, 1912. At this season of the year the stores are busy and their labor force is the largest that is permanently employed. But the extra help for the Christmas rush has not yet been taken on. By studying the payrolls at this season, we are dealing with the regular selling force.

The wages of no girl were copied from the payroll unless she was employed for the entire period of five weeks, nor was her record taken if she was absent for more than three consecutive days. This was judged a reasonable amount of absence. It is rather less than the government allowance of 30 days sick leave during the year without deduction of pay.

Of the 3,768 women whose earnings were thus ascertained from the payrolls, the majority (73%) were saleswomen. They were employed in 76 stores located in New York, Buffalo and Rochester and in five cities of the second class: Albany, Troy, Schenectady, Utica and Syracuse. This wage study is representative of conditions in all the first class cities and in almost all the second cities of the state. The tables afford an opportunity to compare wages in New York and in other cities.

The average earnings have been compiled separately for two classes of mercantile establishments, the five and ten cent stores and the regular department stores. They have also been kept separately for New York and up-state cities.

FIVE AND TEN CENT STORES

There were forty-nine five and ten cent stores that opened their payrolls to us. They employ 1,038 women and girls, all of whom are salesgirls.

CUMULATIVE NUMBER AND PERCENTAGE OF SALESWOMEN EMPLOYED IN FIVE AND TEN CENT STORES ACCORDING TO EARNINGS AND ACCORDING TO CITIES

	AVERAGE WEEKLY EARNINGS					
	Under $5. Per cent.	Under $6. Per cent.	Under $7. Per cent.	Under $8. Per cent.	$8 and over. Per cent.	No. of Saleswomen.
New York City.........	28.8	61.9	81.6	89.5	10.5	772
Buffalo	76.2	95.2	100.0	100.0	......	21
Rochester	24.2	72.5	89	95.6	4.4	91
Second Class Cities....	70.8	89.6	96.1	98.6	1.4	154
All Cities	35.5	67.6	84.8	91.6	8.4	1,038

The employees of stores of this character are usually inexperienced, and no high grade of skill is required of them. It should be noted, however, that the wages of no saleswoman whatever are omitted from this table. Women are thus included who are saleswomen and who, following the practice of these stores, also perform more responsible duties such as assisting the managers. Yet notwithstanding this inclusion of the higher paid workers in the five and ten cent stores, the meagerness of the wages is striking. 67.6% of the girls and women receive less than $6 a week and 91.6% receive less than $8. These amazing figures speak for themselves. They scarcely need comment. It is clearly impossible for any woman to be wholly self-supporting upon such a wage.

DEPARTMENT STORES

Our tables of earnings compiled from regular department store payrolls are somewhat less complete than the table of wages in the five and ten cent stores.

Many of the dry goods merchants of the City of New York refused to permit us to examine their books to ascertain the wages paid to their employees, but after negotiations they submitted to us certain tables of salaries of five different department stores in the City of New York selected by them which showed the wages paid to about 4,000 employees. These tables show higher average wages than those found by our own investigators in stores other than the five referred to. We have no means of verifying these figures. They came to us too late to be incorporated in the report proper, but will be found in Appendix IX.

Wage schedules were obtained for 10% of the total number of saleswomen employed in the department stores. A number of merchants, whose wages are probably among the highest of any paid by New York mercantile establishments, responded to our request for payrolls and at the other end of the scale, a number of firms who sell a cheaper grade of goods and pay lower wages also allowed us to copy their records. However, the data were not secured from the largest New York City establishments. For this reason these wage schedules may not be entirely representative of earnings throughout the department stores of the city. For the largest stores are not represented where older and more experienced saleswomen have to a great extent been replaced by more youthful and less skilled workers.

CUMULATIVE NUMBER AND PERCENTAGE OF SALESWOMEN EMPLOYED IN REGULAR DEPARTMENT STORES ACCORDING TO EARNINGS AND ACCORDING TO CITIES

	AVERAGE WEEKLY EARNINGS.					
	Under $5. Per cent.	Under $6. Per cent.	Under $7. Per cent.	Under $8. Per cent.	$8 and over. Per cent.	No. of Saleswomen.
New York City........	15.4	28.1	44.1	54.5	45.5	877
Buffalo	26.7	53.4	69.1	80.1	19.9	236
Rochester	9.2	21.7	38.4	50.0	50.0	120
Second Class Cities...	23.1	38.2	54.4	64.7	35.3	1,497
All Cities	20.3	35.4	51.1	61.9	38.1	2,730

Twenty per cent. of all the saleswomen reported in all the cities earned less than $5 per week. One-half of all the saleswomen (51.1%) earned less than $7, and 61.9% earned less than $8 a week.

In New York City, where living expenses are highest, the proportion of those earning less than $7 was 44%. These wages, though higher than those paid in five and ten cent stores, are also clearly beneath the level of subsistence. Yet, in some way, the difference must be met between the earnings of the women and their expenses of living. For women who are wholly dependent on their own earnings the difference is made up in one of three ways. They may live in subsidized boarding houses or homes for working girls, where charity pays a part of their maintenance. Secondly they may live with such excessive economy and upon such short rations that health is shattered and future earning capacity is permanently undermined. Thus the worker herself is made to pay unfairly in strength and vitality, instead of receiving a living wage from the industry that employs her. Lastly, in some cases, the impossibility of living upon the pittance which they are paid undoubtedly leads some women to supplement these earnings by leading an immoral life. In this connection, as the Massachusetts Commission on Minimum Wage Board says significantly: *

> "It is remarkable that more saleswomen do not turn to vice. It is impossible to say how many do. No estimate whatever can be made of the extent to which the workers are subsidized because of illicit relations with one or two men. Only a few of the women had the appearance of prostitutes. Women who were making a bravo fight against tremendous odds were many times more often in evidence."

The Massachusetts Report together with the reports of the Federal Government on women in stores (Report on Woman and Child Wage Earners) disposes of the long-lived fallacy that the department store employees are working for pin money, and hence wages may safely be very low because they are not needed for actual self-support. Many store managers acknowledge that they prefer to engage girls who are living at home. The supposition is that they are not entirely dependent on their earnings.

* Report of Mass. Commission on Minimum Wage Boards, 1912, page 90.

Both of these official reports, after intensive study, prove that even when a girl lives at home, her pay is in an overwhelming majority of cases not pin money for herself, but an indispensable part of the family income. Either the chief bread-winner is ill or disabled or is unable to support his wife and children by his own earnings. In many cases women employed in department stores are themselves the chief or sole wage-earners of the family. According to the Massachusetts Report, " throughout the cities of the state about one-quarter of the women workers in stores are dependent on their own resources."

And in Boston, for example, of the 2,276 women and girls employed in retail stores, only 3.3% were working for pin money. All the rest gave their pay envelopes to their families as a necessary part of the family income, or were themselves entirely dependent on their earnings. The United States Government Report gives approximately the same figures, namely, 3.7% pin money workers.

We have thus far considered the wages of saleswomen only, who constitute the best paid group within the stores. The earnings of other workers were also ascertained. In the large establishments where the work is most subdivided there are, besides saleswomen, two main groups—the office force and the younger workers, the stock girls. Of the 76 stores whose payrolls were copied, 69 employed women in their offices and only 22 employed stock girls.

The average weekly earnings of the office help are given below:

CUMULATIVE NUMBER AND PERCENTAGE OF OFFICE HELP EMPLOYED IN DEPARTMENT STORES AND FIVE AND TEN CENT STORES ACCORDING TO EARNINGS AND ACCORDING TO CITIES.

	AVERAGE WEEKLY EARNINGS.					
	Under $5. Per cent.	Under $6. Per cent.	Under $7. Per cent.	Under $8. Per cent.	$8 and over. Per cent.	No. of office employees.
New York City.........	14.1	30.2	51.6	69.1	30.9	149
Buffalo	33.3	50.0	53.3	63.3	36.7	30
Rochester	18.	38.4	56.4	64.1	35.9	39
Second Class Cities...	21.1	35.5	52.2	63.0	37.0	360
All Cities	19.9	35.1	52.4	64.7	35.3	578

It is apparent that the range of wages of the 578 office workers included in this table corresponds closely to the wage scale of the saleswomen in the same stores.

But the younger workers who are employed as stock girls are paid markedly lower wages. The average weekly earnings of 326 are as follows:

CUMULATIVE NUMBER AND PERCENTAGE OF STOCKGIRLS EMPLOYED IN DEPARTMENT STORES ACCORDING TO EARNINGS AND ACCORDING TO CITIES

AVERAGE WEEKLY EARNINGS.

	Under $5. Per cent.	Under $6. Per cent.	Under $7. Per cent.	Under $8. Per cent.	$8 and over. Per cent.	No. of stock-girls.
New York City.........	96.3	96.3	98.1	98.1	1.9	54
Buffalo	85.7	92.8	100.0	100.0	......	14
Rochester	80.0	80.0	90.0	95.0	5.0	20
Second Class Cities....	94.1	97.9	99.5	100.0	......	238
All Cities	90.1	93.2	98.7	99.3	.7	326

It should be noted again that although these girls are undoubtedly young, yet all who are included here are over 16 years of age. They are usually not experienced and do not hold highly responsible positions, but their wages are almost incredibly low; 96.5% earned less than $6. In the absence of further data as to the age and rate of advancement of this group of workers, it is impossible to judge whether we are here considering an initial wage which will increase proportionately with the efficiency of the workers or whether this is, to some extent at least, a standard rate of pay for a body of workers whose chances of advancement are slight.

SUMMARY

This initial inquiry into wages clearly demonstrates a few points:

1. The five and ten cent stores pay the lowest wages; 84.8% of the saleswomen in them receive less than $7.

2. The other retail stores, including the regular department stores, have a higher level of wages; 51.1% receive $7 or less a week.

3. The wages paid in New York City are somewhat higher than in other cities.

4. The wages even of saleswomen are in a great majority of cases not sufficient for self-support.

5. The inadequacy of the earnings and the consequent low standard of living must inevitably undermine the health of the workers.

The previous discussion brings out clearly the limits of this initial inquiry. More intensive study is needed, following the interesting example of the Massachusetts Minimum Wage Commission. In addition to the compilation of actual earnings, the main points to be determined in a study of wages are the age distribution of the workers, the permanence of their employment, and the advancement accorded to experience and increased efficiency. Without such supplementary information no fair judgment can be rendered as to the adequacy of the wages paid.

Concerning the workers themselves, more information should be sought as to the numbers who are wholly self-supporting, or whose wages are an integral part of the family budget. It is not in mercantile establishments only that these facts concerning wages should be made known. It is equally important that the same study should be made of many industries which employ large numbers of young women at approximately the same wage level.

Even with the facts at our disposal now, it can be said with assurance that no business can be carried on without ultimate injury to society, if its wage scale rests on the assumption that its employees are subsidized in some form and therefore do not need to be paid wages sufficient for self-support.

THE MERCANTILE LAW

The mercantile establishments have always been favored by law above the factories of New York State in the number of hours they may employ women and children.

The mercantile law dates back to 1897. The first measure was passed upon the recommendation of the Reinhard Committee, which was appointed by the legislature "to investigate the conditions of female labor in the city of New York," and which held public hearings and heard testimony from employers and employees of department stores.

The original law is substantially in effect at the present day. The hours of work prescribed are as follows: children under sixteen years of age may be employed not more than nine hours a day or fifty-four hours a week and girls under twenty-one years not more than sixty hours a week.

For women above that age there is *no limitation of hours whatever.* During the week preceeding Christmas (December 18th to 24th) except for children, all restriction of hours is removed. There have been no important changes in the law since 1897, except that the working day for children has been reduced from 10 hours to 9 hours and the holiday exemption has been shortened from ten days to seven days before Christmas.

The discrepancy between factory and mercantile laws in this state is striking. In factories children may work only eight hours a day or forty-eight hours a week and women may be employed only fifty-four hours a week. There is a further discrepancy in that the mercantile law omits the provision that work for women must be limited to six days a week. Consequently the employment of women on seven days in mercantile establishments is legalized.

ENFORCEMENT

In 1897 the enforcement of the new law was given to local boards of health instead of being entrusted like other provisions of the labor law and according to the practice of other states, to the labor commissioner. For many years the law was practically a dead letter, for the local boards of health made no adequate attempt to enforce it. In many towns they made inspections only on complaint. In New York City, a corps of special mercantile inspectors of the Board of Health was maintained for only eight months and thereafter the mercantile establishments were inspected, for the most part, by the sanitary inspectors in the course of other duties. They were not trained to enforce a labor law, and in consequence their work was entirely unsatisfactory. The public justly felt that the women and children in stores were not securing the protection which the law intended, and the demand grew year after year for more adequate improvement.

Finally in 1908, to meet this public demand, the legislature passed a law transferring to the labor commissioner the enforcement of the mercantile law in cities of the first class. Thereupon a separate bureau of mercantile inspection was established in charge of the mercantile inspector, who was given 8 deputy inspectors. The number was later increased to 9. During the four years since the change was made, even with a force so clearly inadequate to cover the three largest cities of the state, the bureau has secured a far better enforcement of the law. In the first three years of its existence, the following violations of the child labor law alone were found:

	No. of children illegally employed.	Per ecnt.
1908– 9:	3,121	51.4
1909–10:	2,371	49.
1910–11:	1,575	41.1

There is no large industrial state in the Union which distinguishes so sharply as New York between the protection afforded by law to women and children in mercantile establishments and that afforded to women and children in factories.

In 20 states the hours of labor of *all* women of whatever age employed in mercantile establishments are limited as follows:

Hours in One Day.	Hours in One Week.	State.
8	48	California.
"	"	Colorado.
"	"	Washington.
9	54	Missouri.
"	"	Utah.
10	54	Michigan.
10	55	Wisconsin.
"	58	Connecticut.
"	"	Massachusetts.
"	"	Minnesota.
10	60	Kentucky.
"	"	Louisiana.
"	"	Maryland.
"	"	Nebraska.
"	"	New Jersey.
"	"	Oregon.
10	—	Illinois.
"	—	Virginia (except Saturday).
12	60	Pennsylvania.
"	"	South Carolina.

There are no exceptions to these regulations, save that three states allow holiday overtime, respectively 6, 8, and 20 days preceding Christmas.

New York State is thus in an exceptional position. It, alone, of all the large industrial states fails to protect adult women employed in stores. Owing to this distinction in the law between the women under and over 21 years, even the protection which the law is supposed to extend to the younger women is to a great extent nullified. For it is practically impossible for an inspector to determine the exact age of the women employees. No documentary proofs of age can be demanded, similar to those required for child laborers. Hence the present law does not adequately protect even the young girls under 21 years of age.

This preliminary investigation has not revealed to the Commission any cogent reason why this distinction as to age and hours of work should be made. We do not believe that the conditions of work differ so radically from employment in factories as to justify the discrimination in the laws in favor of mercantile employers. In fact, there have been revealed excessive hours of work which would seem to call for immediate legislation. But the present inquiry, in our opinion, has not been wide enough in its scope to justify at this date recommendations for fundamental changes in the mercantile law.

Thus far the Commission has no information as to conditions of employment in the smaller retail stores, such as the neighborhood stores and the many specialty stores. It has made no investigation of wholesale mercantile houses or of drug and candy stores, restaurants, etc., and has no knowledge whatsoever as to the length of their employees' working hours, and the nature of the work required.

Moreover, in the brief time following the investigation the Commission was unable to formulate tentative bills and to give an opportunity for full discussion of the proposed measures at public hearings. We have followed this procedure in every case before drawing up any final recommendations for the legislature. In view of the short time at our disposal, which precluded the proper amount of publicity and discussion of such important measures, and in view of the incompleteness of our information, we propose no remedial measures, but strongly recommend a far more extended inquiry into conditions of employment in mercantile establishments. We believe that further investigation of these establishments is greatly needed. Our preliminary survey reveals how large is the number of occupations called mercantile and how diverse the classes of workers which are engaged in them. The state should provide for as comprehensive a study of these occupations as it has already done for the factories.

MISCELLANEOUS

One Day Rest in Seven

The attention of the Commission has been called to the fact that a large number of employees in factories work seven days a week and have no opportunity for physical rest and relaxation. Such continuous labor is injurious to the health and morals of workers. We have not, however, had sufficient opportunity to go into this subject so fully as is necessary to propose legislation. We recommend careful investigation into the extent of seven-day labor in the factories of this state and consideration of measures for securing to the worker one day of rest in seven.

City Plan Commission

The Commission has been urged to recommend a plan by which manufacturing shall be confined to certain streets within the city of New York. It is asserted that unless this plan be adopted, property values on Fifth avenue and other important streets will be very much impaired. The Commission, however, does not feel at this time that it can make any recommendations upon this subject.

CONCLUSION

The task laid upon the Commission by the legislature has proved exceedingly arduous. For the inquiry into the conditions under which manufacturing is carried on in New York State involved not only problems of building construction, sanitation, ventilation, the prevention of accident and disease, and the work of women and children, but out of these investigations grew the still more difficult problem of a thorough reorganization of the Department of Labor.

These complex problems have been earnestly and conscientiously considered with due regard to the interests of employee, employer, and consumer. Although the Commission is well aware that a complete solution has not been found, it is nevertheless convinced that if the remedial measures recommended become law and are intelligently enforced they will lighten the burden of the worker and prove of benefit to all the state.

It is of great importance to state clearly that the bills proposed by the Commission have been presented in such form as to justify no modification before enactment into law. We declare distinctly that we have asked for no more remedial legislation than is imperatively demanded by the present conditions in the factories of the state.

The most important recommendation that the Commission presents deals with the reorganization of the Department of Labor. Furthermore, the most important feature of this reorganization is the proposed creation of the Industrial Board. To this board are given large powers for regulating industry, powers that permit the board, with due discretion and reliance both on personal knowledge and the advice of its experts, to make particular regulations with reference to the special industries involved.

Through this plan of reorganization the Department of Labor will be an effective instrument to safeguard the workers of the state. It will be not only an enforcing authority but through its division of Industrial Hygiene it will be also an investigating body which shall study specific dangers and their remedies. Above all, in the Industrial Board the department will have an agency to frame standards and regulations applicable to varying conditions of industry.

The Industrial Board will take under consideration the interests of both employer and employee. There should be no conflict between these interests, for the improved conditions of labor not only conserve the health of the workers but also increase their industrial efficiency. It will therefore be the duty of the Industrial Board to make clear, by the practical application of its standards, that improved conditions of labor are a substantial benefit to business interests. In this way the board will enlist the advice and help of employers.

Our investigation showed that many factories and industrial establishments of the state are conducted by enlightened men who feel deeply the needs of their employees and realize, further, that increased efficiency and enlarged profits will result from proper attention paid to the safeguards which we recommend.

As for the less-enlightened employers, the Industrial Board will act as an educational agency in the sense that it will bring into general practice the best methods of production now in use in establishments of the highest scientific efficiency.

Thus the creation of the Industrial Board within the Department of Labor will harmonize the interests of both worker and employer. Through the exercise of its functions, the labor department will no longer be regarded merely as a bureau invested with police power and as a hostile critic, but also as a source of constructive advice. The achievement of this high ideal calls for the appointment to office in the labor department of men and women of training and high character imbued with the new spirit.

The greater part of the legislation recommended by the Commission must take the form of amendments to the labor law. That statute, since its enactment in 1897, has been subjected to numerous amendments, and has grown to be unwieldy and complicated. It is in need of revision that will simplify its form and arrangement and clarify its meaning. The Commission recommends that the labor law be properly re-codified.

The question of the minimum wage for women has been much discussed. An impartial investigation of all the facts is urgently needed.

The tendency of the age is toward specialization. A further tendency is that of concentration. Both these tendencies are followed in the proposed reorganization of the labor department which will concentrate the specialists in one group, using each with a view to his special knowledge and capacity. Then there will be fought out a hopeful and effective war against ignorance, poverty, disease, and death, for the conservation of the nation's wealth, for the education of the people, for the uplifting of humanity. "And the question of conservation is a great deal bigger than the question of saving our forests and our mineral resources and our waters; it is as big as the life and happiness and strength and elasticity and hope of our people."*

ROBERT F. WAGNER,
Chairman.

ALFRED E. SMITH,
Vice-Chairman.

CHARLES M. HAMILTON,
EDWARD D. JACKSON,
CYRUS W. PHILLIPS,
SIMON BRENTANO,
ROBERT E. DOWLING,
MARY E. DREIER,
SAMUEL GOMPERS.
Commission.

FRANK A. TIERNEY,
Secretary.

ABRAM I. ELKUS,
Chief Counsel.

BERNARD L. SHIENTAG,
Associate Counsel.

---

* Woodrow Wilson; "The New Freedom."

APPENDIX I

List of Bills Submitted to the Legislature by the New York State Factory Investigating Commission.

APPENDIX I

LIST OF BILLS SUBMITTED TO THE LEGISLATURE BY THE NEW YORK STATE FACTORY INVESTIGATING COMMISSION:*

1. Reorganization of Labor Department; Industrial Board.
2. Penalties for violation of labor law and industrial code.
3. Fire proof receptacles; gas jets; smoking.
4. Fire alarm signal systems and fire drills.
5. Automatic sprinklers.
6. Fire-escapes and exits; limitation of number of occupants, construction of future factory buildings.
7. Amendment to Greater New York Charter (Fire Prevention Law).
8. Prohibition of employment of children under fourteen in cannery sheds or tenement houses; definition of factory building; definition of tenement house.
9. Manufacturing in tenements.
10. Hours of labor of women in canneries.
11. Housing conditions in labor camps maintained in connection with a factory.
12. Physical examination of children employed in factories.
13. Amendments to child labor law; physical examination before issuance of employment certificate; school record; supervision over issuance of employment certificates.
14. Amendment to compulsory education law; school record.
15. Night work of women in factories.
16. Seats for women in factories.
17. Bakeries.
18. Cleanliness of workrooms.
19. Cleanliness of factory buildings.
20. Ventilation; general; special.
21. Washing facilities; dressing rooms; water closets.
22. Accident prevention; lighting of factories and workrooms.
23. Elevators.
24. Dangerous trades.
25. Foundries.
26. Employment of children in dangerous occupations; employment of women in core rooms.
27. Labeling of containers of wood alcohol.
28. Extension of jurisdiction of commission.

* All except No. 5 and No. 27 were passed and have become laws.

BILL NO. 1.

AN ACT

TO AMEND THE LABOR LAW, IN RELATION TO THE ORGANIZATION OF THE DEPARTMENT OF LABOR AND ITS VARIOUS BUREAUS, THE CREATION OF AN INDUSTRIAL BOARD, AND THE EXTENSION OF THE DEPARTMENT'S JURISDICTION OVER MERCANTILE ESTABLISHMENTS IN CITIES OF THE SECOND CLASS.

The People of the State of New York, represented in Senate and Assembly, do enact as follows:

Section 1. Article three of chapter thirty-six of the laws of nineteen hundred and nine, entitled "An act relating to labor, constituting chapter thirty-one of the consolidated laws," as amended by chapter five hundered and fourteen of the laws of nineteen hundred and ten, chapter seven hundred and twenty-nine of the laws of nineteen hundred and eleven and chapter three hundred and eighty-two of the laws of nineteen hundred and twelve, is hereby amended to read as follows:*

ARTICLE 3.

DEPARTMENT OF LABOR.

Section 40. Commissioner of labor.
41. Deputy commissioners.
42. Bureaus.
43. Powers.
44. Salaries and expenses.
45. [Sub] *Branch* offices.
46. Reports.
47. Old records.
48. Counsel.

§ 40. Commissioner of labor. There shall continue to be a department of labor, the head of which shall be the commissioner of labor, who shall be appointed by the governor by and with the

* Matter in *italics* is new; matter in [ ] is old law to be omitted.

consent of the senate, and who shall hold office for a term of four years beginning on the first day of January of the year in which he is appointed. He shall receive an annual salary of [five thousand five hundred] *eight thousand* dollars. He shall appoint *and may remove* all officers, clerks and other employees in the department of labor *except as in this chapter otherwise provided.*

§ 41. Deputy commissioners. The commissioner of labor shall forthwith upon entering upon the duties of his office, appoint and may at pleasure remove two deputy commissioners of labor[, who shall receive such annual salaries, not to exceed four thousand dollars and three thousand five hundred dollars, respectively, as may be appropriated therefor. The powers hereinafter conferred upon the first and second deputy commissioners shall not include the appointment of officers, clerks or other employees in any of the bureaus of the department of labor]. *The first deputy commissioner shall receive a salary of five thousand dollars a year; the second deputy commissioner shall receive a salary of four thousand five hundred dollars a year.*

The first deputy commissioner shall, during the absence or disability of the commissioner of labor, possess all the powers and perform all the duties of the commissioner except the power of appointment and removal. During the absence or disability of both the commissioner of labor and the first deputy commissioner of labor, the second deputy commissioner shall possess all the powers and perform all the duties of the commissioner except the power of appointment and removal. In addition to their duties and powers as prescribed by the provisions of this chapter, the deputy commissioners of labor shall perform such other duties and possess such other powers as the commissioner of labor may prescribe.

§ 42. Bureaus. The department of labor shall [be divided into five] *have four* bureaus as follows: [Factory] inspection; [labor] statistics *and information;* mediation and arbitration *and* industries and immigration[, and mercantile inspection]. *There shall be such other bureaus in the department of labor as the commissioner of labor may deem necessary.*

§ 43. Powers. 1. The commissioner of labor, his deputies and their assistants and each [special] agent, [confidential agent,] *chief factory inspector,* factory inspector, mine inspector, tunnel inspector, chief investigator, special investigator[s], *chief* mercantile inspector, [or deputy] *and* mercantile inspector[s] may administer oaths and take affidavits in matters relating to the provisions of this chapter [and may also serve process in criminal actions arising thereunder].

2. No person shall interfere with, obstruct or hinder by force or otherwise the commissioner of labor, *any member of the industrial board, or any officer, agent or employee of the department of labor* [his deputies, their assistants or the special agents, deputy factory inspectors, chief investigator, special investigators, the mercantile inspector, or deputy mercantile inspectors] while in the performance of their duties, or refuse to properly answer questions asked by such officers *or employees* pertaining to the provisions of this chapter, or refuse them admittance to any place [where and when labor is being performed] which is affected by the provisions of this chapter.

3. All notices, orders and directions of *any officer, agent or employee of the department of labor other than the commissioner of labor or the industrial board* [deputies, assistants, special agents, deputy factory inspectors, chief investigator, special investigators, the mercantile inspector, or deputy mercantile inspectors] given in accordance with this chapter are subject to the approval of the commissioner of labor[. A], *and* [all acts, notices, orders, permits and directions by any provisions of this chapter directed to be performed or given by the factory inspector, chairman of the board of mediation and arbitration, chief investigator, special investigators, mercantile inspector or other officer of the department of labor] may be performed or given by and in the name of the commissioner of labor and by any officer *or employee* of the department thereunto duly authorized by such commissioner in the name of such commissioner.

4. The commissioner of labor may procure and cause to be used badges for himself and his subordinates in the department of labor while in the performance of their duties.

§ 44. Salaries and expenses. All necessary expenses incurred by the commissioner of labor in the discharge of his duties shall be paid by the state treasurer upon the warrant of the comptroller issued upon proper vouchers therefor. The reasonable and necessary traveling and other expenses of the deputy commissioners, their assistants, the [special] agents and statisticians, *the chief factory inspectors,* the [deputy] factory inspectors, chief investigator, the special investigators, the *chief* mercantile inspector[s], [deputy] mercantile inspectors, and other field officers of the department while engaged in the performance of their duties shall be paid in like manner upon vouchers approved by the commissioner of labor and audited by the comptroller.

§ 45. [Sub] *Branch* offices. [The commissioner of labor may establish and maintain a sub-office in any city if in his opinion it be necessary. He may designate any one or more of his subordinates to take charge of and manage any such office, subject to his direction.] *The commissioner of labor shall establish and maintain branch offices of the department in the city of New York and in such other cities of the state as he may deem advisable. Such branch offices shall, subject to the supervision and direction of the commissioner of labor, be in immediate charge of such officials or employees as the commissioner of labor may designate.* The reasonable and necessary expenses of such offices shall be paid as are other expenses of the commissioner of labor.

§ 46. Reports. The commissioner of labor shall report annually to the legislature *and shall include in his annual report or make separately in each year a report of the operation of each bureau in the department.*

§ 47. Old records. All statistics furnished to and all complaints, reports and other documentary matter received by the commissioner of labor pursuant to this chapter or any act repealed or superseded thereby may be destroyed by such commissioner after the expiration of six years from the time of the receipt thereof.

§ 48. Counsel. [The commissioner of labor may employ counsel in the department of labor to represent the department or to assist in the prosecution of actions or proceedings brought under the provisions of this chapter. Such counsel shall receive such compensation as may otherwise be provided by law.] *The commissioner of labor shall appoint and may at pleasure remove counsel who shall be an attorney and counsellor at law of the state of New York to represent the department of labor and to take charge of and assist in the prosecution of actions and proceedings brought by or on behalf of the commissioner of labor or the department of labor, and generally to act as legal adviser to the commissioner. Such counsel shall receive a salary of four thousand dollars a year. The commissioner of labor shall have power to appoint and at pleasure remove attorneys and counsellors at law to assist the counsel in the performance of his duties who shall receive such compensation as may be provided by law.*

§ 2. Such chapter is hereby further amended by inserting therein after article three, a new article to be article three-a thereof to read as follows:

ARTICLE 3-A

INDUSTRIAL BOARD.

§ 50. Industrial board; organization. 1. There shall be an industrial board, to consist of the commissioner of labor, who shall be chairman of the board, and four associate members. The associate members shall be appointed by the governor by and with the advice and consent of the senate. Of the associate members first appointed, one shall hold office until December first, nineteen hundred and fourteen, one until December first, nineteen hundred and fifteen, one until December first, nineteen hundred and sixteen, and one until December first, nineteen hundrd and seventeen. Upon the expiration of each of said terms, the term of office of each associate member thereafter appointed shall be four years from the first day of December. Vacancies shall be filled by appointment for the unexpired term. The associate members shall each receive a salary of three thousand dollars a year and each of said associate members shall be paid his reasonable and necessary traveling and other expenses while engaged in the performance of his duties in the manner provided in section forty-four of this chapter.

2. The board shall appoint and may remove a secretary who shall receive a salary to be fixed by the board. The commissioner of labor shall detail, from time to time, to the assistance of the board, such employees of the department of labor as the board may require. In aid of its work, the board is empowered to employ experts for special and occasional services, and to employ necessary clerical assistants. The counsel to the department of labor shall be counsel to the board without additional compensation.

3. The board shall hold stated meetings, at least once a month during the year at the office of the department of labor in the city of Albany or in the city of New York and shall hold other meetings at such times and places as the needs of the public service may require, which meetings shall be called by the chairman or by any two associate members of the board. All meetings of the board shall be open to the public. The board shall keep minutes of its proceedings showing the vote of each member upon every question and records of its examinations and other official action.

§ 51. Jurisdiction of board. The board shall have power: (1) To make investigations concerning and report upon all matters touching the enforcement and effect of the provisions of this chapter and the rules and regulations made by the board thereunder, and in the course of such investigations, each member of the board and the secretary shall have power to administer oaths and take affidavits. Each member of the board and the secretary shall have power to make personal inspections of all factories, factory buildings, mercantile establishments and other places to which this chapter is applicable.

(2) To subpoena and require the attendance in this state of witnesses and the production of books and papers pertinent to the investigations and inquiries hereby authorized and to examine them in relation to any matter which it has power to investigate, and to issue commissions for the examination of witnesses who are out of state or unable to attend before the board or excused from attendance.

(3) To make, alter, amend and repeal rules and regulations for carrying into effect the provisions of this chapter, applying such provisions to specific conditions and prescribing specific means, methods or practices to effectuate such provisions.

(4) To make, alter, amend, or repeal rules and regulations for guarding against and minimizing fire hazards, personal injuries and disease, with respect to (a) the construction, alteration, equipment and maintenance of factories, factory buildings, mercantile establishments and other places to which this chapter is applicable, including the conversion of structures into factories and factory buildings; (b) the arrangement and guarding of machinery and the storing and keeping of property and articles in factories, factory buildings and mercantile establishments; (c) the places where and the methods and operations by which trades and occupations may be conducted and the conduct of employers, employees and other persons in and about factories, factory buildings and mercantile establishments; it being the policy and intent of this chapter that all factories, factory buildings, mercantile establishments and other places to which this chapter is applicable, shall be so constructed, equipped, arranged, operated and conducted in all respects as to provide reasonable and adequate protection to the lives, health and safety of all persons employed therein and that the said board shall from time to time make such rules and regulations as will effectuate the said policy and intent.

§ 52. Rules and regulations; industrial code. 1. The rules and regulations adopted by the board pursuant to the provisions of this chapter shall have the force and effect of law and shall be enforced in the same manner as the provisions of this chapter. Such rules and regulations may apply in whole or in part to particular kinds of factories or workshops, or to particular machines, apparatus or articles; or to particular processes, industries, trades or occupations; and they may be limited in their application to factories or workshops to be established, or to machines, apparatus or other articles to be installed or provided in the future.

2. At least three affirmative votes shall be necessary to the adoption of any rule or regulation by the board. Before any

rule or regulation is adopted, altered, amended or repealed by the board there shall be a public hearing thereon, notice of which shall be published not less than ten days, in such newspapers as the board may prescribe. Every rule or regulation and every act of the board shall be promptly published in bulletins of the department of labor or in such newspapers as the board may prescribe. The rules and regulations, and alterations, amendments and changes thereof shall, unless otherwise prescribed by the board, take effect twenty days after the first publication thereof.

3. The rules and regulations which shall be in force on the first day of January, nineteen hundred and fourteen, and the amendments and alterations thereof, and the additions thereto, shall constitute the industrial code. The industrial code may embrace all matters and subjects to which and so far as the power and authority of the department of labor extends and its application need not be limited to subjects enumerated in this article. The industrial code and all amendments and alterations thereof and additions thereto shall be certified by the secretary of the board and filed with the secretary of state.

§ 3. Such chapter is hereby further amended by inserting therein after section twenty-a, a new section, to be section twenty-b, to read as follows:

§ 20-b. *Protection of employees. All factories, factory buildings, mercantile establishments and other places to which this chapter is applicable, shall be so constructed, equipped, arranged, operated and conducted in all respects as to provide reasonable and adequate protection to the lives, health and safety of all persons employed therein. The industrial board shall, from time to time, make such rules and regulations as will carry into effect the provisions of this section.*

§ 4. Article five of such chapter as amended by chapter seven hundred and twenty-nine of the laws of nineteen hundred and eleven and chapter one hundred and fifty-eight of the laws of nineteen hundred and twelve is hereby renumbered article four, inserted in place of present article four hereinafter renumbered and amended to read as follows:

ARTICLE [5] *4.*

BUREAU OF [FACTORY] INSPECTION.

[§ 60. Chief factory inspector.] § 53. *Bureau of inspection; inspector general; divisions.* [There shall continue to be a bureau of factory inspection.] *The bureau of inspection, subject to the supervision and direction of the commissioner of labor, shall have charge of all inspections made pursuant to the provisions of this chapter, and shall perform such other duties as may be assigned to it by the commissioner of labor.* The first deputy commissioner of labor shall be the [chief factory] inspector *general* of the state, and in charge of this bureau subject to the direction and supervision of the commissioner of labor, *except that the division of industrial hygiene shall be under the immediate direction and supervision of the commissioner of labor. Such bureau shall have four divisions as follows: factory inspection, homework inspection, mercantile inspection and industrial hygiene. There shall be such other divisions in such bureau as the commissioner of labor may deem necessary. In addition to their respective duties as prescribed by the provisions of this chapter, such divisions shall perform such other duties as may be assigned to them by the commissioner of labor.*

[§ 61.] § *54.* [Factory] Inspectors. [The commissioner of labor may appoint from time to time not more than one hundred and twenty-five persons, as factory inspectors, not more than twenty of whom shall be women, and who may be removed by him at any time. The factory inspectors may be divided into five grades, but not more than thirty shall be of the third grade, and not more than eight shall be of the fourth grade and not more than one shall be of the fifth grade. Each inspector of the first grade shall receive an annual salary of one thousand dollars, each of the second grade an annual salary of one thousand two hundred dollars and each of the third grade an annual salary of one thousand five hundred dollars. There shall be after October first, nineteen hundred and eleven, no further appointments in the first grade and no vacancies in the first grade shall be filled. There may be at any time not to exceed ninety persons in the second grade. Each inspector of the fourth grade shall receive an annual salary of two thousand five hundred dollars. Each inspector of the fifth grade shall receive an annual salary of three thousand five hundred dollars. Each inspector of the fifth grade shall be a mechanical engineer] 1. *Factory inspectors. There shall be not less than one hundred and twenty-five factory inspectors, not more than thirty of whom shall be women. Such inspectors shall be appointed by the commissioner of labor and may be removed by him at any time. The inspectors shall be divided into seven grades. Inspectors of the first grade, of whom there shall be not more than ninety-five, shall each receive an annual salary of one thousand two hundred dollars; inspectors of the second grade, of whom there shall be not more than fifty, shall each receive an annual salary of one thousand five hundred dollars; inspectors of the third grade, of whom there shall be not more than twenty-five, shall each receive an annual salary of one thousand eight hundred dollars; inspectors of the fourth grade, of whom there shall be not more than ten, shall each receive an annual salary of two thousand dollars and shall be attached to the division of industrial hygiene and act as investigators in such division; inspectors of the fifth grade, of whom there shall be not more than nine, one of whom shall be able to speak and write at least five European languages in addition to English, shall each receive an annual salary of two thousand five hundred dollars and shall act as supervising inspectors; inspectors of the sixth grade of whom there shall be not less than three and one of whom shall be a woman shall act as medical inspectors and shall each receive an annual salary of two thousand five hundred dollars; inspectors of the seventh grade of whom there shall be not less than four, shall each receive an annual salary of three thousand five hundred dollars; all of the inspectors of the sixth grade shall be physicians duly licensed to practice medicine in the state of New York. Of the inspectors of the seventh grade one shall be a physician duly licensed to practice medicine in the state of New York, and he shall be the chief medical inspector; one shall be a chemical engineer; one shall be a mechanical engineer, and an expert in ventilation and accident prevention; and one shall be a civil engineer, and an expert in fire prevention and building construction.*

2. *Mercantile inspectors. The commissioner of labor may appoint from time to time not more than twenty mercantile inspectors not less than four of whom shall be women and who may be removed by him at any time. The mercantile inspectors may be divided into three grades but not more than five shall be of the third grade. Each mercantile inspector of the first grade shall receive an annual salary of one thousand dollars; of the second grade an annual salary of one thousand two hundred dollars; and of the third grade an annual salary of one thousand five hundred dollars.*

§ 55. *Division of factory inspection; factory inspection districts; chief factory inspectors. For the inspection of factories, there shall be two inspection districts to be known as the first factory inspection district and the second factory inspection district. The first factory inspection district shall include the counties of New York, Bronx, Kings, Queens, Richmond, Nassau and Suffolk. The second factory inspection district shall include all the other counties of the state. There shall be two chief factory inspectors who shall be appointed by the commissioner of labor and who may be removed by him at any time and each of whom shall receive a salary of four thousand dollars a year. The inspection of factories in each factory inspection district shall, subject to the supervision and direction of the commissioner of labor, be in charge of a chief factory inspector assigned to such district by the commissioner of labor. The commissioner of labor may designate one of the supervising inspectors as assistant chief factory inspector for the first district, and while acting as such assistant chief factory inspector he shall receive an additional salary of five hundred dollars per annum.*

§ [62] 56. *Id.; general powers and duties.* 1. The commissioner of labor shall, from time to time, divide the state into *sub*-districts, assign one factory inspector of the [fourth] *fifth* grade to each *sub*-district as supervising inspector, and may in his discretion transfer [them] *such supervising inspector* from one *sub*-district to another; *he shall from time to time, assign and transfer factory inspectors to each factory inspection district and to any of the divisions of the bureau of inspection;* he may assign any factory inspector to inspect any special class or classes of factories or to enforce any special provisions of this chapter; and he may assign any one or more of them to act as clerks in any office of the department.

2. The commissioner of labor may authorize any deputy commissioner or assistant and any [special] agent or inspector in the department of labor to act as a [deputy] factory inspector with the full power and authority thereof.

3. The commissioner of labor, the first deputy commissioner of labor and his assistant or assistants, and every factory inspector and *every person duly authorized pursuant to sub-division two of this section,* may, in the discharge of his duties enter any place, building or room [where and when any labor is being performed] which is affected by the provisions of this chapter and may enter any factory whenever he may have reasonable cause to believe that any [such] labor is being performed therein.

4. The commissioner of labor shall visit and inspect or cause to be visited and inspected the factories, during reasonable hours, as often as practicable, and shall cause the provisions of this chapter *and the rules and regulations of the industrial board* to be enforced therein.

5. Any lawful municipal ordinance, by-law or regulation relating to factories, in addition to the provisions of this chapter

and not in conflict therewith, may be observed and enforced by the commissioner of labor.

§ 57. *Division of homework inspection. The division of homework inspection shall be in charge of an officer or employee of the department of labor designated by the commissioner of labor and shall, subject to the supervision and direction of the commissioner of labor, have charge of all inspections of tenement houses and of labor therein and of all work done for factories at places other than such factories.*

§ 58. *Division of mercantile inspection. The division of mercantile inspection shall be under the immediate charge of the chief mercantile inspector, but subject to the direction and supervision of the commissioner of labor. The chief mercantile inspector shall be appointed and be at pleasure removed by the com- commissioner of labor, and shall receive such annual salary not to exceed three thousand dollars as may be appropriated therefor.*

§ 59. *Id.; general powers and duties. 1. The commissioner of labor may divide the cities of the first and second class of the state into mercantile inspection districts, assign one or more mercantile inspectors to each such district, and may in his discretion transfer them from one such district to another; he may assign any of them to inspect any special class or classes of mercantile or other establishments specified in article twelve of this chapter, situated in cities of the first and second class, or to enforce in cities of the first or second class any special provision of such article.*

2. The commissioner of labor may authorize any deputy commissioner or assistant and any agent or inspector in the department of labor to act as a mercantile inspector with the full power and authority thereof.

3. The commissioner of labor, the chief mercantile inspector and his assistant or assistants and every mercantile inspector or acting mercantile inspector may in the discharge of his duties enter any place, building or room in cities of the first or second class which is affected by the provisions of article twelve of this chapter, and may enter any mercantile or other establishment specified in said article, situated in the cities of the first or second class, whenever he may have reasonable cause to believe that it is affected by the provisions of article twelve of this chapter.

4. The commissioner of labor shall visit and inspect or cause to be visited and inspected the mercantile and other establishments specified in article twelve of this chapter situated in cities of the first and second class, as often as practicable, and shall cause the provisions of said article and the rules and regulations of the industrial board to be enforced therein.

5. Any lawful municipal ordinance, by-law or regulation relating to mercantile or other establishments specified in article twelve of this chapter, in addition to the provisions of this chapter and not in conflict therewith, may be enforced by the commissioner of labor in cities of the first and second class.

§ 60. Division of industrial hygiene. The inspectors of the seventh grade shall constitute the division of industrial hygiene, which shall be under the immediate charge of the commissioner of labor. The commissioner of labor may select one of the inspectors of the seventh grade to act as the director of such division, and such director while acting in that capacity shall receive an additional compensation of five hundred dollars a year. The members of the division of industrial hygiene shall make special inspections of factories, mercantile establishments and other places subject to the provisions of this chapter, throughout the state, and shall conduct special investigations of industrial processes and conditions. The commissioner of labor shall submit to the industrial board the recommendations of the division regarding proposed rules and regulations and standards to be adopted to carry into effect the provisions of this chapter and shall advise said board concerning the operation of such rules and standards and as to any changes or modifications to be made therein. The members of such division shall prepare material for leaflets and bulletins calling attention to dangers in particular industries and the precautions to be taken to avoid them; and shall perform such other duties and render such other services as may be required by the commissioner of labor. The director of such division shall make an annual report to the commissioner of labor of the operation of the division, to which may be attached the individual reports of each member of the division as above specified, and same shall be transmitted to the legislature as part of the annual report of the commissioner of labor.

§ 61. *Section of medical inspection. The inspectors of the sixth grade shall constitute the section of medical inspection which shall, subject to the supervision and direction of the director of the division of industrial hygiene, be under the immediate charge of the chief medical inspector. The section of medical inspection shall inspect factories, mercantile establishments and other places subject to the provisions of this chapter throughout the state with respect to conditions of work affecting the health of persons employed therein and shall have charge of the physical examination and medical supervision of all children employed therein and shall perform such other duties and render such other services as the commissioner of labor may direct.*

§ 5. Article four of such chapter as amended by chapter two hundred and fifty-eight of the laws of nineteen hundred and eleven, is hereby renumbered article five, inserted in place of article four hereinbefore renumbered, and amended to read as follows:

ARTICLE [4]*5.*

BUREAU OF [LABOR] STATISTICS AND INFORMATION.

§ [55]*62.* Bureau of [labor] statistics *and information.* [There shall continue to be a] *The* bureau of [labor] statistics *and information,* [which] shall be under the immediate charge of a chief statistician, but subject to the direction and supervision of the commissioner of labor.

§ [56]*63.* *Divisions;* [D]*duties* and powers. *1. The bureau of statistics and information shall have five divisions as follows: general labor statistics; industrial directory; industrial accidents and diseases; special investigations; and printing and publication. There shall be such other divisions in such bureau as the commissioner of labor may deem advisable. Each of the said divisions shall, subject to the supervision and direction of the commissioner of labor and of the chief statistician, be in charge of an officer or employee of the department of labor designated by the commissioner of labor; and each of the said divisions, in addition to the duties prescribed in this chapter, shall perform such other duties as may be assigned to it by the commissioner of labor.*

2. The [commissioner of labor] *division of general labor statistics* shall collect [assort, systemize and present in annual reports to the legislature, statistical details] *and prepare statistics and general information* in relation to [all departments of labor in the state, especially in relation to the commercial, industrial, social and sanitary condition of workingmen] *conditions of labor* and [to] the [productive] industries of the state.

3. The division of industrial directory shall prepare annually an industrial directory for all cities and villages having a population of one thousand or more according to the last preceding federal census or state enumeration. Such directory shall contain information regarding opportunities and advantages for manufacturing in every such city or village, the factories established therein, hours of labor, housing conditions, railroad and water connections, water power, natural resources, wages and such other data regarding social, economic and industrial conditions as in the judgment of the commissioner would be of value to prospective manufacturers, and their employees. If a city is divided into boroughs the directory shall contain such information as to each borough.

4. The division of industrial accidents and diseases shall collect and prepare statistical details and general information regarding industrial accidents and occupational diseases, their causes and effects, and methods of preventing, curing and remedying them, and of providing compensation therefor.

5. The division of special investigations shall have charge of all investigations and research work relating to economic and social conditions of labor conducted by such bureau.

6. The division of printing and publication shall print, publish and disseminate in such manner and to such extent as the commissioner of labor shall direct, such information and statistics as the commissioner of labor may direct for the purpose of promoting the health, safety and well being of persons employed at labor.

7. *The commissioner of labor* [He] may subpoena witnesses, take and hear testimony, take or cause to be taken depositions and administer oaths.

§ [57]*64.* [Statistics] *Information* to be furnished upon request. The owner, operator, manager or lessee of any mine, factory, workshop, warehouse, elevator, foundry, machine shop or other manufacturing establishment, or any agent, superintendent, subordinate, or employee thereof, and any person employing or directing any labor affected by the provisions of this chapter, shall, when requested by the commissioner of labor, furnish any information in his possession or under his control which the commissioner is authorized to require, and shall admit him *or his duly authorized representative* to any place [where labor is carried on] which is affected by the provisions of this chapter for the purpose of inspection. [All the statistics furnished to the commissioner of labor, pursuant to this article, may be destroyed by such commissioner after the expiration of two years from the time of the receipt thereof.] A person refusing to admit such commissioner, or person authorized by him, for any such establishment, or to furnish him any information requested, or who refuses to answer or untruthfully answers questions put to him by such commissioner, in a circular or otherwise, shall forfeit to the people of the state the sum of one hundred dollars for each refusal or untruthful answer given, to be sued for and recovered by the commissioner in his name of office. The amount so recovered shall be paid into the state treasury.

§ [58] *65.* Industrial poisonings to be reported. 1. Every medical practitioner attending on or called in to visit a patient whom he believes to be suffering from poisoning from lead, phosphorous, arsenic, [or] *brass, wood alcohol,* mercury or their compounds, or from anthrax, or from compressed air illness, contracted as the result of the nature of the patient's employment, shall send to the commissioner of labor a notice stating the name and full postal address and place of employment of the patient and the disease from which, in the opinion of the medical practitioner, the patient is suffering, with such other and further information as may be required by the said commissioner.

2. If any medical practitioner, when required by this section to send a notice, fails forthwith to send the same, he shall be liable to a fine not exceeding ten dollars.

3. It shall be the duty of the commissioner of labor to enforce the provisions of this section, and he may call upon the state and local boards of health for assistance.

§ 6. Sections forty-nine and sixty-three of such chapter are hereby repealed.

§ 7. Section sixty-seven of such chapter is hereby renumbered section twenty-two and inserted in article two after section twenty-one, to read as follows:

§ [67] *22.* Duties relative to apprentices. The commissioner of labor shall enforce the provisions of the domestic relations law, relative to indenture of apprentices, and prosecute employers for failure to comply with the provisions of such indentures and of such law in relation thereto.

§ 8. Section sixty-eight of such chapter is hereby renumbered section ninety-nine-a, inserted at the end of article six, and amended to read as follows:

§ [68] *99.* Laws to be posted. [A copy or abstract] *Copies or digests* of the provisions of this chapter *and of the rules and regulations of the industrial board,* applicable thereto, *in English and in such other languages as the commissioner of labor may require,* to be prepared and furnished by the commissioner of labor, shall be kept posted by the employer in [a] *such* conspicuous place *or places as the commissioner of labor may direct* on each floor of every factory where persons are employed who are affected by the provisions thereof.

§ 9. Section sixty-nine of such chapter as amended by chapter three hundred and thirty-five of the laws of nineteen hundred and twelve, is hereby transferred to and inserted in article six of such chapter, instead of article five.

§ 10. Such chapter is hereby further amended by inserting therein in article nine, before section one hundred and twenty, a new section, to be section one hundred and nineteen to read as follows:

§ 119. *Protection of employees in mines, tunnels and quarries. Every necessary precaution shall be taken to insure the safety and health of employees employed in the mines and quarries and in the construction of tunnels in the state. The industrial board shall have power to adopt rules and regulations to carry into effect the provisions of this article and may amend or repeal rules and regulations heretofore prescribed by the commissioner of labor under the provisions of this article. The rules and regulations heretofore prescribed by the commissioner of labor under this article shall continue in force until amended or repealed by the industrial board.*

§ 11. Section one hundred and twenty of such chapter is hereby amended to read as follows:

§ 120. Duties of commissioner of labor relating to mines, tunnels and quarries; record and report. *1. The commissioner of labor shall enforce the provisions of this article, the rules and regulations adopted by the industrial board pursuant thereto, and the rules and regulations of the commissioner of labor continued in force by this article.*

2. The commissioner of labor shall [see that every necessary precaution is taken to insure the safety and health of employees employed in the mines and quarries in the construction of tunnels of the state and shall prescribe rules and regulations therefor;] keep a record of the names and location of [such] *all* mines, tunnels and quarries, and the names of the persons or corporations owning or operating the same; collect data concerning the working thereof; examine carefully into the method of timbering shafts, drifts, inclines, slopes and tunnels, through which employees and other persons pass, in the performance of their daily labor, and see that the persons or corporations owning and operating such mines, and quarries and constructing tunnels comply with the provisions of this chapter; and such information shall be furnished by the person operating such mine, tunnel or quarry, upon the demand of the commissioner of labor. The commissioner of labor shall keep a record of all mine, tunnel and quarry examinations, showing the date thereof, and the condition in which the mines, tunnels and quarries are found, and the manner of working the same. He shall make an annual report to the legislature during the month of January, containing a statement of the number of mines, tunnels and quarries visited, the number in operation, the number of men employed, and the number and cause of accidents, fatal and nonfatal, that may have occurred in and about the same.

§ 12. Article ten-a of such chapter is hereby renumbered article eleven and inserted in place of present article eleven hereinafter renumbered.

§ 13. Article eleven of such chapter is hereby renumbered article twelve and inserted in place of present article twelve hereinafter repealed.

§ 14. Sections one hundred and sixty-seven, one hundred and sixty-eight, one hundred and sixty-nine, one hundred and seventy-one, one hundred and seventy-two and one hundred and seventy-three of such chapter are hereby amended to read as follows:

§ 167. Registry of children employed. The owner, manager or agent of a mercantile or other establishment specified in section one hundred and sixty-one, employing children, shall keep or cause to be kept in the office of such establishment, a register, in which shall be recorded the name, birthplace, age and place of residence of all children so employed under the age of sixteen years. Such register and the certificate filed in such office shall be produced for inspection, upon the demand of an officer of the board, department or commissioner of health of the town, village or city where such establishment is situated, or if such establishment is situated in a city of the first *or second* class, upon the demand of the commissioner of labor. On termination of the employment of the child so registered and whose certificate is so filed, such certificate shall be forthwith surrendered by the employer to the child or its parent or guardian or custodian. An officer of the board, department or commissioner of health of the town, village or city where a mercantile or other establishment mentioned in this article is situated, or if such establishment is situated in a city of the first *or second* class the commissioner of labor may make demand on an employer in whose establishment a child apparently under the age of sixteen years is employed or permitted or suffered to work, and whose employment certificate is not then filed as required by this chapter, that such employer shall either furnish him, within ten days, evidence satisfactory to him that such child is in fact over sixteen years of age, or shall cease to employ or permit or suffer such child to work in such establishment. The officer may require from such employer the same evidence of age of such child as is required on the issuance of an employment certificate; and the employer furnishing such evidence shall not be required to furnish any further evidence of the age of the child. A notice embodying such demand may be served on such employer personally or may be sent by mail addressed to him at said establishment, and if served by post shall be deemed to have been served at the time when the letter containing the same would be delivered in the ordinary course of the post. When the employer is a corporation such notice may be served either personally upon an officer of such corporation, or by sending it by post addressed to the office or the principal place of business of such corporation. The papers constituting such evidence of age furnished by the employer in response to such demand shall, except in cities of the first *and second* class, be filed with the board, department or commissioner of health, and in cities of the first *and second* class with the commissioner of labor, and a material false statement made in such paper or affidavit by any person shall be a misdemeanor. In case such employer shall fail to produce and deliver to the officer of the board, department or commissioner of health, or in cities of the first *and second* class to the commissioner of labor, within ten days after such demand such evidence of age herein required by him, and shall thereafter continue to employ such child or permit or suffer such child to work in such mercantile or other establishment, proof of the giving of such notice and of such failure to produce and file such evidence shall be prima facie evidence in any prosecution brought for a violation of this article that such child is under sixteen years of age and is unlawfully employed.

§ 168. Wash-rooms and water-closets. Suitable and proper wash-rooms and water-closets shall be provided in, adjacent to or connected with mercantile establishments. Such rooms and closets shall be so located and arranged as to be easily accessible to the employees of such establishments.

Such water-closets shall be properly screened and ventilated, and, at all times, kept in a clean condition. The water-closets assigned to the female employees of such establishments shall be separate from those assigned to the male employees.

If a mercantile establishment has not provided wash-rooms and water-closets as required by this section, the board or department of health or health commissioners of the town, village or city where such establishment is situated, unless such establishment is situated in a city of the first *or second* class, in which case the commissioner of labor shall cause to be served upon the owner, agent or lessee of the building occupied by such establishment a written notice of the omission and directing such owner, agent or lessee to comply with the provisions of this section respecting such wash-rooms and water-closets.

Such owner shall, within fifteen days after the receipt of such notice, cause such wash-rooms and water-closets to be provided.

§ 169. Lunch-rooms. If a lunch-room is provided in a mercantile establishment where females are employed, such lunch-room shall not be next to or adjoining the water-closets, unless permission is first obtained from the board or department of health or health commissioners of the town, village or city where such mercantile establishment is situated, unless such establishment is situated in a city of the first *or second* class in which case such permission must be obtained from the commissioner of labor. Such permission shall be granted unless it appears that proper sanitary conditions do not exist, and it may be revoked at any time by the board or department of health or health commissioners if it appears that such lunch-room is kept in a manner or in a part of a building injurious to the health of the employees, unless such establishment is situated in a city of the first *or second* class, in which case sand permission may be so revoked by the commissioner of labor.

§ 171. Employment of women and children in basements. Women or children shall not be employed or permitted to work in the basement of a mercantile establisment, unless permitted by the board or department of health, or health commissioner of the town, village or city where such mercantile establishment is situated, unless such establishment is situated in a city of the first *or second* class in which case such permission must be obtained from the commissioner of labor. Such permission shall be granted unless it appears that such basement is not sufficiently lighted and ventilated, and is not in good sanitary condition.

§ 172. Enforcement of article. Except in cities of the first *and second* class the board or department of health or health commissioners of a town, village or city affected by this article shall enforce the same and prosecute all violations thereof. Proceedings to prosecute such violations must be begun within sixty days after the alleged offense was committed. All officers and members of such boards or department, all health commissioners, inspectors and other persons appointed or designated by such boards, departments or commissioners may visit and inspect, at reasonable hours and when practicable and necessary, all mercantile or other establishments herein specified within the town, village or city for which they are appointed. No person shall interfere with or prevent any such officer from making such visitations and inspections, nor shall he be obstructed or injured by force or otherwise while in the performance of his duties. All persons connected with any such mercantile or other establishment herein specified shall properly answer all questions asked by such officer or inspector in reference to any of the provisions of this article. In cities of the first *and second* class the commissioner of labor shall enforce the provisions of this article, and for that purpose he and his subordinates shall poseess all powers herein conferred upon town, village, or city boards and departments of health and their commissioners, inspectors and other officers, except that the board or department of health of said cities of the first *and second* class shall continue to issue employment certificates as provided in section one hundred and sixty-three of this chapter.

§ 173 [Copy of article to be posted. A copy of this article shall be posted in a conspicuous place on every floor in each establishment wherein three or more persons are employed who are affected by this provision.] *Laws to be posted. A copy or abstract of applicable provisions of this chapter and of the rules and regulations of the industrial board to be prepared and furnished by the commissioner of labor shall be kept posted by the employer in a conspicuous place on each floor of every mercantile or other establishment specified in article twelve of this chapter situated in cities of the first or second class, wherein three or more persons are employed who are affected by such provisions.*

§ 15. Article twelve of such chapter is hereby repealed.

§ 16. This act shall take effect immediately.

BILL No. 2.

AN ACT

TO AMEND THE PENAL LAW, IN RELATION TO VIOLATIONS OF PROVISIONS OF THE LABOR LAW, THE INDUSTRIAL CODE, THE RULES AND REGULATIONS OF THE INDUSTRIAL BOARD OF THE DEPARTMENT OF LABOR AND THE ORDERS OF THE COMMISSIONER OF LABOR.

The People of the State of New York, represented in Senate and Assembly, do enact as follows:

Section 1. Section twelve hundred and seventy-five of chapter eighty-eight of the laws of nineteen hundred and nine, entitled "An act to provide for the punishment of crime, constituting chapter forty of the consolidated laws," as amended by chapter seven hundred and forty-nine of the laws of nineteen hundred and eleven, is hereby amended to read as follows:

§ 1275. Violations of provisions of labor law; *the industrial code; the rules and regulations of the industrial board of the department of labor; orders of the commissioner of labor.* Any person who violates or does not comply with *any provision of the labor law, and provision of the industrial code, any rule or regulation of the industrial board of the department of labor, or any lawful order of the commissioner of labor;*

[1. The provisions of article three of the labor law, relating to the department of labor;

2. The provisions of article four of the labor law, relating to the bureau of labor statistics;

3. The provisions of artcle five of the labor law, relating to the bureau of factory inspection;

4. The provisions of article six of the labor law, relating to factories;

5. The provisions of artcle seven of the labor law relating to the manufacture of articles in tenements;

6. The provisions of article eight of the labor law, relating to bakeries and confectionery establishments;

7. The provisions of article eleven of the labor law, relating to mercantile establishments, and the employment of women and children therein;

8 A.]and any person who knowingly makes a false statement in or in relation to any application made for an employment certificate as to any matter required by article six and eleven of the labor law to appear in any affidavit, record, transcript or certificate therein provided for, is guilty of a misdemeanor and upon conviction shall be punished, *except as in this chapter otherwise provided,* for a first offense by a fine of not less than twenty nor more than fifty dollars; for a second offense by a fine of not less than fifty nor more than two hundred and fifty dollars, or by imprisonment for not more than thirty days or by both such fine and imprisonment; for a third offense by a fine of not less than two hundred and fifty dollars, or by imprisonment for not more than sixty days, or by both such fine and imprisonment.

§ 2. Section twelve hundred and seventy-three of such chapter is hereby repealed.

§ 3. This act shall take effect immediately.

BILL No. 3.

An Act

To Amend the Labor Law, in Relation to Fire Prevention in Factories.

The People of the State of New York, represented in Senate and Assembly, do enact as follows:

Section 1. Section eighty-three-c of chapter thirty-six of the laws of nineteen hundred and nine, entitled "An act relating to labor, constituting chapter thirty-one of the consolidated laws," as amended by chapter three hundred and twenty-nine of the laws of nineteen hundred and twelve, is hereby amended to read as follows:

§ 83-c. Fireproof receptacles; gas jests; smoking. 1. Every factory shall be provided with properly covered fireproof receptacles, the number, style and location of which shall be approved in the city of New York by the fire commissioner, and elsewhere, by the commissioner of labor. There shall be deposited in such receptacles all inflammable waste materials, cuttings and rubbish. No waste materials, cuttings *or* [and] rubbish shall be permitted to accumulate on the floors of any factory but shall be removed therefrom not less than twice each day. All such waste materials, cuttings and rubbish shall be entirely removed from a factory building at least once in each day[.]*, except that baled waste material may be stored in fireproof enclosures provided that all such baled waste material shall be removed from such building at least once in each month.*

2. All gas jets or lights in factories shall be properly enclosed by globes, wire cages or otherwise properly protected in a manner approved in the city of New York by the fire commissioner of such city, and elsewhere, by the commissioner of labor.

3. [Smoking in a factory] *No person shall smoke in any factory* [is prohibited]. A notice of such prohibition stating the penalty for violation thereof shall be posted *in every entrance hall and every elevator car, and in every stairhall and room* on every floor of such factory in English and also in such other language or languages as the fire commissioner of the city of New York in such city, and elsewhere, the state fire marshal, shall direct. The fire commissioner of the city of New York in such city, and elsewhere, the state fire marshal shall enforce the provisions of this subdivision.

§ 2. This act shall take effect immediately.

BILL No. 4.

AN ACT

TO AMEND THE LABOR LAW, IN RELATION TO FIRE ALARM SIGNAL SYSTEMS AND FIRE DRILLS.

The People of the State of New York, represented in Senate and Assembly, do enact as follows:

Section 1. Section eighty-three-a of chapter thirty-six of the laws of nineteen hundred and nine, entitled "An act relating to labor, constituting chapter thirty-one of the consolidated laws," as amended by chapter three hundred and thirty of the laws of nineteen hundred and twelve, is hereby amended to read as follows:

§ 83-a. *Fire alarm signal systems and* fire drills. 1. *Every factory building over two stories in height in which more than twenty-five persons are employed above the ground floor shall be equipped with a fire alarm signal system with a sufficient number of signals clearly audible to all occupants thereof. The industrial board may make rules and regulations prescribing the number and location of such signals. Such system shall be installed by the owner or lessee of the building and shall permit the sounding of all the alarms within the building whenever the alarm is sounded in any portion thereof. Such system shall be maintained in good working order. No person shall tamper with, or render ineffective any portion of said system except to repair the same. It shall be the duty of whoever discovers a fire to cause an alarm to be sounded immediately.*

2. In every factory *building over two stories in height* in which more than twenty-five persons are [regularly] employed above the ground [or first] floor, a fire drill *which will conduct all the occupants of such building to a place of safety and in which all* [of] the occupants of such building *shall participate simultaneously* shall be conducted at least once *a month* [every three months under the supervision of the local fire department or one of its officers].

In the city of New York the fire commissioner of such city, and in all other parts of the state, the state fire marshal shall cause to be organized and shall supervise and regulate such fire drills, and shall make rules, regulations and special orders necessary or suitable to each situation and in the case of buildings containing more than one tenant, necessary or suitable to the adequate co-operation of all the tenants of such building in a fire drill of all the occupants thereof. Such rules, regulations and orders may prescribe upon whom shall rest the duty of carrying out the same. Such special orders may require posting of the same or an abstract thereof. A demonstration of such fire drill shall be given upon the request of an authorized representative of the fire department of the city, village or town in which the factory is located, and, except in the city of New York, upon the request of the state fire marshal or any of his deputies or assistants. [Appropriate rules and regulations to make effective this provision shall be prepared for the city of New York by the fire commissioner of such city, and for other parts of the state, by the state fire marshal. Such rules and regulations shall be posted on each floor of every factory to which they apply.]

3. In the city of New York the fire commissioner of such city, and elsewhere, the state fire marshal is charged with the duty of enforcing this section.

§ 2. This act shall take effect October first, nineteen hundred and thirteen.

BILL No. 5.

AN ACT

TO AMEND THE LABOR LAW, IN RELATION TO AUTOMATIC SPRINKLERS.

The People of the State of New York, represented in Senate and Assembly, do enact as follows:

Section 1. Section eighty-three-b of chapter thirty-six of the laws of nineteen hundred and nine, entitled "An act relating to labor, constituting chapter thirty-one of the consolidated laws," as amended by chapter three hundred and thirty-two of the laws of nineteen hundred and twelve, is hereby amended to read as follows:

§ 83-b. Automatic sprinklers. In every factory building *heretofore erected* over seven stories or over ninety feet in height in which wooden flooring or wooden trim is used, *and in which any manufacturing is carried on* and more than two hundred people are [regularly] employed above the seventh floor or more than ninety feet above the ground level of such building, *and in every factory building hereafter erected over seven stories or over ninety feet in height in which any manufacturing is carried on above the seventh floor, the owner of the building shall properly install a properly constructed and effective automatic sprinkler system throughout the same. The sprinkler system shall have at least one automatic supply capable of furnishing water at a pressure of not less than fifteen pounds on the highest line of sprinklers. The capacity of the automatic supply shall be ample to furnish water to at least twenty-five per centum of the sprinklers on any one floor area as defined in section seventy-nine-a, subdivision two of this chapter for at least twenty minutes at the average rate of twenty gallons per head per minute. Automatic sprinkler systems shall also be installed in all other factory buildings where the safety of the occupants requires them. The industrial board shall adopt rules and regulations for the installation of automatic sprinkler systems in such cases. The industrial board shall also have power to adopt rules and regulations etsablishing requirements and standards for automatic sprinkler systems in addition to the foregoing requirements and not inconsistent therewith. No person shall tamper with, or render ineffective, any portion of an automatic sprinkler system, except to repair the same.* [The owner of the building shall install an automatic sprinkler system approved as to form and manner in the city of New York by the fire commissioner of such city, and elsewhere, by the state fire marshal. Such installation shall be made within one year after this section takes effect, but the fire commissioner of the city of New York in such city and the state fire marshal elsewhere may, for good cause shown, extend such time for an additional year. A failure to comply with this section shall be a misdemeanor as provided by section twelve hundred and seventy-five of the penal law and t]*T*he provisions hereof shall [also] be enforced in the city of New York by the fire commissioner of such city in the manner provided by title three of chapter fifteen of the Greater New York charter, and elsewhere by the state fire marshal, in the manner provided by article ten-a of the insurance law.

§ 2. This act shall take effect October first, nineteen hundred and thirteen.

BILL No. 6.

AN ACT

TO AMEND THE LABOR LAW, IN RELATION TO FIRE-ESCAPES AND EXITS IN EXISTING FACTORIES; THE FUTURE CONSTRUCTION OF FACTORY BUILDINGS; AND THE LIMITATION OF THE NUMBER OF OCCUPANTS IN FACTORIES.

The People of the State of New York, represented in Senate and Assembly, do enact as follows:

Section 1. Article six of chapter thirty-six of the laws of nineteen hundred and nine, entitled "An act relating to labor, constituting chapter thirty-one of the consolidated laws," is hereby amended by inserting therein after section seventy-nine, six new sections, to be sections seventy-nine-a, seventy-nine-b, seventy-nine-c, seventy-nine-d, seventy-nine-e and seventy-nine-f, to read as follows:

§ 79-a. Construction of factory buildings hereafter erected. No factory shall be conducted in any building hereafter erected more than one story in height unless such building shall conform to the following requirements:

1. All buildings more than four stories in height shall be of fireproof construction. The roofs of all buildings shall be covered with incombustible material or shall be of tar and slag or plastic cement supported by or applied to arches of fireproof material, and the cornices shall be constructed of incombustible material. All exterior walls within twenty-five feet of any non-fireproof building shall be not less than eight inches thick and shall extend three feet above the roof.

2. Floor area and required exits. The term floor area as used in this section signifies the entire space between fire walls, or between a fire wall and an exterior wall of a building, or between the exterior walls of the building where there is no intervening fire wall. From every floor area there shall be not less than two means of exit remote from each other, one of which on every floor above the ground floor shall be an interior enclosed fireproof stairway or an exterior enclosed fireproof stairway, and the other shall be such a stairway or a horizontal exit. No point in any floor

area shall be more than one hundred feet distant from the entrance to one such means of exit. Whenever any floor area exceeds five thousand square feet there shall be provided at least one additional means of exit as hereinbefore described for each five thousand square feet or part thereof in excess of five thousand square feet. In every building over one hundred feet in height there shall be at least one exterior enclosed fireproof stairway which shall be accessible from any point in the building.

3. Stairways. All stairways shall be constructed of incombustible material and shall have an unobstructed width of at least forty-four inches throughout their length, except that hand rails may project not more than three and one-half inches into such width. There shall be not more than twelve feet six inches in height between successive landings. The treads shall be not less than ten inches wide exclusive of nosing, and the rise shall be not more than seven and three-fourths inches. No stairway with "winders" shall be allowed except as a connection from one floor to another. The treads shall be constructed and maintained in such manner as to prevent persons from slipping thereon. Every stairway shall be enclosed on all sides by fireproof partitions extending continuously from the lowest story to which such stairway extends to three feet above the roof and the roof of the enclosure shall be constructed of fireproof material at least four inches thick with a skylight at least three-fourths the area of the shaft. All stairways serving as required means of exit shall extend to the roof and shall lead continuously to the street or to a fireproof passageway independent of other means of exit from the building, opening on a road or street, or to an open area affording unobstructed passage to a road or street. All stairways that extend to the top story shall be continued to the roof. Provision shall be made for the adequate lighting of all stairways by artificial light.

4. Doors and doorways. All doors shall open outwardly. The width of the hallways and exit doors leading to the street, at the street-level, shall be not less than the aggregate width of all stairways leading to them. Every door leading to or opening on a stairway shall have an unobstructed width of at least forty-four inches.

5. Partitions. All partitions in the interior of buildings of fireproof construction shall be of incombustible material.

6. Openings to be enclosed. All elevator and dumb-waiter shafts, vent and light shafts, pipe and duct shafts, hoistways and all other vertical openings leading from one floor to another shall be enclosed throughout their height on all sides by enclosures of fireproof material. Every such enclosure shall have a roof of fireproof material and if the enclosure extends to the top story it shall be continued to three feet above the roof of the building and shall have at the top of a skylight in a metal frame at least three-fourths of the area of the shaft or exterior window with metal frame and sash. The bottom of the enclosure shall be of fireproof material unless the opening extends to the cellar bottom. All openings in such enclosures shall be provided with fireproof doors except that openings in the enclosures of vent and light shafts shall be provided either with fireproof doors or with windows having metal frames and sash and wired glass where glass is used.

§ 79-b. Requirements for existing buildings. No factory shall be conducted in any building heretofore erected unless such building shall conform to the following requirements:

1. Required exits. Every building over two stories in height shall be provided on each floor with at least two means of exit or escape from fire, remote from each other, one of which on every floor above the ground floor shall lead to or open on an interior stairway which in buildings over four stories in height shall be enclosed as hereinafter provided, or to an exterior enclosed fireproof stairway. The other shall lead to such a stairway; or to a horizontal exit; or to an exterior screened stairway; or when, in the opinion of the industrial board the safety of the occupants of the building would not be endangered thereby, to fire-escapes on the outside of the building. No point on any floor of such factory shall be more than one hundred feet distant from the entrance to one such means of exit. Whenever egress may be had from the roof to an adjoining or near-by structure, every stairway serving as a required means of exit shall be extended to the roof. All such stairways shall extend to the first story and lead to the street, or to an unobstructed passageway leading to a street or road or to an open area affording safe passage to a street or road.

2. Stairway enclosures. All interior stairways serving as required means of exit in buildings more than four stories in height and the landings, platforms and passageways connected therewith shall be enclosed on all sides by partitions of fire resisting material extending continuously from the basement. Where the stairway extends to the top floor of the building such partitions shall extend to three feet above the roof. All openings in such partitions shall be provided with self closing doors constructed of fire resisting material except where such openings are in the exterior wall of the building. All such partitions and the doors provided for the openings therein shall be constructed in such manner as the industrial board may prescribe by its rules and regulations. Whenever, in the case of any existing buildings not over six stories in height, the industrial board shall find that the requirements of this and the last preceding subdivision relating to stairway enclosures can be dispensed with or modified without endangering the safety of persons employed in such buildings, the industrial board shall have power to adopt such rules and regulations as may, in its opinion, meet the conditions existing in such buildings, which rules and regulations may make said requirements inapplicable or modify the same in such manner as it may find to be adapted to securing the safety of persons employed therein.

The industrial board shall have power to adopt rules and regulations, permitting, under conditions therein prescribed, as a substitute for the stairway enclosures herein required the use of partitions heretofore constructed in such manner and of such fire resisting material as have heretofore been approved by the local authorities exercising supervision over the construction and alteration of buildings. In such cases, however, every opening in the enclosing partitions shall be provided with fire doors.

3. Doors. Where five or more persons are employed on any floor of a factory building every door on such floor leading to or opening on any means of exit shall open outwardly or be double swinging doors. All exit doors in the first story, including the doors of the vestibule, shall open outwardly.

4. Fire-escapes. All outside fire-escapes shall be constructed of wrought iron or steel and shall be so designed, constructed and

erected as to safely sustain on all platforms, balconies and stairways a live load of not less than ninety pounds per square foot with a factor of safety of four. Wherever practicable, a continuous run or straight run stairway shall be used. On every floor above the first there shall be balconies or landings embracing one or more easily accessible and unobstructed openings at each floor level, connected with each other and with the ground by means of a stairway constructed as hereinafter provided and well fastened and secured. All openings leading to outside fire-escapes shall have an unobstructed width of at least two feet and an unobstructed height of at least six feet and shall extend to the floor level or within six inches thereof, and shall be not more than seven inches above the floor of the fire-escape balcony. Such openings shall have metal frames and be provided with doors constructed of fireproof material with wired glass where glass is used. All windows opening upon the course of the fire-escape shall be fireproof windows. The balconies shall have an unobstructed width of at least four feet throughout their length and shall have a landing not less than twenty-four inches square at the head of every stairway. There shall be a passageway between the stairway opening and the side of the building at least eighteen inches wide throughout except where the stairways reach and leave the balconies at the ends or where double run stairways are used. The stairway opening of the balconies shall be of a size sufficient to provide clear headway and shall be guarded on the long side by an iron railing not less than three feet in height. Each balcony shall be surrounded by an iron railing not less than three feet in height thoroughly and properly braced. The balconies shall be connected by stairways not less than twenty-two inches wide placed at an incline of not more than forty-five degrees, with steps of not less than eight-inch tread and not over eight-inch rise and provided with a hand-rail not less than three feet in height. The treads of such stairways shall be so constructed as to sustain a live load of four hundred pounds per step with a factor of safety of four. There shall be a similar stairway from the top floor balcony to the roof, except where the fire-escape is erected on the front of the building. A similar stairway shall also be provided from the lowest balcony to a safe landing place beneath, which stairway shall remain down permanently or be arranged to swing up and down automatically by counterbalancing weights. When not erected on the front of the building, safe and unobstructed egress shall be provided from the foot of the fire-escape by means of an open court or courts or a fireproof passageway having an unobstructed width of at least three feet throughout leading to the street, or by means of an open area having communication with the street; such fireproof passageway shall be adequately lighted at all times and the lights shall be so arranged as to ensure their reliable operation when through accident or other cause the regular factory lighting is extinguished.

5. The provisions of subdivision four shall not apply where at the time this act takes effect there are outside fire-escapes with balconies on each floor of the building connected with stairways placed at an angle of not more than sixty degrees, provided that such existing outside fire-escapes have or shall be provided with the following:

A stairway leading from the top floor balcony to the roof, except where the fire-escapes are erected on the front of the building; a stairway not less than twenty-two inches wide from the lowest balcony to a safe landing place beneath, which stairway remains down permanently or is arranged to swing up and down by counter-balancing weights; a safe and unobstructed exit to the street from the foot of such fire escapes as provided in subdivision four hereof; steps connecting the sill of every opening leading to the fire-escapes with the floor wherever such sill is more than three feet above the floor level; and all openings leading to the fire escapes provided with windows having metal frames and sash and with wired glass where glass is used, or with doors constructed in accordance with the requirements of subdivision four; and all windows opening upon the course of the fire-escape provided with fireproof windows.

§ 79-c. Additional requirements common to buildings heretofore and hereafter erected. No factory shall be conducted in any building unless such building shall be so constructed, equipped and maintained in all respects as to afford adequate protection against fire to all persons employed therein, nor unless, in addition to the requirements of section seventy-nine-a in the case of a building hereafter erected or of section seventy-nine-b in the case of a building heretofore erected, such building shall conform to the following requirements:

1. Stairways. Stairways shall be provided with proper and substantial hand-rails. Where the stairway is enclosed by fireproof partitions the bottom of the enclosure shall be of fireproof material at least four inches thick unless the fireproof partitions extend to the cellar bottom. All stairways that extend to the top story shall be continued to the roof.

2. Doors and windows. No doors, window or other opening on any floor of a factory building shall be obstructed by stationary metal bars, grating or wire mesh. Metal bars, grating or wire mesh provided for any such door, window or other opening shall be so constructed as to be readily movable or removable from both sides in such manner as to afford the free and unobstructed use of such door, window or other opening as a means of egress in case of need and they shall be left unlocked during working hours. Every door opening on a stairway or other means of exit shall so open as not to obstruct the passageway. A clearly painted sign marked "exit" in letters not less than eight inches in height shall be placed over all exits leading to stairways and other means of egress, and in addition a red light shall be placed over all such exits for use in time of darkness.

3. Access to exits. There shall at all times be maintained continuous, safe, unobstructed passageways on each floor of the building, with an unobstructed width of at least three feet throughout their length leading directly to every means of egress, including outside fire-escapes and passenger elevators. All means of egress shall be maintained in an unobstructed condition. No door leading into or out of any factory or any floor thereof shall be locked, bolted or fastened during working hours.

4. Regulation by industrial board. The industrial board shall have power to adopt rules and regulations and establish requirements and standards for construction, equipment and maintenance of factory buildings or of particular classes of factory buildings and the means and adequacy of exit therefrom in order to carry out the purposes of this chapter in addition to the requirements of this section and of sections seventy-nine-a and seventy-nine-b, and not inconsistent therewith.

§ 79-d. Effect of foregoing provisions; inspection of buildings and approval of plans. 1. Effect of foregoing provisions. The requirements of sections seventy-nine-a, seventy-nine-b and seventy-nine-c are not in substitution for the requirements of any general or special law or local ordinance relating to the construction, equipment or maintenance of buildings, but the provisions of such general and special laws and local ordinances shall be observed as well as the provisions of said sections. The provisions of sections seventy-nine-a, seventy-nine-b and seventy-nine-c shall supersede all provisions inconsistent therewith in any special law or local ordinance, and any provision of law or ordinance which gives power to any officer to establish requirements inconsistent with the provisions of such sections or the rules and regulations adopted by the industrial board under the provisions of this article.

2. Inspection of buildings. The officer of any city, village or town having power to inspect buildings therein for the purpose of determining their conformity to the requirements of law or ordinance governing the construction thereof, shall, whenever requested by the commissioner of labor, inspect any factory building therein and certify to the commissioner of labor in detail whether or not such building conforms to the requirements of this chapter and the rules and regulations of the industrial board, and such certificate shall be filed in the office of the commissioner of labor and shall be presumptive evidence of the truth of the matters therein stated.

3. Approval of plans. Before construction or alteration of a building in which it is intended to conduct one or more factories, the plans and specifications for such construction or alteration may be submitted to the commissioner of labor and filed in his office in such form and with such information as may be required by him or by the rules and regulations of the industrial board, and if such plans and specifications comply with the requirements of this chapter and the rules and regulations of the industrial board, he shall issue his certificate approving the same, which certificate shall bear the date when issued. Whenever any certificate shall be issued by the commissioner of labor under this section the particulars of such certificate shall be recorded and indexed in the records of his office. Before issuing any such cer-

tificate the commissioner of labor may request the officer of the city, village or town in which such building is located having power to examine and pass upon plans for construction of buildings with reference to their conformity to the requirements of law or ordinance governing the construction thereof, to examine such plans and specifications and to certify to the commissioner of labor whether or not such plans and specifications conform to the requirements of this chapter and the rules and regulations of the industrial board, and such officer shall thereupon make such examination and so certify in detail to the commissioner of labor and such certificate shall be filed in the office of the commissioner of labor and shall be presumptive evidence of the truth of the matters therein stated.

4. Certificate of compliance. After such construction or alteration shall be completed, the commissioner of labor shall, when requested by the owner or person filing such plans, ascertain by inspection or in the manner provided in subdivision two of this section, whether such building conforms to the requirements of this chapter and the rules and regulations of the industrial board; and if he finds that it does conform thereto, shall issue his certificate to that effect, which shall bear the date when issued.

§ 79-e. Limitation of number of occupants. The number of persons who may occupy any factory building or portion thereof above the ground floor shall be limited to such a number as can safely escape from such building by the means of exit provided in the building.

1. In buildings hereafter erected no more than fourteen persons shall be employed or permitted or suffered to work on any one floor for every full twenty-two inches in width of stairway conforming to the requirements for a required means of exit except as to extension to the roof, provided for such floor. No allowance shall be made for any excess in width of less than twenty-two inches.

2. In buildings heretofore erected no more than fourteen persons shall be employed or permitted or suffered to work on any one floor for every eighteen inches in width of stairway provided for such floor and conforming to the requirements for a required means of exit except as to extension to the roof, and for any excess in width of less than eighteen inches, a proportionate

increase in the number of occupants shall be allowed. Where the industrial board shall find that the safety of the occupants of any such building will not be endangered thereby, it may allow an increase in the number of occupants of any floor in such building to a number not greater than at the rate of twenty persons for every eighteen inches in width of such stairway provided for such floor, with a proportionate increase in the number of occupants for any excess in width of less than eighteen inches.

3. In any building for every additional sixteen inches over ten feet in height between two floors, one additional person may be employed on the upper of such floors for every eighteen inches in width of stairway leading therefrom to the lower of such floors in buildings heretofore erected, and one for every twenty-two inches in width of such stairway in buildings hereafter erected, provided that such stairways conform to the requirements for required means of exit as to extension to the roof.

4. In any building, if any stairway has steps of the type known as "winders," a deduction of ten per centum shall be made in counting the capacity of such stairway.

5. In any building where the stairways and stairhalls are enclosed in fireproof partitions or where, at the time this act takes effect, the stairways and stairhalls are enclosed in partitions of brick, concrete, terra-cotta blocks or reinforced concrete constructed in a manner heretofore approved by the superintendent of buildings of the city of New York having jurisdiction if in such city, or elsewhere in the state, in a manner conforming to the rules and regulations to be adopted by the industrial board under the provisions of subdivision two of section seventy-nine-b, all openings in which enclosing partitions are or shall hereafter be provided with fireproof doors, in either of such cases so many additional persons may be employed on any floor as can occupy the enclosed stairhall or halls on that floor, allowing five square feet of unobstructed floor space per person.

6. In any building where a horizontal exit is provided on any floor such number of persons may be employed on such floor as can occupy the smaller of the two spaces on such floor on either side of the fireproof partitions or fire walls, or as can occupy the floor of an adjoining or near-by building which is connected with such floor by openings in the wall or walls between the buildings

or by exterior balconies or bridges, in addition to the occupants of such connected floor in such adjoining or near-by building, allowing five square feet of unobstructed floor space per person, provided that the partitions or walls or balconies through which the horizontal exit is provided to such other portion of the same building or to such adjoining or near-by building shall have doorways of sufficient width to allow eighteen inches in width of opening for each fifty persons or fraction thereof so permitted to be employed on such floor in the case of horizontal exits heretofore constructed and twenty-two inches in the case of horizontal exits hereafter constructed.

7. In any building heretofore erected of fireproof construction, where any floor is subdivided by partitions of brick, terra cotta or concrete not less than four inches thick extending continuously from the fireproofing of the floor to the underside of the fireproofing of the floor above with all openings protected by fireproof doors not less than forty-four inches nor more than sixty-six inches in width, and in which all the windows on such floor and on the two floors directly underneath are fireproof windows, such number of persons may be employed on such floor as can occupy the smaller of the two spaces on either side of such partitions, allowing five square feet of unobstructed floor space per person, provided there shall be on each side of said partitions at least one stairway conforming to the requirements for a required means of exit; and provided further that such partitions have doorways of sufficient width to allow eighteen inches in width of openings for each fifty persons or fraction thereof so permitted to occupy such floor, and that such doorways shall be kept unlocked and unobstructed during working hours. The provisions of this subdivision shall apply to any fireproof building heretofore erected which may hereafter be made to conform to the requirements of this section.

8. In any building the number of persons permitted to be employed on any one floor under the provisions of subdivision one, two and three of this section may be increased fifty per centum where there is constructed, installed and maintained throughout the building an automatic sprinkler system conforming to the requirements of section eighty-three-b of this chapter and to the rules and regulations of the industrial board.

9. In any building, the number of persons who may be employed in any one floor shall in no event exceed such number as can occupy such floor, allowing thirty-six square feet of floor space per person if the building is not of fireproof construction, and thirty-two square feet of floor space per person if the building is of fireproof construction.

10. Where one floor is occupied by more than one tenant, the industrial board shall have power to make rules and regulations prescribing how many of the persons allowed to occupy such floor under the provisions of this section, may occupy the space of each tenant.

11. Posting. In every factory, two stories or over in height, the commissioner of labor shall cause to be posted notices specifying the number of persons that may occupy each floor thereof in accordance with the provisions of this section. Every such notice shall be posted in a conspicuous place in every stairhall and workroom. If any one floor is occupied by more than one tenant, such notices shall be posted in the space occupied by each tenant, and shall state the number of persons that may occupy such space. Every such notice shall bear the date when posted.

§ 79-f. Meaning of terms. The following terms when used in this article shall have the following meaning:

1. Fireproof construction. A building shall be deemed to be of fireproof construction if it conforms to the following requirements: All walls constructed of brick, stone, concrete or terra-cotta; all floors and roofs of brick, terra-cotta or reinforced concrete placed between steel or reinforced concrete beams and girders; all the steel entering into the structural parts encased in at least two inches of fireproof material, excepting the wall columns, which must be encased in at least eight inches of masonry on the outside and four inches on the inside; all stairwells, elevator wells, public hallways and corridors enclosed by fireproof partitions; all doors, fireproof; all stairways, landings, hallways and other floor surfaces of incombustible material; no woodwork or other combustible material used in any partition, furring, ceiling or floor; and all window frames, doors and sash, trim and other interior finish of incombustible material; all windows shall be fireproof windows except that in buildings under seventy feet in height fireproof win-

dows are required only when within thirty feet of another building or opening on a court or space less than thirty feet wide; except that in buildings under one hundred feet in height there may be wooden sleepers and floor finish and wooden trim, and except that in buildings under one hundred and fifty feet in height heretofore constructed there may be wooden sleepers, floor finish and trim and the windows need not be fireproof windows, excepting when such windows are within thirty feet of another building.

2. Fireproof material is material which is incombustible and is capable of resisting the effect of fire in such manner and to such extent as to insure the safety of the occupants of the building. The industrial board shall determine and in its rules and regulations shall specify what materials are fireproof materials within the meaning hereof. The industrial board shall also determine and in its rules and regulations shall specify what materials not being fireproof materials, within the meaning hereof, are fire resisting materials. Fire resisting material, when required by any of the provisions of this chapter, shall conform to the requirements of such rules and regulations.

3. Incombustible material is material which will not burn or support combustion.

4. A fire wall is a wall constructed of brick, concrete, terracotta blocks or reinforced stone concrete, and having at each floor level one or more openings each protected by fire doors so constructed as to prevent the spread of fire or smoke through the openings. In buildings of nonfireproof construction fire walls shall be at least twelve inches in thickness and shall extend continuously from the cellar floor through the entire building and at least three feet over the roof and be coped; except that walls heretofore erected not less than eight inches in thickness, but otherwise conforming to the requirements of this subdivision shall be considered fire walls within the meaning of this subdivision. No opening in such wall shall exceed sixty-six inches in width or sixty square feet in area, except that where openings not exceeding eight feet in width exist in fire walls heretofore erected, such walls may be considered fire walls within the meaning of this subdivision, and in the case of fire walls hereafter constructed no two openings in the same wall and at the same floor level shall be nearer than forty feet from the center of one opening to the center of another.

Every opening in a fire wall shall be protected by a fire door closing automatically on each side of the wall. At every opening in the fire wall there shall be an incombustible floor finish extending over the floor for the full thickness of the wall so as to completely separate the woodwork of the floors on each side of the fire wall. In fireproof buildings the fire walls shall comply with the foregoing requirements in all respects excepting that they may be of the thickness required by the provisions of this section with respect to fireproof partitions; such fire walls and fireproof partitions shall be continuous, from the cellar floor to the under side of the fireproof roof.

5. Fireproof partitions shall be built of brick, concrete, reinforced concrete or terra cotta blocks. When built of brick or concrete they shall be not less than eight inches in thickness for the uppermost forty feet, and shall increase four inches in thickness for each additional lower forty feet or part thereof; or, when wholly supported by suitable steel framing at vertical intervals of not over forty feet, they may be eight inches in thickness throughout their entire height. When wholly supported at vertical intervals of not over twenty-five feet, and built of terra cotta blocks, they shall be not less than six inches in thickness and when so supported and built of reinforced stone concrete, they shall be not less than four inches in thickness. The supporting steel framework shall be properly encased on all sides by not less than two inches of fireproof material, securely fastened to the steel work. All openings in such partitions shall be provided with fire doors.

6. Fire doors. Fire doors shall be metal-covered doors, or doors of such other material as shall be specified in the rules and regulations of the industrial board. They shall be provided with self-closing devices and have incombustible sills. The industrial board shall determine, and in its rules and regulations shall specify, the material and mode and manner of construction and erection of such doors.

7. Fireproof windows shall be windows constructed of metal frames and sash and provided with wired glass and of the automatic, self-closing type.

8. Exterior enclosed fireproof stairways shall be stairways completely enclosed from top to bottom by walls of fireproof

material not less than eight inches thick extending from the sidewalk, court or yard level to the roof, and with walls extending above the roof so as to form a bulkhead. The stairway shall in all other respects conform to the requirements of this article in regard to enclosed stairways. There shall be no opening in any wall separating the exterior enclosed fireproof stairway from the building. Access shall be provided to the stairway from every floor of the building by means of an outside balcony or vestibule of steel, iron or masonry. Every such balcony or vestibule shall have an unobstructed width of at least forty-four inches and shall be provided with a fireproof floor and a railing of incombustible material not less than three feet high. Access to such balconies from the building and to the stairway from the balconies, shall be by means of fire doors. The level of the balcony floor shall be not more than seven inches below the level of the door sill of the building. The doors shall be not less than forty-four inches wide and shall swing outward onto the balcony and inward from the balcony to the stairway, and shall be provided with locks or latches with visible fastenings requiring no key to open them in leaving the building. The landings in such stairway shall be of such width that the doors in opening into the stairway shall not reduce the free passageway of the landings to a width less than the width of the stairs. Every such stairway shall be provided with a proper lighting system which shall furnish adequate light and shall be so arranged as to ensure its reliable operation when, through accident or other cause, the regular factory lighting is extinguished. The balconies giving access to such stairways shall be open on at least one side upon an open space not less than one hundred square feet in area.

9. Horizontal exit. A horizontal exit shall be the connection by means of one or more openings not less than forty-four inches wide, protected by fire doors, through a fire wall in any building, or through a wall or walls between two buildings, which doors shall continuously be unlocked and the opening unobstructed whenever any person is employed on either side of the opening. Exterior balconies and bridges not less than forty-four inches in width connecting two buildings and not having a gradient of more than one foot fall in six, may also be counted as horizontal exits when the doors opening out upon said balconies or bridges

are fireproof doors and are level with the floors of the building, and when all doors of both buildings opening on such balconies or bridges are continuously kept unlocked and unobstructed whenever any person is employed on either side of the exit, and when such balconies or bridges are built of incombustible material and are capable of sustaining a live load of not less than ninety pounds per square foot with a factor of safety of four; and when such balconies or bridges are enclosed on all sides to a height of not less than six feet and on top and bottom by fireproof material, unless all windows or openings within thirty feet of such balconies in the connected buildings shall be encased in metal frames and sash and shall have wired glass where glass is used. In any case there shall be on each side of the wall or partition containing the horizontal exit and independent of said horizontal exit, at least one stairway conforming to the requirements for a required means of exit.

10. Exterior screened stairways used as one of the required means of exit in buildings heretofore erected shall be built of incombustible material. The risers of the stairs shall be not more than seven and three-quarters inches in height and the treads not less than ten inches wide. On each floor there shall be a balcony connecting with the stairs. Access to the balconies shall be by means of fire doors that shall open outwardly, so as not to obstruct the passageway, or slide freely, and shall extend to the floor level. All windows or other openings opening upon the course of such stairs shall be fireproof. The level of the balcony floor shall not be more than seven inches below the level of the door sill. The stairs shall continue from the roof to the ground level, and there shall be independent means of exit from the bottom of such stairs to the street or to an open court or to a fireproof enclosed passageway leading to the street or to an open area having communication with the street or road. The balconies and stairs shall be enclosed in a screen of incombustible material.

11. The provisions of subdivisions four to nine inclusive of this section shall apply to all buildings hereafter erected and to all construction hereafter made in buildings heretofore erected. The industrial board shall adopt rules and regulations regulating construction heretofore made in buildings heretofore erected requiring compliance with such of the requirements of the said sub-

divisions or with such other or different requirements as said board may find to be reasonable and adequate to protect persons employed in such buildings against fire.

§ 2. Sections eighty, eighty-two and eighty-three of such chapter are hereby repealed.

§ 3. This act shall take effect October first, nineteen hundred and thirteen, except that section seventy-nine-e of the labor law as added by this act shall take effect February first, nineteen hundred and fourteen.

BILL No. 7.

AN ACT

TO AMEND THE GREATER NEW YORK CHARTER, IN RELATION TO THE BETTER PREVENTION OF FIRES.

The People of the State of New York, represented in Senate and Assembly, do enact as follows:

Section 1. Section seven hundred and seventy-four of the Greater New York charter, as re-enacted by chapter four hundred and sixty-six of the laws of nineteen hundred and one and as added by chapter eight hundred and ninety-nine of the laws of nineteen hundred and eleven, is hereby amended to read as follows:

§ 774. The commissioner shall enforce all laws and ordinances *and the rules and regulations of the industrial board of the department of labor* in respect of

1. The prevention of fires;

2. The storage, sale, transportation or use of combustibles, chemicals and explosives;

3. The installation and maintenance of automatic or other fire-alarm systems and fire-extinguishing equipment;

4. The means and adequacy of exit, in case of fire, from all buildings, structures, enclosures, vessels, places and premises in which numbers of persons work, live, or congregate from time to time for any purpose except tenement-houses *and except factories as defined by the labor law.*

5. The investigation of the cause, circumstances and origin of fires and the suppression of arson.

§ 2. Subdivisions two and three of section seven hundred and seventy-five of such chapter are hereby amended to read as follows:

2. Order, in writing, the remedying of any condition found to exist in, on or about any building, structure, enclosure, vessel, place or premises, except tenement-houses, *and except factories as defined by the labor law,* in violation of any law or ordinance in respect to fires or to the prevention of fires, except the tenement-house law;

3. Require, in writing, the installation, as prescribed by any law or ordinance *or by the rules and regulations of the industrial board of the department of labor,* in any building, structure or enclosure of automatic or other fire-alarm system of fire-extinguishing equipment and the maintenance and repair thereof, or the construction, as prescribed by any law or ordinance, of adequate and safe means of exit *from all buildings and structures except tenement houses and except factories as defined by the labor law;*

§ 3. Section seven hundred and seventy-seven of such chapter is hereby amended to read as follows:

§ 777. The owner, lessee or occupant of any building, structure, vessel, enclosure, place or premises affected by any order of the department, or his agent, may make written demand upon the commissioner for a survey of such building, structure, vessel, enclosure, place or premises to determine whether or not such order is valid and reasonable, which demand for survey must be served upon the commissioner or one of his deputies, or a member of the uniformed force of the department, if personal service cannot be made upon the commissioner or one of his deputies, within forty-eight hours, Sundays and holidays excluded, after the service of the order referred to in such demand. A demand for survey served upon a deputy commissioner or a member of the uniformed force of the department shall be forthwith transmitted to the commissioner. Upon receipt of a demand for a survey the commissioner shall immediately issue an order for the same, naming therein three persons to act as surveyors, one of whom shall be an officer or an employee of the bureau of fire prevention or a member of the municipal explosives commission; another shall be an architect or builder of at least ten years' experience, *nominated by the person demanding the survey,* and the third a person to be chosen *by the fire commissioner* from a list to be furnished by the [board of fire underwriters] *New York Chapter of the American Institute of Architects, if the premises be in the borough of Manhattan, the Bronx or Richmond, or by the Brooklyn Chapter of the American Institute of Architects, if the premises be in the borough of Brooklyn or Queens, or by the New York Society of Architects, or by the American Institute of Consulting Engineers,* or provided by the commissioner, with the approval of the mayor, in the event [of the board of fire underwriters] *that such chapter or such society or institute* shall not furnish such a list. *The date and hour when the survey shall be made shall be stated in the order therefor. A copy of such order shall be served upon the person demanding the survey at least twenty-four hours before the hour fixed in the order for the holding of such survey and he shall have the right to be present and be heard at the same in person, or by agent or attorney; provided that such copy of an order of survey may be served as provided generally in respect of service of orders of the department, by section seven hundred and seventy-five of this act. If the person demanding the survey neglects or refuses to appoint such surveyor, the other two surveyors may make such survey; and in case of disagreement of the latter they may appoint a third person to take part in such survey who shall also be an architect or builder of at least ten years' experience.*

§ 4. Section seven hundred and seventy-five-a of the Greater New York charter, as added by chapter four hundred and fifty-eight of the laws of nineteen hundred and twelve, is hereby repealed.

§ 5. This act shall take effect October first, nineteen hundred and thirteen.

BILL No. 8.

AN ACT

TO AMEND THE LABOR LAW, IN RELATION TO THE EMPLOYMENT OF CHILDREN UNDER FOURTEEN YEARS IN OR FOR A FACTORY, THE DEFINITION OF A FACTORY, FACTORY BUILDING AND TENEMENT HOUSE.

The People of the State of New York, represented in Senate and Assembly, do enact as follows:

Section 1. Section two of chapter thirty-six of the laws of nineteen hundred and nine, entitled "An act relating to labor, constituting chapter thirty-one of the consolidated laws," is hereby amended to read as follows:

§ 2. Definitions. Employee. The term "employee," when used in this chapter, means a mechanic, workingman or laborer who works for another for hire.

Employer. The term "employer," when used in this chapter, means the person employing any such mechanic, workingman or laborer, whether the owner, proprietor, agent, superintendent, foreman or other subordinate.

Factory*; work for a factory.* The term "factory," when used in this chapter, shall be construed to include [also] any mill, workshop, or other manufacturing or business establishment *and all buildings, sheds, structures or other places used for or in connection therewith,* where one or more persons are employed at labor. *Work shall be deemed to be done for a factory within the meaning of this chapter whenever it is done at any place, upon the work of a factory or upon any of the materials entering into the product of the factory, whether under contract or arrangement with any person in charge of or connected with such factory directly or indirectly through the instrumentality of one or more contractors or other third persons.*

Factory building. The term "factory building," when used in this chapter, means any building, shed or structure which, or any part of which, is occupied by or used for a factory.

Mercantile establishment. The term "mercantile establishment," when used in this chapter, means any place where goods, wares or merchandise are offered for sale.

Tenement house. The term "tenement house," when used in this chapter, means any house or building, or portion thereof, which is *either* rented, leased, let or hired out, to be occupied, or is occupied *in whole or in part* as the home or residence of three families or more living independently of each other, and doing their cooking upon the premises, and [having a common right in the halls, stairways, yards, water closets or privies, or some of them,] *includes apartment houses, flat houses and all other houses so occupied,* and for the purposes of this chapter shall be construed to include any building on the same lot with any [dwelling] *such tenement* house and which is used for any of the purposes specified in section one hundred of this chapter.

Whenever, in this chapter, authority is conferred upon the commissioner of labor, it shall also be deemed to include his deputies or a deputy acting under his direction.

§ 2. Section seventy of such chapter is hereby amended to read as follows:

§ 70. Employment of minors. No child under the age of fourteen years shall be employed, permitted or suffered to work in or in connection with any factory in this state **[.]**, *or for any factory at any place in this state.* No child between the ages of fourteen and sixteen years shall be so employed, permitted or suffered to work unless an employment certificate, issued as provided in this article, shall have been theretofore filed in the office of the employer at the place of employment of such child. *Nothing herein contained shall prevent a person engaged in farming from permitting his children to do farm work for him upon his farm. Boys over the age of twelve years may be employed in gathering produce for not more than six hours in any one day subject to the requirements of the Compulsory Education Law, and all acts amendatory thereto.*

§ 3. This act shall take effect immediately.

BILL No. 9.

AN ACT

TO AMEND THE LABOR LAW, IN RELATION TO THE MANUFACTURE OF ARTICLES IN TENEMENT HOUSES.

The People of the State of New York, represented in Senate and Assembly, do enact as follows:

Section 1. Article seven of chapter thirty-six of the laws of nineteen hundred and nine, entitled "An act relating to labor, constituting chapter thirty-one of the consolidated laws," is hereby amended to read as follows:

ARTICLE 7.

Tenement-made Articles.

§ 100. Manufacturing, altering, repairing or finishing articles in tenements. 1. No tenement house nor any part thereof shall be used for the purpose of manufacturing, altering, repairing or finishing therein, any [coats, vests, knee-pants, trousers, overalls, cloaks, hats, caps, suspenders, jerseys, blouses, dresses, waists, waistbands, underwear, neckwear, furs, fur trimmings, fur garments, skirts, shirts, aprons, purses, pocket books, slippers, paper boxes, paper bags, feathers, artificial flowers, cigarettes, cigars, umbrellas, or articles of rubber, nor for the purpose of manufacturing, preparing or packing macaroni, spaghetti, ice cream, ices, candy, confectionery, nuts or preserves] *articles whatsoever except for the sole and exclusive use of the person so using any part of such tenement house or the members of his household,* without a license therefor as provided in this article. But nothing herein contained shall apply to collars, cuffs, shirts or shirt waists made of cotton or linen fabrics that are subjected to the laundrying process before being offered for sale.

2. Application for such a license shall be made to the commissioner of labor by the owner of such tenement house, or by his duly authorized agent. Such application shall describe the house by street number or otherwise, as the case may be, in such manner as will enable the commissioner of labor easily to find the same;

it shall also state the number of apartments in such house; it shall contain the full name and address of the owner of the said house, and shall be in such form as the commissioner of labor may determine. Blank applications shall be prepared and furnished by the commissioner of labor.

3. Upon receipt of such application the commissioner of labor shall consult the records of the local health department or board, or other appropriate local authority charged with the duty of sanitary inspection of such houses; if such records show the presence of any infectious, contagious or communicable disease, or the existence of any uncomplied-with order or violations which indicate the presence of unsanitary conditions in such house, the commissioner of labor may, without making an inspection of the building, deny such application for a license, and may continue to deny such application until such time as the records of said department, board or other local authority show that the said tenement house is free from the presence of infectious, contagious or communicable disease, and from all unsanitary conditions. Before, however, any such license is granted, an inspection of the building sought to be licensed must be made by the commissioner of labor, and a statement must be filed by him as a matter of public record, to the effect that the records of the local health department or board or other appropriate authority charged with the duty of sanitary inspection of such houses show the existence of no infectious, contagious or communicable disease nor of any unsanitary conditions in the said house; such statement must be dated and signed in ink with the full name of the employee responsible therefor. A similar statement similarly signed, showing the results of the inspection of the said building, must also be filed in the office of the commissioner of labor before any license is granted. If the commissioner of labor ascertain that such building is free from infectious, contagious or communicable disease, that there are no defects of plumbing that will permit the [free] entrance of sewer air, that such building is in a clean and proper sanitary condition and that [the] articles [specified in this section] may be manufactured therein under clean and healthful conditions, he shall grant a license permitting the use of such building, for the purpose of manufacturing[, altering, repairing or finishing such articles].

4. Such license may be revoked by the commissioner of labor if the health of the community or of the employees requires it, or if the owner of the said tenement house, or his duly authorized agent, fails to comply with the orders of the commissioner of labor within ten days after the receipt of such orders, or if it appears that the building to which such license relates is not in a healthy and proper sanitary condition, *or if children are employed therein, in violation of section seventy of this chapter.* In every case where a license is revoked or denied by the commissioner of labor, the reasons therefor shall be stated in writing, and the records of such revocation or denial shall be deemed public records. Where a license is revoked, before such tenement house can again be used for the purposes specified in this section, a new license must be obtained, as if no license had previously existed.

5. Every tenement house and all the parts thereof in which any [of the] articles [named in this section] are manufactured, altered, repaired or finished shall be kept in a clean and sanitary condition and shall be subject to inspection and examination by the commissioner of labor, for the purpose of ascertaining whether said garments or articles, or part or parts thereof, are clean and free from vermin and every matter of an infectious or contagious nature. An inspection shall be made by the commissioner of labor of each licensed tenement house not less than once in every six months, to determine its sanitary condition, and shall include all parts of such house and the plumbing thereof. Before making such inspection the commissioner of labor may consult the records of the local department or board charged with the duty of sanitary inspection of tenement houses, to determine the frequency of orders issued by such department or board in relation to the said tenement house, since the last inspection of such building was made by the commissioner of labor. Whenever the commissioner of labor finds any unsanitary condition in a tenement house for which a license has been issued as provided in this section, he shall at once issue an order to the owner thereof directing him to remedy such condition forthwith. Whenever the commissioner of labor finds any [of the] articles [specified in this section] manufactured, altered, repaired or finished, or in process thereof, in a room or apartment of a tenement house, and such room or apart-

ment is in a filthy condition, he shall notify the tenants thereof to immediately clean the same,, and to maintain it in a cleanly condition at all times; where the commissioner of labor finds such room or apartment to be habitually kept in a filthy condition, he may in his discretion cause to be affixed to the entrance door of such apartment a placard calling attention to such facts and prohibiting the manufacture, alteration, repair or finishing of [said] *any* articles therein. No person, except the commissioner of labor, shall remove or deface any such placard so affixed.

6. [None of the] *No* articles [specified in this section] shall be manufactured, altered, repaired or finished in any room or apartment of a tenement house where there is or has been a case of infectious, contagious or communicable disease in such room or apartment, until such time as the local department or board of health shall certify to the commissioner of labor that such disease has terminated, and that said room or apartment has been properly disinfected, if disinfection after such disease is required by the local ordinances, or by the rules or regulations of such department or board. [None of the] *No* articles [specified in this section] shall be manufactured, altered, repaired or finished in a part of a cellar or basement of a tenement house, which is more than one-half of its height below the level of the curb or ground outside of or adjoining the same*; but this prohibition shall not apply to the use of a bakery of a cellar for which a certificate of exemption is issued under section one hundred and sixteen of this chapter.* No person shall hire, employ or contract with any person to manufacture, alter, repair or finish any [of the] articles [named in this section] in any room or apartment in any tenement house not having a license therefor issued as aforesaid. [None of the] *No* articles [specified in this section] shall be manufactured, altered, repaired or finished in any room or apartment of a tenement house unless said room or apartment shall be well lighted and ventilated and shall contain at least five hundred cubic feet of air space for every person working therein, or by any person other than the members of the family living therein; except that in licensed tenement houses persons not members of the family may be employed in apartments on the ground floor or second floor, used only for shops of dressmakers who deal solely in the custom trade direct to

the consumer, provided that such apartments shall be in the opinion of the commissioner of labor in the highest degree sanitary, well lighted, well ventilated and plumbed, and provided further that the whole number of persons therein shall not exceed one to each one thousand cubic feet of air space, and that there shall be no children under fourteen years of age living or working therein; before any such room or apartment can be so used a special permit therefor shall be issued by the commissioner of labor, a copy of which shall be entered in his public records with a statement of the reasons therefor. Nothing in this section contained shall prevent the employment of a tailor or seamstress by any person or family for the purpose of making, altering, repairing or finishing any article of wearing apparel for the use of such person or family. Nor shall this [section] *article* apply to a house if the only [work] *manufacturing* therein [on the articles herein specified] be carried on in a shop on the main or ground floor thereof with a separate entrance to the street, unconnected with living rooms and entirely separate from the rest of the building by closed partitions without any openings whatsoever and not used for sleeping or cooking.

§ 101. Register of persons to whom work is given*; identification label.* [Persons] *Every employer in any factory* contracting for the manufacturing, altering, repairing or finishing of any [of the] articles [mentioned in section one hundred of this article] *in a tenement house* or giving out material from which they or any part of them are to be manufactured, altered, repaired or finished, *in a tenement house,* shall keep a register of the names and addresses plainly written in English of the persons to whom such articles or materials are given to be so manufactured, altered, repaired or finished or with whom they have contracted to do the same, *and shall issue with all such articles or materials a label bearing the name and place of business of such factory written or printed legibly in English.* It shall be incumbent upon *every employer and upon* all persons contracting for the manufacturing, altering, repairing or finising of any [of the] articles [specified in section one hundred of this article] or giving out material from which they or any part of them are to be manufactured, altered, repaired or finished, before giving out [the same] *any such articles or ma-*

terials to ascertain from the office of the commissioner of labor whether the tenement house in which such articles or materials are to be manufactured, altered, repaired or finished, is licensed as provided in this article, and also to ascertain from the local department or board of health the names and addresses of all persons then sick of any infectious, contagious or communicable disease, and residing in tenement houses; and none of the said articles nor any material from which they or any part of them are to be manufactured, altered, repaired or finished shall be given out or sent to any person residing in a tenement house that is not licensed as provided in this article, or to any person residing in a room or apartment in which there exists any infectious, contagious or communicable disease. The register mentioned in this section shall be subject to inspection by the commissioner of labor, and a copy thereof shall be furnished on his demand as well as such other information as he may require. *The label mentioned in this section shall be exhibited on the demand of the commissioner of labor at any time while said articles or materials remain in the tenement house.*

§ 102. Goods unlawfully manufactured to be labeled. Articles manufactured, altered, repaired or finished *in a tenement house* contrary to the provisions [of section one hundred] of this chapter shall not be sold or exposed for sale by any person. The commissioner of labor may conspicuously affix to any such article found to be unlawfully manufactured, altered, repaired or finished, a label containing the words "tenement made" printed in small pica capital letters on a tag not less than four inches in length, or may seize and hold such article until the same shall be disinfected or cleaned at the owner's expense, *or until all provisions of this chapter are complied with.* The commissioner of labor shall notify the person stated by the person in possession of said article to be the owner thereof, that he has so labeled or seized it. No person except the commissioner of labor, *or a local board of health in a case provided for in section one hundred and three,* shall remove or deface any tag or label so affixed. Unless the owner or person entitled to the possession of an article so seized shall provide for the disinfection or cleaning thereof within one month thereafter it may be destroyed.

§ 103. *Powers and duties of boards of health relative to tenement-made articles.* If the commissioner of labor finds evidence of disease present in [a workshop or in] a room or apartment in a tenement house [or dwelling house] in which any [of the] articles [named in section one hundred of this chapter] are manufactured, altered repaired or finished or in process thereof, he shall affix to such article the label prescribed in the preceding section, and immediately report to the local board of health, who shall disinfect such articles, if necessary, and thereupon remove such label. If the commissioner of labor finds that infectious [or] contagious *or communicable* diseases exist in a [workshop,] room or apartment of a tenement [or dwelling] house in which any [of the] articles [specified in section one hundred of this chapter] are being manufactured, altered, repaired or finished, or that articles manufactured or in process of manufacture therein are infected or that goods used therein are unfit for use, he shall report to the local board of health. The local health department or board in every city, town and village whenever there is any infectious, contagious or communicable disease in a tenement house shall cause an inspection of such tenement house to be made within forty-eight hours. If any [of the] articles [specified in section one hundred of this chapter] are found to be manufactured, altered, repaired or finished, or in process thereof in an apartment in which such disease exists, such board shall issue such order as the public health may require, and shall at once report such facts to the commissioner of labor, furnishing such further information as he may require. Such board may condemn and destroy all such infected article or articles manufactured or in the process of manufacture under unclean or unhealthful conditions. The local health department or board or other appropriate authority charged with the duty of sanitary inspection of such houses in every city, town and village shall, when so requested by the commissioner of labor, furnish copies of its records as to the presence of infectious, contagious or communicable disease, or of unsanitary conditions in said houses; and shall furnish such other information as may be necessary to enable the commissioner of labor to carry out the provisions of this article.

§ 104. [Inspection of articles manufactured in other states.] *Manufacturing of certain articles in tenements prohibited.* [Whenever it is reported to the commissioner of labor that any of the articles named in section one hundred of this chapter are being shipped into this state, having previously been manufactured in whole or in part under unclean, unsanitary or unhealthy conditions, said commissioner shall examine said articles and the conditions of their manufacture, and if upon such examination said goods or any part of them are found to contain vermin or to have been manufactured in improper places or under unhealthy conditions, he shall forthwith affix to them the tax or label hereinbefore described and report to the local board of health, which board shall thereupon make such order or orders as the public safety may require.]

No article of food, no dolls or dolls' clothing and no article of children's or infants' wearing apparel shall be manufactured, altered, repaired or finished, in whole or in part, for a factory, either directly or through the instrumentality of one or more contractors or other third person, in a tenement house, in any portion of an apartment, any part of which is used for living purposes.

§ 105. Owners of tenement [and dwelling] houses not to permit the unlawful use thereof. The owner or agent of a tenement house [or dwelling house] shall not permit the use thereof for the manufacture, repair, alteration or finishing of any [of the] article [mentioned in this article] contrary to [its] *the* provisions *of this chapter.* If a room or apartment in such tenement house [or dwelling house] be so unlawfully used, the commissioner of labor shall serve a notice thereof upon such owner or agent. Unless such owner or agent shall cause such unlawful manufacture to be discontinued within ten days after the service of such notice, or within fifteen days thereafter institutes and faithfully prosecutes proceedings for dispossession of the occupant of a tenement house, [or dwelling house,] who unlawfully manufactures, repairs, alters or finishes [such] *any* articles therein, he shall be deemed guilty of a violation of this [article,] *chapter* as if he, himself, was engaged in such unlawful manufacture, repair, alteration or finishing. The unlawful manufacture, repair, alteration or finishing of any [of such] articles by the occupant of a room or apartment of a tenement house [or dwelling] shall be a cause for dispossessing such occupant by summary proceedings to recover possession of real property, as provided in the code of civil procedure.

§ 106. Factory permits. The owner of every factory for which any articles are manufactured in any tenement house shall secure a permit therefor from the commissioner of labor who shall issue such permit to any such owner applying therefor. Such permit may be revoked or suspended by the commissioner of labor whenever any provision of this article or of section seventy of this chapter is violated in connection with any work for such factory. Such permit may be reissued or reinstated in the discretion of the commissioner when such violation has ceased. No articles shall be manufactured in any tenement house for any factory for which no permit has been issued or for any factory whose permit is suspended or revoked. A complete list of all factories holding such permits, together with the name of the owner of each such factory, the address of the business and the name under which it is carried on, and of all tenement houses holding licenses, and a list of all permits and licenses revoked or suspended shall be published from time to time by the department of labor.

§ 2. This act shall take effect October first, nineteen hundred and thirteen.

BILL No. 10.

AN ACT

TO AMEND THE LABOR LAW, IN RELATION TO THE EMPLOYMENT OF WOMEN IN CANNING ESTABLISHMENTS.

The People of the State of New York, represented in Senate and Assembly, do enact as follows:

Section 1. Subdivision three of section seventy-seven of chapter thirty-six of the laws of nineteen hundred and nine, entitled "An act relating to labor, constituting chapter thirty-one of the consolidated laws," as amended by chapter five hundred and thirty-nine of the laws of nineteen hundred and twelve, is hereby amended to read as follows:

3. No female minor under the age of twenty-one years and no woman shall be employed or permitted to work in any factory in this state [before six o'clock in the morning, or after nine o'clock in the evening of any day, or] more than six days or fifty-four hours in any one week; nor for more than nine hours in any one day except as hereinafter provided. *No female minor under the age of twenty-one years shall be employed or permitted to work in any factory in this state before six o'clock in the morning or after nine o'clock in the evening of any day.*

§ 2. Subdivisions two and three of section seventy-eight of such chapter, as amended by chapter five hundred and thirty-nine of the laws of nineteen hundred and twelve, are hereby amended to read as follows:

2. The provisions of subdivision[s] two [and three] of section seventy-seven relating to maximum hours shall not apply to the employment of [women and] *male* minors sixteen years of age and upwards in canning or preserving perishable products in fruit and canning establishments between the fifteenth day of June and the fifteenth day of October each year.

3. *A female eighteen years of age or upwards may, notwithstanding the provisions of subdivision three of section seventy-seven of this chapter, be employed in canning or preserving perishable products in fruit and canning establishments between the fifteenth day of June and the fifteenth day of October in each year not more than six days or sixty hours in any one week nor more than ten hours in any one day; and the industrial board shall have power to adopt rules and regulations permitting the employment of women eighteen years of age and upwards on such work in such establishments between the twenty-fifth day of June and the fifth day of August in each year not more than six days nor more than sixty-six hours in any one week nor more than twelve hours in any one day, if said board shall find that such employment is required by the needs of such industry and can be permitted without serious injury to the health of women so employed. The provisions of this subdivision shall have no application unless the daily hours of labor shall be posted for the infor-*

mation of employees and a time book in a form approved by the commissioner of labor, giving the names and addresses of all female employees and the hours of work by each of them in each day shall be properly and correctly kept and shall be exhibited to him or any of his subordinates promptly upon demand. No person shall knowingly make or permit or suffer to be made a false entry in any such time book.

§ 3. Subdivision three of said section seventy-eight is hereby renumbered subdivision four.

§ 4. This act shall take effect immediately.

BILL No. 11.

AN ACT

TO AMEND THE LABOR LAW, IN RELATION TO THE HOUSING OF FACTORY EMPLOYEES.

The People of the State of New York, represented in Senate and Assembly, do enact as follows:

Section 1. Chapter thirty-six of the laws of nineteen hundred and nine, entitled "An act relating to labor, constituting chapter thirty-one of the consolidated laws," is hereby amended by inserting therein after section ninety-seven, a new section to be known as section ninety-eight, to read as follows:

§ 98. *Labor camps. Every employer operating a factory, and furnishing to the employees thereof any living quarters at any place outside the factory, either directly or through any third person by contract or otherwise, shall maintain such living quarters and every part thereof in a thoroughly sanitary condition. The industrial board shall have power to make rules and regulations to provide for the sanitation of such living quarters. The commissioner of labor may enter and inspect any such living quarters.*

§ 2. This act shall take effect immediately.

BILL NO. 12.

AN ACT

TO AMEND THE LABOR LAW, IN RELATION TO THE PHYSICAL EXAMINATION OF CHILDREN EMPLOYED IN FACTORIES AND CANCELLATION OF THEIR EMPLOYMENT CERTIFICATES BECAUSE OF PHYSICAL UNFITNESS.

The People of the State of New York, represented in Senate and Assembly, do enact as follows:

Section 1. Chapter thirty-six of the laws of nineteen hundred and nine, entitled "An act relating to labor, constituting chapter thirty-one of the consolidated laws," is hereby amended by inserting therein, after section seventy-six thereof, a new section, to be section seventy-six-a, to read as follows:

§ 76-*a*. *Physical examination of children in factories; cancellation of employment certificates. 1. All children between fourteen and sixteen years of age employed in factories shall submit to a physical examination whenever required by a medical inspector of the state department of labor. The result of all such physical examinations shall be recorded on blanks furnished for that purpose by the commissioner of labor, and shall be kept on file in such office or offices of the department as the commissioner of labor may designate.*

2. If any such child shall fail to submit to such physical examination, the commissioner of labor may issue an order cancelling such child's employment certificate. Such order shall be served upon the employer of such child who shall forthwith deliver to an authorized representative of the department of labor the child's employment certificate. A certified copy of the order of cancellation shall be served on the board of health or other local authority that issued the said certificate. No such child whose employment certificate has been cancelled, as aforesaid, shall, while said cancellation remains unrevoked, be permitted or suffered to work in any factory of the state before it attains the age of sixteen years. If thereafter such child shall submit to the physical examination required, the commissioner of labor may issue an order revoking the cancellation of the employment certificate and may return the employment certificate to such child. Copies of the order of revocation shall be served upon the former employer of the child and the local board of health as aforesaid.

3. If as a result of the physical examination made by a medical inspector it appears that the child is physically unfit to be employed in a factory, such medical inspector shall forthwith submit a report to that effect to the commissioner of labor which shall be kept on file in the office of the commissioner of labor, setting forth in detail his reasons therefor, and the commissioner of labor may issue an order cancelling the employment certificate of such child. Such order of cancellation shall be served, and the child's employment certificate delivered up, as provided in subdivision two hereof, and no such child while the said order of cancellation remains unrevoked shall be permitted or suffered to work in any factory of the state before it attains the age of sixteen years. If upon a subsequent physical examination of the child by a medical inspector of the department of labor it appears that the physical infirmities have been removed, such medical inspector shall certify to that effect to the commissioner of labor, and the commissioner of labor may thereupon make an order revoking the cancellation of the employment certificate and may return the certificate to such child. The order of revocation shall be served in the manner provided in subdivision two hereof.

§ 2. This act shall take effect October first, nineteen hundred and thirteen.

BILL No. 13.

AN ACT

TO AMEND THE LABOR LAW, IN RELATION TO EMPLOYMENT CERTIFICATES.

The People of the State of New York, represented in Senate and Assembly, do enact as follows:

Section 1. Subdivision (e) of section one hundred and sixty-three of chapter thirty-six of the laws of nineteen hundred and nine, entitled "An act relating to labor, constituting chapter thirty-one of the consolidated laws," is hereby amended to read as follows:

(e) Physicians' certificates. In cities of the first class only, in case application for the issuance of an employment certificate shall be made to such officer by a child's parent, guardian or custodian who alleges his inability to produce any of the evidence of age specified in the preceding subdivisions of this section, and if the child is apparently at least fourteen years of age, such officer may receive and file an application signed by the parent, guardian or custodian of such child for physicians' certificates. Such application shall contain the alleged age, place and date of birth, and present residence of such child, together with such further facts as may be of assistance in determining the age of such child. Such application shall be filed for not less than ninety days after date of such application for such physicians' certificates, for an examination to be made of the statements contained therein, and in case no facts appear within such period or by such examination tending to discredit or contradict any material statement of such application, then and not otherwise the officer may direct such child to appear thereafter for physical examination before two physicians officially designated by the board of health, and in case such physicians shall certify in writing that they have separately examined such child and that in their opinion such child is at least fourteen years of age such officer shall accept such certificate as sufficient proof of the age of such child for the purposes of this section. In case the opinions of such physicians do not concur, the child shall be examined by a third physician and the concurring opinions shall be conclusive for the purpose of this section as to the age of such child.

Such officer shall require the evidence of age specified in subdivision (a) in preference to that specified in any subsequent subdivision and shall not accept the evidence of age permitted by any subsequent subdivision unless he shall receive and file in addition thereto an affidavit of the parent showing that no evidence of age specified in any preceding subdivision or subdivisions of this section can be produced. Such affidavit shall contain the age, place and date of birth and present residence of such child, which affidavit must be taken before the officer issuing the employment certificate, who is hereby authorized and required to administer such oath, and who shall not demand or receive a fee therefor. Such employment certificate shall not be issued until such child shall further have personally appeared before and been examined by the officer issuing the certificate, and until such officer shall, after making such examination, sign and file in his office a statement that the child can read and legibly write simple sentences in the English language and that in his opinion the child is fourteen years of age or upwards and has reached the normal development of a child of its age, and is in sound health and is physically able to perform the work which it intends to do. [In doubtful cases such physical fitness shall be determined by a medical officer of the board or department of health.] *In every case, before an employment certificate is issued, such physical fitness shall be determined by a medical officer of the department or board of health, who shall make a thorough physical examination of the child and record the result thereof on a blank to be furnished for the purpose by the commissioner of labor and shall set forth thereon such facts concerning the physical condition and history of the child as the commissioner of labor may require.* Every such employment certificate shall be signed in the presence of the officer issuing the same, by the child in whose name it is issued.

§ 2. Sections seventy-three and one hundred and sixty-five of such chapter are hereby amended to read as follows:

§ 73. School record, what to contain. The school record required by this article shall be signed by the principal or chief executive officer of the school which such child has attended and shall be furnished, on demand, to a child entitled thereto or to the board, department or commissioner of health. It shall contain a statement certifying that the child has regularly attended the public schools or schools equivalent thereto, or parochial schools, for not less than one hundred and thirty days during the twelve months next preceding his fourteenth birthday, or during the twelve months next preceding his application for such school record and is able to read and write simple sentences in the English language, and has received during such period instruction in reading, spelling, writing, English grammar and geography and is familiar with the fundamental operations of arithmetic up to and including fractions [.] *and has completed the work prescribed for the first six years of the public elementary school or school equivalent thereto or parochial school from which such school record is issued.* Such school record shall also give the date of birth and residence of the child as shown on the records of the school and the name of its parent or guardian or custodian.

§ 165. School record, what to contain. The school record required by this article shall be signed by the principal or chief executive officer of the school which such child has attended and shall be furnished on demand to a child entitled thereto or to the board, department or commissioner of health. It shall contain a statement certifying that the child has regularly attended the public schools or schools equivalent thereto or parochial schools for not less than one hundred and thirty days during the twelve months next preceding his fourteenth birthday, or during the twelve months next preceding his application for such school record, and is able to read and write simple sentences in the English language, has received during such period instruction in reading, spelling, writing, English grammar and geography, and is familiar with the fundamental operations of arithmetic up to and including fractions [.] *and has completed the work prescribed for the first six years of the public elementary school or school equivalent thereto or parochial school, from which such school record is issued.* Such school record shall also give the date of birth and residence of the child as shown on the records of the school and the name of its parent or guardian or custodian.

§ 3. Section seventy-five of such chapter as amended by chapter three hundred and thirty-three of the laws of nineteen hundred and twelve is hereby amended to read as follows:

§ 75. [Report of certificates issued.] *Supervision over issuance of certificates.* The board or department of health or health commissioner of a city, village or town shall transmit between the first and tenth day of each month, to the [office of the] commissioner of labor, a list of the names of [the] *all* children to whom certificates have been issued *during the preceding month* together with a duplicate of the record of [the physical examination of all such children made as hereinbefore provided] *every examination as to physical fitness, including examinations resulting in rejection.*

In cities of the first and second class all employment certificates and school records required under the provisions of this chapter shall be in such form as shall be approved by the commissioner of labor. In towns, villages or cities other than cities of the first or second class, the commissioner of labor shall prepare and furnish blank forms for such employment certificates and school records. No school record or employment certificate required by this article, other than those approved or furnished by the commissioner of labor as above provided, shall be used. The commissioner of labor shall inquire into the administration and enforcement of the provisions of this article by all public officers charged with the duty of issuing employment certificates, and for that purpose the commissioner of labor shall have access to all papers and records required to be kept by all such officers.

§ 4. Such chapter is hereby amended by inserting therein, after section one hundred and sixty-five, a new section to be known as section one hundred and sixty-six and to read as follows:

§ 166. *Supervision over issuance of certificates. The board or department of health or health commissioner of a city, village or town shall transmit between the first and tenth day of each month to the commissioner of labor a list of the names of all children to whom certificates have been issued during the preceding month, together with a duplicate record of all examinations as to physical fitness, including those resulting in rejection. In cities of the first and second class all employment certificates and school records required under the provisions of this chapter shall be in such form as shall be approved by the commissioner of labor. In towns, villages or cities other than cities of the first or second class, the commissioner of labor shall prepare and furnish blank forms for such employment certificates and school records. No school record or employment certificate required by this article other than those approved or furnished by the commissioner of labor as above provided shall be used. The commissioner of labor shall inquire into the administration and enforcement of the provisions of this article by all public officers charged with the duty of issuing employment certificates, and for that purpose the com-*

missioner of labor shall have access to all papers and records required to be kept by all such officers.

§ 5. This act shall take effect October first, nineteen hundred and thirteen.

BILL NO. 14.

AN ACT

TO AMEND THE EDUCATIONAL LAW, IN RELATION TO SCHOOL-RECORD CERTIFICATES.

The People of the State of New York, represented in Senate and Assembly, do enact as follows:

Section 1. Subdivision one of section six hundred and thirty of chapter twenty-one of the laws of nineteen hundred and nine, entitled "An act relating to education, constituting chapter sixteen of the consolidated laws," as amended by chapter one hundred and forty of the laws of nineteen hundred and ten, is hereby amended to read as follows:

1. A school-record certificate shall contain a statement certifying that a child has regularly attended the public schools, or schools equivalent thereto, or parochial schools, for not less than one hundred and thirty days during the twelve months next preceding his fourteenth birthday or during the twelve months next preceding his application for such school record, and that he is able to read and write simple sentences in the English language and has received during such period instruction in reading, writing, spelling, English grammar and geography and is familiar with the fundamental operations of arithmetic up to and including fractions, *and has completed the work prescribed for the first six years of the public elementary school, or school equivalent thereto, or parochial school, from which such school record is issued.* Such record shall also give the date of birth and residence of the child, as shown on the school records, and the name of the child's parents, guardian or custodian.

§ 2. This act shall take effect October first, nineteen hundred and thirteen.

BILL NO. 15.

AN ACT

TO AMEND THE LABOR LAW, IN RELATION TO PROTECTING THE HEALTH AND MORALS OF FEMALES EMPLOYED IN FACTORIES BY PROVIDING AN ADEQUATE PERIOD OF REST AT NIGHT.

The People of the State of New York, represented in Senate and Assembly, do enact as follows:

Section 1. Chapter thixty-six of the laws of nineteen hundred and nine, entitled "An act relating to labor, being chapter thirty-one of the consolidated laws," is hereby amended by inserting therein, after section ninety-three-a, a new section, to be section ninety-three-b, to read as follows:

§ 93-b. *Period of rest at night for women. In order to protect the health and morals of females employed in factories by providing an adequate period of rest at night no woman shall be employed or permitted to work in any factory in this state before six o'clock in the morning or after ten o'clock in the evening of any day.*

§ 2. This act shall take effect July first, nineteen hundred and thirteen.

BILL NO. 16.

AN ACT

TO AMEND THE LABOR LAW, IN RELATION TO SEATS IN FACTORIES AND OTHER ESTABLISHMENTS FOR FEMALE EMPLOYEES.

The People of the State of New York, represented in Senate and Assembly, do enact as follows:

Section 1. Section seventeen of chapter thirty-six of the laws of nineteen hundred and nine, entitled "An act relating to labor, constituting chapter thirty-one of the consolidated laws," is hereby amended to read as follows:

§ 17. Seats for female employees. Every person employing females in a factory or as waitresses in a hotel or restaurant shall provide and maintain suitable seats, with proper backs where practicable, for the use of such female employees, and permit the use thereof by such employees to such an extent as may be reasonable for the preservation of their health. *Where females are engaged in work which can be properly performed in a sitting posture, suitable seats, with backs where practicable, shall be supplied in every factory for the use of all such female employees and permitted to be used at such work. The industrial board may determine when seats, with or without backs, are necessary and the number thereof.*

§ 2. This act shall take effect October first, nineteen hundred and thirteen.

BILL NO. 17.

AN ACT

TO AMEND THE LABOR LAW, IN RELATION TO BAKERIES.

The People of the State of New York, represented in Senate and Assembly, do enact as follows:

Section 1. Article eight of chapter thirty-six of the laws of nineteen hundred and nine, entitled "An act relating to labor, constituting chapter thirty-one of the consolidated laws," as amended by chapter six hundred and thirty-seven of the laws of nineteen hundred and eleven, is hereby amended to read as follows:

ARTICLE 8.

BAKERIES AND CONFECTIONERIES.

Section 110. [Hours of labor in bakeries and confectioneries.] *Enforcement of article.*
111. Definitions.
112. General requirements.
113. Maintenance.
113a. Prohibited employment of diseased bakers.
114. Inspection of bakeries.

115. Sanitary certificates.
116. Prohibition of future cellar bakeries.
117. Sanitary code for bakeries and confectioneries.

§ 110. [Hours of labor in bakeries and confectioneries. No employee shall be required or permitted to work in a biscuit, bread or cake bakery or confectionery establishment more than sixty hours in any one week, or more than ten hours in any one day, unless for the purpose of making a shorter work day on the last day of the week; nor more hours in any one week than will make an average of ten hours per day for the number of days during such week in which such employee shall work.] *Enforcement of article. In every city of the first class the health department of such city shall have exclusive jurisdiction to enforce the provisions of this article. In the application of any provision of this article to any city of the first class, the words " commissioner of labor " or " department of labor " shall be understood to mean the health department of such city.*

§ 111. Definitions. All buildings, [or] rooms[,] *or places* [except kitchens in hotels and private residences,] used or occupied for the purpose of making, preparing or baking bread, biscuits, pastry, cakes, doughnuts, crullers, noodles, macaroni or spaghetti to be sold or consumed on or off the premises, *except kitchens in hotels, restaurants, boarding houses or private residences wherein such products are prepared to be used and are used exclusively on the premises,* shall for the purpose of this [act] *article* be deemed bakeries. The commissioner of labor shall have the same powers with respect to the machinery, safety devices and sanitary conditions in hotel bakeries that he has with respect thereto in bakeries as defined by this chapter. *In cities of the first class the health department's jurisdiction over hotel bakeries shall not extend to the machinery safety devices and hours of labor of employees therein.* The term cellar when used in this article shall mean a room or a part of a building which is more than one-half its height below the level of the curb or ground adjoining the building (excluding areaways). The term owner as used in this article shall be construed to mean the owner or owners of the freehold of the premises, or the lessee or joint lessees of the whole thereof, or his, her or their agent in charge of the property. The term occupier shall be construed to mean the person, firm or corporation in actual possession of the premises, who either himself makes, prepares or bakes any of the articles mentioned in this section, or hires or employs others to do it for him. Bakeries are factories within the meaning of this chapter, and subject to all the provisions of article six hereof.

§ 112. General requirements. All bakeries shall be provided with proper and sufficient drainage and with suitable sinks, supplied with clean running water for the purpose of washing and keeping clean the utensils and apparatus used therein. All bakeries shall be provided with *proper and adequate* windows, [or] *and* if [deemed necessary by the commissioner of labor,] *required by the rules and regulations of the industrial board,* with ventilating hoods and pipes over ovens and ashpits, or with other mechanical means, to so ventilate same as to render harmless to the persons working therein any steam, gases, vapors, dust, excessive heat or any impurities that may be generated or released by or in the process of making, preparing or baking in said bakeries. Every bakery shall be at least eight feet in height measured from the surface of the finished floor to the under side of the ceiling, and shall have a flooring of even, smooth cement, or of tiles laid in cement, or a wooden floor, so laid and constructed as to be free from cracks, holes and interstices, except that any cellar or basement less than eight feet in height which was used for a bakery on the second day of May, eighteen hundred and ninety-five, need not be altered to conform to this provision with respect to height; the side walls and ceilings shall be either plastered, ceiled or wainscoted. [The furniture, troughs and utensils shall be so arranged and constructed as not to prevent their cleaning or the cleaning of every part of the bakery.] Every bakery shall be provided with a sufficient number of water-closets, and such water-closets shall be separate and apart from and unconnected with the bakeroom or rooms where food products are stored or sold.

§ 113. Maintenance. All floors, walls, stairs, shelves, furniture, utensils, yards, areaways, plumbing, drains and sewers, in or in connection with bakeries, *or* in bakery water-closets and washrooms, *or* rooms where raw materials are stored, [and] *or* in rooms where the manufactured product is stored, shall at all times be kept in good repair, and maintained in a clean and sanitary condition, free from all kinds of vermin. All interior woodwork, walls and ceilings shall be painted or limewashed once every three months, where so required by the commissioner of labor. Proper sanitary receptacles shall be provided and used for storing coal, ashes, refuse and garbage. Receptacles for refuse and garbage shall have their contents removed from bakeries daily and shall be maintained in a clean and sanitary condition at all times; the use of tobacco in any form in a bakery or room where raw material[s] or manufactured product of such bakery is stored is prohibited. No person shall sleep, or be permitted, allowed or suffered to sleep in a bakery, *or* in [a] *any* room where raw material[s are stored,] or [in rooms where] the manufactured product *of such bakery* is stored or sold, and no domestic animals or birds, except cats shall be allowed to remain in any such room. *Mechanical means of ventilation, when provided, shall be effectively used and operated. Windows, doors and other openings shall be provided with proper screens. All employees, while engaged in the manufacture and handling of bread shall wear slippers or shoes and suits of washable material which shall be used for that purpose only and such garments shall be kept clean at all times. Lockers shall be provided for the street clothes of the employees. The furniture, troughs and utensils shall be so arranged and constructed as not to prevent their cleaning or the cleaning of every part of the bakery.*

§ 113-*a*. *Prohibited employment of diseased bakers. No person who has any communicable disease shall work or be permitted to work in a bakery. Whenever required by a medical inspector of the department of labor, any person employed in a bakery shall submit to a physical examination by such inspector. No person who refuses to submit to such examination shall work or be permitted to work in any bakery.*

§ 114. Inspection of bakeries. It shall be the duty of the owner of a building wherein a bakery is located to comply with all the provisions of section one hundred and twelve of this article, and of the occupier to comply with all the provisions of section one hundred and thirteen of this article, unless by the terms of a valid lease the responsibility for compliance therewith has been undertaken by the other party to the lease, and a duplicate original lease, containing such obligation, shall have been previously filed in the office of the commissioner of labor, in which event the party assuming the responsibility shall be responsible for such compliance. The commissioner of labor may, in his discretion, apply any or all of the provisions of this article to a factory located in a cellar wherein any food product is manufactured, provided that basements or cellars used as confectionery or ice-cream manufacturing shops shall not be required to conform to the requirement as to height of rooms. Such establishments shall be not less than seven feet in height, except that any cellar or basement so used before October first, nineteen hundred and six, which is more than six feet in height need not be altered to conform to this provision. If on inspection the commissioner of labor find a bakery or any part thereof to be so unclean, ill-drained or ill-ventilated as to be unsanitary, he may, after not less than forty-eight hours' notice in writing, to be served by affixing the notice on the inside of the main entrance door of said bakery, order the person found in charge thereof immediately to cease operating it until it shall be properly cleaned, drained or ventilated. If such bakery be thereupon continued in operation or be thereafter operated before it be properly cleaned, drained or ventilated, the commissioner of labor may, after first making and filing in the public records of his office a written order stating the reasons therefor, at once and without further notice fasten up and seal the oven or other cooking apparatus of said bakery, and affix to all materials, receptacles, tools and instruments found therein, labels or conspicuous signs bearing the word "unclean." No one but the commissioner of labor shall remove any such seal, label or sign, and he may refuse to remove it until such bakery be properly cleaned, drained or ventilated.

§ 115. *Sanitary certificates.* 1. *No person, firm or corporation shall establish, maintain or operate a bakery without obtaining a sanitary certificate from the department of labor. Application for such certificate shall be made to the commissioner of labor by the occupier of the bakery or by the person, firm or corporation desiring to establish or conduct such bakery. The application for a sanitary certificate shall be made in such form and shall contain such information as the commissioner of labor may require. Blank applications for such certificate shall be prepared and furnished by the commissioner of labor.*

2. *Upon the receipt of such application for a sanitary certificate, the commissioner of labor shall cause an inspection to be made of the building, room or place described in the application. If the bakery conforms to the provisions of articles six and eight of this chapter and the rules and regulations of the industrial board, or in any city of the first class if the bakery conforms to the provisions of article eight of this chapter, and to the sanitary code and the rules and regulations of the department of health of any such city, the commissioner of labor shall issue a sanitary certificate for such bakery. Such certificate shall be for a period of one year and shall be renewed annually by the commissioner of labor if upon a reinspection of the bakery it is found to comply with the aforesaid provisions and regulations. Every certificate granted under the provisions of this chapter shall be posted in a conspicuous place in the bakery for which such certificate is issued.*

3. *Such certificate may be revoked at any time by the commissioner of labor if the health of the community or of the employees of the bakery require such action, or if an order of the department issued under the provisions of this chapter be not complied with within fifteen days after the service thereof upon the person, firm or corporation charged with the duty of complying with such order. The time for such compliance may be extended by the commissioner of labor for good cause shown, but a statement of the reasons for such extension shall be filed in the office of the department of labor as part of the public records thereof. Nothing contained in this subdivision shall be construed to limit in any way the power of the commissioner of labor to seal up an unsanitary bakery as provided in section one hundred and fourteen of this chapter.*

4. *If an application for a sanitary certificate be denied or if such certificate be revoked by the commissioner of labor, he shall file in the office of the department of labor as part of the public*

records thereof, a statement in writing setting forth in detail the reasons for such denial or revocation.

5. *Applications for sanitary certificates for existing bakeries shall be made within four months after this act takes effect, and no such bakery shall be conducted or operated without a sanitary certificate from the department of labor after the first day of January, nineteen hundred and fourteen. In the case of bakeries hereafter established, the application for a sanitary certificate shall be made within ten days after such bakery shall commence business, and no such bakery shall be conducted or operated without a sanitary certificate for more than thirty days after commencing business.*

6. *If a bakery has no sanitary certificate as herein required or if such certificate has been revoked, the commissioner of labor shall, after first making and filing in the public records of his office a written order stating the reasons therefor, at once and without further notice fasten up and seal the oven or other cooking apparatus of said bakery. No one but the commissioner of labor or his duly authorized representative shall remove any such seal, and he shall not remove same until a sanitary certificate has been issued to such bakery.*

§ 116. *Prohibition of future cellar bakeries. No bakery shall hereafter be located in a cellar, and a sanitary certificate shall not be issued for any bakery so located, unless such bakery shall be at least ten feet in height measured from the surface of the finished floor to the under side of the ceiling, and if the bakery is located or intended to be located entirely in the front part of the building, the ceiling of the bakery shall be in every part at least four feet six inches above the curb level of the street in front of the building, or if such bakery is located or intended to be located entirely in the rear part of the building or to extend from the front to the rear, the ceiling of the bakery shall be not less than one foot above the curb level of the street in front of the building and the bakery shall open upon a yard or courts which shall extend at least six inches below the floor level of the bakery, nor unless proper and adequate provision shall be made for the lighting and ventilation of such bakery and for the proper construction of the floor, walls and ceiling thereof, and plans and specifications for the construction and establishment of such bakery, in such form and covering such matters as the commissioner of labor may require, shall have been first submitted to and approved by the commissioner of labor. This prohibition shall not apply to a cellar used and operated as a bakery at any time within one year prior to the date of the passage of this act, provided that satisfactory proof of its use as a bakery as herein specified be furnished to the commissioner of labor in such form as he may require within six months after this act shall take effect. Upon receipt of such proof the commissioner of labor shall issue to the owner of the building in which such cellar is located, a certificate of exemption. This section shall not prevent the local health authorities in any city of the first class from exercising any power of regulation now vested in them.*

§ 117. *Sanitary code for bakeries and confectioneries. All factories wherein any food product is manufactured shall be kept in a thoroughly sanitary condition and shall be properly lighted and ventilated, and all necessary methods shall be employed to protect the food product prepared therein from contamination. The industrial board may adopt rules and regulations for carrying into effect the provisions of this article. Such rules and regulations shall be known as the sanitary code for bakeries and confectioneries and shall not apply to cities of the first class.*

§ 2. This act shall take effect immediately.

BILL NO. 18.

AN ACT

TO AMEND THE LABOR LAW, IN RELATION TO CLEANLINESS OF WORKROOMS IN FACTORIES.

The People of the State of New York, represented in Senate and Assembly, do enact as follows:

Section 1. Section eighty-four of chapter thirty-six of the laws of nineteen hundred and nine, entitled "An act relating to labor, constituting chapter thirty-one of the consolidated laws," as amended by chapter one hundred and fourteen of the laws of nineteen hundred and ten, is hereby amended to read as follows:

§ 84. [Walls, ceilings, floors and receptacles.] *Cleanliness of rooms. Every room in a factory and the floors, walls, ceilings, windows and every other part thereof and all fixtures therein shall at all times be kept in a clean and sanitary condition.* The walls and ceilings of each [work] room in a factory shall be lime washed or painted, *except when properly tiled or covered with slate or marble with a finished surface* [when in the opinion of the commissioner of labor, it will be conducive to the health or cleanliness of the persons working therein]. *Such lime wash or paint shall be renewed whenever necessary as may be required by the commissioner of labor. Floors shall,* at all times, be maintained in a safe condition [and shall be kept clean and sanitary at all times]. No person shall spit or expectorate upon the walls, floors or stairs of any building used in whole or in part for factory purposes. Sanitary cuspidors shall be provided [in the discretion of the commissioner of labor], in every workroom in a factory in [such] *sufficient* numbers [as the commissioner of labor may determine]. Such cuspidors shall be thoroughly cleaned daily. Suitable receptacles shall be provided and used for the storage of waste and refuse; such receptacles shall be maintained in a sanitary condition.

§ 2. This act shall take effect October first, nineteen hundred and thirteen.

BILL NO. 19.

AN ACT

TO AMEND THE LABOR LAW, IN RELATION TO THE CLEAN, SANITARY AND SAFE CONDITION OF FACTORY BUILDINGS.

The People of the State of New York, represented in Senate and Assembly, do enact as follows:

Section 1. Article six of chapter thirty-six of the laws of nineteen hundred and nine, entitled "An act relating to labor, constituting chapter thirty-one of the consolidated laws," is hereby amended by inserting, after section eighty-four, a new section, to be section eighty-four-a, to read as follows:

§ 84-a. *Cleanliness of factory buildings. Every part of a factory building and of the premises thereof and the yards, courts, passages, areas or alleys connected with or belonging to the same, shall be kept clean, and shall be kept free from any accumulation of dirt, filth, rubbish or garbage in or on the same. The roof, passages, stairs, halls, basements, cellars, privies, water-closets, cesspools, drains and all other parts of such building and the premises thereof shall at all times be kept in a clean, sanitary and safe condition. The entire building and premises shall be well drained and the plumbing thereof at all times kept in proper repair and in a clean and sanitary condition.*

§ 2. This act shall take effect October first, nineteen hundred and thirteen.

BILL NO. 20.

AN ACT

TO AMEND THE LABOR LAW, IN RELATION TO VENTILATION IN FACTORIES AND THE REMOVAL OF IMPURITIES AND OF EXCESSIVE HEAT THEREIN.

The People of the State of New York, represented in Senate and Assembly, do enact as follows:

Section 1. Section eighty-six of chapter thirty-six of the laws of nineteen hundred and nine, entitled "An act relating to labor, constituting chapter thirty-one of the consolidated laws," is hereby amended to read as follows:

§ 86. Ventilation. 1. The owner, agent or lessee of [a] *every* factory shall provide, in each work room thereof, proper and sufficient means of ventilation *by natural or mechanical means or both, as may be necessary,* and shall maintain proper and sufficient ventilation *and proper degrees of temperature and humidity in every workroom thereof at all times during working hours.* [; if excessive heat be created or if steam, gases, vapors, dust or other impurities that may be injurious to health be generated in the course of the manufacturing process carried on therein the room must be ventilated in such a manner as to render them harmless, so far as is practicable; in case of failure the commissioner of labor shall order such ventilation to be provided. Such owner, agent or lessee shall provide such ventilation within twenty days after the service upon him of such order, and in case of failure, shall forfeit to the people of the state, ten dollars for each day after the expiration of such twenty days, to be recovered by the commissioner of labor.]

2. *If dust, gases, fumes, vapors, fibers or other impurities are generated or released in the course of the business carried on in any workroom of a factory, in quantities tending to injure the health of the operatives, the person operating the factory, whether as owner or lessee of the whole or of a part of the building in which the same is situated, or otherwise, shall provide suction devices that shall remove said impurities from the workroom, at their point of origin where practicable, by means of proper hoods connected to conduits and exhaust fans of sufficient capacity to remove such impurities, and such fans shall be kept running constantly while such impurities are being generated or released. If, owing to the nature of the manufacturing process carried on in a factory workroom, excessive heat be created therein the person or persons operating the factory as aforesaid shall provide, maintain, use and operate such special means or appliances as may be required to reduce such excessive heat.*

3. *The industrial board shall have power to make rules and regulations for and fix standards of ventilation, temperature and humidity in factories and may prescribe the special means, if any, required for removing impurities or for reducing excessive heat, and the machinery, apparatus or appliances to be used for any of said purposes, and the construction, equipment, maintenance and operation thereof, in order to effectuate the purposes of this section.*

4. *If any requirement of this section or any rule or regulation of the industrial board made under the provisions thereof shall not be complied with, the commissioner of labor shall issue or cause to be issued an order directing compliance therewith by the person*

whose duty it is to comply therewith within thirty days after the service of such order. Such person shall, in case of failure to comply with the requirements of such order, forfeit to the people of the state fifteen dollars for each day during which such failure shall continue after the expiration of such thirty days, to be recovered by the commissioner of labor. The liability to such penalty shall be in addition to the liability of such person to prosecution for a misdemeanor as provided by section twelve hundred and seventy-five of the penal law.

5. *When the commissioner of labor shall issue, or cause to be issued, an order specified in subdivision four hereof, he may in such order require plans and specifications to be filed for any machinery or apparatus to be provided or altered, pursuant to the requirements of such order. In such case, before providing, or making any change or alteration in any machinery or apparatus for any of the purposes specified in this section, the person upon whom such order is served shall file with the commissioner of labor plans and specifications therefor, and shall obtain the approval of such plans and specifications by the commissioner of labor before providing or making any change or alteration in any such machinery or apparatus.*

§ 2. This act shall take effect October first, nineteen hundred and thirteen.

BILL NO. 21.

AN ACT

TO AMEND THE LABOR LAW, IN RELATION TO WASHROOMS, DRESSING ROOMS AND WATER CLOSETS IN FACTORIES.

The People of the State of New York, represented in Senate and Assembly, do enact as follows:

Section 1. Section eighty-eight of chapter thirty-six of the laws of nineteen hundred and nine, entitled "An act relating to labor, constituting chapter thirty-one of the consolidated laws," as amended by chapter three hundred and thirty-six of the laws of nineteen hundred and twelve, is hereby amended to read as follows:

§ 88. Drinking water, washrooms *and dressing rooms* [and water closets]. *1.* In every factory there shall be provided at all times for the use of employees, a sufficient supply of clean and pure drinking water. Such water shall be supplied through proper pipe connections with water mains through which is conveyed the water used for domestic purposes, or, from a spring or well or body of pure water; if such drinking water be placed in receptacles in the factory, such receptacles shall be properly covered to prevent contamination and shall be thoroughly cleaned at frequent intervals.

2. In every factory there shall be provided and maintained for the use of employees suitable and convenient washrooms, *separate for each sex,* adequately equipped with [sinks and proper water service; and] *washing facilities consisting of sinks or stationary basins provided with running water or with tanks holding an adequate supply of clean water. Every washroom shall be provided with means for artificial illumination and with adequate means of ventilation. All washrooms and washing facilities shall be constructed, lighted, heated, ventilated, arranged and maintained according to rules and regulations adopted with reference thereto by the industrial board.* [i]*I*n all factories where lead, arsenic or other poisonous substances or injurious or noxious fumes, dust or gases are present as an incident or result of the business or processes conducted by such factory there shall be provided washing facilities which shall include hot water and *soap and* individual towels.

3. Where females are employed, dressing or emergency rooms shall be provided for their use; each such room shall have at least one window opening to the outer air and shall be enclosed by means of solid partitions or walls. [In brass and iron foundries suitable provisions shall be made and maintained for drying the working clothes of persons employed therein. In every factory there shall be provided suitable and convenient water closets for each sex, in such number as the commissioner of labor may determine. Such water closets shall be properly screened, lighted, ventilated and kept clean and sanitary; the enclosure of each closet shall be kept clean and sanitary and free from all obscene writing or marking. The water closets used by females shall be entirely separated from those used by males and the entrances thereto shall be effectively screened. The water closets shall be maintained inside the factory whenever practicable and in all cases, when required by the commissioner of labor.] *In every factory in which more than ten women are employed, there shall be provided one or more separate dressing rooms in such numbers as required by the rules and regulations of the industrial board and located in such place or places as required by such rules and regulations, having an adequate floor space in proportion to the number of employees, to be fixed by the rules and regulations of the industrial board, but the floor space of every such dressing room shall in no event be less than sixty square feet; each dressing room shall be separated from any water closet compartment by adequate partitions and shall be provided with adequate means for artificial illumination; each dressing room shall be provided with suitable means for hanging clothes and with a suitable number of seats. All dressing rooms shall be enclosed by means of solid partitions or walls, and shall be constructed, heated, ventilated, lighted and maintained in accordance with such rules and regulations as may be adopted by the industrial board with reference thereto.*

§ 2. Such chapter is hereby amended by inserting after section eighty-eight a new section, to be section eighty-eight-a, to read as follows:

§ 88-a. *Water closets.* 1. *In every factory there shall be provided suitable and convenient water closets separate for each sex, in such number and located in such place or places as required by the rules and regulations of the industrial board. All water closets shall be maintained inside the factory except where, in the opinion of the commissioner of labor, it is impracticable to do so.*

2. *There shall be separate water closet compartments for females, to be used by them exclusively, and notice to that effect shall be painted on the outside of such compartments. The entrance to every water closet used by females shall be effectively screened by a partition or vestibule. Where water closets for males and females are in adjoining compartments, there shall be*

solid plastered or metal covered partitions between the compartments extending from the floor to the ceiling. Whenever any water closet compartments open directly into the workroom exposing the interior, they shall be screened from view by a partition or a vestibule. The use of curtains for screening purposes is prohibited.

3. *The use of any form of trough water closet, latrine or school sink within any factory is prohibited. All such trough water closets, latrines or school sinks shall, before the first of October, nineteen hundred and fourteen, be completely removed and the place where they were located properly disinfected under the direction of the department of labor. Such appliances shall be replaced by proper individual water closets, placed in water closet compartments, all of which shall be constructed and installed in accordance with rules and regulations to be adopted by the industrial board.*

4. *Every existing water closet and urinal inside any factory shall have a basin of enameled iron or earthenware, and shall be flushed from a separate water-supplied cistern or through a flushometer valve connected in such manner as to keep the water supply of the factory free from contamination. All woodwork enclosing water closet fixtures shall be removed from the front of the closet and the space underneath the seat shall be left open. The floor or other surface beneath and around the closet shall be maintained in good order and repair and all the woodwork shall be kept well painted with a light-color paint. All existing water closet compartments shall have windows leading to the outer air and shall be otherwise ventilated in accordance with rules and regulations adopted for that purpose by the industrial board. Such compartments shall be provided with means for artificial illumination and the enclosure of each compartment shall be kept free from all obscene writing or marking.*

5. *All water closets, urinals and water closet compartments hereafter installed in a factory, including those provided to replace existing fixtures, shall be properly constructed, installed, ventilated, lighted and maintained in accordance with such rules and regulations as may be adopted by the industrial board.*

6. *All water closet compartments, and the floors, walls, ceilings and surface thereof, and all fixtures therein, and all water closets and urinals shall at all times be kept and maintained in a clean and sanitary condition. Where the water supply to water closets or urinals is liable to freeze, the water closet compartment shall be properly heated so as to prevent freezing, or the supply and flush pipes, cisterns and traps and valves shall be effectively covered with wool felt or hair felt, or other adequate covering.*

7. *All water closets shall be constructed, lighted, ventilated, arranged and maintained according to rules and regulations adopted with reference thereto by the industrial board.*

§ 3. This act shall take effect October first, nineteen hundred and thirteen.

BILL No. 22.

AN ACT

TO AMEND THE LABOR LAW, IN RELATION TO THE PROTECTION OF EMPLOYEES OPERATING MACHINERY, DUST-CREATING MACHINERY, AND THE LIGHTING OF FACTORIES AND WORKROOMS.

The People of the State of New York, represented in Senate and Assembly, do enact as follows:

Section 1. Section eighty-one of chapter thirty-six of the laws of nineteen hundred and nine, entitled "An act relating to labor, constituting chapter thirty-one of the consolidated laws," as amended by chapter one hundred and six of the laws of nineteen hundred and ten, is hereby amended to read as follows:

§ 81. Protection of employees operating machinery*; dust-creating machinery; lighting of factories and workrooms. 1.* The owner or person in charge of a factory where machinery is used shall provide, [in the discretion of the commissioner of labor] *as may be required by the rules and regulations of the industrial board,* belt shifters or other mechanical contrivances for the purpose of throwing on or off belts on pulleys. Whenever practicable, all machinery shall be provided with loose pulleys. [All vats, pans, saws, planers, cogs, gearing, belting, shafting, set-screws and machinery, of every description, shall be guarded.] *Every vat and pan wherever set so that the opening or top thereof is at a lower level than the elbow of the operator or operators at work about the same shall be protected by a cover which shall be maintained over the same while in use in such manner as effectually to prevent such operators or other persons falling therein or coming in contact with the contents thereof, except that where it is necessary to remove such cover while any such vat or pan is in use, such vat or pan shall be protected by an adequate railing around the same. Every hydro-extractor shall be covered or otherwise properly guarded while in motion. Every saw shall be provided with a proper and effective guard. Every planer shall be protected by a substantial hood or covering. Every hand-planer or jointer shall be provided with a proper and effective guard. All cogs and gearing shall be boxed or cased either with metal or wood. All belting within seven feet of the floors shall be properly guarded. All revolving shafting within seven feet of the floors shall be protected on its exposed surface by being encased in such a manner as to effectually prevent any part of the body, hair or clothing of the operators or other persons from coming in contact with such shafting. All set-screws, keys, bolts and all parts projecting beyond the surface of revolving shafting shall be countersunk or provided with suitable covering, and machinery of every description shall be properly guarded and provided with proper safety appliances or devices. All machines, machinery, apparatus, furniture and fixtures shall be so placed and guarded in relation to one another as to be safe for all persons. Whenever any danger exists which requires any special care as to the character and condition of the clothing of the persons employed thereabouts, or which requires the use of special clothing or guards, the industrial board may make rules and regulations prescribing what shall be used or worn for the purpose of guarding against such danger and regulating the provision, maintenance and use thereof.* No person shall remove or make ineffective any safeguard *or safety appliance or device* around or attached to machinery, vats or pans, [while the same are in use unless for the purpose of immediately making repairs thereto *or adjustment thereof,* [and all such safeguards so removed shall be promptly replaced] *and any person who removes or makes ineffective any such safeguard, safety appliance or device for a permitted purpose shall immediately replace the same when such purpose is accomplished. It shall be the duty of the employer and of every person exercising direction or control over the person who removes such safeguard, safety appliance or device, or over any person for whose protection it is designed to see that a safeguard or safety appliance or device that has been removed is promptly and properly replaced. All fencing, safeguards, safety appliances and devices must be constantly maintained in proper condition.* [If] *When in the opinion of the commissioner of labor* a machine or any part thereof is in a dangerous condition or is not properly guarded *or is dangerously placed,* the use thereof [may] *shall* be prohibited by the commissioner of labor and a notice to that effect shall be attached thereto. Such notice shall not be removed *except by an authorized representative of the department of labor, nor* until the machinery is made safe and the required safeguards *or safety appliances or devices* are provided, and in the meantime such unsafe or dangerous machinery shall not be used. *The industrial board may make rules and regulations regulating the installation, position, operation, guarding and use of machines and machinery in operation in factories, the furnishing and use of safety devices and safety appliances for machines and machinery and of guards to be worn upon the person, and other cognate matters, whenever it finds such regulations necessary in order to provide for the prevention of accidents in factories.*

2. All grinding, polishing or buffing wheels used in the course of the manufacture of articles of the baser metals shall be equipped with proper hoods and pipes and such pipes shall be connected to an exhaust fan of sufficient capacity and power to remove all matter thrown off such wheels in the course of their use. Such fan shall be kept running constantly while such grinding, polishing or buffing wheels are in operation; except that in the case of wet-grinding it is unnecessary to comply with this provision *unless required by the rules and regulations of the industrial board.* All machinery creating dust or impurities shall

be equipped with proper hoods and pipes and such pipes shall be connected to an exhaust fan of sufficient capacity and power to remove such dust or impurities; such fan shall be kept running constantly while such machinery is in use; except where, in case of wood-working machinery, the [commissioner of labor, after first making and filing in the public records of his office a written statement of the reasons therefor,] *industrial board* shall decide that it is unnecessary for the health and welfare of the operatives.

3. All passageways and other portions of a factory, and all moving parts of machinery which are not so guarded as to prevent accidents, where, on or about which persons work or pass or may have to work or pass in emergencies, shall be kept properly and sufficiently lighted during working hours. [When, in the opinion of the commissioner of labor, it is necessary] *The* [workrooms] halls and stairs leading to the workrooms shall be properly *and adequately* lighted, and [in cities of the first class, if deemed necessary by the commissioner of labor,] a proper *and adequate* light shall be kept burning by the owner or lessee in the public hallways near the stairs, upon the entrance floor and upon the other floors on every workday in the year, from the time when the building is open for use in the morning until the time it is closed in the evening, except at times when the influx of natural light shall make artificial light unnecessary. Such lights shall be [independent of the motive power of such factory] *so arranged as to insure their reliable operation when through accident or other cause the regular factory lighting is extinguished.*

4. All workrooms shall be properly and adequately lighted during working hours. Artificial illuminants in every workroom shall be installed, arranged and used so that the light furnished will at all times be sufficient and adequate for the work carried on therein, and so as to prevent unnecessary strain on the vision or glare in the eyes of the workers. The industrial board may make rules and regulations to provide for adequate and sufficient natural and artificial lighting facilities in all factories.

§ 2. This act shall take effect October first, nineteen hundred and thirteen.

BILL No. 23.

AN ACT

TO AMEND THE LABOR LAW, IN RELATION TO ELEVATORS AND HOISTING SHAFTS IN FACTORY BUILDINGS.

The People of the State of New York, represented in Senate and Assembly, do enact as follows:

Section 1. Section seventy-nine of chapter thirty-six of the laws of nineteen hundred and nine, entitled " An act relating to labor, constituting chapter thirty-one of the consolidated laws," as amended by chapter two hundred and ninety-nine of the laws of nineteen hundred and nine, is hereby amended to read as follows:

§ 79. [Inclosure and operation of e]*Elevators and hoistways.* [Hoisting shafts; inspection. If, in the opinion of the commissioner of labor, it is necessary to protect the life or limbs of factory employees, the owner, agent or lessee of such factory where an elevator, hoisting shafts or well-hole is used, shall cause, upon written notice from the commissioner of labor, the same to be properly and substantially inclosed, secured or guarded, and shall provide such proper traps or automatic doors so fastened in or at all elevator ways, except passenger elevators, inclosed on all sides, as to form a substantial surface when closed and so constructed as to open and close by action of the elevator in its passage either ascending or descending. The commissioner of labor may inspect the cable, gearing or other apparatus of elevators in factories and require them to be kept in a safe condition.] 1. *Inclosure of shafts. Every hoistway, hatchway or well-hole used for carrying passengers or employees, or for freight elevators, hoisting or other purpose, shall be protected on all sides at each floor including the basement, by substantial vertical inclosures. All openings in such inclosures shall be provided with self-closing gates not less than six feet high or with properly constructed sliding doors. In the case of elevators used for carrying passengers or employees, such inclosures shall be flush with the hatchway and shall extend from floor to ceiling on every open side of the car, and on every other side shall be at least six feet high, and such enclosures shall be free from fixed obstructions on every open side of the car. In the case of freight elevators the enclosures shall be flush with the hoistway on every open side of the car. In place of the inclosures herein required for freight elevators, every hatchway used for freight elevator purposes may be provided with trap doors so constructed as to form a substantial floor surface when closed and so arranged as to open and close by the action of the car in its passage both ascending and descending; provided that in addition to such trap doors, the hatchway shall be adequately protected on all sides at all floors, including the basement, by a substantial railing or other vertical inclosure at least three feet in height.*

2. *Guarding of elevators and hoistways. All counter-weights of every elevator shall be adequately protected by proper inclosures at the top and bottom of the run. The car of all elevators used for carrying passengers or employees shall be substantially enclosed on all sides, including the top, and such car shall at all times be properly lighted, artificial illuminants to be provided and used when necessary. The top of every freight elevator car or platform shall be provided with a substantial grating or covering for the protection of the operator thereof, in accordance with such rules and regulations as may be adopted with reference thereto by the industrial board.*

3. *Elevators and hoistways in factory buildings hereafter erected. The provisions of subdivisions one and two of this section shall apply only to factory buildings heretofore erected. In all factory buildings hereafter erected, every elevator and every part thereof and all machinery connected therewith and every hoistway, hatchway and well-hole shall be so constructed, guarded, equipped, maintained and operated as to be safe for all persons using the same.*

4. *Maintenance of elevators and hoistways in all factory buildings. In every factory building heretofore erected or hereafter erected, all inclosures, doors and gates of hoistways, hatchways or well-hole, and all elevators therein used for the carrying of passengers or employees or freight, and the gates and doors thereof shall at all times be kept in good repair and in a safe condition. All openings leading to elevators shall be kept well lighted at all*

times during working hours, with artificial illumination when necessary. The cable, gearing and other apparatus of elevators used for carrying passengers or employees or freight shall be kept in a safe condition.

5. *Powers of industrial board. The industrial board shall have power to make rules and regulations not inconsistent with the provisions of this chapter regulating the construction, guarding, equipment, maintenance and operation of elevators and all parts thereof, and all machinery connected therewith and hoistways, hatchways and well-holes, in order to carry out the purpose and intention of this section.*

§ 2. This act shall take effect October first, nineteen hundred and thirteen.

BILL No. 24.

AN ACT

TO AMEND THE LABOR LAW, IN RELATION TO PROTECTING THE LIVES, HEALTH AND SAFETY OF EMPLOYEES IN DANGEROUS TRADES.

The People of the State of New York, represented in Senate and Assembly, do enact as follows:

Section 1. Chapter thirty-six of the laws of nineteen hundred and nine, entitled "An act relating to labor, constituting chapter thirty-one of the consolidated laws," is hereby amended by inserting therein, after section ninety-eight, a new section to be section ninety-nine, to read as follows:

§ 99. *Dangerous trades. Whenever the industrial board shall find as a result of its investigations that any industry, trade or occupation by reason of the nature of the materials used therein or the products thereof or by reason of the methods or processes or machinery or apparatus employed therein or by reason of any other matter or thing connected with such industry, trade or occupation, contains such elements of danger to the lives, health or safety of persons employed therein as to require special regulation for the protection of such persons said board shall have power to make such special rules and regulations as it may deem necessary to guard against such elements of danger by establishing requirements as to temperature, humidity, the removal of dusts, gases or fumes and requiring licenses to be applied for and issued by the commissioner of labor as a condition of carrying on any such industry, trade or occupation and requiring medical inspection and supervision of persons employed and applying for employment and by other appropriate means.*

§ 2. This act shall take effect immediately.

BILL No. 25.

AN ACT

TO AMEND THE LABOR LAW, IN RELATION TO FOUNDRIES.

The People of the State of New York, represented in Senate and Assembly, do enact as follows:

Section 1. Chapter thirty-six of the laws of nineteen hundred and nine, entitled " An act relating to labor, constituting chapter thirty-one of the consolidated laws," is hereby amended by inserting therein, after section ninety-six, a new section, to be section ninety-seven, to read as follows:

§ 97. *Brass, iron and steel foundries.* 1. *Foundries shall be subject to all the provisions of this chapter relating to factories.*

2. *All entrances to foundries shall be so constructed and maintained as to minimize drafts, and all windows therein shall be maintained in proper condition and repair.*

3. *All gangways in foundries shall be constructed and maintained of sufficient width to make the use thereof by employees reasonably safe; during the progress of casting such gangways shall not be obstructed in any manner.*

4. *Smoke, steam and gases generated in foundries shall be effectively removed therefrom, in accordance with such rules and regulations as may be adopted with reference thereto by the indus-*

trial board, and whenever required by the regulations of such board, exhaust fans of sufficient capacity and power, properly equipped with ducts and hoods, shall be provided and operated to remove such smoke, steam and gases. The milling and cleaning of castings, and milling of cupola cinders, shall be done under such conditions to be prescribed by the rules and regulations of the industrial board as will adequately protect the persons employed in foundries from the dust arising during the process.

5. *All foundries shall be properly and thoroughly lighted during working hours and in cold weather proper and sufficient heat shall be provided and maintained therein. The use of heaters discharging smoke or gas into workrooms is prohibited. In all foundries suitable provision shall be made and maintained for drying the working clothes of persons employed therein.*

6. *In every foundry in which ten or more persons are employed or engaged at labor, there shall be provided and maintained for the use of employees therein suitable and convenient washrooms of sufficient capacity adequately equipped with hot and cold water service; such washrooms shall be kept clean and sanitary and shall be properly heated during cold weather. In every such foundry lockers shall be provided for the safe-keeping of employees' clothing. In every foundry in which more than ten persons are employed or engaged at labor where water closets or privy accommodations are permitted by the commissioner of labor to remain outside of the factory under the provisions of section eighty-eight of this chapter, the passageway leading from the foundry to the said water-closets or privy accommodations shall be so protected and constructed that the employees in passing thereto or therefrom shall not be exposed to outdoor atmosphere and such water closets or privy accommodations shall be properly heated during cold weather.*

7. *The flasks, molding machines, ladles, cranes and apparatus for transporting molten metal in foundries shall be maintained in proper condition and repair, and any such tools or implements that are defective shall not be used until properly repaired. There shall be in every foundry, available for immediate use, an ample supply of lime water, olive oil, vaseline, bandages and absorbent cotton, to meet the needs of workmen in case of burns or other*

accidents; but any other equally efficacious remedy for burns may be substituted for those herein prescribed.

§ 2. This act shall take effect October first, nineteen hundred and thirteen.

BILL No. 26.

AN ACT

TO AMEND THE LABOR LAW, IN RELATION TO THE PROHIBITION OF THE EMPLOYMENT OF CHILDREN IN THE OPERATION OF DANGEROUS MACHINERY AND IN TRADES, OCCUPATIONS OR PROCESSES OF MANUFACTURE DANGEROUS OR INJURIOUS TO THEIR HEALTH AND IN RELATION TO THE PROHIBITION OF THE EMPLOYMENT OF WOMEN IN THE COREROOMS OF FOUNDRIES.

The People of the State of New York, represented in Senate and Assembly, do enact as follows:

Section 1. Section ninety-three of chapter thirty-six of the laws of nineteen hundred and nine, entitled " An act relating to labor, constituting chapter thirty-one of the consolidated laws," as amended by chapter one hundred and seven of the laws of nineteen hundred and ten, is hereby amended to read as follows:

§ 93. Prohibited employment of women and children. 1. No child under the age of sixteen years shall be employed or permitted to work in operating or assisting in operating any of the following machines. Circular or band saws, woodshapers, woodjointers, planers, sandpaper or wood polishing macinery; picker machines or machines used in picking wool, cotton, hair or any upholstery material; paper lace machines; burnishing machines in any tannery or leather manufactory; job or cylinder printing presses having motor power other than foot; wood-turning or boring machinery; drill presses; metal or paper cutting machines; corner staying machines in paper box factories; stamping machines used in sheet metal and tinware manufacturing or in washer and nut factories; machines used in making corrugating rolls; steam boilers; dough brakes or cracker machinery of any description; wire or iron straightening machinery; rolling mill machinery; power punches or shears; washing, grinding or mixing machinery; calendar rolls in rubber manufacturing; or laundering machinery; *or in operating or assisting in operating any other machines or machinery which may be found by the industrial board to be dangerous and specified as such from time to time in rules and regulations adopted by such board.*

2. No child under the age of sixteen years shall be employed or permitted to work at adjusting or assisting in adjusting any belt to any machinery, oiling or assisting in oiling, wiping or cleaning machinery; or in any capacity in preparing any composition in which dangerous or poisonous acids are used; or in the manufacture or packing of paints, dry colors, or red or white lead; or dipping *or* dyeing [or packing] matches; or in the manufacture, packing or storing of powder, dynamite, nitroglycerine, compounds, fuses, or other explosives; or in or about any distillery, brewery, or any other establishment where malt or alcoholic liquors are manufactured, packed, wrapped, or bottled; and no female under the age of sixteen shall be employed or permitted to work in any capacity where such employment compels her to remain standing constantly. No child under the age of sixteen years shall be employed or permitted to have the care, custody or management of or to operate an elevator either for freight or passengers. No person under the age of eighteen years shall be employed or permitted to have the care, custody or management of or to operate an elevator either for freight or passengers running at a speed of over two hundred feet a minute. No male persons under eighteen years or woman under twenty-one years of age shall be permitted or directed to clean machinery while in motion. No male child under the age of eighteen years, nor any female, shall be employed in any factory in this state in operating or using any emery, tripoli, rouge, corundum, stone, carborundum or any abrasive, or emery polishing or buffing wheel, where articles of the baser metals or of iridium are manufactured.

3. In addition to the cases provided for in the foregoing subdivision, the industrial board, when as a result of its investigations it finds that any particular trade, process of manufacture, or occupation, or particular method of carrying on any trade, process of manufacture, or occupation, is dangerous or injurious to the health of minors under eighteen years of age employed therein, shall have power to adopt rules and regulations prohibiting or regulating the employment of such minors therein.

4. No female shall be employed or permitted to work in any brass, iron or steel foundry, at or in connection with the making of cores where the oven in which the cores are baked is located and is in operation in the same room or space in which the cores are made. The erection of a partition separating the oven from the space where the cores are made shall not be sufficient unless the said partition extends from the floor to the ceiling, and the partition is so constructed and arranged, and any openings therein so protected that the gases and fumes from the core oven will not enter the room or space in which the women are employed. The industrial board shall have power to adopt rules and regulations regulating the construction, equipment, maintenance and operation of core rooms and the size and weight of cores that may be handled by women, so as to protect the health and safety of women employed in core rooms.

§ 2. This act shall take effect October first, nineteen hundred and thirteen.

BILL No. 27.

AN ACT

TO AMEND THE PUBLIC HEALTH LAW, IN RELATION TO THE SALE OF WOOD ALCOHOL.

The People of the State of New York, represented in Senate and Assembly, do enact as follows:

Section 1. Chapter forty-one of the laws of nineteen hundred and nine, entitled "An act in relation to the public health, constituting chapter forty-five of the consolidated laws," is hereby amended by inserting therein, after section three hundred and eighteen-a, a new section, to be section three hundred and eighteen-b, to read as follows:

§ 318-*b*. *Sale of wood alcohol. No person shall sell any wood alcohol nor any fluid containing wood alcohol unless the bottle, vessel or other container in which the same is sold or transported shall bear a label containing the following words conspicuously printed in red ink:*

POISON

WOOD ALCOHOL

Do not use except where there is sufficient ventilation.

§ 2. This act shall take effect October first, nineteen hundred and thirteen.

BILL No. 28.

AN ACT

TO CONTINUE THE COMMISSION CREATED BY CHAPTER FIVE HUNDRED AND SIXTY-ONE OF THE LAWS OF NINETEEN HUNDRED AND ELEVEN, ENTITLED "AN ACT TO CREATE A COMMISSION TO INVESTIGATE THE CONDITIONS UNDER WHICH MANUFACTURE IS CARRIED ON IN CITIES OF THE FIRST AND SECOND CLASS IN THIS STATE, AND MAKING AN APPROPRIATION THEREFOR," AND TO ENLARGE THE SCOPE OF THE INVESTIGATION OF THE COMMISSION AND MAKING AN APPROPRIATION THEREFOR.

The People of the State of New York, represented in Senate and Assembly, do enact as follows:

Section 1. The commission created by chapter five hundred and sixty-one of the laws of nineteen hundred and eleven, entitled "An act to create a commission to investigate the conditions under which manufacture is carried on in cities of the first and second class in this state, and making an appropriation therefor," is hereby continued with all the powers conferred by said chapter, as amended by chapter twenty-one of the laws of nineteen hundred and twelve.

§ 2. In addition to the powers heretofore conferred upon it by such chapter, as amended, the said commission shall have power to inquire into the wages of labor in all industries and employments and the conditions under which labor is carried on throughout the state, and into the advisability of fixing minimum rates of wages or of other legislation relating to the wages or conditions of labor in general or in any industry. Said commission shall also have power to subpoena and require the attendance of witnesses and the production of books and papers pertaining to the investigation and inquiries hereby authorized and to take the testimony of all such witnesses and to examine all such books and papers in relation to any matter which it has power to investigate.

§ 3. The said commission shall make a report of its proceedings, together with its recommendations, including a revision of the labor law, to be prepared by the said commission if deemed advisable by it, to the legislature on or before the fifteenth day of February, nineteen hundred and fourteen.

4. The sum of fifty thousand dollars ($50,000), or so much thereof as may be needed, is hereby appropriated for the actual and necessary expenses of the commission in carrying out the provisions of chapter five hundred and sixty-one of the laws of nineteen hundred and eleven, as amended, and of this act, payable by the treasurer on the warrant of the comptroller on the order of the chairman of said commission.

§ 5. This act shall take effect immediately.

INDEX TO COMMISSION'S REPORT.

www.ingramcontent.com/pod-product-compliance
Lightning Source LLC
LaVergne TN
LVHW011159110826
845150LV00006B/1265

9781425573348